RESISTING COLONIALISM AND COMMUNAL POLITICS

Resisting Colonialism and Communal Politics

Maulana Azad and the Making of the Indian Nation

RIZWAN QAISER

MANOHAR
2018

First published 2011
Paperback edition 2013
Reprinted 2018

ISBN 978-93-5098-014-9

Published by
Ajay Kumar Jain *for*
Manohar Publishers & Distributors
4753/23 Ansari Road, Daryaganj
New Delhi 110 002

Typeset by
Ajay Arts
New Delhi-110002

Printed by
Shri Ganpati Enterprises
Delhi-110052

In memory of
my parents and grandparents
who
taught me early lessons in secular values

Contents

Preface to the Paperback Edition

It gives me immense pleasure in writing this preface to the paperback edition. In the preface of the hardback edition, I had confessed that the book was in the making for a long time, however, now it seems that the delay has hugely been compensated by the interest shown by individuals as well as institutions, which is self-manifest in the publication of the present edition in less than a year and a half. My apprehension at the time of its publication in 2011 was that many would treat this as yet another biography of Maulana Azad whereas it is 'less a biography of an individual and more a story of the political process of late colonial India', where he occupies a significant place. The scholarly community has been discerning enough not to confuse such works with hagiography/ biography as some would have liked others to believe. The proof is that hardback edition of the book has been hosted by the websites in languages such as German, French, Spanish, Dutch, Italian, Polish, Slovenian and Japanese.

It is certainly an occasion to sincerely acknowledge all individuals and institutions for their support. While I do so, I express my gratitude to my teachers, Professors Romila Thapar and Muzaffar Alam at the Centre for Historical Studies, JNU. I thank Professor Barun De for his kindness. I also thank Mrs. Purnima Ghosh of Kharagpur, for her affection.

I thank many friends, whom I inadvertently skipped acknowledging earlier for their support. Special ones are Venu Rajamony, Madhu Kumar Reddy, Anuradha Duda, Rahul Kulshreshtha, Sanjay Verma, Sangeeta Matta Verma, Salil Misra, Hulas Singh, Neerja Singh, Javed Alam, Shashi Bhushan Upadhya, Padma J. Anagol and late E.H. Qadri.

I thank Syed Ali Kazim, Sarfaraz Nasir, Firoz Ansari, Zahid Ashraf and Abdul Aziz for their love and affection.

I thank many family members, whose affection and care I have enjoyed all these years. They are Rana Perveen, Mojeeb Alam, Fauzia Perveen, Shahin Iqbal, Aftab Taiyab, Imtiaz Husain and Shadab Taiyab.

Once again, I thank my wife Farah and son Miraan for their unqualified support and sharing the joy of success of the hardback edition.

December 2012 RIZWAN QAISER

Preface

Maulana Abul Kalam Azad (1888-1958), became conscious of the role he would play in the nationalist movement quite early. The most interesting illustration of this consciousness was seen in the beginning of 1922 when he issued a pamphlet titled *Qaul-i-Faisal* (Final Verdict) during his trial following his arrest in the wake of the Non-Cooperation–Khilafat movement at Calcutta in December 1921. He issued written statements instead of defending himself in a court of law. While addressing the magistrate, he wrote

> Mr. Magistrate, I do not wish to take more time of the court. This is an interesting chapter of history in which we both are engaged: I stand in the dock of an under trial and you in the chair of a magistrate. I admit that the chair of a magistrate is as important as the dock. Let's finish the task fast. The historian and the future are awaiting us. We shall meet more often as this process shall go on till such time as the door of another court of law opens up, however it shall be the court of divine laws of God, the time shall be its judge, and a final judgment shall be written.[1]

The timing of issuing this statement was indeed crucial—the Non-Coöperation–Khilafat movement was still going on and several top leaders of the Congress as well as the Khilafat Committee were under arrest. In this statement Maulana Azad had launched a scathing attack on the British government and many of its repressive policies. At this stage of political development Azad's contributions to the ongoing nationalist movement had not grown to warrant the attention of a historian, as it was to be in the days to come.

Azad emerged on the Indian horizon simultaneously as an intellectual and a nationalist. He enjoyed an impeccable reputation on both counts. In the realm of his intellectual life he drew upon a large number of resources from within as well as outside India. The creative calibre of Azad made him blend several strands in order to produce a viable intellectual world-view which he claimed to be his own. In the realm of political life, even though he started his political career as an underground activist by joining *Yugantar*, an extremist group active in the wake of the partition of Bengal, in 1905, he made a quick shift to embrace pan-Islamism as a tool to generate an anti-colonial nationalist ideology particularly among the Muslims. This shift was apparent particularly during the *Al-Hilal* period, which lasted through the Non-Cooperation–Khilafat movement. However, soon after the withdrawal of the movement, Azad was convinced that the efficacy of pan-Islamism was no longer valid under the changed circumstances and a new order of political engagement had become a necessity. This realization brought him closer to the Congress, which he presided over in 1923. After joining the Congress, his central concern was to strengthen the Congress and bring the Muslims of India closer to it in order to make the on-going nationalist struggle for freedom stronger. He strove hard to fight the growing alienation of Muslims from the Congress, particularly in the 1920s and 1930s. At the same time, he wanted the Congress to be more accommodative towards Muslims in the party structure as well as the government formation, particularly after the election of 1937. His unflinching commitment to the cause of Indian nationalism again earned him the chair of the president of the Indian National Congress in 1940.

This brief sketch of Azad's political trajectory shows that he was a historical personality of significance and yet very little was known about him for a long time. The truth of the matter is that Azad was not willing to put on record all the facts of his personal and political life. Even in *Tazkirah*, which he wrote while he was interned at Moorabadi, in Ranchi during 1916-19, he was reticent about himself and concentrated more on highlighting the achievements of his ancestors. There was an element of reticence in Azad to let others peep into his life and yet a palpable desire was apparent that some day, perhaps a historian would pick-up the loose threads to weave a story for the world to take interest in his intellectual and political life. During his lifetime two biographical works of his were published. One was by Mahadev Desai, published in 1941 under the title *Maulana Abul Kalam Azad: The President of Indian National Congress, a Biographical Memoir*, in which Desai, gave some basic details about his ancestry and political ascendancy which would justify his election as president of the Indian National Congress in 1940. However, it is difficult to consider this biography as a work borne out of the rigours of scholarship of a historian. Later in 1946, A.B. Rajput published *Maulana Abul Kalam Azad*, but this too was a work of hagiography rather than serious scholarship. The scholarly silence was finally broken by Azad when *India Wins Freedom* was published posthumously soon after his death in 1958. It attracted the attention of historians but mostly from a perspective of material to challenge some of Azad's assertions like that the process of the making of Pakistan started from the time Jawaharlal Nehru went against accommodating two Muslim League members in government formation in the United Provinces in 1937. Another assertion by Azad in his memoir was concerning his role in negotiations with the Cabinet Mission, in which the federal structure of the future government of India was clinched, but this was undone because of a statement issued by Nehru on 10 July 1946 that the Congress was bound only to enter the Constituent Assembly. Azad argued that because of this statement the Muslim League, which had earlier agreed with broader formulations of the Cabinet Mission, decided to pull out, leading to a total failure of the whole process of negotiations. Historians have challenged even this assertion of Azad.

This assertion apart, *India Wins Freedom* was caught in another bout of controversy when the '30 pages' of the volume which was earlier withheld in 1958 were published in 1988 coinciding with his birth centenary the same year. The 30 pages did not add anything startling yet led to a serious uproar in academic and political circles. Many scholars went to the extent of claiming that *India Wins Freedom* was not by Maulana Azad at all. Two scholars who challenged its authenticity were V.N. Datta,[2] and

Syeda Saiyidain Hameed.[3] They both seem to suggest that Azad dictated the said autobiography to Humayun Kabir and it was published posthumously. They also argued that it does not reflect the literary style that the Maulana had adopted rather early in life.

Any serious study on Azad has to take place against the backdrop of an academic debate among historians, political scientists and others whether there is compatibility between Islam and particularistic nationalism since he had invoked the authority of Islam in the service of Indian nationalism. Many have argued that there is an essential contradiction between the two on account of the notion of *umma*, believers in Islam which presupposes the existence of a trans-national community of Muslims. Some would argue that Muslims tend to organize their collective life in a manner to actualize the larger world-view of the *sharia,* a set of religious laws, which may not be possible in a pluralistic society. In such societies the desire to organize life conditioned by the *sharia* would lead Muslims to a politics of separatism.[4] Robinson has been pursuing this line of enquiry for quite some time.[5] This line of enquiry was attempted to be further reinforced by Farzana Sheikh when she argued

> The elements of Indo-Muslim discourse and the assumptions that followed there from are also crucial if we are to understand fully the significance of Muslim separatism as the triumph of the 'minority politics'. What is important is to recognize that these concerns had as much to do with the status of the Muslims as minority as with the espousal of a view that presupposed this minority's pre-eminent claim to power. Such a view was shaped not only by the ingredients of a Mughal political culture nurtured in the context of Muslim political domination in India but by a religious tradition whose relationship to power was deemed to be both necessary and divinely endorsed.[6]

The proponents of such a line of enquiry have largely ignored the findings in an important work where it has been argued that separatism was not inherent in Muslim politics. It occurred due to the several difficulties associated with the demands of many Muslim leaders and formations, which the Congress was not able to accommodate. It was this lack of accommodation which pushed many Muslims towards separatism, particularly after the failure to arrive at a consensus on the Nehru Report. It has been argued that the

> Change cannot be explained by pointing out to an ever present antagonism between Hindus and Muslims as some scholars tend to do. There were certainly occasions when antagonism between the two communities surfaced itself, but this cannot be described as having been always present. Nor can the change in the nature of Muslim politics be described as an inevitable manifestation of a separate Muslim nationalism.[7]

It has been further argued from time to time that there were difficulties in terms of cordiality of relations between the two communities, however, there were many opportunities as well, which made it possible for the two to come together on several occasions.[8] 'The emergence of the demand for India's partition, therefore, was not inherent in the situation from the beginning, but was primarily the result of the development between 1928 and 1940.'[9] In the light of arguments such as the above, it does not seem tenable to argue that there was inherent separatism in Muslim politics.

In some of the recent works it has been argued that 'the rise of pan-Islamism helped to establish the credentials of particularistic nationalism'.[10] In the context of Arab nationalism it is argued that pan-Islamism generated the possibility of a larger community of *ummas* and the smaller nation of *watan*, the place of birth.[11] In the context of the larger pan-Islamic ideology it can be pointed out that Jamaluddin Afghani, the chief proponent of pan-Islamism, was caught in some kind of contradiction where it was argued that there was a need for reform within the Islamic community. However, this reform was not possible without independence from imperialist domination, which could take place only in a limited and particularistic context. It is further pointed out that in the scheme of Afghani, pan-Islamism was the ultimate goal but the more proximate goal was to rid the Muslims of Western colonialism. Therefore, while Islamic unity was perceived to be essential, national unity was more important.[12] Afghani had an opportunity to stay in India during 1880-2 when he interacted with many Indians. In the course of his stay he was able to write many essays and deliver several lectures where he laid emphasis on those factors that united Indians and distinguished them from the British.[13] He focused his arguments on two fronts: 'against traditionalists who wished to maintain traditional learning in the old language as it was, and against modernizers who supported the British method of higher education and the spread of modern ideas through the medium of English'.[14] He did not argue for any kind of religious unity since he desired that all Indians should be united against the British. Nor did he express any sectarian or separatist tendencies in relation to India.[15] In another context of a multi-religious society such as Indonesia, Islam emerged as an equally potent factor to mobilize nationalist political forces. In 1912 a political formation called the *Sarekat Islam* was founded. Its immediate objective was not the independence of Indonesia but to promote Islamic values and rid society of many false beliefs.[16] However, the same formation soon graduated to become a force to reckon with, in the context of nationalist political mobilization. In its second congress in 1917, it made many demands such as self-government and elimination of 'sinful capitalism'.[17] It emerges from the preceding arguments that in several colonial societies, the indigenous resources such as language, culture and religion were utilized in the course of the nationalist political mobilization.

Jamaluddin Afghani seemed to have left a much deeper influence on several leaders engaged in similar exercises of mobilizing indigenous resources to promote the cause of Indian nationalism. One of them was Maulana Abul Kalam Azad, whose writings and political activities in the initial years seemed to fall within this framework. He was able to make use of religion for political mobilization but made little efforts to revive religious institutions of a bygone era. His invocation of Islam had the limited purpose of letting Muslims develop a sense of confidence in the context of colonial cultural hegemony. Imagery from Islam was invoked only to embolden the community for the politics of confrontation. Envisaging a politics such as this was in a way a historical necessity. However, Azad was conscious to remind Muslims that their becoming partners in freedom along with Hindus should not be borne out of a sense of diffidence, but from a point of strength. He followed such a line of thinking particularly during the *Al-Hilal* phase. He attacked the conservative *ulema*, religious scholars, for their views that were caught up in a time warp, and the modernists for their attempts to reconcile Indians at large, and Muslims in particular, with British rule. He treated pan-Islamism as a source to reinforce Indian nationalism. He maintained this line of thought and action till the Non-Cooperation and Khilafat movement. However, soon after this movement was withdrawn, Azad was convinced that the relevance of pan-Islamism was lost forever and was inexorably drawn to the Congress, which he presided over in 1923 for the first time. From this time onwards he did not look back to his earlier thoughts, though he kept referring to them later as well in a manner to emphasize some continuity, which, ironically was not there. However, even after joining the Congress, Azad's major concern was to draw Muslims closer to Indian nationalism as it was articulated by the Congress, but at the same time he persisted in impressing upon the Congress to agree to accommodate Muslims in the power structure. Such a line of thinking acquired salience, particularly in the 1930s and 1940s. In independent India, Maulana Azad was the Minister of Education, and in that capacity his concern was to expand the social base of education, including the scientific and technological. His role was crucial in the founding of many cultural and literary institutions, which are still serving the nation well.

In pursuit of the present study to understand the dynamics of relationship between a leader and society in political processes, a number of unexplored primary sources such as writings by Azad, including correspondences and speeches, private papers of several important nationalist leaders, government records, institutional papers like AICC files and the Transfer of Power volumes have been made use of. For the sixth chapter of the present work, the files of the Ministry of Education have been extensively consulted. For the purpose of a complete picture of the historical circumstances in which Azad was active as an ideologue, a leader, and a minister, secondary sources too have been utilized. The present work consists of six chapters followed by a conclusion.

The first chapter discusses Azad's attempts to seek ideological and political moorings, which led him in various directions. He began his political career as an extremist and later moved on to embrace pan-Islamism but only in consonance with Indian nationalism. The second chapter discusses his engagements with building bridges with pan-Islamism. The third chapter deals with efforts to fight the growing tide of communalism in the 1920s, while exhorting Muslims to join the cause of an integrative politics in order to strengthen Indian nationalism. The fourth chapter discusses his efforts to convince the Congress leaders to adopt a policy of greater accommodation of Muslims in the power structure, while being sensitive to their identity and cultural concerns. The fifth chapter discusses his election as the Congress president in 1940 and the series of negotiations that he carried out with the Cripps Mission in 1942 and the Cabinet Mission in 1946 in order to win India's freedom without conceding the Muslim League's demand for partition of the country. The sixth chapter discusses Maulana Azad's role as the Minister of Education during 1947-58, a period fraught with possibilities and challenges. Maulana Azad met these challenges with vision and wisdom to guide the nation through.

NOTES

1. Abul Kalam Azad, *Qaul-i-Faisal*, Taj Publishers, Delhi, 1967, p. 141.
2. V.N. Datta, *Maulana Azad*, Manohar, Delhi, 1990, p. ix.
3. Syeda Saiyidain Hameed, *Islamic Seal on India's Independence, Abul Kalam Azad: A Fresh Look*, Oxford University Press, Karachi, 1998, p. 263.
4. Francis Robinson, *Islam and Muslim History in South Asia*, Oxford University Press, Delhi, 2000, Robinson has argued that, 'Where Muslims form a minority, there frequently springs up a demand that Muslims should be organised as a separate political community, either as a separate nation state or as a state within a state', p. 177.
5. Francis Robinson, 'Islam and Muslim Separatism: A Historical Debate', in Mushirul Hasan, ed., *Communal and Pan-Islamic Trends in Colonial India*, rev. edn., Manohar, Delhi, 1985.
6. Farzana Sheikh, *Community and Consensus in Islam: Muslim Representation in Colonial India, 1860-1947*, Cambridge University Press, Cambridge, 1989, p. 9.

7. Uma Kaura, *Muslims and Indian Nationalism: The Emergence of the Demand for India's Partition, 1928-40*, Manohar, Delhi, 1977, p. 163.
8. Ibid., 164.
9. Ibid.
10. James P. Piscatori, *Islam in a World of Nation-States*, Cambridge University Press, Cambridge, 1986, p. 77.
11. Ibid.
12. Nikki R. Keddi, *An Islamic Response to Imperialism, Political and Religious Writings of Syed Jamaluddin al Afghani*, University of California Press, Berkeley, 1968, p. 43.
13. Ibid., p. 57.
14. Ibid., p. 58.
15. Ibid.
16. Hans Kahler, 'A Short History of Indonesia', in *The Muslim World: A Historical Survey Part IV Modern Times*, tr. and adaptation by F.R.C. Bagley, E.J. Brill, Leiden, 1981, p. 302.
17. Ibid., p. 303.

Acknowledgements

This book has been in the making for a long time and now that it has taken shape, the immediate realization is that I have incurred a huge debt to a large number of people, including my teachers, family members, friends and all those who play an important role in keeping the sources of history safe for posterity. I can never pay them back but I would like to thank them from the bottom of my heart, knowing that it is still an inadequate expression of my gratitude for adding meaning to my work and life.

My deepest gratitude is to Professor Bimal Prasad, who not only taught me affectionately but also ensured that I had a place to stand in the academic world. I am equally grateful to Professor Uma Singh under whose supervision I obtained my research degrees at the South Asian Studies Division of the School of International Studies, Jawaharlal Nehru University, New Delhi. She has been a constant source of confidence and support. I thank Professors Kalim Bahadur, S.D. Muni and I.N. Mukherji. I thank my teachers at the Centre for Historical Studies, especially Professors Bipan Chandra, K.N. Pannikar, Harbans Mukhia and Savyasachi Bhattacharya. I thank Professors V.N. Datta and Asghar Ali Engineer for their help and the remarkable insight into the life of Maulana Azad.

I owe a deep sense of gratitude to many teachers at Munger, my native town in Bihar. I fondly remember Hafiz Abdur Razzaq Saheb, who taught me the fundamentals of Urdu and recitation of the Quran. He advised me to have patience in moments of desperation. Alas! Hafiz Saheb is not here to see this work, which essentially is the outcome of the formula he shared with me years ago. My middle school teacher, whom all of us fondly addressed as Idris Master Saheb, taught us English grammar and left a lasting impression on all his students. Bal Govind Mishra, Principal of

Zila School taught me a strong sense of discipline. Professor Shamshad Sahar, with the help of Urdu literature taught me how to develop a critical sense of the relationship between literature and society. I pay my homage to all of them for their extraordinary contribution to my ordinary life.

I thank all my colleagues in the Department of History and Culture, Jamia Millia Islamia, especially Professors Rafaqat Ali Khan, Narayani Gupta, G.P. Sharma, Mushirul Hasan, Azizuddin Husain, Drs. Neshat Manzar and Farhat Nasrin. I also thank my colleagues in other departments of the University. They are Professors Mujtaba Khan, M. Rais Khan, Sharfuddin Ahmad, Anisur Rahman and Ameena Kazi Ansari.

My sincere thanks are due to all the staff members of the Zakir Husain Library, Jamia Millia Islamia, Central Library, Jawaharlal Nehru University, National Archives of India and the Nehru Memorial Museum & Library, especially Neelam Vats, Shazia Faridi, Soumya Mohanty, Dharmendra Rawat and Shashi Anand. I also thank Jaya Ravindran of the National Archives of India, for her help. The photographs used in this volume except Plate 11 is courtesy the Director, NMML, New Delhi.

My friends have always known that without their support, it would have been difficult to sustain the rigours of life and research. They stood by me in moments of despair. In the long list of such friends, special ones are Shibli, Rashid Taraz, Abdisalam, K. Krishna Reddy, Shekhar Singh, Shikha Sen, Saroj Thapa, Ajit Jha, Rashid Zeya, Perwaiz Nazir, Mohammad Sajjad, Subrat Raut, Musarrat Jabeen, Nandita D. Majumdar and Zafar Naeem. Many former students, Mujahid Raza, Ahmadulla Khan and Manju, who now are more like friends, I thank them all.

Ann Ninan, of all my friends, deserves special thanks for editing my work. She painstakingly proof-read the book to make it error free. However, if there are any, I alone am responsible.

I thank my uncles Taha Ashique, Mohammad Taiyab, Tahir Husain and Zahid Husain for their support ever since the early loss of my parents and grandparents. I thank my eldest brother Amin Arshad for his encouragement. I thank Ejaz Husain, for his sustained interest in the progress of the work. My father-in-law,

Ishrat Husain has been a source to rely on under all circumstances. I thank Anil Nauriya, and Uma Rani, a mother figure, for their encouragement. And Ghosh Babu (Kamal Kumar Ghosh) of Kharagpur who along with his family took care of me and my brothers in the dark days of 1964.

My brothers Perwaiz Ahmad and Imran Ahmad would have been happy seeing this work, had they been around. I fondly hope that Irfan Haidar, my youngest brother will one day return home to share the joy of completing this work.

Special thanks are due to Shri Ramesh Jain of Manohar Publishers & Distributors for his consistent cooperation and encouragement. I thank Siddharth Chowdhury, for his patience with my innumerable questions, while expediting the publication of the volume.

Finally, my wife Farah and son Miraan, who were ever willing to put up with my long absences, deserve special thanks. It is no exaggeration that the present work is an outcome of my labour and their sacrifice. Thanking them will never be enough.

I have dedicated this work to the memory of my parents, Mohammad Yaseen and Akbari Begum and grandparents, Ashiq Ali and Fatima Khatoon for their love, which I enjoyed as a child. I cherish their commitments to secular values, which they never compromised with even under the most trying conditions.

RIZWAN QAISER

CHAPTER ONE

The Historical Background: Azad's Search for Ideological and Political Moorings, 1906-1918

Maulana Abul Kalam Azad was one of the few nationalist leaders who stood out among a galaxy of leaders on account of his intellectual prowess and deep commitment to the on-going nationalist political processes in twentieth-century India. Azad's contributions towards the national as well as intellectual life of India are multifaceted and call for serious attention from historians. Any study on Azad would have to take into account certain important points; the larger theoretical considerations of the relationship between an individual, society and political processes at large, particularly in the context of the anti-imperialist struggle. It is important to examine as to what kindled Azad's imagination and made him dedicate himself to the cause of India's freedom? How did Azad negotiate the turns in his personal and political life either by way of resolving contradictions in his thoughts or the confirmation of his ideas and action? How did Azad maintain an extremely complex relationship with the Congress leaders? These are issues concerning Azad's life that have remained unexplored. The present study makes a serious attempt to understand the process of a search for ideological and political moorings that Azad struggled for before charting out a course in consonance with the Congress.

Azad was able to blend the liberal political ethos with the mobilization of religio-cultural resources of Islam and Muslims in order to strengthen Indian nationalism. The course of his political journey did not move in a linear manner, as he confronted all kinds of trials and tribulations. The terrain of his journey was marked by periodic shifts and adjustments depending on the exigencies of the historical circumstances and the possibilities of practical politics. However, despite shifts and adjustments he was steadfast to Indian nationalism. He was committed to bringing Muslims within the fold of the Indian nationalist movement; however, in the course of the movement he also wanted the Indian National Congress to accommodate Muslims in the party structure as well as in the government, particularly in the context of ministry formation after the 1937 provincial elections. In March 1940 Azad took charge as the president of the Indian National Congress and strove hard against the 'two-nation' theory of the Muslim League and the Pakistan movement from within as well as outside the Congress. He walked extra miles to negotiate with various missions such as the Cripps Mission in April 1942 and the Cabinet Mission in March-April 1946, sent by the British government in order to make a strong case for India's independence and against the making of Pakistan. At the same time he worked hard to mobilize political resources of those Muslim political formations that were outside the fold of the Congress yet committed to the cause of Indian nationalism.

After India's independence, Azad was entrusted with the responsibility of looking after the Ministry of Education as minister. The irony was that at the time he presided over the ministry, education was not even in the Concurrent List, but only in the State List. Despite these limitations, he strove hard to lay deep foundations for academic, scientific and cultural institutions so that they could serve the new nation. At one stage, Azad thought of introducing conscription in order to overcome the paucity of qualified teachers. Education for Azad was a means to deepen the roots of democracy through democratization of knowledge by establishing educational institutions, accessible to the larger mass of the people. Another concern of Azad was scientific and technological education to meet the challenges of the time. Challenges such as these were daunting in the face of financial difficulties, which the nascent republic faced, however, it was the considered view of Azad that irrespective of these difficulties, the nation had to move on.

Despite the serious role played by nationalist Muslims in reinforcing Indian nationalism at different stages of its evolution, many historians and political scientists have laid emphasis on separatism among them, whether in an instrumentalist manner or as an essential part of the Muslim community's collective life. Two instances should suffice. Paul R. Brass has argued that the 'ideology of Muslim separateness did not flow necessarily and inexorably out of the objective differences between Hindus and Muslims, but out of the uses which were made of those differences through manipulation of symbols of Muslim unity and Hindu-Muslim separateness by an elite concerned to preserve its political privileges'.[1] It has to be noted that contrary to Brass's formulation that separatism was an instrument in the hands of the Muslim elite, Francis Robinson has recently argued that 'in development of Muslim separatism many Muslim leaders had been constrained by political ideas derived from the Islamic culture, indeed, on occasions they had been constrained by religious belief itself'.[2] Such a trend in historical thinking has persisted among historians for quite some time. In *The Muslims of British India*, Peter Hardy has surveyed the political landscape of Muslims in India in general in the context of relationship between religion and politics and argued that 'In 1920-2 Abul Kalam Azad and *Jamiyyat* were advocating the mental partition of India'.[3] Peter Hardy's contention has been that Azad and *Jamiyyat* were indeed talking about Indian independence but only to become in free India 'members of *imperium* in *imperio*'.[4] What Hardy has missed out while making an argument such as this was that people like Azad were simply making use of religious idioms to convince Muslims about the necessity of their participation in the freedom struggle. In one of his papers, 'Islam and Muslim Separatism: A Historical Debate', Francis Robinson has argued that it is rather surprising that the Ulema of Jamiatul-Ulema-i-Hind were able to strike conciliation with nationalism, considering that 'separatism in Islam is inherent'. He also stated that 'Hasrat Mohani, Mohammad Ali and Maulana Azad all were working only towards an Islamic goal'.[5] Moin Shakir in *Khilafat to Partition 1919-1947* did not accuse Azad of generating separatism, nonetheless he said that his basic political philosophy was highly romantic and the goal he pursued was the unity of Muslims and the attainment of *Sharia*.[6]

In all these studies the Maulana's life was not the central theme of discussion. Remarks were made in the larger context of Muslim politics in the subcontinent. However, there are works available on the Maulana written by those who were at some stage or the other closely associated with him. Mahadev Desai[7] has uncritically suggested that the Maulana studied at Al-Azhar University at Cairo. In the course of delineating Azad's political career Desai does not take into account the complexity of historical circumstances in which Azad operated. A.B. Rajput too makes a similar point that Azad studied at Al-Azhar, which he never did. Apart from highly generalized statements there are factual inaccuracies in the book too. For instance, at one point the author argues that the Maulana was responsible for starting the 'Mass Contact Movement',[8] after he became the president of the Congress, which, however, was not the case. H.L. Kumar's *The Apostle of Unity: A Biographical Study of Maulana Azad*, is a preliminary but laudatory study on Azad, which covers the period only till July 1941. Other than these, there are studies in Urdu, for instance Asar bin Yahya Ansari in an exaggerated manner has argued that the Medical Mission sent to Turkey in the context of the Balkan Wars was inspired by the formation of *Hizbollah* by Azad,[9] which is not in conformity with the actual historical developments. The formation of *Hizbollah* by Azad took place much after the Mission had left the Indian shores. Similarly, in disregard to factual accuracy he argues that on 15 April 1940 at a meeting at Wardha, it was on the insistence of Gandhiji that Azad relented to become the president of the Congress.[10] Abdul Qavi Dasnavi in a voluminous book *Hayat Abul Kalam Azad* has given immense details without any distinct perspective. For instance, Chapter Four consists of about 250 pages dealing with the period from 1928 to 1947 and has relied heavily on the Urdu translation of *India Wins Freedom*. Other highly limited sources relied upon are *Tabarrukat-i-Azad* and *Naqsh-i-Azad*, which contain essays written by Azad, compiled and edited by Ghulam Rasool Meher. Other than these, very few sources have been used to construct the history of a period full of complex historical developments. In an interesting study, Mohammad Farooq Qureshi has argued that in the course of the Pakistan movement and after the making of Pakistan, the Muslim League reviled the lives of all those who were opposed to the making of Pakistan.[11] While talking about Azad's conviction he points out that he was opposed to all sectarian considerations in regard to Indian nationalism. As a consequence he did not waver in his conviction and could not bring himself around to accept the partition of India.[12]

There have been other scholars too who have examined Azad's Islamic world-view and his political stand as regards the freedom of the country. In *Destiny of Indian Muslims*, Abid Husain is of the opinion that the Maulana, endowed with tremendous talent, was able to develop a better understanding of Islam, which he presented to the Muslim community with the help of the *Tarjumanul Quran*. While doing so, he lacked consistency because of his own 'ambition to reform not only the religious thought but also the religious life of the Muslims, and the need of the time was that in the critical phase of Indian history through which they were passing, he should have led his community and his nation in the fight for freedom'.[13] Abid Husain has further argued that Maulana Azad failed in his first endeavour since he did not lead an austere life, which could have attracted the mass of the Muslims. But as far as his political objective was concerned, he was only partially successful.[14] Abid Husain's formulation is helpful in understanding Azad only to a limited extent, for after all he could not be called someone who failed in his political objective. The viability of the political thought and actions of Azad could be seen also from another angle that after Independence Indian Muslims had no one to look to, except the Maulana.

Contrary to the perception of Abid Husain, Mohammad Mujeeb is of the opinion that the Maulana's attempt to invoke the notion of *Umma Vahida* (one nation), in the wake of the Khilafat did not carry conviction with everybody and he was isolated. He further argues, 'Perhaps there would come a time when Indian Muslims will discover for themselves the farsightedness of the Maulana in discovering a precedent such as this.'[15] He further argues that even though the Maulana did not have a large following, he was consulted on important matters because of his political acumen. He never bothered about individuals, and did not indulge in political gossip and manipulation.[16]

Abid Husain and M. Mujeeb both wrote during 1965-7 and were able to assess the Maulana on terms which Azad himself was trying to lay down in terms of ideology and mobilization technique. Since then, there was no really serious work on him for a long time, barring Mushirul Haq's *Muslim Politics in Modern India*, in which certain aspects of Azad's politics were analysed. The academic silence on him was broken with the publication of Ian Henderson Douglas' work[17] in which for the first time the intellectual as well as political life of the Maulana was the subject of serious study. However, it must be said that he focuses more on the intellectual life of Azad than the political. Douglas has tried to establish that in the formation of the intellectual life of the Maulana, the influences of an array of scholars from Shah Waliullah to Allama Shibli can be seen. Jamaluddin Afghani and other scholars of the *al-Manar* group too had their share of influence on Azad.[18] However, while analysing Azad's political life he commits a serious error of judgement when he argues that the nationalist strand of Azad's politics can be seen only from the time he became the president of the Indian National Congress in 1923.[19] Such an assertion seriously undermines the nationalist political activities of the Maulana prior to 1923.

Another serious study on Azad is by V.N. Datta[20] who has examined the contributions made by him against the background of nationalist Muslim politics. Datta, despite a sympathetic approach to Azad, argues that the nationalist content of his political endeavours took shape only in the context of the Non-Cooperation–Khilafat movement. It is further argued that only in the context of the said movement did Azad talk about Hindu-Muslim unity.[21] Subsequently Azad made serious attempts for the Muslims' (particularly those who had remained under the influence of Indian nationalism) acceptance of the Nehru Report. It is to be noted that efforts had already been launched by various Muslim political formations to arrive at a consensus in order to work out a constitutional mechanism, which would ensure a share in power for Muslims, particularly in Muslim majority provinces. But the

Hindu Mahasabha's intransigent attitude at the All Party Conference in Calcutta, December 1928, resulted in failure to generate consensus on the Nehru Report. It resulted in the alienation of Muslims from the Congress. In order to stem such tendencies Azad became an integral part of the launching of the All-India Nationalist Muslim Party in July 1929 in order to seek Muslim support for the Congress and the ongoing nationalist movement. All these efforts established that he was a 'confirmed nationalist'.[22] Despite his sympathetic treatment, certain problems of perception persist. For instance, if we accept the notion of 'confirmed nationalist' as given by Datta, it would create a difficulty in categorizing his earlier political activities, which too can be considered to fall in the category of nationalist political activities. For instance, it was out of his nationalist political zeal that he became a part of the underground political endeavours in 1906. Even during the *Al-Hilal* phase, his essential emphasis remained on India's liberation from British rule as well as Hindu-Muslim unity. P.N. Chopra has tried to study Azad in the context of the unfolding historical circumstances in which he was working for the reinforcing of nationalist political processes, however, on occasions many of his formulations about Azad appear sketchy. There are instances of factual inaccuracies too. For instance at one place Chopra argues that Azad in the beginning years of the first decade of the twentieth century 'visited Egypt where he met such great men of the time as Syed Jamaluddin al Afghani, who was hailed as the champion of pan-Islamism'.[23] Such assertions are contrary to historical facts. For instance, it is true that Maulana Azad was under the influence of the thoughts of Jamaluddin Afghani and many of his disciples such as Sheikh Abduh and Rasheed Rida but he could not have had any opportunity to meet Afghani since he had passed away in 1897.[24]

Ejaz Ahmad in his essay on Azad argues that despite the fact that Azad could have contributed towards secularism, and to the enlightenment and emancipation of the average Muslim, he chose not to do so. Azad was more interested in religious fundamentalism and revivalism; so much so that he started dreaming of becoming *Imam-al-Hind*.[25] It is argued that Azad failed to mobilize a programme for social and religious reform, which could have detached Muslims from separatist politics by linking anti-colonial, secular political vision with demands of social and economic justice.[26] These formulations about the ideology and politics of Azad represent extreme views.

Syeda Saiyidain Hamid[27] has made a survey of Azad's personal and political life. There are, however, several contradictions in her assessment. For instance, she strongly questions the authenticity of *India Wins Freedom*. She argues,

> What creates doubt about *India Wins Freedom* as Azad's work is not only that Kabir's prose was an inadequate vehicle for his literary style or the intricacy of his mind but the errors and the virtual absence of style. Kabir's insistence that Azad gave a blanket approval confirms the hypothesis. Azad never gave such hearty approval.[28]

It is ironical that despite such a strong view about the authenticity of *India Wins Freedom*, the author goes on to use the same narrative as a source to construct an argument about a crucial period of the 1940s, which experienced successive attempts to hammer out constitutional arrangements, which would satisfy the Congress and the Muslim League. For instance she uses arguments extended by Azad in his autobiography as regards the Cabinet Mission negotiations and accepts his assertions uncritically as she argues, 'the by now famous statement of Nehru which altered the "course of history" and undid all that Azad had managed to accomplish by way of negotiation, is given detailed analysis in *India Wins Freedom*'.[29] S.R. Mehrotra in a recent study has challenged Azad's assertion that the failure on the part of the Congress to form a coalition ministry in the United Provinces led to the partition of the country. Even though Mehrotra recognizes the fact that the failure of the talks 'exacerbated relations between the Congress and the League'.[30] While talking about the failure of the Cabinet Mission Plan, Maulana Azad had said that had Nehru not given his press statement on 10 July 1946 the Muslim League would not have withdrawn from its commitment to the said Plan. Mehrotra has challenged this assertion too. He argues that Azad's main concern was as stated in *India Wins Freedom* that 'The only result of the creation of Pakistan was to weaken the position of the Muslims in the subcontinent of India.'[31] Contrary to these formulations, V.N. Datta argues that Maulana Azad 'had realised that with the growing popularity of the Muslim League, the Cabinet Mission Plan was the best option available to thwart the idea of Pakistan'.[32] Keeping in view the arguments of historians of all shades, one can assess the role that Azad played.

II

In the beginning of the twentieth century there were two distinct political choices before Indian Muslims. First, the politics of loyalism as represented by the Muslim League, founded in 1906. The self-professed objective of the party was to promote the interest of Muslims while seeking the goodwill of the government. Second, was the choice of politics of conflict and resistance. Similar choices had been available to them even in the late nineteenth century. On one side of the spectrum was Sir Syed Ahmad Khan who wanted to promote the interest of the community through education but with government support, whereas on the other side there were the Ulema of the Darul Uloom at Deoband, who challenged British rule.[33] The Muslim political leaders in the mould of the Deoband Ulema were convinced of the efficacy of Islam being pressed into the politics of resistance to the British. This political approach of the Ulema at Darul Uloom got a fillip with the emergence of pan-Islamism, an ideology articulated by Jamaluddin Afghani in the late nineteenth century. Apart from several issues that Afghani touched upon, his anti-colonial formulations were quite strong.[34]

The emergence of pan-Islamic tendencies generated anti-British consciousness among some sections of Indian Muslims who looked upon the West with great suspicion because several Muslim countries were overrun by Western imperialism. It was perceived that the Christian West was bent upon destroying several centres of Muslim political control.[35] This perception was strengthened with the outbreak of the Balkan wars. The conflict in the Balkans provided a backdrop to the rise of several nationalist Muslim leaders. A formidable figure among nationalist Muslims was Mukhtar Ahmad Ansari, who began his political career by leading a Medical Mission in 1912 to Constantinople to provide medical help to the Turkish army.[36] The Ali Brothers too were involved in similar activities. Maulana Mohammad Ali had launched the *Comrade* and *Hamdard* with the purpose of communicating with Muslims on a range of political issues. He raised many questions uncomfortable to the British rulers and incurred their wrath.[37] Hakim Ajmal Khan, another prominent figure of Delhi, was involved with pan-Islamic activities and reached a position of prominence in mounting a challenge to British rule. Zafar Ali Khan, the editor of *Zamindar*, Lahore, too was carrying forward the ideology of resistance to British rule in the context of growing pan-Islamism. However, long before these nationalist Muslim leaders, Hasrat Mohani had embarked on a course of resisting colonial domination through *Urdu-i-Mualla* in 1903. The only difference between Mohani and the others was that he was attracted to the ideology of extremism as advocated by Tilak and other leaders.[38]

It is against this background of the contributions made by nationalist Muslim leaders that we can make an assessment of the rise of Maulana Abul Kalam Azad on the Indian political firmament as a scholar of Islam and a staunch nationalist. The pages of *Al-Hilal*, which Azad had launched in July 1912 from Calcutta, became the main carrier of Azad's viewpoint with regard to politics and religion—essentially attempts to seek Islamic legitimization for his ideas. With the help of *Al-Hilal* he was able to establish a political dialogue with the members of his community and was convinced that engendering political consciousness was a duty incumbent upon him, where Muslims could be ideologically prepared to confront the British. But Azad was also convinced that Muslims as a whole were suffering from an acute sense of diffidence on account of the ideological and cultural hegemonic influence of British rule and due to the absence of a clear objective of demanding freedom. The lack of clarity dictating a course of political action was in a large measure also due to the emerging communalism in the late nineteenth century. In order to overcome a sense of cultural diffidence, Hindus and Muslims both sought their respective roots. The trends ran parallel to each other; and on many occasions either reinforced each other or generated conflict, and laid the basis of the Hindu-Muslim problem.[39] The most serious aspect of revivalism in India in the nineteenth century was when Hindus and Muslims went beyond the last thousand years to search for traditions and heroes, away from one another.[40]

Azad was aware that both the communities had moved away from each other in the realm of politics and culture. It was a daunting task to bring them closer. This would require immense intellectual and political energies. Quite consciously he chose to blend both kinds of energies in order to seek reconciliation between the communities so that it would be easier to challenge colonial domination. Even though Azad's rise to a prominent position in the political and intellectual world was seen only with *Al-Hilal*, he had already started his journey on both counts much earlier. For instance, his politics had acquired a distinct tone in the wake of the partition of Bengal. The short-lived phase of revolutionary terrorism saw Azad as a member of a revolutionary terrorist group about which he writes in his autobiographical narrative, *India Wins Freedom*.[41] However, such statements about an early political career went unnoticed till the historian Rajat Ray detailed the track record of Azad's underground political association with several revolutionaries.[42]

Similarly, in the realm of intellectual pursuit, Azad had already shown his prowess in 1902, when he addressed a letter to Hakeem Mohammad Tabeeb Ali (editor of a journal, *Muraaqqua-e-Alam*) in which he dwelt upon many issues of importance. He said that the protagonists of English education wished to spread Western sciences, but English had been accepted as a means of securing jobs. As a result there was hardly any emphasis on learning science and philosophy. The need of the hour was to translate the works of the West in the languages of the country. Azad went on to say that it was time that the fallacy of the perception that those who believed in sciences were turning to atheism was challenged as also the argument that Islam and science were contradictory.[43] Assertions such as this are significant in the light of the fact that Muslims at large had for long perceived Western education with suspicion since it was thought to be not in conformity with religious injunctions. Syed Ahmad Khan had started a Scientific Society at Ghazipur as early as 1866; a major component of its work was to translate Western scientific literature into Indian languages, particularly

Urdu. Even Jamaluddin Afghani in the course of articulating a pan-Islamic ideology talked about reconciling Islam with modern sciences. The Delhi College in the middle of the nineteenth century had undertaken similar exercises.

It is remarkable that Azad should have advocated the learning of Western sciences, since he himself belonged to a family in which anything Western was anathema. His father Maulana Khairuddin, an *alim* (scholar) of stature, had opposed any possibility of his children picking up Western influences, even in the realm of knowledge and language such as English. Maulana Khairuddin's attitude was not at all surprising considering the backdrop of Muslim antipathy towards English education, particularly in Bengal. How far Maulana Azad agreed with this perception of his father is difficult to ascertain. However, what is certain and revealed later by Azad himself is that he gradually started moving away from the ambit of the family where the ambience of *piri-muridi* was strong.[44] It was in this religious ambience that Azad was born in 1888 in Mecca where his father had gone with the intention of settling down, and later married an Arab lady.

Maulana Khairuddin Dihlawi belonged to the *Naqshbandi Silsilah* of *pirs* and had a large following among the business community of *Suratee Nakhudars* of Calcutta. Maulana Khairuddin was perceived to be a serious scholar of the Quran, Hadith and Islamic theology. It is said that in the post-1857 period, he moved to Mecca with an intention of staying there; there he got married to Aliya, the niece of Shaikh Mohammadd Bin-Zahir Watri, the Mufti of Mecca. The marriage of Maulana Khairuddin into a family of scholars of Mecca provided him with the opportunity of interacting with scholars there. It is also said that Maulana Khairuddin had no desire to return to India, but was compelled by circumstances, when he broke his leg. He along with his family returned to Calcutta perhaps in 1890.[45] V.N. Datta[46] states this but then writes, 'It is not clear when Khairuddin reached Calcutta and how old Azad was at that time. It was probably around 1895 that Khairuddin arrived in Calcutta.'[47]

Maulana Khairuddin had spent a considerable part of his life following a strict regimen in Arabia, which he followed in Calcutta. The children of Khairuddin were only to be brought up in a religious atmosphere, where obligatory performance of *namaz* and other duties was to be followed strictly. In brief, the atmosphere in the family was highly religious and *piri-muridi* was its dominant overtone. Khairuddin wanted that his sons, Abu Nasir (the elder brother of Azad) and Azad himself should succeed him as *pirs*.[48] Any influence, which was external to Islam was anathema to him, and even more so an influence associated with the West.[49]

III

How did Azad receive his father's teachings and practices? It is argued that Azad rejected his father's attitude towards *taqlid* (blind imitation) and the structure of *piri-muridi*.[50] However, for Azad the choice was not clear since he belonged to the tradition of his father and in many ways sought to continue it.[51] But the ever-enquiring mind that Azad was endowed with could not have gone on much longer accepting all this. Slowly but surely Azad began chafing against his domineering father. But this was not enough for a man like him. He had to find a path for himself, as he was to say later,

> I could not reconcile myself with the prevailing customs and belief and my heart was full of a new sense of revolt. The ideas I had acquired from my family and early training could no longer satisfy me. I felt that I must find the truth for myself. Almost instinctively I began to move out of my family orbit and seek my own path.[52]

Seeking his own path, simply meant confronting various aspects of life all by himself, which was not an easy task. Azad had to undergo a process of spiritual tumult and he 'passed from one phase to another and a stage came when all the old bonds imposed on my mind by family and upbringing were completely shattered'.[53] And with this shattering of old influences and ties began a journey of definition of life, its purpose spiritual or political. Azad was to say, 'I felt free of all conventional ties and decided that I would chalk out my own path'.[54]

Chalking out his own path was not an easy task, for he was to undergo the travails of a broken spiritual journey where, as he himself said, he lost faith in religion and became an atheist even though outwardly he followed the rituals of worship. As Azad put it himself, 'I was by now a complete atheist. I took great pride in my belief in materialism and rationalism and saw in religion only ignorance and conjecture'.[55]

The course of his loss of faith and later its recovery around 1910 lasted about eight years, the youthful days from fourteen to twenty-two. In the course of it, Azad had to undergo a process of agony, 'My outward appearance was that of a man who wanted to reconcile religion with reason and intellectual discussion, but within, I had renounced all beliefs and in practice was a sinner. This was the final stage of my despair.'[56]

The loss of faith as well as its recovery marked a distinct phase in the life of Azad. It can be argued that in the travails of an intellectual's journey one finds something of Ghazali's experience as depicted in *Al-Manqizaminzalal*. His rationalism was a stage in the evolution of his religious thought. He believed in contemplation and ratiocination. Having covered all stages of scepticism, doubt, agnosticism, atheism, etc., he came back to his original faith, but it was now his own discovery, not an inherited legacy.[57]

Undergoing the process of loss of faith and its recovery was no easy experience for Azad since he suffered its pangs and indulged in 'various forms of misconduct and there was scarcely any degree of sinfulness which escaped the poor wretched that I was'. While suffering the pains, Azad all along was actually conscious of it. It is not clear how much regret he had while undergoing this, but on discovery of his lost faith he certainly felt quite excited.

> Suddenly the light of hope shone before me. Just as I could not say from where had come the hand, which pushed me into the darkness, so, I cannot explain the hand, which suddenly pulled me out into the light. Nevertheless, the fact is that the light was suddenly manifest and after nine years of groping in the dark, I found the goal I was seeking around me. All doubts faded, all disappointments disappeared and I found the faith and tranquillity I had been seeking.[58]

Azad rarely talked about the period of his tribulations as regards his conviction. But his abundant metaphorical explanations in *Tazkirah* and some personal letters give the impression that during the period under discussion he let his youthful life have full play. It has been argued that all this was taking place while Azad was already married. It is possible to argue that he was looking for personal gratification outside the marriage. However, it is abundantly clear that the affair was a short-lived experience for Azad. The loss on the emotional front was a definite gain on the political front, since by this time he seemed to have matured personally and politically.

While he was caught in the spiritual wilderness of the loss and recovery of faith, he was also simultaneously engaged in defining a political course for himself. He was to do so in the absence of any background of politics in the family, which largely boasted of only spiritual and academic achievements, which Azad was extremely conscious of. In the name of politics, there was nothing explicit; if at all there was anything it was a spirited opposition to the Wahhabi movement about which Azad has talked about so much[59] and was a bit confused himself. However, the Wahhabi movement generally speaking, was opposed to British rule, a fact largely ignored by his father. The Maulana's father Khairuddin was also opposed to any contact with the Western world and its influence on Islamic society. Perhaps this was one of the reasons why Azad was never sent to school. Other than all this, there is hardly any evidence to suggest any significant political atmosphere in the family.

Then how did Azad embark on a political course, that too in the direction of India's freedom from British rule? Historians have barely been able to establish an immediate reason which led Azad to plunge into the freedom struggle. In the absence of evidence, what is widely known is that he started his political career when Bengal was in the throes of the Swadeshi movement in the wake of the partition of Bengal. Azad has given hints about his revolutionary political affiliations in *India Wins Freedom* where he wrote, 'Bengal did not take the measure (partition of Bengal) lying down. There was an unprecedented outburst of political and revolutionary enthusiasm.' He went on,

> It was during this period that I came in contact with Shri Shyam Sunder Chakravarty, who was one of the important revolutionary workers of the day. Through him I met other revolutionaries. I remember having met Shri Aurobindo Ghosh on two or three occasions. The result was that I was attracted to revolutionary politics and joined one of the groups.[60]

Similar indications were seen elsewhere too. 'Not many people knew that the Maulana was involved in the revolutionary struggle and was preparing for a violent overthrow of British rule. He maintained his contacts with the revolutionaries of Bengal while at the same time his agents were active among certain tribals of the Frontier.'[61]

Despite such clear indications, the Maulana's early political career of a revolutionary did not receive attention from historians till Rajat Ray wrote a paper[62] in which the primary evidence culled from archival sources such as Secret Reports, constructed a plausible narrative to establish that Azad had a revolutionary political background. Though Azad himself had argued that, 'In those days the revolutionary groups recruited their members exclusively from the Hindu middle classes. In fact, all the revolutionary groups were actively anti-Muslim.'[63] The statement was not free from substance. Among extremist groups, the use of Hindu ritual and symbols, especially in the vows of initiation, excluded Muslim participation, so much so that the manual of Dacca's Anushilan Samiti, perhaps the biggest of all revolutionary groups, especially laid down that Muslims were not eligible as members.[64] Another major group was Yugantar, which did not have an anti-Muslim bias, but nonetheless was exclusively Hindu.[65]

Under these circumstances, after having come in contact with Shyam Sunder Chakraborty, the Maulana became part of the revolutionary-terrorist world and was introduced to other revolutionaries. When they found that Azad was willing to join them, they were greatly surprised.[66] Thus he became involved with the fringe of the extremist movement.[67] He also made claims that he played a significant role in setting up cells in Bombay and in north Indian towns.[68] Rajat Ray is sceptical of these claims and argues that it is doubtful if the Maulana even penetrated beyond the fringe of the revolutionary circles. However, after the launch of *Al-Hilal*, the intelligence branch conducted enquiries about his antecedents and established that he had been active in the Punjab during 1907-8, was an active helper of the extremists in Lahore, and had contacts with Sufi Amba Prasad and Ajit Singh and other Punjab extremists.[69]

What is also clear from the nature of the Maulana's association with revolutionary politics is that he believed in violence as a method to free India. Abdur Razzaq Malihabadi has reported, 'In the beginning the Maulana believed in violence and was in constant touch with the revolutionaries'.[70] Abdur Razzaq went on to say,

> When I came in contact with the Maulana in 1920 he was still convinced of a violent overthrow of the British. Once he sent me to fetch a few dozen pistols which I did. Later these pistols were sent away for some people. However, during those days Maulana went through a realisation that a violent overthrow of the British may not be possible at all.[71]

With the passage of time Azad developed a new understanding about violence, different from the earlier phase. In reply to a question by Abdur Razzaq Malihabadi, he argued, 'Under the circumstances as they prevail in India and countries like her it is important to pursue a policy of non-violence. So far as the question of non-violence as a moral principle is concerned it is acceptable only in the light of the *Quranic* definition. However, in many cases, violence is also the law of Nature.'[72] This may have been one of the reasons that when the Non-Cooperation movement started Maulana Azad was not willing to accept non-violence as a creed. At best he agreed with the principle of non-violence as a strategy rather than a belief.[73]

Despite Azad's understanding about violence as a method, it may not have proved fruitful in the long run, since such a position did not take the might of the colonial state into account. Gandhi in more ways than one had close encounters with the violent nature of the colonial state during his South African days. Azad was not alone in believing in violence as a method to fight the British; many others shared similar views.

IV

Azad's participation in revolutionary activities could be seen as an indication of his personal conviction. He must have been aware of their limitations since the Muslim masses could barely be involved. It required a different approach and strategy to mobilize them, which in due course of time became Azad's major concern.

He embarked on the course of mobilizing them only with the publication of *Al-Hilal* in July 1912. But the question that historians have persistently asked is what did Azad do between his revolutionary days and the starting of *Al-Hilal*. An answer is yet to be found, though Azad himself has made certain statements: 'It was during this period that I had occasions to go out of India and tour in Iraq, Egypt, Syria and Turkey.'[74] He does not explain whether his trip was on a mission or a personal visit. If it was a personal visit, and that too with his brother, why was it so prolonged?

About this tour Azad made a statement,

> When I came to Iraq, I met some Iranian revolutionaries. In Egypt I came in contact with the followers of Mustafa Kamal Pasha. I also met a group of Young Turks who had established a centre in Cairo and were publishing a weekly from there. When I went to Turkey, I became friends with some of the leaders of the Young Turk Movement. I kept my correspondence with them for many years after my return to India.[75]

Many questions have been raised about Azad's extended trip to West Asia and developing contacts with the nationalists of those countries. Abid Reza Bedar has reconstructed part of Azad's journalistic activities for those years, establishing that between January 1907 and August 1908 Azad worked for *Dar-al-Sultanat* of Calcutta and the *Vakil* of Amritsar, and was in Calcutta at the time of his father's death in August 1908.[76] What is less certain is Azad's claims to have established connection with the Bengal revolutionaries and to have travelled to West Asia all within less than two years.[77] It is further argued that if he was in Calcutta trying to build a relationship of trust with the revolutionaries, he probably did not have time for an extended foreign tour.[78] Moreover, Azad need not have actually visited these countries in order to be in touch with the climate of revolutionary opinion there.[79]

V.N. Datta argues that when after the death of his father Azad journeyed to Islamic countries, he found a new world astir with ideas of liberty, progress and revolutionary Islam. His contacts with these revolutionaries made him lament the indifference of Indian Muslims towards the freedom of their country. 'This made a great impression on Azad.'[80] Datta goes on to argue that Syed Sulaiman Nadvi had raised doubts about Azad's trip to the Middle East, but there is no reason to doubt the account of this visit given by Humayun Kabir.'[81] Azad's visit to the Middle East remains clouded in doubts. Yet there is some fragmentary evidence, which may help establish the credentials of his journey. 'Professor Louis Massignon told me that when he met the Maulana at the residence of Shaikh Alusi in Baghdad in 1908 he felt particularly attracted by his charming features.'[82] This merely confirms Azad's presence in Baghdad in 1908.

His trips to the Middle East seem to have been given importance by Azad himself, particularly as regards his desire to mobilize his co-religionists towards the freedom movement. He said that his contact with one or the other type of revolutionaries convinced him that Muslims should have taken the lead against British imperialism.[83] 'I decided that on my return to India I would take up political work with greater earnestness.'[84] However, Datta argues that it would be naïve to think that it was his Middle East experience alone that inspired Azad to take a plunge in the journalistic venture of *Al-Hilal* and *Al-Balagh*.[85] Datta goes on to invoke psychoanalysis in order to explain the *Al-Hilal* endeavour. 'The bitter experiences of frustration in love, made Azad employ a relatively mature defence mechanism of sublimation. He began to experience henceforth a genuine satisfaction in the cause of his community and his personal ambitions found an appropriate expression through his sublimating channel of social service.'[86] However, Datta provides us with no credible evidence to make his case stronger. Azad returned to his faith towards the end of 1909 or at the beginning of 1910. By then the headiness of his 'love affairs' was also over. Why then did Azad have to wait for another two and a half years to 'sublimate' his emotions in the service of the community? It is important to look for the explanation elsewhere.

A plausible explanation for starting *Al-Hilal* is crucial since this venture put Azad on the national map as an easily recognizable face particularly among those engaged in India's freedom struggle. Datta argues, 'It was the impact of the plight of Muslim countries and the degrading condition of Muslims in India that moved Azad to launch *Al-Hilal* and *Al-Balagh*.'[87] This repudiates his own statement about Azad's sublimating experience. The question then does arise as to what led Azad to start *Al-Hilal*, since this was not merely a journal in the normal sense of the term; it combined Azad's personal journey in the freedom struggle with a clarion call to his co-religionists to be partners in the freedom struggle. Both were couched in profound Islamic expressions, something which came easily to Azad and was easily comprehensible to readers.

V

The Maulana had been given to writing essays since quite early in life, though he may not have got them published. As he put it, 'A serious reading of newspapers and journals had already started off and it inspired me to write a few things. I do not remember having written anything serious. Yet by 1899-1900 I did start scribbling a few things, however I never had the courage to get them published'.[88] Azad was barely twelve years old when he began writing, and got the first chance of editing a paper called *Al-Misbah*.[89] He benefited from his association with *Ahsan-al-Akhbar* brought out by Abdul Ghaffar of Calcutta, who owned a press. Here, according to Azad's own narration, he got a chance to browse through papers and journals, which came in exchange from far-off places such as Egypt, Constantinople, Tripoli, Tunis, Algeria and America. Most of these were in Arabic.[90]Azad got to see two Egyptian journals, *Al-Hilal* and *Al-Muqtatif*. He also got to read *Al-Manar*. Of all these journals and papers, *Al-Manar* seemed to have made a profound influence on Azad.

> From the point of literary style as well as journalistic value the *Al-Manar* was quite a new experience. In matters of religion it did not have so much of impact since Sir Sayyid's ideas had already cast its influence upon me, but it was a fine example of inspiring Arabic literature, and turned out to be so fruitful in the future. Without an iota of doubt I am indebted to the *Al-Manar*.[91]

After his initial brush with the world of journalism, Azad was noticed. Shibli Nomani entrusted him with the responsibility of editing a journal, *Al-Nadwa*, brought out by Nadwatul-Uloom of Lucknow. In his chequered career of journalism Azad seems to have given a pride of place to the *Vakil,* which he edited for a while. 'Around that time the *Vakil* was the most serious of all Urdu newspapers, which took deep interest in national issues and therefore had earned a place of respect for itself.'[92]

After having edited the *Vakil* for about a year he left Amritsar for Calcutta and was associated with another paper called *Darus-Sultanat*. His brother had passed away and his father strongly wished him to stay back in Calcutta. However, after a short while, Azad once again took over the editorship of the *Vakil.*

> About after eight or nine months once again the editorship of the *Vakil* was with me. However by this time my political views had undergone all kinds of metamorphosis, which guided me during my *Al-Hilal* days. These changes were not in tune with the thinking of Shaikh Ghulam Majeed, *therefore, I came back to Calcutta with a firm understanding that in order to speak out openly it was important to have one's own press and bring out a paper*.[93] (Emphasis added)

Azad strongly felt the need to start his own journal in order to give expression to his political thoughts as well as to discuss other issues of the corporate life of Muslims. But he did not have any political platform to articulate his view to his co-religionists. The question that arises is what those issues were on which he felt like speaking out so strongly, in other words, did he really undergo any change of political ideas that made him seriously disagree with Shaikh Ghulam Mohammad, a person with whom Azad seemed to agree and share so much, particularly with regard to Sir Syed and his ideas.

One suggestion that can be offered is that Azad was in constant touch with developments in the Islamic world, since he had been reading so much of the literature from those societies. He stated that he had come under the influence of the *Al-Manar* group, which was carrying forward the ideological legacy of men such as Jamaluddin Afghani. Afghani was the ideologue of pan-Islamism, a phenomenon which had emerged during the last quarter of the nineteenth century. The agenda of pan-Islamism as articulated by Afghani largely consisted of bringing reforms within the Islamic community and confronting the growing hegemony of Western imperialism. Both the issues posed challenges to the Muslim world.

In order to achieve it then it was necessary to revitalize Islam and for this it was crucial that there was an Islamic centre in the form of the Khilafat.[94] This concern necessitated a pan-Islamic upsurge, seeking solidarity among Muslims the world over. However, since colonial domination by the West had given rise to particularism in such societies, Afghani seemed to have taken due recognition of this also.[95] In the long run this produced a strong tendency of particularistic nationalism. In other words, Afghani carried along both tendencies, which cannot be said to be free from contradictions. But the same was true about pan-Islamism itself. For instance, for Afghani pan-Islamism was an ultimate goal, but liberating Muslims from colonial domination was immediate.[96] In the same vein Afghani had argued that while achieving Islamic unity was important it was much more important to achieve national unity.[97]

Jamaluddin Afghani's thoughts profoundly influenced thinking sections of Muslims everywhere. He had paid visits to India, and on a couple of occasions had got into debate with Syed Ahmad Khan and repudiated him for his collaborative politics with the British government.

It was not Afghani alone but his followers such as Shaikh Abduh and Rasheed Rida too who pursued a similar line of thinking and wrote extensively on political and social issues concerning Muslims. In a *fatwa* Rasheed Rida dwelt upon Islam and its compatibility with nationalism.

> The contemporary notion of patriotism expresses the unity of the people of different religions in their homeland and their co-operation in defending the homeland they share. They co-operate to preserve its independence, to win it back if it was lost and to develop it. The type of patriotism that should adorn Muslim youth is that he be a good example for the people of the homeland, no matter what their religious affiliation, and co-operating with them in every legitimate action for independence.[98]

It has already been pointed out that Azad had conceded rather early that he was indebted to *Al-Manar.* He made it clear that he had absorbed influences from these thinking men, whose theoretical articulation established that Islam and particularistic nationalism were compatible and that Muslims should forge links with others to combat colonial domination, while still pursuing a pan-Islamic agenda.

Such was the background of long years of ideological and theoretical preparedness for Azad's endeavours, where various streams of political thought produced a blend of tradition, religion and liberalism to create a new brand of politics with specific reference to Muslims. By June 1912 Azad 'took a momentous step of publishing the *Al-Hilal*'. Contrary to common assumption, *Al-Hilal* did not start with the outbreak of the Balkan wars in October 1912, which had stirred the Muslim mind and given rise to a countrywide pan-Islamic agitation.[99] What then was the immediate inspiration? It has been argued that, 'it was revolutionary nationalism as well as the fate of Turkey which inspired its publication'.[100]

It may be added on the basis of the reading of *Al-Hilal* that political education formed the core of the efforts where Muslims would be able to define their own political identity *vis-à-vis* the colonial rulers, and forge political links with Hindus. Certain domestic issues in a way provided the context. At the Durbar of December 1911, the partition of Bengal was publicly revoked. This dismayed Muslims in general since they had benefited from it in areas such as bureaucratic recruitment and other sectors of employment. The revoking of the partition was seen as an act of betrayal of Muslim sentiments. Around the same time, attempts to seek elevation of the M.A.O. College to the status of a university, were being ignored by the government, which further incensed Muslims. The Italian invasion of Tripoli in July 1912 had convinced Muslims that Britain had acquiesced in this act and that the entire European world was bent upon dismantling the Ottoman Empire, which was also the seat of the *Khalifa*.

The upheaval taking place in the minds of Muslims on account of these developments was reflected in various papers, like Mohammad Ali's *Comrade* (started at the beginning of 1911 in Calcutta, later shifted to Delhi when the capital was shifted there), and *Hamdard*. In 1912, Zafar Ali Khan had made his weekly *Zamindar*, a daily. The press, the Urdu press in particular, had acquired credibility in the political life of the country. This was the immediate context in which *Al-Hilal* was launched on 13 July 1912.

Al-Hilal swept its readers off their feet. Humayun Kabir has characterized Azad's style as unique in the history of the Urdu language and literature, capturing the imagination of the youth of the community with its poetic grace and its formulation of a new faith. This was the greatest appeal of *Al-Hilal*.[101] Not Humayun Kabir alone but Syed Sulaiman Nadvi too who never hid his bitterness towards Azad, once commented,

> I must in all fairness say one thing, the time Maulana Abul Kalam Azad was bringing out *Al-Hilal,* the Muslims' mind was set on fire by his passionate words. He sounded loudly and fiercely the trumpet of *Jihad*, whose name people were afraid to mention, so that the forgotten lessons were on the tongues of the people again. . . .[102] *Al-Hilal* spoke in the language of a 'High souled prophet', throughout he had the stamp of a *Mujtahid*.[103]

What were the subjects concerning Muslims that Azad wanted to touch upon? Very clearly at that moment two issues were of crucial importance; Islam and its fresh interpretation, and, secondly, the political education of his co-religionists so that they could be an equal partner in the freedom struggle.[104] Azad treats Muslims as a distinct political community, potentially if not actually under the current circumstances, capable of working for common enterprises because its members shared the values of Islam.[105] He argued that the duty of every Muslim was to 'bid [*sic*] the good and forbid the evil'. His call was to develop cooperative efforts with non-Muslims for political action. 'Azad was endowed with creative genius in writing as well as speech. His command over Urdu prose was extraordinary. He could be witty, charming, refined and subtly humorous, bitterly satirical and compulsively exhortatory.'[106] Azad could go on at length without losing the appeal and power of his arguments.

The first issue of *Al-Hilal* came out on 13 July 1912. This issue did not discuss the objective of the paper. The third issue barely hinted at it. However, later, Azad discussed quite elaborately that *Al-Hilal* would call upon Muslims to follow the true spirit of the Quran and *Sunnah* (Practices of the Prophet Muhammad) in all spheres of life—education, culture or politics. In brief, *Al-Hilal* called upon Muslims to be true Muslims.[107] In another issue Azad argued that once Muslims truly followed the Quran, they would experience a new life.[108] *Al-Hilal*'s content and message initially baffled its readers since religious issues were enmeshed with political issues. There were innumerable queries as to what *Al-Hilal* stood for on these questions. In response to one such query Azad wrote,

> The question whether political discussion should be separated from religious education is very important. But you must know that this is the very foundation on which one intends to build the whole edifice of *Al-Hilal*. If you say that the arch is not beautiful, one may try to alter its shape, but if you wish that the keystone be removed then one cannot accede to your wishes. There will be nothing left with us if we separate politics from religion.[109]

With these pronouncements, Azad had clearly begun to advocate cultural nationalism, where to return to the roots was to derive strength from one's religion and culture in order to challenge the colonial hegemony. Amilcar Cabral had argued, 'The national liberation of a people is the regaining of the historical personality of that people, its return to history through the destruction of imperialist domination to which it was subjected.'[110]

'Regaining of historical personality' also meant redefining the political identity of a people. In the case of Indian Muslims, to be a Muslim in a religious or cultural sense was not enough since it required a clearly defined political position. It was crucial to Azad's scheme of thinking that Muslims were brought to the forefront of the freedom struggle with the help of Islam and associated symbols. He described the fight against the British as *Jihad*. Once he argued, 'Thus, like many other things, the call of *Al-Hilal* is that neither trust the government nor follow the Hindus. Take only the right path, "*Seerat-Ul Mustuqeem*", as suggested by Islam.' He further added, 'If we take to the political path as suggested by Islam then of course we shall be a group not to be daunted by anything. We shall express ourselves fearlessly as we should not be afraid of anyone but God.'[111]

By invoking rather frequently the expression *Sirat-al-Mustaqeem* (the Right path) Azad was basically working towards constructing a model of cultural personality that in a manner would give birth to a new and confident Islamic political person, who would wage *Jihad* against the British. The agenda of *Jihad* would encompass many other things too, for instance establishing democracy and the founding of a parliamentary and constitutional government. As he put it:

Islam stands for freedom and is against those who wish to perpetuate an autocratic rule through brute force. It (Islam) wants its followers to be in action in order to attain freedom. It is the soul of democracy and equality and considers that government to be against the will of God, which is not parliamentary and constitutional. This lesson is not to be learnt from the Hindus but from the *Quran*, and should be as such made the motto of life.[112]

These concerns formed the core of *Al-Hilal.* Azad touched upon many other issues of contemporary politics concerning Muslims. For instance while surveying contemporary political developments; Azad came down heavily upon the Muslim League, whom he considered nothing more than a *Naya Khilona* (new toy), which was thrust upon the Muslims. Apparently, the objective of the Muslim League was to awaken the community but, to Azad, it was a reflection of political stupor and the humiliation of Muslims.[113] Azad was aware that the Muslim League enjoyed the support of the government.[114] He accused the Muslim League leadership of misguiding and channelling the energy of the community in a wrong direction and as such considered the existence of the League unfortunate for the whole community.[115] He further contended that the Muslims would have been better off if they had united with the Hindus.[116] There were others who held different views about the Muslim League. Aurobindo Ghosh considered the emergence of the League as the self-expression of Muslims and welcomed it. 'We do not fear Mohammadan opposition so long it is an honest swadeshi article and not manufactured in Shillong or Simla. We welcome it as a sign of life and aspiration.'[117]

To Azad the provisions of separate electorates was unacceptable since he did not think of it as more than a crumb thrown to Muslims as a reward of loyalty, which was unfortunately considered a big gain by the misguided leadership.[118] A survey of the political scene brought total disappointment to Azad. He concluded that there were two kinds of leadership among the Muslims—the Ulema and those Muslims who had acquired modern education. Neither group was competent to provide leadership, since one was caught in obscurantism and the other was openly loyalist.[119] Such a state of affairs reduced the entire community to nothing more than a pawn in the hands of the government.[120]

The outcome was that the Muslims became a stumbling block to the progress of India. Whenever the government desired, it used the Muslims as stones to crush the aspiration of the country. First of all the Muslims alienated themselves from the Hindus who have been the most politically active group. Thus, the government felt quite assured of the failure of the demands of the nationalists.[121]

Despite this dismal picture, Azad retained a strong streak of hope where he saw in religion a beacon of light for the future, and a possibility of sections of the Muslims closing ranks. He also hoped that with the help of religion it was possible to explain that Islam and slavery were contradictory and therefore it was incumbent upon a Muslim to cut through the chains of bondage.

The pertinent question was as to what course of political action Muslims should take? While answering a query as to which group of Hindus *Al-Hilal* identified itself with, Azad argued that the followers of Islam themselves need to determine their political course and not follow others. He exhorted thinking Muslims to form their own organization and provide leadership.[122] Azad must have been acutely aware that his utterances could remain mere exhortations, since many Muslims were in a state of inertia and defeatism. He was equally aware that Muslims were caught in a fear of the Hindu majority overriding their interests and aspirations. But to Azad sheer numerical size was inconsequential. What was of consequence was the historical importance of a group. Muslims should have felt confident since they had provided leadership to the world ever since Islam emerged. Here Azad clearly indulged in the selective use of history to delineate the political identity of the community,[123] so as to inspire them to shed defeatism.

Apprehension regarding the minority and majority is not something which has emanated from within. Rather it has been imposed from without and now it has become centre of our ills. There is fear in joining the Congress because the Muslims are in a minority and Hindus would override them.[124]

He further ridiculed the community, 'No doubt the conditions that you are in do not require the majority of the Hindus. Your defeatism alone is enough to destroy you.'[125]

After ridicule, it was the turn of reassurance. Muslims needed to be told that they must have faith in themselves and trust Hindus and work out a scheme of lasting cooperation with them, since they were the main flag-bearers of the freedom movement. The freedom movement would lack teeth without active cooperation between the two communities. He argued, 'There is no need to fear Hindus. If at all you fear anyone you should fear God. If you want to live in India then embrace your neighbours. You have seen the consequence of keeping aloof from them, now you should join them.'[126] Hindu–Muslim unity was not conditioned by convenience nor was it a matter of exigencies. For Azad, indeed it was a matter of conviction, throughout his political life. However, one point must be noted in the context of the present discussion—that, by arguing in favour of unity, he was merely advocating a case where various religious communities would come together to act in unison towards the political end, i.e. freedom for the country.

Here Azad treats religious communities as political entities who could enjoy autonomy of political thought and action. He always visualized active cooperation with other social groups, particularly in the realm of political action. By the time the Non-Cooperation–Khilafat movement was launched, Azad's thought was to undergo a transformation, since he began visualizing Indians as a single political entity. However, what remained of intrinsic value is that even during the *Al-Hilal* phase Azad's plea for Hindu–Muslim unity was not based on the notion of seat-adjustment or power-sharing. It was a case of political unity based on spiritual considerations.

While Azad was concerned about Hindu–Muslim understanding in the national arena, he was no less concerned about Muslims developing a sense of solidarity on an international scale, more so in the light of a perpetual threat to the existence of Turkey. In his view, the Christian West was bent upon destroying the last outpost of Islamic power. Developments concerning Turkey had already agitated the minds of Muslims but from 1910 many developments took place, which stirred the minds of Indian Muslims.

It has already been pointed out how Azad had come under the influence of *Al-Manar* and the writing of Shaikh Abduh and Rasheed Rida in the years preceding the launching of *Al-Hilal*. However, since its publication, the pan-Islamic thoughts of these leaders found more than adequate space in the pages of *Al-Hilal*. There was a purpose in it, since Azad wished his readers too to be familiar with these contemporary thinkers and ideologically prepare them for a long drawn-out struggle against the Raj. The Balkan wars were given a prominent place in *Al-Hilal*.[127]

These international developments too shaped Azad's view on pan-Islam, which found adequate space in the pages of *Al-Hilal*. He solicited support for Turkey, spiritual or material.

> It becomes a religious duty that the seat of *Khalifa* should be held dear to every Muslim purely as a matter of religious relationship. Any government, which is Khilafat's enemy should be considered enemy of Islam and one which is friendly towards it a friend. Because the friendship and enmity for a Muslim should not depend on personal losses and gains rather it should be for the sake of religion.[128]

Such a stance was to serve the purpose of generating anti-British sentiments among Muslims. Therefore it is possible to argue that Azad's pan-Islamism was in consonance with Indian nationalism.[129]

While delivering a speech in Calcutta on pan-Islamism, after the First World War had broken out, he argued as if Khilafat was not only the religious centre but also a political centre of Muslims the world over. 'As we know, no nation can survive without a political centre. And if there is any political centre of Islam then it is Khilafat.'[130] Azad must have known that talking in terms such as these might bring a charge of extra-territorial loyalty against him as well as against Muslims at large, particularly in India. However, it cannot be ignored that Azad's enthusiasm was essentially directed towards arousing Muslims to political action against the British.[131] Yet it is difficult to deny that in his scheme of things pure pan-Islamic concerns remained equally pronounced.

VI

When the war began, Azad clearly sympathized with Germany as an ally of Turkey. Azad emphasized that Germans were superior to the British in the war theatre, in terms of material resources as well as discipline and training. His bias in favour of Germany aroused government suspicion about the man and his newspaper.

V.N. Datta argues that Azad's pro-German attitude cost him the security deposit of Rs. 2,000 initially. Later the government took a pretty serious view of the anti-British and pro-Turkish and pro-German views of *Al-Hilal* and this became a subject of discussion in pro-government papers, which provoked the government to take action against Azad.

However, a reading of the secret files prepared by government agencies leaves a clear impression that Azad had been a suspect in the eyes of the government for quite some time. Intelligence agencies kept a close watch on this 'dangerous man' since the time he had protested legally against the government for its action against the *Comrade* for publishing an article, 'The Choice of Turks'. The article had caused quite a stir in official circles, as a result the security deposited in respect of the *Comrade* and *Hamdard* press was forfeited.[132]

As a reaction to this, on 30 November 1914, Abul Kalam Azad, editor of the *Al-Hilal* newspaper, forwarded to the Commissioner of Police under protest, a copy of the issue of the *Comrade* and asked for an acknowledgement, if it was seized.[133] On its confirmation, the next best thing Azad could do to protest against the high-handedness of the administration was to legally challenge the validity of the orders of confiscation of the *Comrade*.[134] On his petition, a special Bench of the High Court of Calcutta was appointed under the Indian Press Act 1910 and proceedings were to take place on 11 January 1915.[135] Azad's pleading took a strange turn when he argued that the article had exhorted Indian Muslims to remain loyal to the government established by law even if the Turks participated in the war against his Majesty and his allies 'and does not contain any thing to cause disaffection'.[136]

But the official opinion was that the article was potent enough to cause disaffection. Eventually the special Bench of the High Court dismissed Azad's petition on technical grounds.[137]

Azad's writings in *Al-Hilal* and his protest against the measures taken against the *Comrade* convinced the government that,

> the Editor (Maulana Azad) does his best to make his readers believe in the bad chances of the Allies and in the prospects of German victory. Mohammad Ali in the *Hamdard* is playing the same game. The insidious disloyalty of these people in spite of warning and promises is most

discreditable. They are unfit to be allowed to publish newspapers at the present time.[138]

The Maulana was suspected to be part of a Turkish and German intrigue not only from the time the war began, but since the winter of 1911-12 when a German emissary moved about in pan-Islamic circles and 'consorted' with the friends of the editor of *Al-Hilal*.[139]

Such a suspicion led C.R. Cleveland, the Director of Intelligence, to suggest that the paper be thoroughly searched and confiscated. If possible, the provision of the Press Act and the Indian Penal Code should be invoked.[140] What was the immediate provocation for the governmental agencies to sound so harsh about Azad? The reasons were articles carried by *Al-Hilal* in August 1914, which analysed various aspects of the war theatre and the prospects of different warring countries with an obvious anti-British touch. Certain articles carried in the September 1914 in *Al-Hilal* too were a cause of serious concern to the British authorities.

Finally, official circles recognized that, 'the editor of the *Al-Hilal* is a dangerous man, that his private feelings which probably lead him to regard Germany as the friend of Turkey and that no chance should be lost checking his activities'.[141] It was further assessed 'that the Editor, Maulana Abul Kalam Azad is a well informed man, who is quite capable of discussing strategic and political questions from a wide point of view'.[142]

In the course of the World War, *Al-Hilal* and its editor had become a source of anxiety to various provincial governments such as Bengal, Punjab, Bihar, Orissa, as also princely states such as Hyderabad. All the provincial governments began asking the central government if measures were being suggested to put a halt to the dissemination of Azad's thoughts in *Al-Hilal*. The Lt. Governor of the Punjab, Sir M.O. Dwyer showed serious anxiety over a likely visit to the Punjab by Mohammad Ali and Shaukat Ali accompanied by Azad. Referring to their earlier visits which had caused quite a stir, particularly among Muslims, M.O. Dwyer asserted, 'If I find any of the above trio in the Punjab, I won't hesitate to use the War Act to exclude them, but it is of course much better to restrict their movements from the source.'[143]

Finally, action was initiated against Azad's paper on 16 November 1914, at the press and his residence, 13-14, Macleod

Street, Calcutta. At the time of the raid it seems Azad was away in Delhi to meet Mohammad Ali.[144] Copies of *Al-Hilal* were seized and with this came to an end Azad's efforts to be in communication with his co-religionists on matters of politics as well as religion. The government may have thought that they had won but it was a temporary victory, since Azad's conviction helped him withstand such pressures.

After a brief respite, Azad started another paper *Al-Balagh* from Calcutta itself (the address was Ripon Lane, Calcutta). The first issue appeared on 12 November 1915, and it lasted till the end of March 1916, when Azad was externed from Calcutta for his continuous exhortation to Muslims for education including political education which essentially meant building up self-confidence to resist British rule. The 'well informed' and yet 'dangerous' man, i.e. Azad, had become a thorn in the side of the government. He was externed from Calcutta in April 1916 under the Defence of India Regulation.

The externment of Azad from Calcutta brought his political as well as journalistic and literary activities to a sudden halt. In Ranchi he was compelled to live in confinement where any contact with the outside world was impossible. And yet it did not dishearten him. Even in confinement he felt free but only in the realm of ideas. His messages through *Al-Hilal* and *Al-Balagh*, which had been moulded in the light of the Quran were reverberating in the minds of his readers.

However, Azad was convinced that Muslims must get access to the Quran in a language which they understood easily. Thus, there arose the need to translate the Quran into Urdu and write a commentary on it. Azad had begun the task during his *Al-Hilal* and *Al-Balagh* days, but confinement in Ranchi gave him the gift of time, which went into the making of *Tazkirah* and the translation of the Quran.

NOTES

1. Paul R. Brass, *Language, Religion and Politics in North India*, Vikas Publishing House, Delhi, 1975, p. 120.
2. Francis Robinson, *Islam and Muslim History in South Asia*, Oxford University Press, Delhi, 2000, p. 13.

3. Peter Hardy, *The Muslims of the British India,* Cambridge University Press, Cambridge, 1973, p. 195.
4. Ibid.
5. Francis Robinson, 'Islam and Muslim Separatism, A Historical Debate', in Mushirul Hasan, ed., *Communal and Pan-Islamic Trends in Colonial India*, Manohar, Delhi, 1985, p. 356.
6. Moin Shakir, *Khilafat to Partition: A Survey of Major Political Trends Among Indian Muslims–1919-1947*, Kalamkar Prakashan, Delhi, 1970, p. 142.
7. Mahadev Desai, *Maulana Abul Kalam Azad: The President of Indian National Congress, A Biographical Memoir*, George Allen and Unwin, London, 1941, p. 27.
8. A.B. Rajput, *Maulana Abul Kalam Azad*, Lion Press, Lahore, 1946, p. 163.
9. Asar bin Yahya Ansari, *Maulana Azad ek Siyasi Diary*, Aaliya Publication, Dholia, 1982, p. 72.
10. Ibid., p. 294.
11. Mohammad Farooq Qureshi, *Maulana Abul Kalam Azad aur Qaum Parast Musalmanon ki Siyasat*, Takhliqat, Lahore, 1997, p. 21.
12. Ibid., p. 36.
13. S. Abid Husain, *Destiny of Indian Muslims*, Asia Publishing House, Bombay, 1965, p. 135.
14. Ibid.
15. M. Mujeeb, *The Indian Muslims*, George Allen and Unwin, London, 1967, p. 463.
16. Ibid., p. 442.
17. Ian Henderson Douglas, *Abul Kalam Azad: An Intellectual and Religious Biography*, Oxford University Press, Delhi, 1988.
18. *Al-Manar* was an influential journal started by Rasheed Rida at Cairo in 1897. This journal had made an impact on Azad because of its efforts to move away from the influence of traditional Ulema of al-Azhar in Cairo, ibid., p. 109.
19. Ibid., pp. 189-96.
20. V.N. Datta, *Maulana Azad*, Manohar, Delhi, 1990.
21. Ibid., p. 40.
22. Ibid.
23. P.N. Chopra, *Maulana Abul Kalam Azad: Unfulfilled Dreams*, Interprint, Delhi, 1990, p. 9.
24. Nikki R. Keddi, *An Islamic Response to Imperialism: Political and Religious Writings of Syed Jamaluddin al Afghani*, University of California Press, Berkeley, 1968, p. 3.

25. Ejaz Ahmad, 'Azad's Careers, Roads Taken and Not Taken', in Mushirul Hasan, ed., *Islam and Indian Nationalism: Reflections on Abul Kalam Azad*, Manohar, Delhi, 1992, p. 166.
26. Ibid.
27. Syeda Saiyidain Hameed, *Islamic Seal on India's Independence: Abul Kalam Azad—A Fresh Look*, Oxford University Press, Karachi, 1998.
28. Ibid., p. 263.
29. Ibid., p. 271.
30. S.R. Mehrotra, 'Maulana Abul Kalam Azad on Jawaharlal Nehru's "Blunders" Leading to the Partition of India in 1947', in Mahavir Singh, ed., *Maulana Abul Kalam Azad: Profile of a Nationalist*, Anamika Publishers, Delhi, 2003, p. 25.
31. Ibid., p. 29.
32. V.N. Datta, 'An Intimate Relationship, Maulana Azad and Jawaharlal Nehru', in Mahavir Singh, ed., op. cit., p. 41.
33. For a detailed discussion refer to Barbara D. Metcalf, *Islamic Revival in British India: Deoband, 1860-1900*, Princeton University Press, New Jersey, 1982.
34. John L. Esposito, *Islam the Straight Path*, Oxford University Press, New York, 1991, pp. 127-8.
35. For a detailed discussion refer to B.R. Nanda, *Gandhi, Pan-Islamism, Imperialism and Indian Nationalism*, Oxford University Press, Bombay, 1989.
36. Mushirul Hasan, *A Nationalist Conscience: M.A. Ansari, the Congress and the Raj*, Manohar, Delhi, 1987, p. 39.
37. Mushirul Hasan, *Mohammad Ali: Ideology and Politics*, Manohar, Delhi, 1991, pp. 25-7 and Aparna Basu, 'Mohammad Ali in Delhi', in Mushirul Hasan, ed., *Communal and Pan-Islamic Trends in Colonial India*, op. cit., p. 116.
38. For details refer to Khalid Hasan Qadri, *Hasrat Mohani*, Adara-i-Adabiyat-i-Delhi, Delhi, 1985 and Khaliq Anjum, *Hasrat Mohani* Publications Division, Delhi, 1994.
39. Beni Prasad, *The Hindu-Muslim Questions*, Kitabistan, Allahabad, 1941, pp. 18-19.
40. Ibid., p. 25. Recently K.N. Panikkar, in *Communal Threat Secular Challenge,* Earthworm Books, Madras, 1997, has acknowledged that such tendencies as a matter of fact undid all that has been the hallmark of a corporate life between Hindus and Muslims in India, p. 18.
41. Azad, *India Wins Freedom: The Complete Version* (hereafter *India Wins Freedom*), Orient Longman, Madras, 1988, p. 5.
42. Rajat K. Ray, 'Revolutionaries, Pan-Islamists and Bolsheviks: M.A.K. Azad and Political Underworld of Calcutta', in Mushirul Hasan,

ed., *Communal and Pan-Islamic Trends in Colonial India,* op. cit., p. 157.

43. Azad's letter to Hakeem Mohammad Ali Tabeeb, 11 June 1902 in Malik Ram, ed., *Khutoot Abul Kalam Azad*, vol. 1, Sahitya Akademi, Delhi, 1991, pp. 22-3.
44. Azad, *India Wins Freedom*, op. cit., p. 3. (The institution of *piri-muridi* was preceded by the notion of *Beit* in order to express allegiance to the Khalifa and subsequently any ruler, which in due course of time became the hallmark of Sufic practices.)
45. Peter Hardy, *Partners in Freedom and True Muslims*, Greenwood Press Publishers, London, 1985, p. 47.
46. Datta, *Maulana Azad*, op. cit., p. 6.
47. Ibid.
48. Ibid., p. 8.
49. Ibid.
50. Douglas, op. cit., p. 37.
51. Ibid.
52. Azad, *India Wins Freedom*, op. cit., p. 3.
53. Ibid., p. 4.
54. Ibid. (This experience of Azad has not been explained either by any historian or Azad himself. However, it is possible to surmise that the intensity of indecisiveness led him ideologically astray from religious practices.)
55. As quoted in Douglas, op. cit., p. 67.
56. Abdur Razzaq Malihabadi, *Zikr-e-Azad*: *Maulana Azad ki Refaqat Mein Anrtees Saal*, Ujala Press, Calcutta, 1960, pp. 259-60.
57. Asghar Ali Engineer, 'Theological Creativity of Abul Kalam Azad' (unpublished paper), Delhi, 1988, As regards his return journey towards religion there is another explanation available. It can be argued that it might have been just a personal experience. However, it is interesting to note that this is the same period when Azad was able to go through exposure to various political currents at home and abroad.
58. Abdur Razzaq Malihabadi, *Azad ki Kahani Khud Azad ki Zubani,* Maktaba Ishatul-Quran, Delhi, 1965, p. 400.
59. Ibid., pp. 145-6 also pp. 337-9.
60. Azad, *India Wins Freedom,* op. cit., pp. 4-5.
61. Malihabadi, *Zikre Azad,* op. cit., p. 272.
62. Ray in Mushirul Hasan, ed., *Communal and Pan-Islamic Trends in Colonial India*, op. cit.
63. Azad, *India Wins Freedom*, op. cit., p. 5.
64. Intelligence Branch Report as cited in Ray, op. cit., p. 102.

65. Ray, op. cit., p. 102.
66. Azad, *India Wins Freedom*, op. cit., p. 5.
67. Ray, op. cit., p. 103.
68. Azad, *India Wins Freedom*, op. cit., p. 6.
69. Ray, op. cit., p.104.
70. Malihabadi, *Zikre Azad*, op. cit., p. 272.
71. Ibid., p. 222.
72. Ibid., p. 274.
73. Azad, *India Wins Freedom,* op. cit., p. 5.
74. Ibid., p. 6.
75. Ibid., p. 7.
76. Gail Minault, 'The Elusive Maulana, Reflections on Writing Azad's Biography', in Mushirul Hasan, ed., *Islam and Indian Nationalism: Reflections on Abul Kalam Azad*, op. cit., p. 24.
77. Ibid., p. 21.
78. Ibid.
79. Ibid., p. 22.
80. Datta, op. cit., p. 51.
81. Ibid.
82. K.A. Nizami, *Abul Kalam Azad: An Assessment*, in a commemorative volume of Iran Society, Calcutta, 1988, p. 25.
83. Azad, *India Wins Freedom*, op. cit., p. 7.
84. Ibid., p. 8.
85. Datta, op. cit., p. 51.
86. Ibid.
87. Ibid., p. 52.
88. A.R. Malihabadi, *Azad ki Kahani*, op. cit., p. 249.
89. Ibid., p. 252.
90. Ibid., p. 254.
91. Ibid., p. 255.
92. Ibid., p. 293.
93. Ibid., p. 300.
94. Shan Muhammad, *Sir Syed Ahmad Khan: A Political Biography*, Minakshi Publications, Meerut, 1969, p. 26.
95. Esposito, op. cit., pp. 127-8.
96. James Piscatori, *Islam in a World of Nation-States*, Cambridge University Press, Cambridge, 1986, p. 87.
97. Ibid., p. 78.
98. Rasheed Rida, as quoted in ibid., p. 79.
99. Ray, op. cit., p. 107.
100. Ibid.
101. Douglas, op. cit., p. 99.

102. Nadavi, as quoted in ibid., p. 100.
103. Ibid.
104. Ibid.
105. Hardy, *Partners in Freedom and True Muslims*, op. cit., p. 23.
106. Tara Chand, *History of the Freedom Movement in India*, vol. III, Publications Division, Delhi, 1971, p. 266.
107. *Al-Hilal*, vol. 1, no. 9, 8 September 1912.
108. Ibid., vol. 1, no. 11, 22 September 1912.
109. Ibid., vol. 1, no. 9, 8 September 1912.
110. Amilcar Cabral, *Revolution in Guinea, Selected Text*, tr. Richard Handyside, Monthly Review Press, New York, 1969, pp. 104-5.
111. *Al-Hilal*, vol. 1, no. 9, 8 September 1912.
112. Ibid.
113. Ibid.
114. Ibid.
115. Ibid.
116. Ibid
117. Bande Matram, 17 December 1907 as quoted in Prabha Dixit, 'Ideology of Hindu Nationalism', in Thomas Panthem and Kenneth L. Deutisch, eds., *Political Thought in Modern India*, Sage Publications, Delhi, 1986, p. 124.
118. *Al-Hilal*, vol. 1, no. 8, 1 September 1912.
119. Ibid., vol. 1, no. 4, 4 August 1912.
120. Ibid., vol. 1, no. 8, 1 September 1912.
121. Ibid.
122. Ibid., vol. 1, no. 9, 8 September 1912.
123. A.P. Cohen, *The Symbolic Construction of Community*, Ellis Horwood Limited, Chichester, 1985. Cohen has argued that for most people at most moments of history the past is inchoate, transmitted only selectively according to contemporary purpose and recalled selectively without historiographical rigour.
124. *Al-Hilal*, vol. 1, no. 8, 1 September 1912.
125. Ibid.
126. Ibid.
127. B.R. Nanda, *Gandhi, Pan-Islamism, Imperialism and India Nationalism*, Oxford University Press, Bombay, 1989, pp. 105-6.
128. *Al-Hilal*, vol. 1, no. 16, 6 November 1912.
129. Douglas, op. cit., p. 149.
130. Azad, *Taqreer-i-Ittehad-Islami*, speech delivered by Azad at Calcutta on 27 October 1914 in Malik Ram, ed., *Khutbat-i-Azad*, Sahitya Akademi, Delhi, 1990, pp. 13-26.
131. Douglas, op. cit., p. 149.

132. Home Political A, February 1915, no. 265-92 k&w.
133. Ibid., p. 19.
134. Ibid.
135. Ibid., p. 20.
136. Ibid., p. 21.
137. Ibid.
138. Home Political A, February 1915, nos. 178-204, p. 4.
139. Ibid., p. 15.
140. Ibid., p. 1.
141. Ibid., p. 10.
142. Ibid., p. 12.
143. Government of India, Home Dept. Pol. Deposit proceedings, May 1915, no. 36.
144. Ibid.

CHAPTER TWO

Building Bridges between pan-Islamism and Indian Nationalism, 1919-1922

At the time when Azad wrote in *Al-Hilal* and *Al-Balagh*, he had as if cast a spell on his readers so that they became equal partners in the long journey of the freedom struggle. However, it also made him a strong suspect in the eyes of the British government who came to regard him as a 'dangerous man' and 'fanatic' capable of rousing the ordinary mass of Muslims against the British government established by law. When the First World War broke out, *Al-Hilal* became a major cause of concern for the government as it feared the paper was spreading disaffection and mischief about the government,[1] particularly when the government needed all possible support in its war efforts.

During the early years of the war, it was not *Al-Hilal* alone but other papers such as *Comrade* and *Hamdard* of Mohammad Ali and Zafar Ali Khan's *Zamindar* too which caused sufficient anxiety in government circles. Punitive action against all these editors who were championing the cause of pan-Islamism, considered to be anti-government, was being mooted for quite some time. Eventually, the axe first fell on the Ali Brothers, who were initially kept in confinement at Mehrauli[2] and later shifted to Chhindwara in Madhya Pradesh, where they spent four long years of quiet life. Their arrest led to protests by many sections of the Muslim public. Azad too expressed his sympathy for the Ali Brothers. However, he did not realize that a similar fate awaited him, and at the end of March 1916 Azad too was ordered to leave Calcutta. Then came the turn of Zafar Ali Khan, whose paper *Zamindar* had antagonized the government. All these steps were the outcome of a fear in the government that, 'We must not allow pro-German writings in the Indian press. They travel far and give wrong and dangerous impressions both in India and Turkey.'[3]

For Azad, the externment from Calcutta meant going to a place where he would have to live a life of confinement. But the question was where to send him? In a short span, ever since the publication of *Al-Hilal*, Azad had earned nothing but notoriety in the eyes of the government. Most secret reports prepared on Azad described him as mentioned earlier, as a 'dangerous man' and a 'fanatic', 'capable of rousing the Muslim masses'. In such a situation not many provincial governments were willing to keep him as a political prisoner. The provincial governments who refused to admit Azad were Bombay, Bengal, the United Provinces, the Punjab and Delhi. 'These local governments consider the man dangerous from their point of view and their action is therefore justified.'[4] However, it was hoped that Madras or the Central Provinces might finally accept him since he was considered not so dangerous in those places.[5] At one time it was mooted that Azad should be allowed to have the option of staying either at Ranchi or Purulia in Bihar, once he was interviewed by a 'tactful officer' and Azad himself gave an undertaking of a 'quiet behaviour'.[6] Finally, at the initiative of the governments of Bihar and Orissa it was agreed that Azad would be kept at Moorabadi on the outskirts of Ranchi.[7] Here Azad was to spent four years, a life of not high political drama but of contemplation. It was a journey towards quietude.

Even after Azad's internment in Ranchi, the government continued to remain uneasy about his conduct. His remaining quiet was the only condition for him not to have undergone 'compulsory residence'. It was also contemplated that Maulana Abul Kalam Azad could be verbally warned by a tactful and responsible officer that future action regarding him will depend on his behaviour.[8]

What guarantee could Azad give to the government regarding his conduct? As a matter of fact Azad too was perhaps yearning for a life of solitude for a while. Even before he had started *Al-Hilal*, Azad had been travelling widely throughout the country, sometimes editing a paper or attending educational conferences.

With the publication of *Al-Hilal*, the demand on Azad's time had increased manifold, denying him the luxury of time when he could indulge himself in a contemplative life, something which he apparently had desired, 'for long I had yearned for peace of heart and freedom of thought and action but the pressure of work and the entanglement of relationship never permitted this to happen so far. I have it now.'[9]

In Moorabadi, a place largely inhabited by the Munda and Oraon tribes, Azad found himself bereft of the comfort of a home and the company of the learned in Calcutta. And yet rather philosophically he said that he 'yearned for peace of heart and freedom of thought and action'. Azad was to have plenty of time to contemplate any subject of his choice and write extensively, which he actually did. But so far as 'action' was concerned, perhaps Azad was able to realize his limitations, only in the course of his stay there, since the government agencies had kept a strict watch on the 'dangerous man'. Therefore, it is difficult to establish when Azad had made this statement. Azad's yearning for freedom of political action may never have been fulfilled for the government was quite serious about him. In one of the secret government reports it was argued. 'Abul Kalam Azad was deeply involved in the "Silk letter Conspiracy". He is interned in Ranchi and first of all subjected to numerous restrictions under the Defence of India Act, but these were subsequently removed, with the exception of the condition that he should not leave that station without first obtaining the consent of the local Government.'[10] The government's resolve was quite firm as regards Azad, so much so that even his personal correspondencc was checked.[11] Under no circumstances the restrictions imposed upon him were to be relaxed.[12] The government's concern about Azad grew in view of the peace terms with Turkey which were likely to be harsh. Any talk of releasing Azad was unlikely, because it was thought to be taking a grave risk.[13]

Under the watchful eyes of the government, was it possible for Azad to enjoy freedom of thought and action? Freedom of thought may have been possible, but action must have remained a bit problematic, since the government at best would have allowed Azad to carry out some religious activities not having a direct bearing upon contemporary political developments. The question then arises as to what were Azad's thoughts during his Ranchi days?

When Azad came to Ranchi to take up residence, it may seem that he would be depressed at the turn of events. But on the contrary, he seemed to be much more concerned about his journal *Al-Balagh*, which he had started soon after the closure of the *Al-Hilal*. Immediately on reaching Ranchi, Azad wrote to Syed Suleiman Nadavi and the very first sentence is highly reflective of his mind and resolute determination. He wrote, 'I have just reached Ranchi. The *Al-Balagh* will continue.'[14] He went on to ask him to write an article of eight columns every two weeks for *Al-Balagh* and also request Maulvi Abdussalam to write an article of a similar length. 'Thus two forms shall easily be ready. And the remaining three forms I shall write myself.'[15] Despite Azad's best of intentions not a single issue of the paper could be brought out after he was externed from Calcutta.

Azad's externment generated a sense of scare among those who earlier used to correspond with him. On one occasion he happened to remark that he didn't write to people till he received letters from them, since many had become wary of the government agencies who kept a close watch on his correspondences.[16] But he didn't give up corresponding with the people who really mattered to him. For instance, he kept corresponding with Syed Suleiman Nadavi on several issues of academic importance and showed keen interest in activities of the *Darul-Mussanifin*,[17] and advised him not to snap his association with this centre of learning started by Allama Shibli.

It is commonly believed that the only occupation of Azad during his stay at Ranchi was to write *Tazkirah* and begin his *magnum opus*, the *Tarjumanul Quran*.[18] On the contrary, Azad did not remain quiet during the Ranchi days but indulged in several activities. Ranchi was not a place with any significant concentration of educated people, but still the Maulana's presence evoked a warm response, where men started to flock around him. Gradually Azad began giving the Friday *khutba* (sermons) in one of the local mosques of Ranchi, which not only attracted local people but in several cases people travelled from far off places such as Calcutta.[19]

In Ranchi the Maulana, established one *Anjuman-i-Islamia* under whose auspices later a madrasa was also founded. To undertake a job such as this was not easy for Azad, considering that Ranchi was a new place for him and the paucity of resources could easily hamper any venture of this kind. However, by this time Azad had gained so much in stature that his appeal for the purpose was responded to rather warmly by both Hindus and Muslims alike.[20] In this endeavour of Azad the financial support came from Calcutta also, a city with many prosperous Azad followers.

During those days, a controversy arose among the Hanafis and Wahhabis. Common Muslims remained susceptible to all kinds of influences, but a person like the Maulana, who frequently reflected on this issue as well took the stance of a non-conformist, which looked akin to Wahhabiat and earned him several critics who described him as a *ghair muqallid* (non-conformist). However, this controversy subsided quickly.[21]

For his other activities, the Maulana was to receive a stream of visitors in Ranchi who wanted to meet him. These included men with distinct political leanings, *ulema* of all hues and even students. His visitors also included those who needed financial assistance, which he gave generously even though he was financially not very comfortable himself. The stipend paid to him by the government was too inadequate considering his expenditure on books and journals.[22] Yet he never betrayed any sign of pecuniary constraint and continued to remain generous with the needy. In a general sense, Azad's stay at Ranchi had a profound impact on the spiritual and cultural life of the local people.

During the years of a relatively quiet life at Ranchi, Azad remained in touch with friends and others who gave him intellectual company. Letters that Azad wrote from Ranchi clearly give the impression of his being in touch with the political developments in the country, exploring the unfathomable depths of intellectual as well as spiritual realms. The correspondence that the Maulana carried out from Ranchi may defy any chronological order; however, from time to time the Maulana kept on reflecting on issues of larger concern. For instance, in one of his letters addressed to Maulvi Mohiuddin Ahmad Saheb Qasoori, he supported the just cause for which the Rowlatt agitation was started by Gandhi and felt that, 'the people should participate in it'.[23] However, the Maulana was sceptical of its protagonists. At one point he argued,

> Barring Gandhi I am not quite sure of the tenacity and perseverance of those who seem to have signed the pledge. After all Mr. Sharma has already resigned and despite his resignation Mr. Madan Mohan Malaviya is still seen in the Council. Even if twenty members had resigned, it would have shaken the India office within twenty-four hours and intervened in the matter. Let us wait and see as to what happens. . . .[24]

The passing of the Rowlatt Acts was a desperate attempt by the British government of India at a time when in several cases Indians at large had extended moral and material support to the government in its war efforts in the hope that after the war was over India's aspiration would be adequately paid attention to. Instead, the government slapped the Rowlatt Acts in an attempt to clamp down on the civil rights of Indians. It evoked wide condemnation among Indians of all hues and finally Gandhi decided to launch a mass agitation. It is common knowledge that the Rowlatt agitation was the first ever attempt to launch an agitation across the country. As it was also a first major attempt of Indians to emerge as a political society.[25] Azad's moral support for this agitation, even though he himself was in confinement, clearly establishes his political leanings, which were to grow stronger in the days to come.

It was in the course of this agitation that the bloody incident of the Jallianwala Bagh massacre took place on 13 April 1919 and clearly exposed the brutal character of British rule. However, it was the same incident which also galvanized the Indians. On this incident Azad was to comment much later rather movingly.

> This is the land where the death had given a new life to our freedom struggle. The blood of the Hindus, Muslims and Sikhs was shed together and it gave us a new lease of life. Twenty years have passed since the incident and we gather here to commemorate this inci-

dent. This is an occasion to remind our Hindu, Muslim and Sikh brethren whether they have preserved the memory and the message of this tragedy or have completely forgotten the sacrifices of the people.[26]

The Anjuman-i-Islamia founded by the Maulana under extreme pecuniary conditions started flourishing within a short period. As a matter of fact, once Azad narrated to G.R. Meher that in the beginning in order to run the Anjuman, a handful of flour were collected in the town. However, soon enough the source of income stabilized and annual functions came to be organized. It was on the occasion of the second annual function that the Maulana so keenly invited Syed Suleiman Nadavi to Ranchi. He requested him, 'your participation is essential. No matter what happens, you have to come. Your not coming would hurt me'.[27]

This function was to take place on 24-6 October 1919 and for this Azad's unbridled enthusiasm was clearly discernible in the above letter. To spread education including a political one, among his co-religionists remained his main agenda; however, he lamented that Bihar hardly showed any enthusiasm in these endeavours and he wanted Suleiman Nadavi to highlight the academic achievements of Bihar as a reminder to its people in one of the sessions of the annual function.[28]

Behind all these activities of Azad, the guiding motive was to spread Islamic education among his less fortunate co-religionists at Ranchi. He tried to do so to sustain an image that he had projected about himself that he was an Islamic scholar who was committed to uphold Islamic ideals in public as well as private life. He was quite self-conscious of it all though. In one of the letters that he wrote from Ranchi, while responding to objections raised about his arguments not being in the light of the Quran, he asserted that he never said anything, which was beyond the Quran.[29] He reiterated the same with much greater emphasis when he said, 'Till such time that I have control over my tongue it is impossible that I could ever suggest any thing which is against the Quran.'[30] Azad went on to lament the fact that the correspondent doubted Azad's credentials in terms of his arguments not being in the light of the Quran.[31]

In the same letter perhaps for the first time the Maulana, regretted the fact that he was not a free man. As he put it,

Quite often I feel that I am helpless. Believe me that for the first time I have developed such feelings. My wife is not well and I have received a telegram about her illness. However I think that the God has given me enough courage to withstand such miseries and I am sure these things won't break my resolve.[32]

The above mentioned letter seems to be the only one of its kind where Azad lamented his internment since it prevented him from discharging many obligations. Whereas, most other letters of his contained discussions only on issues of academic and political concerns, and rarely betrayed any sense of lamentation.

Another place where Azad seemed to lament his internment is in *Tazkirah*, which was written in the initial months of his confinement. At one place he laments, 'While I am writing this, I am put away all by myself in a place called Moorabadi, in the outskirt of Ranchi town.'[33]

At another place too in the same volume, he gave expressions to similar feelings but a bit differently 'For the first time I seem to be missing all the humdrum of the month of *Ramdan* (month of fasting) and the pleasure of congregation (*namaz*). By now the conditioning of my heart is such that I don't seem to be much bothered.[34]

Despite such bouts of occasional depression Azad strove to fight back these feelings. He in a manner of self-assurance once said, 'Somehow if I have to stay longer in this confinement then I must start my work here itself. The world has seen my work when I was free, whereas it is a matter of real test to work under such trying conditions of confinement.'[35]

Azad did strive to achieve certain objectives that he had set before himself, but the most memorable has been the writing of the *Tazkirah*. Apart from the efforts that he made on so many fronts, he never gave up on his creativity. But for the solitude it would not have been possible for Azad to write *Tazkirah*, which is described as a biography in symbols. But as a matter of fact the *Tazkirah* contains hardly any facet of Azad's personal life. He preferred to write more on his exalted ancestry. One plausible reason for doing so might have been to let the world know what his ancestors had achieved much in the realm of learning and religious studies. Secondly but equally significantly, Azad may have wanted to seek better recognition for himself since he belonged to such an illustrious family. This consciousness must have weighed heavily on his mind for some time. Malik Ram, the editor of *Tazkirah* noted in the Foreword, 'It appears that he (Azad) intended to project himself as a descendant of the intellectuals of the past whose message he wanted to bring to the world in general and the Muslims in particular as a model to emulate.'[36]

In *Tazkirah*, Azad while making laudatory claims about the achievements of his ancestors seems to be caught in contradictions. For instance in the Preface (*Tamheed*), the Maulana argues, 'That for a person it is his personal achievements which should really count rather than accomplishments of his ancestors'. He argues, 'We should be such that the family should be recognised because of our achievements rather than depending on the family for any recognition.'[37] However, while describing the confluence of three streams of learned men as his ancestors, the Maulana seems to contradict himself when he says, 'The three streams of illustrious families together constitute my forefathers. And if at all achievements of any family matters then certainly I could take the liberty of using expressions about my family which might bring charges of arrogance.'[38]

While on the one hand achievements of his ancestors made him so very proud, on the other he laid a lot of emphasis on the ideal Islamic constructs of a man and his recognition as such for performance of duties and achievements. Despite this irony, his pride in the achievements of his family seemed to overwhelm him so much that while describing his mother and her family, he wrote, 'My mother was a niece of Shaikh Mohammad bin Zaheer Watari, who was the Mufti of Medina.'[39]

Since Shaikh Mohammad Watari was a man of many accomplishments, Azad talked about him with great pride, but in the course of his narration Azad completely missed out informing about his mother's father (maternal grandfather) who may not have earned distinctions. Therefore, what comes out clearly is that, Azad consciously and carefully chose to write about only those of his ancestors who were achievers of some kind and did not mention the rest.

Aside from these highly personalized statements about his ancestors such as Maulana Jamaluddin and many others, Azad delved into several lively areas of discussion. For instance, one such issue was the biography of Prophet Muhammad where he said that not many scholars have paid attention to the fact whether a biographical sketch of the Prophet could easily be constructed merely on the basis of the information provided in the Quran. He wondered, 'And the way the Quran doesn't depend on any external source for its authenticity, similarly it is important to find out if constructing a biography of its propagator, i.e. Muhammad is possible or not.'[40]

While Azad wondered on this question, he didn't wait as he himself proceeded to answer his own query as regards the Prophet's life and said that even if all books on the history of Islam disappear and only the Quran survives then also it would be possible to write his biography.[41]

Azad looked upon the Quran as a major source of the biography of the Prophet Muhammad and in *Tazkirah* he does not attempt at all to write the biography of the Prophet, contrary to a suggestion made.[42] As a matter of fact, what Azad did was to formulate all conceivable questions which would form the bedrock of any biographical study of the Prophet. For instance,

> Who was he? What was his age? Which country was he born? How did he look like? What were the conditions of his followers? How did he and the world interact with each other? How did he spend his domestic life and external life? The conditions of life and at the time he was born and the time he bade goodbye to this world?[43]

According to Azad, these questions could easily be answered with the help of the Quran. As he put it, 'Any information required could be obtained from the Quran itself. For the purpose the Quran does not depend upon any other authority.'[44] In the light of the above it is interesting to argue that he posed lively questions, which could be attractive to a biographer of the Prophet. However, Azad's purpose in formulating these questions was to explore if it was possible to construct a biographical account of the Prophet, perhaps contrary to what has been suggested by V.N. Datta.[45]

Talking about the biographical construction of the Prophet Muhammad was only one aspect of the *Tazkirah*. There are innumerable other issues on which Maulana Azad seriously reflected upon. And not surprisingly almost all issues in one form or the other concerned Islam and the socio-political conditions of Muslims at large. In the course of such reflections Azad expressed another concern regarding the Muslims following the 'real path' suggested by Islam in all areas of life. He quite clearly expressed his preference for scriptural Islam rather than Sufic Islam. Such a standpoint of Azad seems to clearly establish his non-preference for a culture of *piri-muridi*, which he had experienced during the period till his father was alive. In *Tazkirah*, Azad is clear about his preference as he argues, 'The problem in India was that every body was under the influence of *tasavvuf* (meditation). Without a reference to it nothing was considered complete. However the same *tasavvuf* was thoroughly tainted.'[46]

He goes on to argue 'The entire country seemed to be ignorant of the *sharia*. And every body seemed to be only bothered about the *khanquah* (hospices) and the *sajjada nashins* (spiritual heirs of a sufi).[47]

Azad seemed to follow the same agenda which he had set before the *Al-Hilal* and *Al-Balagh* where Islam does not appear merely as a means of spiritual fulfilment but a storehouse of principles around which Muslim society could be organized and in the absence of such a possibility, degeneration was bound to follow, which would appear in three stages; 'firstly, pious people are not able to attract others; secondly, people neither follow the right path nor allow others to do so; thirdly, there comes a stage when distinctions between good and evil is completely lost'.[48]

Islam as a central theme as well as some related issues never escaped Azad's attention. He was a keen observer of several developments regarding the evolution and spread of Islamic learning in India. In the same context, Azad talks about one of his ancestors Maulana Jamaluddin, who had attained the remarkable distinction of an exalted *mohadith* (a scholar of Hadith) in the age of Akbar, and could be said to be associated with the spread of Islamic learning in India.[49]

Towards the end, Azad does get back to briefly talking about himself, which was the original objective of writing *Tazkirah*. The idea was to not give any clear picture of his autobiographical accounts, instead he talked about his highly personalized experiences of wandering in the wilderness of emotions and recovery from all this and embarking upon a path of self-discovery. He was to state, 'whatever I have gained in life is not indebted to any body not even training in the family. It has all been the result of emotional tumult in his life. It was so painful and this pain alone was the panacea.'[50]

Azad made a categorical statement about his own self that in his search for Truth he had embarked upon a lonely journey in which he felt indebted to none, neither any individual nor even his family. Finally, Azad seems to make a highly sublime statement when he says, 'It was He (God), who opened the door to knowledge. It was He (God) alone who showed the way of action.'[51]

Tazkirah was the product of the early phase of Azad's internment at Ranchi. Another more formidable task that he had undertaken was to write the *Tarjumanul Quran* and a commentary thereupon. But it could not be completed during the course of his stay there and whatever portion was completed was also destroyed during the frequent searches of his house. In one such search, the manuscript of the *Tarjumanul Quran*, was lost. Azad lamented it intensely[52] and he gave up the effort of writing for quite a while.

Azad's internment had upset a large number of his admirers and supporters. A series of meetings were organized in several towns of north India where his internment was protested and demands for his release were raised.[53] Even Azad stated about it in *Tazkirah*,

> Friends and admirers didn't leave any stone unturned to demand my release. It was perhaps for the first time that sixty thousand signatures were collected to send a memorandum. I have come to know that many members of the government too realize their mistake. So much so that even Lord Carr Michael had shown his willingness for the release. These developments did affect me initially, however, later on my feelings had turned hard.[54]

The British government of India was not to succumb to these pressure tactics to release Azad. More so, when the First World War was on. It was not Azad alone, but the Ali Brothers, Zafar Ali Khan, Hasrat Mohani and so many others whose pan-Islamic and anti-colonial feelings had become a source of anxiety to the British government in India and therefore it tried its best to shut their voices.[55] The British government's anxiety about the Muslims response to a possible harsh treatment to Turkey was raised even though the war was coming to an end, since it was obvious that the same fate awaited so many other vanquished nations, at the Versailles Peace Conference.[56] Despite these apprehensions, the government had no option but to release many leaders whose voices were gagged during the war years. However, unless the government felt absolutely sure of its act it did not wish to rush into releasing these men. And Azad, of all the others, was a major concern for them.

The correspondence between various agencies of th government continuously harped on Azad's underground contacts and therefore his being 'quite dangerous'. In one such correspondence the government of Bengal stated, 'Abul Kalam Azad was deeply involved in the Silk Letter Conspiracy case. He is interned in Ranchi and first of all subjected to numerous restrictions under the Defence of India Act, but these were subsequently removed. . . .'[57]

There were occasions when Azad's correspondence was thoroughly scrutinized and in several cases intercepted,[58] even though he largely refrained from discussing political issues overtly. Azad did not have permission to leave the station without prior sanction since he was perceived as hostile to the government.[59] It was also observed that 'this man (Azad) is extremely able and dangerous and that the same considerations apply to him as to the Ali Brothers'.[60] He was also proclaimed to hold 'pro-Turkish sympathies', therefore extreme caution was suggested to be exercised in considering the case of his release.

The year 1919 was of great significance for the British government of India as well as the Indian struggle towards the freedom of the country. The First World War had come to an end and the Paris Peace Conference was set in motion to work out the finer points of the international power structure, where dictating terms to the vanquished nations was a dominant agenda. Turkey could not have escaped the fate, which was due, to all vanquished countries.

Britain had hardly enjoyed the fruits of victory in the war when its anxiety grew over the Muslims of India who were anxious about the fate and future of Turkey. During the course of the war itself the Muslims had shown concern as to what would happen to Turkey, whose capital was also the seat of the *khalifa* of the Muslims, particularly the Sunnis. The *khalifa* was also the custodian of the holy places of Islam, therefore, the concern was heightened as to who would look after these holy places once the Turkish Empire disintegrated. The British government was fully aware of these disturbed feelings of the Indian Muslims. The government made every effort to smoothen out their feelings. Turkey was projected as having been duped by German intrigues. It also solemnly promised that the holy places of Islam would remain immune from attack or molestation.[61] The Viceroy also assured the Imperial Legislative Council that under any circumstances 'the holy places will remain inviolate and that Islam will still be one of the great world forces'.[62]

But in spite of government assurances, the Muslim sentiments aroused in favour of Turkey went on unabated. It was with dismay that Austin Chamberlain, the Secretary of State for India, noted 'the Muslim community of India is I think, the only community under the British flag which habitually prays for a foreign sovereign and does not offer prayers for the king'.[63]

However, what Chamberlain did not realize was that both the sovereigns were alien to Indian Muslims in particular and Indians in general. And yet the religious affiliations of Indian Muslims marked a very special relationship with Turkey. The defeat of Turkey produced fresh pan-Islamic convulsions among the Muslims since the dismemberment of Turkey was strongly feared as the Turkish army had been driven back into their home territory, Constantinople was occupied by allied troops; the Ottoman Empire was in the process of liquidation.[64]

The general expectations were that the peace settlement with Turkey would be announced by May 1919. But the entire issue was indefinitely postponed and could be announced only by 20 May 1920. However, the government had made efforts to face all possible consequences in the wake of the announcements of peace terms with Turkey right from the beginning. As a matter of fact the delay in the announcement had dissipated several efforts made towards it.[65]

Meanwhile in March 1919, for the first time with the formation of the Khilafat Committee under the chairmanship of Seth Chotani, an institutional basis was created in order to channellize the pan-Islamic feelings.[66] This was just the beginning. Within months, several provinces and towns followed suit.[67] In other words, the network of the Khilafat Committee started spreading its tentacles far and wide, where not only provincial cities but the smaller towns as well as *qasbas* were touched, and the Khilafat propaganda carried on relentlessly. The impact of this propaganda was widely manifest on 17 October 1919, which was observed as Khilafat Day. It was organized on an all-India basis and various regions responded to it rather enthusiastically.[68] The significance of Khilafat Day was established in several ways. First, it enjoyed the support of a wide range of groups among the Muslims. However, it also established another trend within the Khilafat movement that the constitutional methods seemed to give way to the militant approach.[69] And finally the realization that the only way to save the Khilafat was to keep the pressure on the government by intensifying the agitation.[70]

The government noted that 'on the 17 October 1919, Khilafat Day was observed generally throughout India'. To their surprise they found the speeches and resolutions rather moderate in tone.[71] However, their concern and anxiety did not disappear completely since it observed that the Khilafat Committee, which sat along with Gandhi and many other Hindu leaders on 23 and 24 October 1919, 'passed violent resolution advocating total abstention from the peace celebrations, the gradual boycott of British goods, the abandonment of co-operation with the government as regards the civil and military services, etc.'[72]

Such trends in the Khilafat movement had forced the government to sit up and think of a strategy which would enable it to contain the consequences that the announcement of the peace terms with Turkey would produce. Preparation in this regard had already been done earlier and towards the close of the year it was imminent that the peace terms would be announced anytime. In a government report it was observed, 'the idea has nevertheless made headway in towns and greater the delay in the announcement of the peace terms, greater is the danger that the agitation may extend to rural areas and sweep even moderate minded Mohammedans, off their feet'.[73]

Such was the perception of the government as regards the announcement of the peace terms and its impact on the Muslim masses. It has already been said that many Muslim leaders were out of the scene either because of internment or imprisonment. However, towards the closing months of 1919 a discussion regarding the release of many such leaders was carried out in official circles. About Azad too, a similar possibility was discussed but the government still had quite a stern view on him. It observed, 'It would be taking a grave risk to release this man at present, pending the announcement of the Turkish peace terms and the question seems to be whether the restrictions now in force should not be made more stringent.'[74] The government finally was of the view that no fresh restriction be imposed on him but only the one which prevents him from leaving Ranchi must be maintained.[75] However, the government thought that this might be considered later on once the peace terms with Turkey were announced.

The announcement of the peace terms appeared to have been delayed further and the political detenues could not be kept in confinement indefinitely. As the Director of the Central Intelligence C.R. Cleveland was willing to say, 'I am in favour of taking the risks involved' to release Azad as many others even in the face of a contrary suggestion made by the government of Bengal.[76] The Ali Brothers along with many others had already been released and they plunged into the heat of the Khilafat agitation and the freedom of the country. Azad was finally released only on 27 December 1919.[77]

From the time of Azad's internment till he was released, more than 3½ years had elapsed. During this period the politics of the freedom struggle had begun changing its character from being elite—middle-class based to a mass-based agitation. The period had experienced two Home Rule league movements, which in their own limited way had tried to reach out to the masses. Gandhi, ever since he had come back to India and after familiarizing himself with Indian realities afresh, had already experimented with the Kheda and Champaran mode of mass-based agitation. The maiden attempt of forging a political society[78] in the context of the Rowlatt Satyagraha, had borne some fruit and at the same time had also exposed the repressive character of the British rule, when its forces indulged in white terror in the Jallianwala Bagh on 13 April 1919. All these developments coalesced with the Khilafat issue in the context of Turkey's participation in the First World War and her subsequent defeat.

These were certain developments which provided the larger political backdrop against which Azad was released. Even though officially released on 27 December 1919, he stayed put in Ranchi till 2 or 3 January 1920.

After his release Azad found himself tormented by the pulls of the two extremes. On the one hand there was this charm of seclusion and solitude where time could be spent in pursuing studies and on the other hand, freedom of the country was a call equal to the first, which Azad could not ignore either. As Azad himself put it 'One of the programmes that I wanted to carry out was to return to some secluded place with a group of companions and disciples and start teaching and writing.'[79] But it was not going to be a clear choice for Azad since the pull to work for the freedom of the country was as strong and powerful. Azad summed up his feelings 'it was a torrent in consonance with my will and intent, a torrent in which I could hear the voice of heavens, calling a man to accept God's will instead of his own'.[80] Ultimately, Azad upheld 'God's will' and surrendered his own, thus making a sacrifice for the cause of the country.[81]

Even while Azad was trying to steer through the conflict of choice between personal volition and God's will, his preference was clearly towards national issues. On 2 January 1920 he wrote a letter to Syed Suleiman Nadavi in which apart from many other issues he made a keen enquiry if he (Nadavi) had gone to Amritsar[82] to participate in the programmes of the Congress which had held its annual session there against the macabre background of the Jallianwala Bagh massacre, which he himself could not attend since he was released only 1 January 1920,[83] a thing he may have liked to do himself.

It was around this time that Azad met Gandhi on 18 January 1920 for the first time. The meeting seemed to have had a profound impact on both of them. Gandhi had tried seeing Azad at Ranchi, while he was interned there but the government did not permit this,[84] and the meeting could not materialize.

By the time Azad met Gandhi, the Khilafat Conference had already decided to send a deputation to the Viceroy to present the Muslim point of view as regards the Khilafat. A memorandum was signed by prominent Muslim leaders, Maulana Azad too was a signatory to this memorandum but declined to join the deputation to the Viceroy, since he considered, 'Old methods of begging, petitioning, waiting in deputation and so on could not be of much avail. We had to try to find some means of exerting direct pressure.'[85]

The deputation of the Khilafat leaders, under the leadership of M.A. Ansari on 19 January 1920 met the Viceroy Lord Chelmsford. The response of the Viceroy was discouraging. However, he assured all help in case any delegation wished to visit England. Shortly, under the leadership of Mohammad Ali, a delegation comprising Syed Husain Ali, Syed Suleiman Nadavi and Hasan Mahmood Hayat left India on 1 February 1920 to impress upon the imperial government[86] led by Lloyd George, whose response too was less than encouraging and it became a source of resentment. Later trips to other European countries including the venue of the Peace Conference were organized. In all these places the delegation stressed upon three central demands that the Sultan of Turkey, who was also the *khalifa,* must be able to retain the control over the Muslim sacred places. Secondly, he must be left with sufficient territory to enable him to defend the Islamic faith and finally, the *Jazirat-ul-Arab* (Arabia, Syria, Iraq, Palestine) must remain under Muslim sovereignty.[87] All these efforts made by the Khilafat leaders did not produce any desired result.

While the delegation to the Peace Conference was touring various countries, the Khilafat agitation back home was gaining momentum. Many Khilafat stalwarts toured different parts of the country and addressed several meetings and raised funds.[88] In all these meetings constant reference was made to seeking support from the Hindus at large. Gandhi had already begun espousing the cause of the Khilafat and was in constant touch with several Khilafat leaders including the firebrand Maulana Abdul Bari of Firangi Mahal. The way Gandhi rationalized his support to the Khilafat was simple. He said, 'It was his duty to stand by the Muslims in the hour of their peril.' Later Gandhi observed in May 1920,

> If I kept aloof from the Khilafat question I, would consider myself as having lost all my worth. That work is my dharma par-excellence. It is through the Khilafat that I am doing the triple duty of showing to the world what ahimsa means, of uniting Hindus and Muslims and of coming in contact with one and all.[89]

It was no surprise to anybody that by September 1919 the All India Muslim Conference and the All India Khilafat Conference had unofficially begun accepting overall leadership of Gandhi as regards the Khilafat agitation.[90] With the commencement of the Third Khilafat Conference in Bombay from 15-17 February 1920, it was clear that the Khilafat leaders had been pushed to the brink. This Conference produced two documents, the Khilafat Manifesto and the constitution of the All India Khilafat Committee. The Conference while laying down Muslim demands also warned the government of dire consequences if the Ottoman Empire was not left the way it was before the war,[91] and the *Jazirat-ul-Arab* must remain under the suzerainty of the Caliph.

The constitution of the All India Khilafat Committee defined four aims of the organization: (1) to preserve the Khilafat as a centre for the Muslim world, (2) to keep the *Jazirat-ul-Arab* free from non-Muslim control, (3) to work in India for the attainment of self rule, and (4) social and economic upliftment of the common people. The method to achieve all this would include solidarity among Muslims world over, working towards the national movement and seeking cooperation with the Hindus while non-cooperating with the government.[92]

The Khilafat Conference, which met in February 1920 was to act as a catalytic agent in organizing many more such meetings in the provinces and other smaller cities and towns. It was in this wake, that a series of meetings of the Bengal Provincial Khilafat

Conference was held in Calcutta from 28-9 February 1920. It was in this meeting, while other established leaders of Khilafat indulged in great elocution, Maulana Azad got an opportunity to speak for the first time after his release, that too on his home ground.[93] He spoke at great length, elaborating upon the historical and spiritual importance of the institution of the Khilafat. Azad further emphasized the need to build on internal solidarity among the Muslims and to launch an anti-British struggle. The desire and need of internal solidarity convinced Azad to bring the Shias too within the fold of the Khilafat movement. He argued that Sunnis and Shias are agreed on the need to obey the Imam, they differ only on the method of choosing him. According to him, it was the duty of all Muslims to uphold and defend the institution of the Khilafat or else they would fall into disunity.[94]

All the above points made by Azad were new only in the manner of presentation since many such points he had already made during the *Al-Hilal* days and several speeches before his internment.[95] Even as regard to his distinction of a friendly non-Muslim and an inimical non-Muslim and the need to align with the friendly non-Muslim, Azad was breaking no new ground since that was a line he had already taken during the *Al-Hilal* days.[96] Despite the repetition of many of the points, Azad's skill of oratory had made them look fresh.

The Calcutta Session of the Khilafat Conference had adopted quite a militant posture where a direct talk of non-cooperation with the government had begun taking place, even though the moderates based in Bombay had no desire to endorse such a stand at this moment.[97] The leaders who had assembled in Bengal also called for 19 March 1920 to be observed as Khilafat Day.

As it was decided, 19 March 1920 was observed as Khilafat Day. It was a day of strikes, special prayers and public meetings in major cities all over India, where non-cooperation with the government and the boycott of foreign goods was mostly favoured.[98] The impact of Khilafat Day was felt throughout the country. Bombay Presidency and Bombay city in particular experienced the cessation of business activities. In Sind, four honorary magistrates resigned, since they thought the government pursued anti-Islamic politics. Calcutta, Dacca, Chittagong all observed Khilafat Day with a renewed resolve to resist the government on the question of Khilafat.[99] Public meetings were organized at Amritsar, Lahore, Multan, Sialkot and Peshawar where fasting and prayers were also organized. Delhi too witnessed a very warm response to Khilafat Day, so did several towns of U.P.[100] While the Khilafat cauldron had begun simmering on apprehension of a harsh treatment to Turkey, however, the publication of the Turkish Peace terms on 14 May 1920 led it to boil over. By the time the mood to launch a relentless campaign against the government[101] had acquired definite shape, Gandhi had felt highly resentful and declared that the non-cooperation was the only effective remedy for healing the wounds inflicted upon Mohammedan opinion.[102]

Almost around the same time, the Hunter Commission Report on the Punjab disturbances was also out and the way brazen attempts were made to whitewash the Jallianwala Bagh tragedy, further fuelled the fire. All sections of Muslims were already stunned by the terms of the peace,[103] and were raring to go into action.

Prior to the publication of the peace terms the programme of non-cooperation had already been formulated and was finally announced by Gandhi at the U.P. provincial Khilafat Conference held at Meerut on 21-3 March 1920. The four-stage programme of non-cooperation was to be as follows: (1) renunciation of titles, (2) resignation from government services, (3) resignation from the police and military, and (4) non-payment of taxes.[104] Each stage of the programme was to follow the other with great care and only when the previous stage had been carried out fully.

The stage for political action was all set. A sufficiently viable structure of the Khilafat Committee at all levels was in order. The consensus that Gandhiji would lead the agitation was reached. So much so that even the method of the agitation was almost formulated, with non-violence being a crucial component on the insistence of Gandhiji, despite reservations in certain quarters. With these preparations everybody waited with bated breath for the peace terms to be announced. Once they were declared, Indians at large and Muslims in particular were straining at the leash to surge. The only hitch that remained to be overcome was to get the Congress' approval since it remained sceptical about the efficacy of any mass movement at this stage. Once the peace terms were out, Gandhiji could no longer have waited for Congress approval. He perhaps knew that the approval would come surely but only in the course of the movement.

1 August 1920 was the date to start the agitation. From the time of the publication of peace terms till the agitation started, Gandhi and Shaukat Ali were tirelessly moving across the length and breadth of the country in order to give finishing touches to all the preparations so far.[105] It was pre-formulated that the first stage of the movement would include surrendering of the titles and honorary positions as also the boycott of government schools, the elections to the reformed councils, and the law courts.[106] Exactly as per the plans, on 1 August 1920, Gandhi went to the Viceroy personally and surrendered his title of Kaiser-i-Hind and Zulu war medals, which he had won during his South African days.

Once the wheels of the Non-Cooperation–Khilafat movement were set rolling, there was no stopping it. What options did the Congress as a national body have, except supporting the movement? Finally, the Calcutta Congress took place in September 1920 and after great deliberations it put the seal of approval on the movement, even though the margin was quite slender. After Calcutta it was the annual session of the Congress in December 1920 and similar programmes of the movement were endorsed.

While the ideological as well as political preparations for the Khilafat movement were underway, it was observed that Azad had very clearly thrown himself in the midstream. He was not even willing to exercise restraint, therefore taking an extreme step of advocating non-cooperation right from the start, though the Khilafat leaders of moderate predilections did not agree with such a stand initially. Azad put his felicity with pen and oratory to the best use in campaigning on the issue of Khilafat. His deep interest in Islamic history as well as theology, were distinct advantages with which he could keep his listeners spellbound. Azad had a great capacity of providing religious justification to all his political activities.

Of the various efforts made by Azad in the wake of the Non-Cooperation–Khilafat movement, the most remarkable was engendering a political society by utilizing religious resources. Prior to such efforts of Azad, it was Gandhi who in his own inimitable manner had tried much the same thing.[107] But there was a difference between the two approaches. While the Rowlatt Satyagraha was a political act, the methods employed by Gandhi too were political though occasionally they touched the borders of religiosity. But Azad solely relied upon religious and spiritual resources in order to work out the possibility of a political society consisting of various religious groups. Though it is a different matter that during his *Al-Hilal* days, Azad was treating respective religious communities as political entities too and only then he advocated a policy of cooperation between Hindus and Muslims. However, it is to be noted that Azad's suggestion of Hindu-Muslim ententé was not based on the notion of power sharing, rather this too had the backing of religious and spiritual sanctions.

In the course of all these developments, Azad does not seem to follow a unilinear line of progression from one stage to another. On the contrary, he seemed to be caught in many contradictory situations, which shall be observed shortly.

During the course of the movement, the issue of *Hijrat* as a method of political protest has been the focus of historians' attention. It has mostly been argued that Azad's *fatwa* of *Hijrat* was responded to overwhelmingly but at the same time it caused untold miseries to those who migrated to Afghanistan. The *fatwa* was issued in an emotionally charged atmosphere in July 1920, almost a month in advance of the launch of the movement. The *fatwa* of Maulana Azad argued,

> After having considered all dimensions of the issue the conviction has been reinforced that for the Muslims of India there is no option left but to migrate. Those Muslims who are presently staying in India and wish to conduct their life according to Islamic preaching must migrate. However those who for some reasons cannot migrate must help those who are migrating in a manner as if they themselves are emigrating.[108]

It was further added, '*Hijrat* before the World War I was desirable now it has become mandatory'.[109]

However, a lesser-known fact is that even before Maulana Azad, or for that matter Maulana Abdul Bari of Firangi Mahal, issued the *fatwa* of *Hijrat*, one Khilafat zealot called Aziz Hindi had mooted the idea of *Hijrat*. It was only when Aziz Hindi himself had migrated to Afghanistan that Azad took it upon himself to issue such a *fatwa*.[110]

In the same *fatwa*, Azad also argued that it would not be impossible for every single Muslim to migrate nor would it be desirable according to the Sharia. However, *Hijrat* will continue and the Muslim would stay in India as well. Those who would stay back in India would have to fulfil one condition, 'Thus those who stay back in India, it would be imperative on them not to have any truck with the government. In case any body happened to have any thing to do with the government it would be considered an act against Islam.'[111]

In the religiously charged atmosphere of the Khilafat mobilization, Azad's advocacy of the *Hijrat*, was popular only in pockets of Sindh and NWFP, that too only among the lower and ill-educated classes, who were under the influence of local *pirs* and *alims*. Azad's *fatwa* was also caught in a quirk of logic where safeguarding one's faith took precedence over everything else. For instance, he argued, 'In my considered opinion which is free from all speculations that the motto of the Muslims is not so much to save Constantinople but safeguard our own faith.'[112]

What turns out to be surprising is that a person like Azad overemphasized the concern for the Khilafat and he expected an overwhelming response from the community on the issue. But the point which must not be missed is that he insisted that those Muslims who would stay back will not cooperate with the government failing which they may not be counted among Muslims.

Azad's *fatwa* has been evaluated by historians rather harshly and described as a case of 'Islamic supra-nationalism'[113] but later developments suggest contrary to such assumptions. For instance, the founding of the educational institutions such as Jamia Millia Islamia, Kashi Vidyapeeth and Gujarat Vidyapeeth were products of the collective effort of several nationalist leaders. While these institutions were the fruits of joint efforts of many, the Madrasa Islamia, Calcutta, was the brainchild of Azad alone. Singlehandedly he took pains to establish the Madrasa Islamia

(Jama Masjid, Calcutta) with a view to provide an alternative to the government-aided institutions of Arabic learning. The madrasa was formally inaugurated by Gandhi on 13 December 1920 where he acknowledged the singular courage of those students who responded to the call of Azad and gave up the comfort of government-run institutions.[114]

Preparation to establish this Madrasa had begun some time ago. In a letter dated 20 September 1920 to A.R. Malihabadi, Azad had written,

> In the wake of the non-cooperation it has become essential to withdraw from the government aided schools most particularly government aided Arabic schools. There are two thousand students enrolled in such (government aided) schools. If such a big group of students decide to withdraw from the government aided school it will have far reaching impact.[115]

Even though mobilizing financial resources to run the Madrasa was a tall task,[116] the students showed quite an enthusiasm. In keeping with the programmes of the non-cooperation movement to wear khadi, the students asked for *charkhas* for themselves, which were promptly arranged.[117] In this project of Azad, contrary to his expectations, not many people volunteered to take up teaching assignments at his madrasa, which did dishearten him even though he remained undaunted.

Azad's first tour as an ideologue of the Khilafat movement came when he became the secretary of the Central Khilafat Committee after the arrest of Maulana Shaukat Ali in mid-September 1921. Azad took over the secretaryship on 22 September 1921 and remained so till he was arrested. His major responsibility was to propagate the Khilafat and Non-Cooperation ideas. In order to intensify the movement, he began touring the country to hold meetings and deliver lectures.[118]

In many such meetings that Azad addressed, he dwelt upon various nuances of the Khilafat and the Non-Cooperation movement. In most such meetings, Azad reminded his audience,

> It is the most decisive moment of discharging our duties enjoined upon by Islam, which has come to us in the form of Khilafat issue and India's independence. There are about ten crore Muslims in India

who were caught in a state of inertia, however now they have woken up to the cause of the Khilafat as well India's freedom.[119]

The next moment in the same breath, Azad warned that having undertaken the responsibility of defending the *Khilafat-i-Islamia* and *Jazirat-ul-Arab* as well as waging a struggle to free India would not be easy.[120] He went on to argue, 'You are faced with a daunting task of taking away the *shikar* (prey) from the most formidable power on this earth. Therefore life is not going to be easy. Those who are not given to bear pains must vacate the arena in favour of those who are willing to put up a struggle.'[121]

The question of violence or for that matter of non-violence as a method of the Non-Cooperation movement had largely been resolved even before the movement was formally launched. So much so that a person like Maulana Abdul Bari who ideally would have liked to retain violence as a method also gave in to Gandhi's wishes. Though most Khilafat leaders agreed with non-violence only as a tactic and not as a creed since that was the only position, which enjoyed the sanction of Islam. Therefore in certain quarters serious objections were raised that adhering to non-violence on Gandhi's advice was against the *sharia* and thus unacceptable.[122] Azad took it upon himself to answer these questions. The manner in which Azad answered reflected clear signs of creative politics. For instance, he argued, 'Violence means oppression and usurping the rights of the others. And Islam has never permitted any such thing. It has never permitted committing any excess.'[123] He argued further that Islam while it permits violence, which could be said to be in tune with human nature, it does not permit violence in the sense of oppression and persecution. Thus violence in this sense has never enjoyed the sanction of Islam.[124]

Having dwelt at length in order to convince his co-religionists that there was a distinction between violence as coercion and waging a war, which Islam does permit for a just cause. So if this was the Islamic position then the alternative in the present context could only be non-violence. Azad argued, 'The path suggested by the Jamiatul-Ulama is the path of peace enjoined upon by *sharia*. As a matter of fact this is the only correct *sharia* position in this matter and we should be able to take it to its logical end.'[125]

The question of violence or non-violence was only a matter of method of the Non-Cooperation movement. But the declared objective was to attain *swaraj* as well as the defence of *khalifa* and the *Jazirat-ul-Arab*. Regarding *swaraj* Azad said,

> There is another problem which pertains to a Hindi word called *swaraj*. It must be made clear that this is not a new thing. It is not a new message for the Muslims since they should know that there is hardly any corner on this earth where the message of the Prophet and God has not been resounding for the last thirteen hundred years.[126]

While attainment of *swaraj* was a task enjoined upon Muslims for the last thirteen hundred years, however, fighting for the dignity and upholding the sanctity of the *Jazirat-ul-Arab* was an entirely new challenge, which had come up in the wake of Turkey's participation in the First World War and her subsequent defeat. He candidly expressed this point,

> The demands of the Muslims in this regard were to keep the *Jazirat-ul-Arab* free from non-Muslim control. Till such time as even the tiniest area of the *Jazirat-ul-Arab* is in the control of the British, it is impossible for a Muslim to extend a hand of co-operation to the British government. It may be easy for a Muslim to buy peace with a beast but the British.[127]

Azad kept on arguing with his listeners in a firm tone that this was the time to resist the highhandedness of the British government. But according to Azad this was not possible till Hindus and Muslims joined hands in their common fight against the foreign rule. He gave full expressions to his conviction, 'For the sake of India and her freedom, for the sake of the truth and duty it is important that the Muslims and the Hindus join together.'[128]

Azad made a powerful case of this unity between the Hindus and Muslims in the context of the Non-Cooperation movement. He had already put forward similar arguments during the *Al-Hilal* days. So it would appear that there was consistency in Azad's argument on this count. And yet a distinction can be discerned in his arguments during the two different phases of his political and intellectual life. For instance, during the *Al-Hilal* days, Azad quite clearly treated religious communities such as Hindus and Muslims as political entities as well. And yet all through the Maulana made a strong case for Hindu-Muslim unity a pre-condition to the struggle against the Raj. According to Azad, even Muslims shall remain a distinct community not only in the religious sense but also politically.[129]

But in the course of the Non-Cooperation Azad went through a process of self-evaluation and took several steps beyond the *Al-Hilal* phase when he argued,

> First of all I would use a word of our own language then one of another language. Actually I wish to say that the Hindus and Muslims must unite in a manner that they together form one '*Qaum*' and one nation. Now I shall address the Muslims in particular and remind them that after the Quran it is the Prophet whose voice is the most authentic and he had said that he extended the hands of friendship to all those who lived in the vicinity of Medina and declared that we should be '*Umma Vahidah*', one people. 'Umma' means 'Qaum' and 'Vahidah' means one.[130]

Azad was seeking an alliance between Hindus and Muslims sanctioned by Islam itself and took a step towards visualizing a political society consisting of various religious communities in the struggle against the British rule. In the same context, Azad invoked the Quran with reference to *Surah Mumtahina* in order to make a distinction among non-Muslims where it was said that there were two kinds of non-Muslims, one who are friendly towards Muslims and the other who are inimical. He went on to argue that such groups which have never harmed Muslims and nor wish to do so, should be made friends by the Muslims.[131]

According to Azad, this alliance was a pre-condition for launching a joint political action against the British since the issue of Khilafat had re-opened the agenda of India's freedom as well.[132] Azad implied that only when there was a political alliance among the religious communities would a joint political action be possible or else all efforts for it were doomed from the start. This was a very clear step towards the formation of a political society because in a colonial context, where multiplicity of religious groupings existed, it needed a strong and viable political welding, which in this context Azad was working at. While working at it, Azad had hoped, 'In these moments all Indians be they the Hindus, Muslims, Sikhs, and Zoroastrians, need to come together and wish for India's success.'[133]

But the finest moment of Azad's reflections and articulation as regards the religious communities merging into each other in order to make a political society or community, came in the context of the movement under discussion. According to Azad, all these efforts were not based on the exigencies and political tactic of the present time, rather they drew their sanction from the Quran. Invoking religious authority in order to work out the basis of a political society was a novel method adopted by Azad. He seemed to take this articulation to a greater height when he argued the case of Hindus and Muslims joining each other in a manner as if they were one nation.[134]

Thus Azad sought religious sanction of a political nature where people of a given territorial unit in the course of a political process could transform themselves into a nation. There were so many other national leaders who since the last quarter of the nineteenth century were grappling with this problem of hastening the process of the formation of a nation. Those who invoked the Hindu religion and culture in a similar direction, kept other religious communities out of its purview,[135] whereas Azad's argument in this regard was rather unique. To what extent such arguments had an impact on his audience, it is difficult to say, but what is certain is that the Maulana laid an ideological basis for a nation to emerge from the fermentation of the Non-Cooperation movement.

The Maulana took pains to elaborate upon the plan of action for the people who were expected to follow it. However, there were some plans, which were exclusively addressed to Muslims alone. For instance he argued, 'Till such time as the British remain our adversary and does not fulfil demands concerning the Khilafat, and till such time it does not grant *swaraj* it is possible that a Muslim may do any thing but extend the hand of friendship to the British.'[136]

It comes out quite clearly that in Azad's perception, the objective of the Khilafat and Non-Cooperation movement was the formation of a political society and attainment of *swaraj*. Referring to the issue, the Maulana argued,

> In this regard one was confronted with two tasks; one was in the arena of India itself rather than of Iraq, Asia Minor or Smyrna where the blood of the Muslims had already been spilt. And this was truly the arena to test your determination. As regards the Khilafat movement the first task pertained to India, Muslims and other communities living

in India. And the world recognised it as such. Therefore it does not come as a surprise that the Hindus and Muslims have succeeded in attaining it.[137]

At another time Azad was clearly appealing to all sections of Indian society to quit military service. Azad exhorted, 'Even if one was not to commit a sin in the British army and were asked merely to pray in a mosque or temple then also it was not justified for any of them to enter the services of the British army.'[138]

In the same breath, he went on to establish the rationale of his call to quit the British Indian army. He clarified that the army was meant for two objectives of security; one was internal and the other was external. 'External was well understood by everybody. But its internal objective was only to oppress Indians at large, it enslaves the Indians and spills their blood.'[139] He further argued that if anybody was still in doubt regarding the internal objective of the army, then, 'He need not answer that question. It was the land of the Jallianwala Bagh drenched with the blood of the Hindus and Muslims, which would answer that question. We should also know who had fired bullets on the Indians? They were Indian soldiers only.'[140] Obviously, Azad saw the British Indian army as a means of oppression and exploitation of India and since the army was full of Indians, it was all the more lamentable.[141]

Exhortations apart, Azad also adopted the method of shaming the audience for their indirect support to mechanisms of exploitation of the British by buying foreign goods, particularly foreign clothes. Azad's logic of boycott of foreign goods particularly was double-edged. In one context he argued that every year about Rs. 90 crore were drained out of India on account of people buying foreign clothes. The same money had been used to wipe out Islam from the face of the earth. Therefore, Azad appealed to the people to give up wearing foreign clothes and adopt locally produced clothes. He said, 'till such time the boycott of foreign clothes does not take place it is simply not possible to attain the set goal (freedom from British rule).'[142] Maulana Azad did not stop at that. In the same speech he reiterated the appeal but added more force in it and he addressed every common man and exhorted that if they could sacrifice their lives why could they not give up wearing foreign clothes, which was incumbent upon them.[143]

Shifting from the general to the specific while addressing Muslims he argued that, 'particularly for the Muslims it is important that they sacrifice certain comfort of their body. That they must stop wearing fine clothes imported from Manchester and Lancashire because these clothes are destructive to their country and as such they should be thrown away.'[144]

With these arguments the Maulana clearly and cleverly tried to convey the mechanism of colonial exploitation in idioms, which were comprehensible to his audience. While Azad remained an integral part of the non-violent Non-Cooperation–Khilafat movement, he did not give up his underground activities, where the use of violence was considered legitimate in order to overthrow the government. In 1921 he reactivated his association with the Secret Society in Calcutta, developed contacts with the Bolsheviks, and revived his contacts with other underground revolutionaries of Bengal.

However, eventually all these efforts of Azad did not go beyond a point. But they clearly established his zeal in the service of his country's freedom.[145]

Asking Indians at large and Muslims in particular to quit the British Indian army must have been received with alarm in government circles. Not only quitting the army was being advocated, but in general, Azad had declared, 'To take up any government job was *Haram* (forbidden) for a Muslim.'[146]

As the movement progressed the government was uneasy about it and decided to crack down. Many top non-cooperators and Khilafat leaders had already been arrested, and by the end of September 1921, Azad was quite sure that his own arrest was in the offing for having exhorted Indians to quit the army, which was no small offence to have committed. It also seems Azad was willing to suffer the privations of gaol as he said, 'Thus if the government was making preparations for arrests then we too were openly inviting this. And ever since these arrests began being made I nurtured a desire to go to gaol. However if the Government stops making more arrests then disappointments would know no bounds.'[147]

Azad's desire to be arrested became more intense with the passage of time. The fact that leaders such as Mohammad Ali, Shaukat Ali, Maulana Husain Ahmad, Dr. Saifuddin Kitchlew, Peer Ghulam Mujuddid, Maulana Nisar Ahmad, Jagat Guru Shankaracharya, Maulana Ahmad Saeed and Abdul Aziz Saheb had been arrested and Azad was still moving about freely was something unbearable to Azad, as if being arrested would bring about a halo of martyrdom in the cause of the Non-Cooperation–Khilafat movement. After a point he began lamenting,

> I am tired of waiting to be arrested. For the last two months I have carried the arguments to the extremes anticipating that it would result in my arrest. However while the whole lot of people are being arrested I am still waiting around.[148] Am I expected not to call the government by its real name? I refuse to call black as white.[149]

He also took the opportunity to remind Indians at large and Muslims in particular that if they wished to have rights and justice, then the only recourse was to attain *swaraj*. This would mean the government of Indians in India and for Indians.[150] In *Qaul-i-Faisal* (the final verdict), Azad was at his theoretical best in explaining the character of colonial rule, its mechanism of exploitation of local people and reactionary attitude towards the just demands of Indians in general.

Azad did not have to wait for long to be arrested, since his turn came shortly on 10 December 1921. The charges against him were the speeches which he had delivered in Mirzapur Park at Calcutta on 1 and 15 July 1921 and these were presented in the court of the Presidency Magistrate. After the trial he was awarded a year's rigorous imprisonment on 9 February 1922, under Section 124-A of the Indian Penal Code.[151] Azad thought that the punishment awarded to him was too slight compared to the magnitude of his crime.

However, the highlight of the court trial was that Azad did not defend himself since the CWC's decision had clearly laid down that 'in the event of prosecution or a civil suit being brought against non-cooperators, they should not participate in the proceedings beyond making before the court a full statement of facts in order to establish their innocence before the public'.[152]

Accordingly Azad, rather than defending himself issued a written statement titled *Qaul-i-Faisal* which turned out to be an important piece of political as well as literary writing. In *Qaul-i-Faisal*, Azad referred to the same speech which was made the basis of his arrest and reiterated his statement, 'Undoubtedly, I said that the present government is a tyrant.' While Azad's trial was still on and the punishment was yet to be awarded, on 5 February 1922 at Chauri-Chaura in Gorakhpur, a violent incident of burning 22 policemen alive took place, which rendered Gandhi helpless and without any option other than withdrawing the movement itself. It was Gandhi's solitary act since no consultations were made with other leaders of the movement. Withdrawal of the movement dismayed all sections of Indians, who were enthusiastic about the movement, but the Muslims in particular were thoroughly disappointed, since for many Muslims and their leaders the Khilafat question remained a vital issue and the suspension of the movement, 'took the sting out of their agitation'.[153] In various meetings of the Jamiat-ul-Ulama-i-Hind and Central Khilafat Committee, Gandhi was attacked, which continued even after his arrest on 10 March 1922.[154]

Withdrawal of the movement resulted in a schism in the edifice of solidarity between Hindus and Muslims, which was built so assiduously during the course of the movement. However, what was also discernible in bold relief was the schism among the Muslims themselves, when the disappointment of withdrawal of the movement led some to move towards communal politics, while others still remained committed to nationalism based on the politics of integration. Azad followed the latter path.

NOTES

1. Home Political A, February 1915, nos. 265-92 k&w.
2. Mushirul Hasan, *Mohammad Ali: Ideology and Politics*, Manohar, Delhi, 1981, p. 26.
3. Home Political A, February 1915, nos. 178-204.
4. Home Political A, May 1916, nos. 455-6.
5. Ibid.
6. Ibid., p. 3.
7. Ibid.

8. H. Wheeler, Secretary to the G.O.I., to the Chief Secretary, 20 May 1916.
9. As quoted in Arsh Malsiyani, *Abul Kalam Azad*, Publications Division, Delhi, 1976, p. 27.
10. G.O.I., Home Political A, proceeding nos. 180-92, November 1919.
11. Ibid.
12. Ibid.
13. Ibid.
14. A letter to Syed Suleiman Nadavi, letter no. 11 in Ghulam Rasool Meher, ed., *Tabarrukat-i-Azad*, Adabi Duniya, Delhi, 1963, p. 112.
15. Ibid.
16. Ibid., letter no. 13, p. 115.
17. Ibid., letter no. 17, pp. 122-3.
18. Suhail Azimabadi, 'Maulana Azad Ranchi Mein', *Payam-i-Watan,* Azad Number, Delhi, 1977, p. 69.
19. Ibid.
20. Ibid., p. 9.
21. Ibid.
22. Ibid.
23. Azad's letter to Maulana Mohiuddin Qasuri, undated, but it is suggested by the editor that this letter was written towards the end of his confinement in Ranchi, in Ghulam Rasool Meher, op. cit., p. 20.
24. Ibid., p. 22.
25. Ravinder Kumar, ed., *Essays on Gandhian Politics: The Rowlatt Satyagrah of 1919*, Clarendon Press, London, 1971, p. 16.
26. Maulana Azad papers, Messages, Nehru Memorial Museum & Library (NMML), New Delhi.
27. Azad to Suleiman Nadavi, undated but perhaps written in August or September 1919, in Ghulam Rasool Meher, ed., op. cit., p. 128.
28. Ibid.
29. A letter written from Ranchi (name of the person is not clear), 20 May 1919, *Azad Papers*, NMML, p. 1.
30. Ibid., p. 2.
31. Ibid.
32. Ibid.
33. Azad, *Tazkirah*, Sahitya Akademi, Delhi, 1993, p. 333.
34. Ibid.

35. Ibid., p. 336.
36. Ibid., Foreword, pp. 10-11.
37. Ibid., p. 26.
38. Ibid.
39. Ibid., p. 25.
40. Ibid., p. 204.
41. Ibid., p. 206.
42. V.N. Datta, *Maulana Azad*, Manohar, Delhi, 1990, p. 98.
43. Azad, *Tazkirah*, op. cit., p. 206.
44. Ibid.
45. Datta, op. cit., p. 98, Datta has argued that Azad was perhaps interested in 'writing the biography of the Prophet'.
46. Azad, *Tazkirah*, op. cit., p. 266.
47. Ibid.
48. Ibid., pp. 284-5.
49. Ibid., p. 301.
50. Ibid., p. 330.
51. Ibid.
52. Malsiyani, *Abul Kalam Azad*, op. cit., p. 30.
53. The listing of files of Home Political, deposited with the National Archives of India, does show such meetings took place. But actual files are not available since they are categorized as 'not transferred'.
54. Azad, *Tazkirah*, op. cit., p. 335.
55. B.R. Nanda, *Gandhi: Pan-Islamism, Imperialism and Nationalism*, Oxford University Press, Bombay, 1989, p. 204.
56. Ibid., p. 205.
57. Home Political A., proceeding nos. 180-92, November 1919.
58. Ibid.
59. Ibid.
60. Ibid.
61. Nanda, op. cit., p. 203.
62. Ibid.
63. Ibid., p. 204.
64. Nanda, op. cit., p. 205.
65. Home Political, nos. 284-5, February 1920.
66. Nanda, op. cit., pp. 209-10.
67. Mushirul Hasan, *Nationalism and Communal Politics in India 1916-1928*, South Asia Books, Delhi, 1979, pp. 149-50.
68. Ibid., pp. 152-4.
69. Ibid., p. 155.

70. Ibid.
71. Home Political B, nos. 284-5, February 1920, p. 2.
72. Ibid.
73. Ibid., p. 3.
74. Home Political A, proceeding nos. 180-92, November 1919, p. 6.
75. Ibid., p. 7.
76. Ibid.
77. Datta, op. cit., p., 106. However, Ghulam Rasool Meher informs us that Azad was released on 1 January 1920.
78. Kumar, op. cit., p. 16.
79. Azad, as quoted in Arsh Malsiyani, op. cit., p. 33.
80. Azad as quoted in ibid.
81. J.B. Kriplani, 'The Voice of Reason', in Humayun Kabir, ed., *Maulana Abul Kalam Azad: A Memorial Volume*, Asia Publishing House, Bombay, 1959, p. 36.
82 Azad to Suleiman. Nadavi, in Ghulam Rasool Meher, op. cit., p. 132.
83. Meher, ibid., p. 132 fn.
84. Datta, op. cit., p. 106.
85. As quoted in Mahadev Desai, *Maulana A.K. Azad: A Biographical Memoir*, George Allen and Unwin, London, 1946, p. 4.
86. Datta, op. cit., p. 109.
87. Sumit Sarkar, *Modern India*, Macmillan, Delhi, 1983, p. 195.
88. Datta, op. cit., p. 109.
89. A letter to Maganlalbhai, 3 May 1920 in Mahadev Desai, ed., *Day-to-Day with Mahatma Gandhi (Secretary's Diary)*, Sarva Seva Sangh Prakashan, Varanasi, 1968, p. 154.
90. Mushirul Hasan, *Nationalism and Communal Politics, 1885-1930*, Manohar, Delhi, 1991, p. 129.
91. Gail Minault, *The Khilafat Movement: Religious Symbolism and Political Mobilisation in India*, Oxford University Press, Delhi, 1982, p. 92.
92. Ibid., p. 93.
93. Ibid.
94. Ibid., p. 94.
95. A particular reference can be made to his speech at *Ittihad-i-Islami*, Calcutta, 27 October 1914, in Malik Ram, ed., *Khutbat-i-Azad*, Sahitya Akademi, Delhi, 1990, pp. 13-36.
96. *Al-Hilal,* vol. 1, no. 8, September 1912.
97. Minault, op. cit., p. 96.

98. Ibid.
99. Hasan, op. cit., p. 131.
100. Ibid., p. 132.
101. Ibid.
102. Ibid.
103. Minault, op. cit., p. 99.
104. Ibid., p. 98.
105. Ibid., p. 108.
106. Ibid.
107. Kumar, op. cit., p. 16.
108. Azad, *Hijrat ka Fatwa*, in Ghulam Rasool Meher, op. cit., p. 164.
109. Ibid.
110. For details see I.H. Qureshi, *Ulema in Politics: A Study Relating to the Political Activities of the Ulema in South-Asian Subcontinent from 1556-1947*, Ma'aref Ltd., Karachi, 1972.
111. Azad, in Ghulam Rasool Meher, op. cit., p. 165.
112. Ibid., p. 166.
113. Prabha Dixit, 'Political Objectives of the Khilafat Movement in India' in Mushirul Hasan, ed., *Communal and Pan-Islamic Trends in Colonial India*, Manohar, Delhi, 1985, p. 74.
114. *Makateeb-i-Abul Kalam Azad*, ed. Abu Salman Shahjahanpuri, Urdu Academy Sindh, Karachi, 1968, p. 110.
115. Ibid., pp. 111-13.
116. Ibid., pp. 114-19.
117. Ibid., p. 118.
118. Datta, op. cit., p. 119.
119. Azad, *Khutbat-i-Sadarat, Ajlas Jamiatul Ulema-i-Hind*, Lahore, 18-21 November 1921 in Malik Ram, ed., op. cit., p. 132.
120. Ibid., p. 134.
121. Ibid. pp. 134-5.
122. Syed Jamaluddin, 'The Barelvis and the Khilafat Movement', in Mushirul Hasan, ed., *Communal and Pan-Islamic Trends in Colonial India*, op. cit., p. 44.
123. Azad, *Khutbat-i-Sadarat, Jamiatul-Ulema-i-Hind*, Lahore, 18 November 1921 in Malik Ram, ed., op. cit., p. 148.
124. Ibid.
125. Ibid., p. 151.
126. Ibid., p. 154.
127. Ibid., p. 140.
128. Azad, *Khutbat-i-Azad, Majlis-i-Khilafat*, Agra, 25 August 1921 in Malik Ram, ed., op. cit., p. 46.

129. *Al-Hilal*, vol. 1, no. 9, 8 September 1912.
130. Azad, *Khutbat-i-Sadarat-i-Iftitahia,* in Malik Ram, ed., op. cit., p. 51.
131. Azad, *Khutbat-i-Sadarat, Majlis-i-Khilafat*, in Malik Ram, ed., Agra, 25 August 1921, p. 47.
132. Ibid., p. 46.
133. Ibid., p. 57.
134. Ibid., p. 51.
135. For details refer to Hulas Singh, 'Cultural Consciousness in 19th Century Maharashtra', unpublished M.Phil dissertation, JNU New Delhi, 1984.
136. Azad, *Khutbat-i-Sadarat, Majlis-i-Khilafat*, in Malik Ram, ed., op. cit., Agra, 25 August 1921, p. 50.
137. Ibid., pp. 43-4.
138. Azad, *Khutbat-i-Ikhtimamiya, Majlis-i-Khilafat*, in Malik Ram, ed., op. cit., Agra, 26 October 1921 p. 77.
139. Ibid.
140. Ibid.
141. Ibid.
142. Azad, *Khutbat-i-Sadarat*, in Malik Ram, ed., op. cit., p. 65.
143. Ibid., p. 66.
144. Ibid.
145. Rajat K. Ray, 'Revolutionaries', Pan-Islamists and Bolshevikis: M.A.K. Azad and the Political Underworld in Calcutta', in Mushirul Hasan, ed., op. cit., pp. 118-19.
146. Azad, *Khutbat-i-Ikhtimamiya, Majlis-i-Khilafat*, in Malik Ram, ed., op. cit., p. 77.
147. Ibid. p. 74.
148. Azad, *Khutbat-i-Sdarat, Ajlas-i-Jamiatul-Ulema-i-Hind*, Lahore, 18-21 November 1921, in Malik Ram, ed., op. cit., p. 98.
149. Azad, *Qaul-i-Faisal*, Taj Publishers, Delhi, 1967, p. 91.
150. Ibid., p. 118.
151. Datta, op. cit., p. 121.
152. A.B. Rajput, *Maulana Abul Kalam Azad*, Lion Press, Lahore, 1946, p. 81.
153. Mushirul Hasan, 'Religion and Politics in India: The Ulema and Khilafat Movement', in Mushirul Hasan, ed., *Communal and Pan-Islamic Trends in Colonial India*, op. cit., p. 34.
154. Ibid.

CHAPTER THREE

Integrative Politics: Azad and the Indian National Congress, 1923-1934

Disturbing trends in the Hindu–Muslim relationship marked the immediate post-Khilafat period. The close political collaboration during the Non-Cooperation–Khilafat movement started developing cracks and it was feared that the entire edifice of the partnership, so assiduously built, would crumble. While this was disconcerting enough, there was another disturbing trend within Muslim politics, one section of Muslim leadership gravitated towards communal politics and argued that Muslim interests remained largely autonomous of other sections of society and sometimes at loggerheads with them, particularly the Hindus. This section of Muslim leadership suggested a course of politics with a much narrower perspective. On the other hand, another section of Muslim politicians took a moderate view of the political developments in the post-Khilafat period and remained steadfast to the same political world-view, which was its hallmark during the Non-Cooperation–Khilafat movement. In other words, these leaders continued believing in Hindus and Muslims maintaining a collaborative relationship in order to emerge as a political society so that a united fight against the British was possible. They also believed that pursuing a separate course of politics would be highly injurious to the community and the freedom struggle. The first group was represented by the Ali Brothers, the second by men such as M.A. Ansari and Maulana Azad.

I

Despite the ideal of a collaborative politics between Hindus and Muslims[1] during the Non-Cooperation–Khilafat movement, fissures in the grand alliance had already appeared due to the excesses committed by the Moplahs in Malabar. Several factors are ascribed to the Moplah rising of 1921. The most dominant was economic, since the Moplah peasants had evinced economic discontent for some time. This, along with the call for the Non-Cooperation–Khilafat movement generated religious fervour among the peasants, and two distinct symbols of authority and oppression—the landlords who were mostly Hindus, and the government—were the targets. Besides several estates, many Hindu temples were burnt and there were cases of forced conversion.[2] Some historians have argued that the Moplah uprising had a distinct class rather than communal character.[3]

The violence committed by the Moplahs was disapproved of and in several cases condemned by many individuals as well as by the Jamiatul-Ulema-i-Hind as a body.[4] Azad took a critical view of the Moplah violence, and argued that once non-violence was adopted as a method of agitation by some Muslims, including the Jamiatul-Ulema-i-Hind, then violence indulged in by any section of Muslims in India could not be condoned.[5]

Regarding forcible conversion of non-Muslims, Azad used strong expression to condemn it. He vehemently argued, 'Any one who is knowledgeable about the *sharia* would know that if at all there have been cases of forced conversion then it is certainly not an act in consonance but against the *sharia*. It never permits forced conversion.'[6]

Having condemned violence against landlords and forced conversions, Azad was somewhat sceptical about the veracity of reports coming from Malabar. 'We are not very sure about the authenticity of the reports reaching us. A number of incidents, which were reported earlier turned out to be fictitious. Even I have received some letters from Malabar in this regard.'[7] Doubts persisted in his mind. He reiterated that it was difficult for him to say what the realities were.[8] At one point he appeared deeply introspective, and argued that even if the Moplahs revolted in the manner that they did, they must have done so as a last resort. He obliquely hinted that since atrocities had occurred in the rest of the country the Moplahs could not have remained an exception and when the capacity to bear these atrocities collapsed, frustration and anger might have spilled over.[9]

The repression of the Moplah uprising in many ways was a crude reminder of the 1857 days. The Podnaur incident, in which 56 Moplahs died of asphyxiation because they were shut in a boxcar while being transported to jail,[10] turned some of the hostility back on the government. But Hindu-Muslim understanding had been irrevocably violated by the Moplah rebellion.[11] And this was bound to overshadow the future of inter-community relations and act as an impediment in the emergence of a political community not limited to a single religious group.

It was not the Moplah episode alone but other contentious issues as well which contributed to strain the relations between Hindus and Muslims. One such incident was a speech delivered by Mohammad Ali on 2 April 1921 in Madras in which he went to the extent of conjuring up the bogey of an Afghan invasion in order to oust the British from India.[12] Certainly, such assertions were nothing more than the reflection of excitement in the course of the movement. However, these statements affected several Hindu leaders such as Pt. Madan Mohan Malaviya, who reacted to it rather strongly.[13] There were others who joined Malaviya on this issue and did not appreciate such statements since it generated the spectre of Muslim rule even though they knew that it was virtually impossible. Gandhi obliquely defended him by arguing that the basic essence of Mohammad Ali's speech remained within the boundary of patriotism.[14] Even though critics were calmed by Gandhi's support of Mohammad Ali, doubts persisted and the Hindu–Muslim alliance was definitely in jeopardy by the monsoon of 1921.[15]

These issues, when added to Muslims zeal to start civil disobedience as a protest against the prescription of the *fatwa*, the religious decree, and Gandhi being circumspect about it then, had also made the political air heavy.[16] Another issue was the boycott call given by Gandhi on the eve of the arrival of the Prince of Wales on 17 November 1921. Even though the call was for a peaceful boycott, incidents of violence were frequent in which Christians, Parsis and Anglo–Indians were targeted, particularly in Bombay. Violence in any case went against Gandhi's grain, and he chastized Muslims, without adequate evidence for being the major perpetrators of violence.[17] Such statements of Gandhi perplexed the Muslims.

The strains on the Hindu–Muslim relationship had become apparent even while the movement was on. The withdrawal of the Non-Cooperation–Khilafat movement on 5 February 1922 was, considered by many Muslim leaders as an indication of scant regard for their feelings, a case of betrayal. As a result of all this, the gap in perception of Hindus and Muslims kept growing with the passage of time. The collapse of the Non-Cooperation–Khilafat movement on the one hand impeded the growth of the process of formation of a political community, while on the other it created enough space for communalism to re-emerge with intensity. Both processes were interlinked. The relative strength and weakness of both phenomena affected each other in a proportionate manner. Since during the movement the mobilization of the masses had brought them into politics, the emergence of communalism too was bound to affect them, which it did in abundant measure. The Shuddhi and Sangathan movements[18] as also the Tabligh and Tanzeem movements[19] were some crude manifestation of this phenomenon.

The emergence of communalism had brought certain questions of political choice before the leaders, as well as the masses. There were two courses open to them: one was to carry forward the same programme of turning various religious communities into a single political community, the other was to move in the direction of narrow politics where each religious community would chalk out its own line of politics and therefore inevitably weaken the voice of the freedom struggle.

How did Azad articulate his responses to these issues? He was in jail when the movement was withdrawn by Gandhi and, like many Congress and Khilafat leaders, felt quite disheartened but had no choice except to remain quiet. In Alipore jail (Calcutta) there were innumerable occasions when he went into deep contemplation, confining himself to his cell, refusing to meet and entertain anyone,[20] though it is not clear as to what he was contemplating upon while in jail.

Some idea about Azad's political understanding at this time is available from Abdur Razzaq Malihabadi's account, which he collected in the course of his conversations with Azad. One question he raised was about the nature of *swaraj*. Azad replied that *swaraj* to him meant a good government, which was conditioned upon two factors: its being national in character and democratic in functioning.[21] In yet another significant reflection in the context of the withdrawal of the movement Azad expressed regrets that the surest way to success was to have remained steadfast on the principles of democracy and to build a national alliance of Indians, but the opportunity was lost by withdrawing the movement. As he put it, 'I think that by following democratic principles and remaining united as a nation it is possible to win India's freedom. I strongly feel that if a historic blunder of withdrawing the movement was not committed then the immediate outcome would have been highly positive.'[22]

Commenting on non-violence, without giving way to despair, he expressed hope for the future, provided concerted action was initiated and mistakes were not committed.

> Experimentation with non-violence and non-cooperation has convinced me further about its efficacy. After the first bout of struggle, halting at a station was unavoidable. However it is important that we learn a lesson of not committing the same mistakes that we did. Then I have no doubts that we are bound to be a success.[23]

These were serious reflections on the contemporary as well as the future politics of the freedom movement. While Azad seemed quite critical of the withdrawal of the movement, he did not give up optimism about a concerted and united political action. But these were mere ideas since no political action was possible inside the jail.

Azad was released on 1 January 1923. The political climate, in the post-withdrawal phase could only be described as disappointing on several counts. First, Hindu–Muslim relationship had become embittered on account of Shuddhi and Sangathan, and Tableegh and Tanzeem. Second, the Khilafat movement was in a state of disarray, and had lost all sense of purpose and direction. Finally, even the Indian National Congress was faced with a crisis where a split appeared imminent, on account of the conflict between the 'No-changers' and 'Pro-changers'.

From the high hopes of the Non-Cooperation–Khilafat days, Azad confronted, on his release, a dismal political atmosphere. He felt quite disoriented in the absence of any defined political agenda. He must have also faced another dilemma because he had never engaged himself in organized and structured politics notwithstanding his association with revolutionary organizations and attempts to start his own organization such as the Hizbullah. Considering all this, the question that arises is what Azad's political plan was? He could no longer have remained content with mere conceptual formulations only, as he had done during the *Al-Hilal* days. The historical opportunity came to Azad when an offer was made to him to preside over the special session of the Congress.

It is common knowledge that in June 1922 a Civil Disobedience Committee was set up by the All India Congress Committee with the express purpose of suggesting the future course of action. In the committee Vallabhbhai Patel, Rajendra Prasad, M.A. Ansari, Rajagopalachari and Srinivas Iyengar advocated concentration on Gandhi's constructive work, whereas Motilal Nehru, Vittahalbhai Patel, Hakim Ajmal Khan and C.R. Das were in favour of participation in the Council elections. The tussle between the two groups acquired ominous proportions at the Gaya session of the Congress in December 1922 where C.R. Das put forward a resolution recommending the principle of entry, which was defeated by the combined strength of the followers of Gandhi and several Khilafat leaders.[24] Consequently C.R. Das, Motilal Nehru and others decided to found the Swaraj Party in March 1923. Such a division among the leaders made a split in the Congress imminent. It was at this juncture that the Congress decided to hold a special session in Delhi. This was held in September 1923, and elected Maulana Azad as its president. He was only 35, an unusually young age to occupy the chair of the Congress, which was unprecedented in its history.

Why did the Congress choose Azad as its president bearing in mind that he had only a brief association with it so far? Was it because of the deteriorating communal situation in the country? Or did the Congress indulge in damage control in the post-

Khilafat period since as an organization it had to shoulder the blame for not having consulted other constituents of the movements such as the Central Khilafat Committee and the Jamiat-ul-Ulama-i-Hind? So far there has been no answer to these questions.

Azad took his job seriously and embarked on a course of conciliation between the two competing factions of the Congress, which could have caused a split in the party. Azad was equal to the challenge and made every effort to bring about reconciliation between the two groups. He enjoyed the confidence of both the factions for his was an image of a man of balanced disposition. Azad, in order to strike a note of conciliation in his presidential speech said, 'The differences have arrayed the leaders in two groups. The members in both the groups enjoy immense respect and esteem for their stature and learned dispositions from me as well as those who hold similar opinion.'[25]

Having made these preliminary statements, Azad went on to argue that ideally he personally would prefer the policy of non-cooperation with the government as had been done earlier.[26] This remained the central issue in the whole scheme, the rest was a matter of detail as to whether to enter the council or boycott it.[27] In either case the crucial point was to keep the ranks of the freedom fighters united, which required discipline in the party and upholding of Hindu–Muslim unity.[28] With these arguments, first of all Azad clearly tried to underplay the importance attached by both groups in the Congress to the issue of council entry. He went out to argue as if this issue was just one of many facing the country. He said,

> After having considered various dimensions of the issue I have reached certain conclusion that boycotting the council may not be desirable. In the last elections the boycott was necessary. However this time around it would be good if we enter the councils and assemblies and capture seats and conduct ourselves in a manner as if even these councils become another arena of our struggle for freedom.[29]

Those who wished to enter the council should also be seen as freedom fighters since these councils too would become the arena of conflict. However, entry into the council should be seen merely as a stopgap arrangement rather than a long-term programme. He warned, 'If at all we are going to be diffident about our struggle then I would not even for a minute ever give an advice to enter the council.'[30] Azad wished to make another point quite clear that the All India Congress Committee would regulate both the case of council entry as well as its boycott.[31]

It must have been quite a task for Azad to argue this out, particularly in the face of a rigid stand taken by both factions that the entry into the councils as well as boycott, would both have to have the permission of the Congress. Thus at one stroke both the boycott and the entry of the councils were co-opted by the Congress. This saved the organization from a major blow at a time when its spirit was already at a low point.

The manner and the sense of involvement with which Azad attempted to avert the crisis in the Congress, gave the impression that he had a long association with it, which was not the case. Even though his contacts with the Congress were recent Azad took this opportunity to reflect on several issues of national concern such as the assessment of the national movement carried out so far, future course of the political plans, the Hindu–Muslim relationship, etc. With this he himself embarked on a new course of politics, which for the sake of convenience could be described as integrative politics where religious communities would not be treated as political entities, instead they would merge into a single political community. In the course of developing these ideas Azad was also delineating a course of politics, which would carry along his co-religionists and the country as a whole. Such a stance was markedly different from the agenda he had set before himself during the *Al-Hilal* days. Azad argued, for instance, that Muslims kept aloof from the Congress because they feared their interests would be overridden by the Hindu majority.[32] He went on to point out, 'They (Muslims) should not fear their Hindu brethren, join the Congress and make freedom of the country the motto of their life.'[33]

In the course of his speech Azad had referred to *Al-Hilal* and argued that his present stance was in tune with the policies of the paper since the beginning.[34] Such an assertion was contrary to facts. It remains common knowledge that during the *Al-Hilal* days Azad had favoured the idea of Muslims forming their own party, committed to the cause of the freedom of the country rather than joining anybody,[35] or the Congress. Therefore such an assertion was directed towards the future course of politics rather than indicating continuity with the past.

But the stand on Hindu–Muslim unity remained part of Azad's unflinching commitment from the *Al-Hilal* days. Even though, he had favoured the idea of Muslims following their own course he had vigorously argued for a cordial relationship between the two religious communities.

> I am hinting at the Hindu-Muslim unity. This unity is the first step not only towards laying the foundations of India's freedom but for every thing else which is important for any nation to survive and prosper. Without this unity there can be no freedom, it will be impossible to develop values of humanism.[36]

In taking a position such as this Azad moved beyond *Al-Hilal* without which he thought not only would the attainment of the freedom be impaired, but also the basic question of a civil human relationship.

Having said this, he launched a scathing attack on the communal mindset where fear of each other among both Hindus and Muslims seemed to have become the order of the day and as a result the ideals of Swaraj and Khilafat had been replaced by instances such as Shuddhi, etc. All this was taking place at the cost of India's freedom's struggle.[37] He castigated the Hindu communal organizations for creating the same mindset of a fear psychosis that Muslims would overwhelm the Hindus even though the latter constituted more than three quarters of the total population.

After having cautioned against the nefarious designs of the communal groups, Azad made another statement with a sense of prophetic finality, 'I can argue without any hesitation that today India doesn't need any Hindu sangathan or Muslim sangathan. It needs only one sangathan, i.e. Indian National Congress.'[38]

II

From now onwards Azad's agenda as regards the freedom movement was clearly defined—the spiritual-religious resources would continue to be invoked in order to arouse patriotism but not outside the fold of the Congress. Thus he himself accepted the Congress as the sole legitimate body to carry forward the freedom struggle. This was the final seal of confirmation of the political metamorphosis that Azad underwent since the Non-Cooperation–Khilafat movement.

Acceptance of the Congress as the legitimate vehicle of the freedom struggle took Azad in yet another direction of defining programmes for the Congress. While doing so he was sensitive to developments such as the emergence of a working-class movement, as also the role of the vernacular press in spreading the message of freedom even in rural areas. However, his basic emphasis was on a constructive programme. He argued on several points: first, as part of the constructive programme we should work for Hindu–Muslim unity from scratch; second, by ignoring the ongoing working-class movement we may not be able to achieve much; third, we must impress upon the common man the values of national unity, non-cooperation, non-violence and civil disobedience. All these things must be accepted purely out of love for the country. Finally, literature regarding the freedom struggle should be produced in the vernacular. Congress workers must fan out in remote areas and spread the message of freedom.[39]

After having defined the future course of programme for the Congress Azad went on to comment on the issue of leadership. He unambiguously declared, 'I strongly believe that Mahatma Gandhi is the only true leader. As and when India will achieve freedom it would only be under his leadership.'[40]

From then on, Azad became an integral part of the Congress and remained so till the end. As always he wished to carry along his co-religionists but the timing he chose to embark on integrative politics was inauspicious for several reasons. First, the withdrawal of the movement had made Muslims in particular resentful of the Congress and of Gandhi; second, the Shuddhi and Sangathan movement, as also recurring communal riots in places like Saharanpur and Agra, had vitiated the political atmosphere; finally, the drift among the Muslim rank and file did not seem to augur well for integrative politics.

The years after the Non-Cooperation–Khilafat period were marked by one distinct feature, i.e. national political activities were overshadowed by communalization of the society and frequent communal riots. This became a major concern for nationalist leaders. Azad also engaged himself in the task of stemming the tide of communalism.

Azad was convinced that recurring communal riots would not only hamper good relations between the two communities but also impede the formation of a united nationhood. 'The need of the hour is a single and united nationhood. As we all are aware that so long shouting of slogans such as *"malechcha"* and *"kafir"* would rent the air, it is impossible that we can build a culture of tolerance and brotherhood, without which the unity can't exist.'[41]

Even before Azad delivered his presidential speech, he had visited Agra, which was the nerve-centre of the Shuddhi movement launched by the Arya Samaj. The Shuddhi movement in particular targeted the Malkan Rajputs, who had converted to Islam a long time ago. Azad did not have any objection to these Rajputs going back to Hinduism in case they wished it that way.[42] But he felt that this was not the case, and that the movement was one orchestrated by the Arya Samajists. Azad argued that they (Arya Samajists) did not take the larger national interest into account. 'I am convinced that those who have started such a thing have simply ignored the national interest. They were duty-bound to have avoided raking up issues such as this since the attention is diverted from national unity to communal discord.'[43]

Azad also expressed his concern about the use of coercion in the re-conversion of the Malkan Rajputs.[44] This was being done on the assumption of Swami Shraddhanand that the Malkan Rajputs were Hindus, and being brought back to their original fold,[45] whereas there was a need to ameliorate the conditions of innumerable untouchables,[46] who had suffered immeasurably for centuries. Azad appealed to the Shuddhi leaders to give up their policy of coercion but he doubted whether he would be paid any attention, and that Hindu leaders and the press must play their role to stop such coercion.[47]

Ever since Azad became a public figure with the publication of *Al-Hilal*, pan-Islam remained a significant plank of his religio-political formulations. This was partly the result of Azad's conviction that in order to maintain cohesion in the community, it was necessary that the Khalifa was looked upon with reverence, and allegiance was expressed, not only spiritually even politically. However pan-Islam, gave him a handle to mobilize his co-religionists for political action against colonial domination. Both these aspects were abundantly evident during the *Al-Hilal* days as well as during the Non-Cooperation–Khilafat movement, when a mass upsurge occurred.

Gradually but steadily a shift in Azad's position as regards the Khilafat issue had started taking place. During the Khilafat movement most leaders had focused their attention on Turkey while being equally concerned about India's independence. In contrast to several Khilafat leaders Azad took the unique position of describing the Khilafat issue as nothing but the struggle to free India, a point, which has already been discussed in the previous chapter. Azad first attempted to equate the two issues as the same and then focused attention on India alone, thus making a complete departure from his earlier stand. This was perhaps the reason that when the movement was withdrawn, he did feel disappointed but it did not drive him to despair. Azad had forcefully argued that withdrawal of the movement was a blunder, which must never have been committed.

Meanwhile the situation in Turkey itself had undergone drastic changes. The first blow to the Khilafat came in November 1922, when the Turkish Grand National Assembly abolished the Ottoman Sultanate itself. Sultan Wahiduddin Muhammad VI was deposed and in his place Abdul Mejid Effendi was declared to be the new khalifa.[48] Thus in one blow the Khilafat was separated from the Turkish state. There was a mixed response by Indians to these developments, which ranged from disbelief to acceptance. In any case Indian Muslims had little option but to accept the state of affairs in Turkey.[49]

The final blow to the institution of Khilafat was yet to follow. The Turkish National Assembly met on 1 March 1924 and deliberated upon the issue and finally voted to depose the khalifa, abolish the Khilafat and banish all surviving members of the Ottoman dynasty.[50] This decision of the Assembly caused total disarray in the Indian Khilafat camp.[51] Most Khilafat leaders went through a phase of disorientation and views ranging from disappointment to a vain hope that the Khilafat could not cease to exist were expressed. Maulana Abdul Bari, the Ali Brothers,

Hakim Ajmal Khan and Maulana Azad differed from one another. Most leaders retained the hope in one form or the other of the revival of the Khilafat, even though they knew in their heart of hearts that it was a lost cause.

Azad's reaction was quite different from that of the other Khilafat leaders. He did not betray any emotion nor was he mortified by the development in Turkey. To Azad, Khilafat as an issue of political mobilization was no longer relevant since he had already embarked on the course of integrative politics, even more so after he became the president of the Congress in September 1923. The irrelevance of Khilafat as an issue was manifest in his response in the series of articles entitled, 'Masala-i-Khilafat aur Jamhoria Turkiya' published in the *Zamindar* of Lahore in 1924. Azad's articulation on the subject followed a particular logic. 'Islamic Khilafat in reality is nothing but a government. And the khalifa is the head of this government, which in common parlance is known as the state. Thus on the basis of certain reasons the present government may be treated as Khilafat' and khalifa could be easily be substituted by any head of the state in the context of Turkey.[52]

Azad went on to discuss the Turkish Assembly and its decision to bifurcate the Sultanate from the Khilafat, transforming Turkey into a democracy. As such there was nothing wrong in it, however, what should not have taken place was

> to declare the *Khalifa* a separate entity. *Khalifa* after all is another name of the head of the state. So long as the regime was monarchical the king was its head and *Khalifa* as well. Now that the state has become democratic its president should become the *Khalifa* as well, and if the Turkish Assembly was not particularly against the House of Ottomans, Abdul Majeed should have been made the *Khalifa*. However, unlike the status of the Pope, there should be changes in the Islamic political structure too.[53]

Azad was highly critical of those who did not show restraint in expressing their opinion. It was important that they should have taken some time to grapple with the issue. 'Out of excitement everybody seems to have given up balance. Even the best of brains did not have the patience to wait for a few days before reacting to an issue of grave importance.'[54]

While reflecting on the subject Azad did admit,

> It is true that for centuries the institution of *Khilafat* has been personalised. Barring the first thirty years of Islam and two or three years of Umar bin Abdul Aziz the entire history of Islam is that of personalised rule. However, the solution of the problem is not to abolish the institution itself. The answer is to create a proper Islamic Khalifa. Creation of such an institution won't be against the larger principles of democracy and national liberation. On the contrary it would be well in accordance with its spirit.[55]

Azad's stand on the abolition of the Khilafat was quite characteristic of his personality. He clearly sidestepped the issue by arguing that Khilafat as such was not abolished, since the Republic of Turkey still remained an Islamic power its government could be still considered the same. This was certainly not a stand which enjoyed the sanction of Islam and *sharia,* as there was no precedent in the history of Islam to justify this. However, in arguing this Azad drew his strength from logic in the manner of casuistry. It seemed an attempt on his part to wriggle out of the issue without risking the susceptibilities of his co-religionists. Finally it can be argued that it was a political move *par excellence*. Now that he had become a part of the only Indian 'Sangathan', i.e. the Indian National Congress, the issue of Khilafat was irrelevant.

What was the impact of Azad's formulations on the abolition of the Khilafat? No answer could be found to this question, since the political agenda in the country too had undergone drastic changes. The agenda of the Hindu–Muslim alliance during the Non-Cooperation–Khilafat days had given way to communalism and there was no clarity of thought as to how the Congress and others would fight this out. Thus the Khilafat as an issue had been consigned to history.

To Azad, other issues had acquired a new urgency. First of all, he was to devote his energy to stemming the tide of communalism, which he considered terribly injurious to India's national health. He feared that the cause of the freedom struggle was impeded by frequent riots, particularly in northern India. The savagery of the Kohat riots had shaken many, including Gandhi who undertook a twenty-one-day fast as penance.[56] To stem communalism now became a religious mission for him.

In the Unity Conference, under the chairmanship of Gandhi, on 16 September1924 in Delhi, Azad played a significant role, specially in the passing of the resolution which stated,

> The conference declares that it is not only wrong against law but also against religion for any one to take the law in his hands, either for the purpose of retaliation or punishment and therefore declares that all points in dispute shall be decided by reference either to private arbitration or where it is possible by reference to a court of law.[57]

In the charged climate of communal animosity and suspicion among the members of the Hindu and Muslim communities, any pretext was good enough to launch a vitiated campaign against each other. A similar situation had arisen in Nagpur, where the question of playing music before mosques had the potential to cause communal disturbances. In order to resolve the issue Pandit Motilal Nehru and Maulana Azad played a crucial role by engaging the representatives of both communities and tried to impress upon them that neither playing music before the mosque was a religious issue for the Hindus nor making attempts to stop it a religious issue for Muslims.[58] In the course of deliberations the Muslim group pointed out that it was a convention for a long time that the Hindus had stopped playing music when any religious procession passed by any mosque. However, B.S. Moonje resisted such a contention. In a letter addressed to Gandhiji he argued that, 'so far I am able to judge, I am of the opinion that there is no reliable evidence to support their claim. But how could there be any such custom in Nagpur? Any man with a grain of common sense can decide it for himself.'[59] Moonje continued,

> There was hardly 25 years Mohammedan rule in Nagpur, it was subverted by the Marathas about 200 years ago and the Maratha rule was in turn subverted by the British about 60 years ago. During the Maratha rule, one can imagine, there could have been no power, which could by force stop the Hindu Music. Old Hindu gentlemen of light and leading all testify to the fact that until 1904, there was no restriction to the playing of music.[60]

In the same letter while concluding, Moonje also said, 'That until the time this dispute is settled to mutual satisfaction the Hindus have to be always prepared for self-defence but they will never provoke a fight. The provocation has always come from the side of Mohamedans.'[61] Moonje's apprehensions proved more imaginary than real. Three months of hammering the issue bore fruits in the beginning of 1925, when Motilal Nehru and Maulana Azad issued a joint statement, congratulating both the communities of Nagpur for resolving the issue in an amicable manner. It was agreed that Muslims would not insist on total stopping of music, and left it to the goodwill of Hindus and they in turn agreed to not to play music before five mosques of Nagpur, which were: (1) Big Samdar Masjid, (2) Lonasath Masjid of Cutchi Musalman, (3) Sanichar Masjid, (4) Azam Shahi Masjid, and (5) Chatnis Park Masjid. The interesting part of the entire concluding episode was a public meeting was convened which was presided by none other than B.S. Moonje, who 'assured the Musalmans on behalf of the Hindus of Nagpur that the brotherly feelings of the former would be fully reciprocated by the latter'.[62]

Azad was growing in stature, so were his responsibilities. As stated earlier, the mid-1920s happened to be a period of deep communal distress and it became his preoccupation to think about the issue and devise means to find solution to the problem. He did not miss any opportunity to articulate his point of view in the matter. When Azad was invited to preside over the All India Khilafat Conference held on 29 December 1925 at Kanpur, he briefly referred to the latest development in Arabia and then quickly came to issues which had a larger relevance to India. He said, 'Under no circumstances we can ignore the fact that what matters are developments and activities to be carried out in our own country.'[63] But the prevailing political climate was depressing, as all around an atmosphere of mutual suspicion, rancour and animosity was thick.[64] Focusing on the Muslims he argued that during the Non-Cooperation movement, for the first time they had risen in collaboration with others but the sudden withdrawal of the movement had shaken them beyond measures, resulting in bitter animosity and violence.[65] He urged them not to give up optimism. 'If ignorance and inaction have impeded the path, it must never deter us in accepting the goal of freedom even if these developments might have made the task a little more difficult. This must also not mean that we start fighting among ourselves.'[66] He assured the Muslims that they in particular must remain undaunted. If necessary they must start a new journey, 'Let us start all afresh. After all for us it is a march, of communities and the nation.'[67]

He exhorted Muslims not to look back, even if the current political atmosphere looked gloomy. He argued, 'Under the present circumstances of gloom and despondency if the Muslims can do nothing then at least they must never look back.'[68] Looking back would not be in tune with the requirements of the time, since the need of the hour was political action. He reiterated certain basic commitments of the Khilafat Committee towards building a united nationhood.

> The Muslims must not feel alienated from their Hindu brethren and become a tool against the unity between the communities. They must never become friendly with the government so that it does not use them against the unity of the country. If they (Muslims) have to demand justice and cordial relationship with the Hindus, they must do so but at the same time care must be taken so that difficulties in relations between the two communities are kept away from the arena of the freedom movement.[69]

Azad did concede that differences between Hindus and Muslims must be resolved but was not willing to allow differences to enter the arena where a confrontation with the British government had been taking place. The near-absence of any political programme should not dishearten anybody, as it should be treated as a recess before a new programme of national action was launched. The intervening period must be utilized to educate the masses not in texts and grammar but politically, since that held the key to the future. He put a condition, that for all this to materialize it was important that the attitude of the present generation be put in order. That alone was the solution.[70]

Political education for his community, as well as for the country as a whole indeed, had been a passion with Azad ever since he started *Al-Hilal*. The language and method employed by him kept on changing from time to time, according to changing political developments. The vitiated communal situation was a hindrance to imparting the kind of political education Azad desired. The intensity with which the Maulana had felt about communalism was reflected in his correspondence with Gandhiji. In a telegram he implored Gandhiji to convene a special session of the Congress to thrash out the Hindu–Muslim question. His anxiety to see an end to this problem was evident. 'Please try for special Congress session in July or August to consider Hindu-Muslim question. This is the last chance, if disregarded all efforts useless for long time and instead of nationalism and patriotism the whole country will plunge in communal and religious strife.'[71] His passionate concern brought him to collaborate with all those who struggled in similar direction. It was at his instance that a meeting of the CWC was convened at Calcutta on 4 July 1926. In the meeting it was resolved that a permanent publicity bureau be established to develop sound 'national life'. This meeting authorized Motilal Nehru, Sarojini Naidu and Maulana Azad to take necessary steps to organize such a bureau[72] with a view to educate the masses out of communal conflicts and differences.

It was with this important objective in mind that Motilal Nehru and Azad issued a manifesto about the formation of the Indian National Union, on 31 July 1926. This endeavour enjoyed the support of leaders such as Jawaharlal Nehru, Tej Bahadur Sapru, Ajmal Khan, Sarojini Naidu, M.A. Ansari, Syed Mahmud, Duni Chand, Khaliquzzaman, P.C. Ray and Srinivas Iyenger.[73] The express objective was to unite those who agreed that communalism was against everything that was national.[74] The Union was meant to be a non-political national platform, membership of which was open to those who had no affiliation with any communal organization.[75] It clearly stated 'the only remedy which can save us from disaster is the deliberate establishment in our midst of a national consciousness and a national atmosphere in which religious and communal conflicts and passions will be relegated to a subordinate and a lower plane'.[76] In spite of the pious intention in launching this Union, it was welcomed with mixed feelings. Many 'Hindu newspapers in the Punjab' did not look at these efforts with any sense of conviction as they suspected Pandit Motilal Nehru's capacity to deliver goods beneficial to the

Hindu community.[77] In a similar vein Swami Shraddhanand too attacked such a formation, 'I have gone through the Nehru–Azad manifesto carefully and do not see what it aims at. . . . I consider that the Conference made a mistake in keeping itself clear of the political issues involved in Hindu-Muslim unity.'[78] In certain Muslim quarters too such attempts were decried. For instance the *Muslim Outlook* of Lahore described it as 'The Latest Fraud'. These objections notwithstanding the Union had prepared an interesting pledge: 'the only way to India's lasting prosperity and freedom lies in the realisation by all communities of India of a common united nationality and harmonious cooperation between them all', 'I neither am nor will be a member of any organisation declared communal by the Central Board of the Union.'[79] However, there was a flaw in not clearly stating as to which organizations would be treated as communal. The only thing the Central Board of this Union had said was, 'A communal organisation is one whose present activities are calculated to retard or obstruct the growth of a common Indian nationhood.' Such a loose definition left much to be desired since there was any number of political and quasi-political outfits, which were engaged in communal activities, but the Union wanted to avoid naming any one as such.

While Azad's concern both in words and action was to engage himself in activities which could stem the tide of communalism, there erupted a controversy over the issue of pamphlets by certain Arya Samajists, clearly targeted at the personal life of Prophet Muhammad, to hurt the religious sensibilities of Muslims. Three caricatures of the life of Prophet Muhammad had appeared during the 1920s. The first was *Vichitra Jeevan* by Pandit Kalicharan Sharma, first published in Agra in November 1923, the second was *Rangila Rasool* by Pandit Chamupati published by Mahashay Rajpal in Lahore in May 1924, and the third was *Sair-i-Dozakh* by Devi Sharan Sharma in Amritsar in May 1927.[80]

The pamphlet *Rangila Rasool* was the most controversial and attracted wide publicity. Innuendos and insinuations about the Prophet was its basic content, with the potential to vitiate the communal atmosphere further. The Muslims protested and the Punjab government sanctioned the prosecution of Rajpal, the publisher, under Section 153A of the Indian Penal Code. Though the hearing of the case began in October 1927, the final disposal of the case was in May 1928.[81]

The lengthy proceedings gave it wide publicity and the pamphlet surreptitiously reached far-off places such as Calcutta and Bombay. The magistrate, Mr. Phailbus found Rajpal guilty of creating enmity between the classes as also of incensing Muslims. He ordered that the penalty be rigorous imprisonment for eighteen months and a fine of Rs.1,000 in lieu of an additional period of six months imprisonment.[82] The magistrate's judgement was challenged in the Lahore Sessions Court where the conviction was upheld. But the final appeal was made to the High Court at Lahore, where Justice Dalip Singh, due to infirmities in the provisions of Section 153A of the I.P.C. to try cases such as this, acquitted Rajpal.[83] The final judgement angered Muslims beyond measure. The Punjab Governor Haile reported, 'There was really a very serious danger of disorder, for an attack on the Prophet was a concrete offence against Islam that stung them to the quick and they could not bear the thought that Hindus could repeat it with impunity.'[84]

The *Rangila Rasool* controversy cast a pall of gloom on the political climate of the country. The Muslim reaction was intense and violent particularly in the Punjab. The intensity of feelings had already claimed the life of Swami Shraddhanand, a leader of the Arya Samaj. The North West Frontier Province saw the expulsion of Hindus of one area from their homes.[85]

In response to the *Rangila Rasool* controversy Azad wrote a detailed article under the title 'Punjab High Court Ka Ek Faisla' published in the issue of *Al-Hilal* of 1 and 8 July 1927. He had argued that contrary to Justice Dalip Singh's assertion, the pamphlets' author could have been tried under the provisions of Section 153A. However, since the High Court of a province had ruled, then it became imperative that an unambiguous law was enacted, which would effectively put a check on blasphemous statements.[86] Many people took serious objection to Azad's statements, saying they were based more on legal interpretation rather than the *sharia* and Islamic tradition. One such person was Maulvi Mohiuddin Ahmad Qasuri, who wrote to Azad making similar objections to which the Maulana gave a lengthy reply defending his position that the parameters of the discussion could be legal provisions only and nothing else.[87]

Azad felt indignant about the tendency towards violence on the slightest pretext and *Mazhabi Ahkam* (religious commandments) among certain sections of Muslims. He did not agree with the contention that an attempt such as *Rangila Rasool* could belittle the persona of the Prophet. 'I would disagree that if in 1927 or in earlier years some despicable characters or somebody wrote something bad against the greatest of personalities known to human civilisation, this could ever dishonour him and it has become a matter of life and death for the Muslims.'[88]

Azad's disgust with the book was clear when he described the author as a *keeda makoda* (insect) but at the same time he appeared extremely critical of those who committed excess towards other faiths and practices.[89] Azad thought that such ugly behaviour was unbecoming of a Muslim. As he put it, 'It is distressing that such behaviour is against the values of patience, restrain and self respect of the community. Instead all this has given way to narrow mindedness and ill behaviour. And all this is being described as sacrifices of the *Fidayan-i-Rasool*.'[90]

Apart from the *Rangila Rasool* controversy, there were other factors such as the question of playing music before mosques and the cow-protection movement, which added to the deteriorating inter-community relations. Maintaining a balanced disposition was difficult. Yet it was expected of the men who were shaping contemporary politics that they should maintain sanity in public life. Keeping the above in view, the president of the Congress, Srinivas Iyengar, convened a Unity Conference at Simla on 30 August 1927 in order to deal with the question of the cow slaughter and music before mosques. Subsequently another conference was convened between 16 to 22 September 1927 at Simla again in order to thrash out the issue at hand. It constituted a committee of eminent political personalities such as Pandit Malaviya, Dr. Moonje, Jairam Das, Sardar Sardul Singh, Hakim Ajmal Khan, Maulana Azad and Dr. Ansari. The members debated the issues, however, nothing much came of it.[91] It did not dampen the spirit of Srinivas Iyengar as he convened another Unity Conference on 27 October 1927 at Calcutta to consider the issue of music before mosque and cow slaughter. The Conference experienced animated arguments on both the issues and despite differences the Conference managed to pass a resolution which was unanimously agreed by all. The resolution said, 'Hindus are at liberty to take procession and play music before mosques at any time for religious and social purposes.' While addressing Muslims it said, 'Moslems shall be at liberty to sacrifice or slaughter cows in exercise of their rights in any town or village in any place not being thoroughfare nor one in the vicinity of a temple or a mandir nor one exposed to the gaze of a Hindu.'[92]All this was done under the aegis of the Congress. The members of this Conference must have derived satisfaction for having reached an unanimous position such as this but then soon after Srinivas Iyenger was flooded with letters and telegrams protesting against the decision to permit Muslims for cow slaughter.[93] There were other Hindu organizations too who strongly protested against such a permission granted to Muslims. What is interesting in this context is that telegrams of protest, which originated from Calcutta, used almost similar language.[94] It is interesting to note that while hurt Hindu feeling were given expression, there was an element of threat too that many Hindus would be alienated from the Congress, therefore it was not in the national interest.

In view of the growing polarization in the society whether on the *Rangila Rasool* controversy or the question of cow slaughter and music it was expected of leaders to steer clear of the maze. There were two ways of doing it. One was to play to the gallery and become popular, however, the other way of doing was not to succumb to popular pressures and hold on to one's conviction. In case of Azad there was an additional aspect to it that he was a scholar and irrespective of circumstances he was not expected to compromise with his conviction. Such an approach helped him in reinforcing his conviction but did not bring him any political dividends. From this time onwards the gap between him and his co-religionists started widening. The reason was obvious that Azad was convinced that in matters of politics he would follow his own agenda rather than be influenced by others. Azad chose to speak a language which was his own. His co-religionists began drifting away from him, as Azad stood firm on his ground, yet he never missed an opportunity to articulate his views on several issues concerning Muslims which were in consonance with Indian nationalism.

Azad's stand as regards several issues, which affected religio-cultural life of the Muslims, did not go well with his co-religionists, particularly since the ending of the Non-Cooperation–Khilafat movement. Moreover, the political language used by Azad no longer carried the same religious appeal, and left little scope for Muslims to be convinced that participation in the freedom struggle would bring them spiritual fulfilment. The absence of a political language and metaphor, which Muslims had been accustomed to during the Khilafat movement, generated a hiatus between them and Azad, as there emerged a new reality of political accommodation and adjustments in the evolving power structure.

III

It was a historical coincidence that against this background of deteriorating inter-community relations the government announced a decennial review of the working of the Government of India Act of 1919 popularly known as the Montague–Chelmsford Reforms. Under this in certain departments power was devolved to popularly elected representatives in the provinces. While this was accepted as a welcome arrangement as regards the power-spaces being made available to Indians, it brought communal tensions in its wake. Punjab and Bengal were two provinces, which had experienced bitter communal animosity over power sharing.

The realization among those with nationalist concerns was acute that if the communally tense situation was allowed to persist it would do grave damage to the long-term political interests of India. It was no ordinary event that the Gauhati session of the Congress devoted attention to the question of resolving Hindu–Muslim differences.[95] Various groups of Muslim leadership showed similar concern when they met in Delhi, on 20 March 1927, under the presidentship of M.A. Jinnah and discussed the issue of Muslim representation in the legislatures.[96]

It was unanimously resolved that separate electorates would be given up provided certain other conditions were met. These were: (1) Sind to be separated from Bombay and made into a separate province, (2) North West Frontier Province to be brought on par with other provinces in India, (3) in the Punjab and Bengal, the proportion of representation be made in accordance with the population, (4) one-third reservation of seats for Muslims at the Centre.[97] However, there were voices of resentment emanating from certain quarters of the Muslims particularly in Bihar and Madras on the question of giving up separate electorates.[98]

These demands have been known as the Delhi Proposals or alternately the Muslim Proposals and they seemed to be endorsed by the Congress. The Madras session of the Congress in 1927 assured Muslims that their legitimate interests would be secured by the reservation of seats in joint electorates on the basis of population in every province and in the Central Legislature.[99] At this session of the Congress a resolution was introduced on religious and other rights, which was seconded by Maulana Azad. While seconding the resolution he elaborated upon the rationale for accepting the principle of joint electorates. He said, '... but now we have taken a step. We are going to have joint electorate in the country. Hereafter the Musalmans will not have separate electorate and feel certain that this will settle the differences in the country towards unity.'[100] He expressed confidence about its acceptance by all Muslims. The Muslim League too endorsed the Delhi Proposals in its Calcutta session on 20 December 1927.[101]

While such efforts were on, the appointment of an all-British Statutory Commission was announced to look into the functioning of the Government of India Act of 1919 and make recommendations regarding further devolution of power. Its composition prompted a quick response for boycott by most Indian political groups. Dr. Ansari in his presidential speech underlined the importance of Indians making their own constitution in view of the near total boycott of the Simon Commission. He said, 'To frame a constitution for the people consisting of 320 million souls, professing different religions and speaking different languages, will be most unique and gigantic experiment in democracy ever attempted.' He further added, 'As soon as the Draft Constitution is ready the Congress should take steps to call a national convention consisting of representatives of all interests, communities and political parties to consider it and give it a final shape.'[102] Dr. Ansari had also suggested a federal constitution for India. Subsequently a sub-committee consisting of representatives of several political formations was constituted under the chairmanship of Pandit Motilal Nehru to draft a constitution.

The first meeting of the All-Parties Conference was held in Delhi on 12 February 1928. In its second meeting on 9 March 1928 it resolved to appoint a committee to work out the framework for a constitution of India while looking for means to deal with the communal problem.[103] In the course of its deliberations, two issues turned out to be contentious; first, the basis of power-sharing among communities in various provinces with varying percentages of the respective population, second, not unrelated to the first, the character of the constitution; whether it would be unitary or federal. The resolution of these problems was the real challenge before the Committee particularly when all kinds of pressures were brought upon it. The two issues were a clear indication that in the emerging power structure the competition among various communities to occupy bigger space was considered crucial to their future. Many Muslims felt that the power-base of the Muslim-majority provinces could be secure only in a federal structure with a clear demarcation of central and provincial lists of subjects and the residuary power vested with the provinces rather than the centre. Their argument was that in the Punjab and Bengal there should be proportionate reservation of seats for Muslims for they were mostly backward agricultural labours.

The Hindu Mahasabha, claiming to champion the interests of Hindus, was in no mood to concede any further space to the Muslims than what was already available. Thus stiff resistance was put up to demands such as proportionate reservation of seats in the Punjab and Bengal and one-third reservation of seats in the central legislature. The demand for separation of Sind from Bombay Presidency was anathema to them. It was not the Hindu Mahasabha alone which was opposed to separation of Sind from Bombay, but there were many associations of the Sindhi Hindus who strongly protested against any such proposal.[104] In an interesting manner it added that it was 'politically dangerous to split frontiers of India into small provinces having a population which have predominantly communal and pan-Islamic outlook and have admittedly developed little national feeling.'[105] It further reflected the minority complex in a Muslim majority area when it said, 'Already proposal has raised in Mahomadan mind exaggerated hopes of communal Raj. Those few Sindhis attending this session of the Congress who are in favour of separation do not represent voice of Sind.'[106] However, counter pressures for Sind's separation too was being organized. The Sind Mohamedan Association in a telegram to the General Secretary of the Congress suggested not only that Sind be separated but it should be made an autonomous province on historical, political, economic and linguistic considerations.[107]

It was against this background of pressures and counter-pressures from various quarters that negotiations and parleying were carried out in a series of meetings of the All Parties Conference. The Congress in general and the Chairman of the drafting committee Motilal Nehru in particular, despite his strong liberal and secular credentials, came under the influence of the Mahasabha, the members of which perpetually threatened to walk out of the negotiations.

When the Nehru Report was made public on 15 August 1928, it turned out to be a document of historical importance, the first attempt by Indians to work out a constitution on their own. An attempt such as this one was not appreciated in the British media. The *Manchester Guardian* was particularly critical, 'that the proposal to transfer ultimate responsibility to an entirely new and untried Assembly elected by new and untried and a mainly illiterate constituency is a mere lunacy'.[108]

The main recommendations of the report were as follows: (1) The constitution gives India Dominion Status modelled on the lines of self-governing countries like Canada and South Africa. (2) While the Committee is agreed that nothing short of Dominion Status will suit India, it takes particular care to point out that this does not mean any individual Congressman has given up or moderated the demand for complete independence. (3) Whatever might be the difficulties in the way of establishing full independence, the committee is emphatically of the opinion that there is no halfway house between the present hybrid system and a responsible self-government of the Dominion Status type. (4) The real problem being the transference of power from the people of England to the people of India, the Committee suggests the abolition of the Secretary of State for India and his council. (5) The fears of the European commercial interests and that of Indian minorities are assuaged by the provision that the Commonwealth of India Act will provide for a declaration of the rights of citizens.[109] As regards the questions of redistribution of provinces and communal representation the report suggested the following: 're-distribution of provinces should take place on the linguistic basis and on the demand of a majority of people and subject to financial and administrative considerations. Sind is to be separated and formed into a new province',[110] subject to financial and administrative considerations. And regarding the communal representation the report said the following: 'There shall be joint-mixed electorates, there shall be no reservation of seats for the majority. There shall be strict proportional representation for Muslim minority except in Punjab and Bengal and for the non-Muslim minority in NWFP, with a qualification that such a privilege shall be there only for ten years.' In a separate note Shuaib Qureshi, a member of the Nehru Committee said that one-third of seats in the central legislature shall be reserved for the Muslims.[111]

The Report accepted two of the Delhi proposals—the separation of Sind, and the elevation of NWFP as a full province. It clearly rejected separate electorates and the principle of weightage.[112] The Report favoured a unitary character for the constitution rather than federal. Another feature of the Report was that it debarred Muslims from reservation of seats in provinces where they constituted a majority.[113] The Report did not demand complete independence, instead it asked for Dominion Status, though this was opposed by the radical elements in the Congress such as Jawaharlal Nehru and Subhas Chandra Bose.[114] A Declaration of Rights guaranteeing religious liberty and cultural autonomy was also incorporated.[115] The Report also believed that adult franchise would solve the problem of Muslim representation, once religious liberty and cultural autonomy were guaranteed.

Those claiming to represent the 'Hindu interest' appeared to have agreed with the Committee's report, since they thought that it did not concede the Muslims' demands, known as Delhi declaration or Muslim declaration, which were in the public domain since the beginning of 1927 and endorsed by the Congress. The Report did not enjoy the backing of the entire Muslim community.[116] However, the support extended to the exercise by a section of Muslims enabled the chairman Motilal Nehru to claim unanimity,[117] which was factually not correct. Among Muslims, there were certain sections, which strongly felt that the Report compromised with the aspirations of Muslims. Those who challenged the Committee's recommendations included the Ali Brothers, Shafi Daudi, etc. They persistently attacked those Muslims who had extended their support to the Report such as M.A. Ansari, Maulana Azad and Ali Imam.[118] However, what is little known is that many Muslims leaders who extended their support to the Report were not uncritical of its many recommendations and hoped that at some stage, their concerns would be addressed.[119] They came up with their own suggestions; they wanted the report to have taken clearer position on the separation of Sind, and said that while they did not insist on reservation of seats in the Punjab and Bengal in the hope that adult suffrage was introduced or failing which some other means were devised whereby Muslims maintained the same proportion on the electoral roll that they have to other communities in population.[120] In order to accommodate the apprehensions of the Muslim majority provinces, they said the Report should also contain a provision that each amendment was just not carried out by two-third majority of the central legislature but supported by similar strength in the provincial legislatures as well.[121] The manner in which these leaders had articulated issues which occupied Muslims' concern were given blunt expression by many Khilafatists such as Maulana Shaukat Ali and others. A week after the Report was made public, in an article, Shaukat Ali had spoken against it. He argued that it was unnecessary to have made a reference to the British as the permanent power. Secondly he said the Report had compromised on the Congress' resolution adopted in the Madras session of 1927. He further justified the demand for reservation of seats in the Punjab and Bengal.[122]

He was not alone in criticizing the Report. A number of leading Muslim members from the Punjab and Bengal met at the residence of Malick Firoz Khan Noon, Minister, Local-Self-Government, Government of Punjab and took a critical view of the Report. The criticism was based on eight points and argued that it (Report) tried to centralize all powers at the cost of the autonomy of the provinces. They wanted guarantees for minorities on a uniform basis throughout India. As regards redistribution of provinces it was said,

> *we are prepared to support their platitudes subject to an extremely important provision, which was first enunciated in the Indian Muslim League of 1924 to the effect that in no circumstances should the Punjab, Bengal, N.W.F.P., Sind and Baluchistan be so added to or reorganized as to take away the Muslim majority from them.*[123] (Emphasis added)

Leaders such as M.A. Ansari and Maulana Azad had taken upon themselves to canvass among the Muslims that the Report adequately took care of interests and aspirations.[124] Their assumptions were not unfounded. It can also be argued that there were many Muslim groups, who shared similar thoughts on many political questions, including the Nehru Report. For instance, in Lahore, 10,000 Muslims had gathered to deliberate upon various provisions of the Nehru Report under the chairmanship of Syed Ataullah Bukhari. In the course of the deliberations violence broke out and brickbating was resorted to, which injured many speakers sitting on the dais, including the editor of the *Zamindar*, Maulana Zafar Ali Khan. Despite provocation, the organizers maintained calm and finally a resolution was moved supporting the Nehru Report. Ten thousand hands went up in support of the Report as only 20 people voted against it.[125] In the course of the speeches Hindu–Muslim unity was repeatedly emphasized. The meeting was called off by 11 p.m. but the audience lingered on and was willing to listen to more on the subject. Zafar Ali Khan again addressed them in front of the *Zamindar* office and the crowd cheered him lustily.[126]

Maulana Azad was keenly involved in the campaign for the Report's acceptance. He asked his one time secretary A.R. Malihabadi to write essays in Urdu newspapers and journals favouring its acceptance. In one of the meetings, Maulana said to him, 'It would be in the fitness of things if you campaigned for the acceptance of the Report in the newspapers. *Time spent on this shall adequately be compensated by the Congress*.'[127] (Emphasis added)

It is rather intriguing that Maulana Azad in a way desired to hire the services of men like Malihabadi to campaign for the acceptance of the Nehru Report. Malihabadi started off his campaign in the Urdu press and unwillingly accepted the remuneration.[128] Azad too wrote essays supporting the Report, which were published in the name of Malihabadi.[129] Azad was a little wary of Malihabadi's enthusiasm in his article in *Zamindar* and cautioned him that the support for the Report should not be exaggerated. He advised moderation and argued that Muslims could not have got a better deal than what the Nehru Report has given them. He argued that the Report and the Conference had determined certain broader principles, which were favourable to Muslims. They should ensure that nothing came in the way of their collective progress and the struggle for freedom.[130]

Despite support that Maulana Azad extended to the Nehru Report, he was sceptical that it would face tough resistance from many Muslim quarters. However, if the Congress in general and Motilal Nehru in particular were serious in convincing Muslims that the Report was as much favourable to them in taking care of their aspirations, then they needed to do much more. In this regard Azad repeatedly emphasized that vigorous propaganda was the need of the hour and the ground for it must be prepared much before the All Parties Conference (Convention) proposed to be held at Calcutta in December 1928. He argued that two things were necessary. First, a series of essays must be published in newspapers along with pamphlets to distribute among Muslims. Second, he suggested that reliable and knowledgeable Muslim workers must be enlisted to carry out the propaganda work among

Muslims.[131] His suggestions were based on the consideration that before the ordinary mass of Muslims were misled on the Report, adequate arrangements must be made to educate them.[132] Azad was aware of the activities of people like Shaukat Ali, who was carrying out campaigns against the Report. As Azad said, Shaukat Ali had issued a statement in *Hamdard*, which insinuated that Muslims' interests were sacrificed at the All Parties Conference in Lucknow, as he had also activated the Khilafat Committee and was using it as a platform to mobilize opinion against the Report.[133] Motilal Nehru shared Azad's concern with regard to the Report. In a telegram to Azad, Motilal Nehru indicated that Azad could go ahead in getting propaganda material, etc., published on behalf of the Committee, as he should also try enlisting the support of prominent Bengali Muslims for the Lucknow resolutions.[134]

Azad sounded quite reassuring to Motilal Nehru that he was already preparing essays to be published in newspapers including the material, which would be published as pamphlets. However, Azad was apprehensive that 'there is hardly much time left in the face of adverse circumstances. If extraordinary efforts are not put in from now till December then it is likely that a favourable climate for the convention might not be generated.[135] He also warned that Shaukat Ali was leaving no stone unturned in campaigning against the Report. He was also using the office and fund of the Khilafat Committee against the Report as he was funding the activities of the Calcutta Khilafat Committee, which was starving of resources, only to make noises.[136] Azad said that Shaukat Ali was visiting Calcutta by 20 September 1928 as he was also planning a conference of the Khilafat Committee in Calcutta in December. The most interesting part of the letter is the suggestion made by Azad that only if there were adequate resources then it would not be difficult to win over Urdu and Bangla papers, which would help alter the wind of opposition in our favour.[137] He further argued that the groups, particularly in Calcutta and the Punjab, which were working against the Report, would work for us if we were to spend about Rs. 100-200 on each worker for a period of three months. He also requested Motilal Nehru to make arrangements for financing these activities, for which Azad not only expressed enthusiasm but confidence too.[138] It is interesting to note that Azad was willing to walk the extra mile to garner support for the Report. In doing so he showed eagerness to use all possible means including money in winning over opponents.

Azad was conscious of the fact that even at the Lucknow conference, Dr. M.A. Ansari and he had to exercise personal influence in convincing the extremist elements in the Central Khilafat Committee[139] that the Nehru Report was by all means Muslim-friendly, and they were confident that with certain reservations, most parties would be able to extend support to the Report. However, such expectations required hard work too in order to fructify, which Azad was doing. In the context of the Bengal Provincial Muslim League, he tried to influence opinion in favour of the Report. In a letter to Motilal Nehru he admitted that he influenced the decision of the provincial League and it was willing to accept the decision of the Conference with an additional factor of adult suffrage.[140] In a tone of confidentiality and secrecy he said, 'How did these changes occur? I shall tell you personally. In order to get this unanimous decision I did not care for any impediment. Had the Bengal Muslim League's decision been postponed then the entire edifice would have remained hung in the air.'[141]

Azad's concern as regards the Nehru Report was growing, particularly in the face of the campaign that was launched by Shaukat Ali and many detractors of the Report. In a letter addressed to Motilal Nehru, he pointed out that in his absence from Calcutta, Shaukat Ali had held three meetings in the city and published highly provocative statements with regard to the report. For instance he had said that at Lucknow, Hindus had resolved that in future Muslims would have no right to send their representatives to the councils. He also said that the report was a declaration of 'Hindu Raj' or for that matter it was a question of life and death for Muslims.[142] Azad felt concerned that the Khilafat Committee might try to mobilize more people in order to influence the decision at the All-Parties Convention, which must be checked. He further emphasized that a sustained campaign particularly among Muslims was the need of the hour, which required financial resources.[143] It was clear for some time that

Maulana Shaukat Ali was consistently opposed to the Nehru Report and was seriously engaged in mobilizing support against it. He also exuded confidence that even his younger brother Maulana Mohammad Ali too would go along with him. He had said this in view of the fact that a difference of opinion seemed to be there. Shaukat Ali retorted, 'I am a very mild man compared with my brother. He is returning shortly to India and you will then hear his views definitely. In the meantime let me assure the Public that he feels ten times more strongly than myself on the Nehru Report.'[144] He further stated that had Mohammad Ali been on the Nehru Committee in place of Shuaib Qureshi, the Nehru Conference would not have made the blunder it has made.[145] It is another matter that when it came to the crunch, Maulana Mohammad Ali was persuaded to accept the Report, with the exception of the Dominion Status clause[146] as he also assured M.A. Ansari that he would not carry out any campaign detrimental to the Nehru Report.

However, it was difficult to trust such an assurance as there was a potential for throwing the spanner in the smooth passage of the Report at the All-Parties Convention at Calcutta.[147] In these conditions hope and anxiety were both visibly manifested. There were many nationalist leaders who maintained a safe distance from the Khilafatists, who were opposing the Nehru Report such as Dr Ansari, Saifuddin Kitchlew, Maulana Daud Ghaznavi, Ghazi Abdur Rahman, Dr Mohammad Alam and Maulana Abul Kalam Azad.[148] Apart from these leaders there were others too, who voiced similar opinion in support of the Nehru Report. For instance M.C. Chagla while addressing a public meeting of Muslims vehemently repudiated the allegations that the Report ignored the Muslim community's rights and asserted that Nehru's recommendations were the best for the minority community.[149] He further argued that it would be suicidal under the joint electorate to ask for reservation for Muslims in the Punjab and Bengal where they were in a majority. In the same meeting, which was presided over by S.A. Barelvi, editor of the *Bombay Chronicle,* he argued that adult suffrage, as embodied in the Nehru Report was the cardinal principle of Islam. Barelvi said that to ask for the reservation of seats was un-Islamic. He further appealed for the formation of a Muslim association to fight the cry for reservation of seats.[150] In a similar manner, support for the Nehru Report was coming from still other quarters. For instance, it was reported by the *Hindustan Times*, 'General support was accorded to the Nehru Report at a meeting of the Behar Provincial Moslem League held on Sunday last. Mr. Mahmud, Bar at Law presided. A resolution moved by Mr. Abdul Bari appreciating the labour of the members of the Nehru Committee was carried.'[151]

Earlier M.A. Jinnah had spoken on the theme of the Nehru Report in a conciliatory tone. He said, 'No doubt that signatories to the Nehru Report and the various men who met at Lucknow have made an effort towards Hindu-Moslem settlement and one cannot help appreciating the great endeavour they have made.'[152] In the same breadth he went on to add, 'the Nehru Report and the Lucknow decisions are not the laws of the Medes and Persians and certainly they are not the last word, because the Lucknow Conference had decided that the proposals should be placed before a convention to be called shortly'.[153] Jinnah sounded a note of caution to those Muslims who were sceptical of the Report, 'I should particularly appeal to Musalmans not to be alarmed. I see no reason for consternation and stampede but Musalmans must organise themselves and stand united. They should press every reasonable point for the protection of their community.'[154] However, the contrasting point that several Muslim leaders who were critical of the Report were also focusing on was their criticism that why did the Report ask for only dominion status for India and not complete independence. Whereas Jinnah seemed to be satisfied, 'I have always maintained that India's policy can only be for the establishment of dominion status.'[155]

Against the background of caution and mixed but yet considerable support to the Nehru Report, Azad seemed to be convinced that there was still enough room for amendments, thus the finality of the Report was not yet accepted. He said to Malihabadi that it must be impressed upon the Muslims that there was scope for revision. Thus Azad harboured the hope that the Report might still be reconsidered,[156] perhaps to accommodate the divergent points of view that were emerging from within the Muslims. While the Maulana entertained the hope that the last word on the making of the constitution may not have been said as yet, M.A. Ansari thought that the Report gave the 'minorities of India more real and more solid safeguards than have been granted by the League of Nations to the racial minorities of any of the newly constituted states of Europe'.[157]

It seems that support for the Nehru Report particularly among Muslims was considerable, from the point of view of the leaders as well as the masses, which was amply demonstrated since the time it was made public, dissenting voices notwithstanding. The Congress and others could have easily capitalized on the general mood of the Muslims if they were prepared to make some concessions in order to accommodate Muslim aspirations, which were more directed towards future political arrangements. Three crucial points still engaged their attention: first, separation and creation of Muslim majority provinces; second, the nature of the state being federal rather than unitary so that provinces enjoyed more autonomy; third, one-third reservation of seats for Muslims in the centre.

Despite protestations of secular ideals in the Nehru Committee Report, the real problem was that the Congress' strategy of mass mobilization was flawed from the beginning. The Congress, instead of emphasizing the Hindu–Muslim interest, sought the support of the respective communities by exploiting religious issues.[158] Such alignments did not cut across caste, community and regional barriers. At the same time, Muslims who had enjoyed concessions under the Act of 1919 could not have been easily swayed by the sanctimonious argument of the Nehru Committee Report.[159] However, on the other hand, it remains a fact that due to the intransigence of the Hindu Mahasabha and the Sikh groups from the Punjab, the Congress refused to meet Muslim demands.[160] Many Muslim leaders were convinced that the Delhi Proposals were quite legitimate[161] and should have been accepted as such. In the wake of the Nehru Report's partial approval by Muslims the political air was heavy with suspicion and disappointment. It was against this background that an All-Parties Convention was held at Calcutta towards the end of December 1928. Here Jinnah proposed three amendments to the Nehru Report: first, that one-third seats in the central legislature should be reserved for Muslims; second, in the event of adult suffrage not coming into effect, Bengal and Punjab Muslims should have seats reserved for them for ten years; third, residuary powers must be vested with the provinces.[162] But in Calcutta at the All Parties Convention there were not many who were willing to listen to him as most of his amendments to the Report were rejected. The person who launched a frontal attack on Jinnah was M.R. Jayakar, a leading light of the Hindu Mahasabha. However, two of his suggestions were endorsed: first, that no changes be made in the Constitution except by four-fifth majority of either House of Parliament and by four-fifths majority of two houses of the Parliament; second, incorporating in the constitution, the Hindu–Muslim agreement of Lucknow.[163] Rejection of Jinnah's amendments was perceived as rejection of the major points, which were raised by various Muslim groups from time to time. Maulana Azad reacted to such an outright rejection rather indignantly. He remarked, 'the Muslims were fools to put forward their proposals and the Hindus were greater fools to reject them'.[164]

Why did Azad react to the developments at the All-Parties Convention so strongly? One plausible explanation could be that he was intensely involved with the Constitution-making process right from the beginning. When opposition to the Report started surfacing, then M.A. Ansari and Maulana Azad took it upon themselves to iron out differences among Muslim ranks so that a consensus was built for its acceptance. He had voiced concern about some of the provisions of the Report and signed a joint statement along with Ansari, M.C. Chagla, Sir Ali Imam, T.A.K. Sherwani and others, which was published in newspapers. He had exchanged many letters with Pandit Motilal Nehru and confided to him about the efforts that he made to turn Muslim opinion in favour of the Report. Despite all this even Azad had felt that it (the Report) was still not the final word as he also hoped that at some stage many of its provisions might be reconsidered. But all those expectations came to naught with the rejection of Jinnah's proposed amendments.

'The Muslim demands became commonly known as Jinnah's Fourteen Points, but in substance they represented the same demands which the Muslim leaders had been pressing since

1927.'[165] However, such assertions by Jinnah did not go unchallenged. There were many who found holes in the Fourteen Points as propounded by him. For instance, it was argued that, 'redundancy is apparent in the "demand" for religious liberty and communal education autonomy. These have been already and very elaborately and specifically provided for in the Report and the Congress constitution.'[166] Abdur Rahim further clarified that, 'No redistribution of provinces has been hinted at "to adversely affect the Muslim majorities in Bengal and Punjab" or even in New Sind, N.W.F.P. and Baluchistan.'[167] It seemed that many issues of concern raised in the Fourteen Points were not based on solid grounds, as they were more in the form of conjectures and apprehensions. The Muslim League and M.A. Jinnah continuously made attempts in a similar direction so that the Nehru Report was completely rubbished. However, these attempts were resisted in the process.[168] A few days later in an interview to the *Free Press*, Azad, reflected on the subject and openly hinted that to persons like Jinnah and Mohammad Ali, no proposal or resolution with regard to Muslim interest would be acceptable till it rejected the Nehru Report. Such an assertion was unacceptable to Azad and many like him in the Subjects Committee of the Muslim League.[169] Yet he was willing to go with the majority view in the Subjects Committee, which suggested amendments but not its complete rejection. What is interesting in this interview is that at one stage Azad suggested that no amendment in the 'Nehru constitution' was acceptable to him. This assertion seems quite contrary to statements he had made to A.R. Malihabadi that this Report might not be taken as the last word as there was room for its reconsideration.

Despite serious postulations by men like Azad and others that there was no cause to worry with regard to securing the rightful place for Muslims in view of the making of the Nehru Report, dissenting voices had become loud. It was apprehended that in the days to come this dissent might lead to a drift among them, which would be harmful to the political health of the nation in general and Muslims in particular. The challenge before them was to sound convincing to the Muslims without compromising on their nationalistic conviction. This required political balancing skills, which Azad, Dr Ansari and many others had in plenty. The challenge was to assure them that the best of India's interest would be served only when these two communities worked together. The task was daunting in view of the fact that the Hindu Mahasabha was gearing up for a long haul in attacking those who were asking for safeguards for Muslims as well as those Hindus who were sympathetic to their cause.[170]

Two kinds of responses were emerging from within the Muslims; one kind of response had an all-India appeal and the second kind was largely confined to Bombay city and Bombay presidency. As early as April 1929 a large number of Muslims, representing different provinces had met at Dr. Ansari's residence in Delhi to consider forming a party to counteract the activities of 'the so-called All Parties Muslim Conference'.[171] Many prominent Muslims had participated in this meeting. Their names were as follows: Maulana Azad, Dr. Ansari, Maulana Mujibur Rahman, Abdul Qadir Kasuri, Shah Mohammad Zubair, Maulana Zafar Ali Khan, Choudhary Khaliquzzaman and others. Rafi Ahmad Kidwai was its secretary (perhaps as a stop gap arrangement), who put out a notice for a meeting, which was to take place at Mr. Sherwani's house in Allahabad on 27 July 1929 inviting all those Muslims who were to respond to the call of duty to the nation.[172] This notice was immediately endorsed by Dr Ansari, who said, 'the community must be made to participate effectively in our common struggle for freedom. . . . Let it be not said that the Musalmans with their great Islamic tradition of freedom and chivalry failed their motherland at a critical and turning point in its history.'[173] With this in mind a conference of All India Nationalist Muslims was organized at Allahabad, which elected Maulana Azad as president, Dr Ansari as treasurer and T. Sherwani as secretary. The members of the central executive consisted of prominent names such as Rafi Ahmad Kidwai, Professor Abdul Bari and Shah Mohammad Zubair, Khaliquzzaman, Syed Mahmood, Khan Abdul Ghaffar Khan, Dr Mahmud Alam and others.[174] The larger objectives that it set before itself were: 'promotion of a spirit of nationalism, inducement of Muslims to take a proper share in the national struggle and creation of such relations between the majority and minority communities leading to the former considering the rights of the minorities in a spirit of broadminded patriotism.'[175] These aims and objectives were formulated by a committee, which was set up on 27 July 1929, consisting of Maulana Azad, Khaliq-uzzaman, Mahmud Alam and others.[176] This event of forming a party such as this was greeted by goodwill messages from different parts of India. For instance it received messages from as far a place as Madras, Bombay and Lahore.[177] It was further resolved that state-wise activities of the Nationalist Muslim Party would be organized.[178] In this party, there were representatives from across the length and breadth of India.[179]

Even though the Nationalist Muslim Party did not have an independent identity and was guided by the Congress ideology and programme[180] these efforts were misinterpreted as a scheme designed to change the decisions of the All-Parties Convention and to bring the Congress around to the acceptance of one-third Muslim representation in the central legislature and the unconditional separation of Sind.[181]

Similarly, another effort was made in the Bombay Presidency to form a political organization called the Congress Muslim Party with its headquarters at Bombay. The larger objectives of this party were to work towards attaining the much desired Hindu–Muslim unity, helping the Congress to achieve freedom for the country, persuade Muslims to join the Congress and finally to carry out the campaign to propagate the programmes and policies of the Congress.[182] It is interesting in the context of the formation of this Party that a paper such as *The Pioneer*, known for its pro-government policy, too welcomed it: 'the formation of the Congress Muslim Party in Bombay is a move which must be applauded and encouraged'.[183] It further suggested that such a formation was important in view of the likely changes in the Constitution and to present a united representation of communities. Welcoming the formation of the Congress Muslim Party, Mahatma Gandhi had sent them a goodwill message.[184] The Party held elections for positions of the office bearers. S.A. Barelvi, editor of the *Bombay Chronicle* was elected as the president, while Abbas S. Tayabji and Mohammad Ali were elected as vice-presidents. Yusuf J. Meherally and Abid Ali Jafferbhoy were elected as secretaries and Dr Mazharul Haq Gour was elected as the treasurer. With these elections the Party had developed a certain structure and began work in right earnest.[185] The party had an ambitious job at hand. The constitution of the party suggested that the 'Bombay presidency Congress Muslim Party will be controlling and organising divisions or branches in Bombay, and its suburbs, Gujarat, Karnataka, Maharashtra, Sind, Ahmedabad, Belgaum, Poona and Hyderabad.'[186] Contrary to Mahatma Gandhi's apprehension, 'if it does not go to sleep' the Congress Muslim Party kept itself awake and organized several public meeting in different parts of Maharashtra and Gujarat. For instance, a public meeting was organized at Jalgaon, where several people spoke on the necessity of Muslims coming forward to take part in the ongoing freedom struggle. Many speakers also invoked the authority of Islam that it taught the whole world lessons of freedom, and therefore the Muslims of India could not afford to stay aloof. They also emphasized the Hindu–Muslim unity as vital for India's progress.[187] It was reported that the Party had organized another meeting at Dhulia. However, no meeting could take place at Malegaon due to an outbreak of plague. Earlier, while addressing a meeting organized by the Congress Muslim Party at Broach, Maulvi Mohammad Ali, a party leader, argued that 'Muslims could not claim themselves to be true Muslims so long India was in bondage'. He added that to fight to free India was not only their national but religious duty too.[188]

Thus despite such efforts, the political atmosphere remained vitiated by mutual distrust and lack of understanding. A power-sharing formula in a manner where every community's interest was accommodated was not to be since most Muslims feared that attempts to get a fixed share in the power structure would be challenged by the Hindus. It was a classic example of the fear of the future, which had a partly real and partly imaginary basis. However, the leaders of both communities were concerned about securing a political future for themselves at the cost of the other. While these issues were being debated and the knotty ones were yet to be resolved, the Viceroy Lord Irwin on 31 October 1929 announced that the intention of his Majesty's government was the constitutional progress of India towards Dominion Status.[189] It was simultaneously announced that a Round Table Conference of the representatives of British India, Indian states and British political parties would be held in London in order to lay down the basis of the future constitution.[190] Meanwhile, the Congress session in Lahore in December 1929 resolved that complete independence shall be its goal and the All-India Congress Committee was authorized to launch a Civil Disobedience movement whenever it considered it fit.

Initially the general reaction to the announcement was quite encouraging.[191] However, when the Lahore delegation of Mahatma Gandhi, Tej Bahadur Sapru and Motilal Nehru, met Irwin on 23 December 1929 to work out the modalities of the announcement, the Viceroy reminded them of their internal differences, which the Congress as a whole emphatically denied.[192] In the light of the communally tense years prior to the Nehru Committee Report and the controversy which surrounded the Report, such a claim by the Congress lacked conviction. The Muslims were apprehensive that the 'Hindus' aim was to gain political domination.[193] Jinnah was of the opinion that the Hindu–Muslim problem was a 'national problem' without which no constitutional advancement was possible. Even Sapru tried his best to contact various political formations in order to thrash out the issue. While all the others responded to this, the Hindu Mahasabha refused to cooperate.[194] The Mahasabha felt encouraged because of the attitude of the Congress leaders who had been lukewarm in trying to solve this problem.[195] Many Muslim Congress members too, such as M.A. Ansari, Shoaib Qureshi and Khaliquzzaman did not approve the attitude of the Congress on the communal problem.

In order to thrash out the issue, an All-Parties Conference was convened by Sapru in February 1930 in New Delhi in which a manifesto was released with the warning that if various communities were to go their own ways they would not be able to achieve anything. It was also resolved that a consultative meeting would take place in March, the same year. This in principle accepted the demands of the Muslims and other minorities for safeguarding their religion, education and culture.[196]

While all this was going on Gandhi was making preparations to launch the Civil Disobedience movement, even though M.A. Ansari had strongly advised against starting off the agitation until the Hindu–Muslim question was resolved. Whereas Mahatma Gandhi was of the opinion that differences among the communities could be resolved only when there was a mass political action launched in view of the mandate of the Lahore Congress in order to attain 'Purna Swaraj'. And to address this question to the Viceroy, he prepared a draft note and sent it to Jawaharlal Nehru for comment. It was a scathing criticism of colonial rule and its consequences. He said,

> The British Government of India has not only deprived the Indian people of their freedom but has based itself on the exploitation of the masses and has ruined India economically, politically, culturally and spiritually. We believe therefore that India must sever the British connection and attain Purna Swaraj or complete independence.[197]

He talked about the destruction of village industries, manipulation of customs and currencies, which heaped further burden on the peasantry and compulsory disarmament, which made Indians unmanly as if they could not protect themselves. He asserted, 'culturally the system of education has torn us from our moorings and our training has made us hug the very chains that bind us'.[198] In view of all this Gandhiji was emphatic that it would be a crime against man and God to submit any longer to a rule 'that has caused this fourfold disaster to our country'.[199] Subsequently he submitted a memorandum to the Viceroy containing the famous 11 points,[200] in order to free India from colonial bondage, as he started preparing the ground for launching the Civil Disobedience.

The newly constituted Congress Working Committee, soon after the Lahore Congress, included Maulana Azad apart from many others, had begun making preparations for the movement. In its meeting held on 2 January 1930, the CWC passed many resolutions, one of them was to observe a Purna Swaraj Day and the date chosen was 26 January 1930. It said,

> In order to carry the message of *Purna Swaraj*—Complete Independence—to the remotest village in India, this Committee appoints Sunday the 26th of January 1930, as the day of celebration when the declaration to be hereafter issued by the Working Committee will be read to the meeting in the provincial language and the members present at the meeting will be invited to signify by show of hands their assent to the declaration.[201]

With these preparations underway, Gandhiji started contemplating the timing and manner of launching the movement, which he did on 12 March 1930 when he embarked upon the long march, along with a band of 78 Satyagrahis from Sabarmati Ashram to Dandi, a coastal town of Gujarat, to break the salt law. Despite the declared policy of Gandhiji and the Congress that the movement would remain non-violent under all circumstances, the government resorted to large-scale repression and in this context the experience at Dharsana was the worst case. Another spot as regards the use of violent repression was in the NWFP, despite the fact that the Khudai Khidmatgars under the leadership of Khan Abdul Ghaffar Khan were committed to non-violence. It was on 25 April 1930 that the government had unleashed its brute force at Peshawar, resulting in casualties and the Congress had taken strong exception to such an attitude of the government. It was not satisfied with the government explanation about the incident as it decided to constitute the Peshawar Enquiry Committee under the chairmanship of V.J. Patel to find out the circumstances leading to the happening at Peshawar and consequences thereof. The members of this Committee were Maulana Azad, Abdul Qadir Kasuri, Sardar Sardul Singh Caveeshar, Lala Duni Chand and Dr. Syed Mahmud. The Committee did not have the permission of the Commissioner of NWFP to visit Peshawar to conduct an enquiry, so it had to make alternate arrangements. Its mandate was to submit the report at its earliest.[202] The hard work of the Committee led to filing a report with the CWC, which acknowledged it as such. The major finding of the Committee was that the unnecessary use of force at Peshawar was a deliberate attempt on the part of the Deputy Commissioner of NWFP to strike terror in the hearts and minds of the people of Peshawar as the firing was not confined to the bazaar but it was extended to side streets, bylanes and balconies and other places round about. The number of people killed would be in the range of 125 or more.[203]

The Congress leaders also consulted Maulana Azad for suggesting names of Muslims, who would propagate the Congress point of view.[204] He was active in mobilizing support for the movement. As acting president[205] of the Congress, Maulana Azad had visited Meerut on 7 August 1930, where he was taken through the city in a procession and at the end he addressed a largely attended meeting, in which, 'he emphasized that the country had made tremendous sacrifices but he appealed for still more sacrifices. He also appealed to Muslims to join the movement—not to fight for communal rights and representation in the councils now. Their case was safe in the hands of the Congress.'[206]

On an earlier occasion too, Maulana Azad addressed a largely attended meeting in Bombay along with Lala Duni Chand and Deep Narayan Singh, while they were in the city to attend the CWC meeting on 3 August 1930. They all congratulated Sardar Patel and Pandit Madan Mohan Malaviya on their arrest. Here, Maulana Azad was greeted with rousing cheers when he rose to address the meeting. In the course of his speech he denounced the use of force by the police on the unresisting crowd of satyagrahis at Bori Bundar, the same morning. In this context, he denounced all attempts at peace negotiations as 'fraudulent', while brutal repressions were going on. He asserted, 'you cannot get peace by asking for it. You have to win it by sacrifice. You must prepare yourself for any sacrifice for that freedom.'[207]

After Bombay it was the turn of Delhi to host Maulana Azad, acting president of the Congress, in a mass meeting held at Queen's Park on 6 August 1930. He was welcomed with tremendous applause and when he started speaking he was heard with rapt attention. He surveyed the movement and argued that it was a huge success and nearing the final stage. He pointed out that, 'the success in defying the Salt Act was really unparalleled. The Salt Act was not only defied but it was trampled under feet. . . . The foreign cloth boycott had proved so effective that England was keenly feeling its effect and it was therefore all news about the economic conditions in England effectively being censored.'[208] On behalf of the CWC, he congratulated the foreign cloth merchants for the success and advised them not to go back on their pledge and remain steadfast till the nation achieved its goal.[209] He exhorted the members of the audience to sacrifice for the cause of the country's freedom. He made a passionate appeal, 'freedom will come out of sacrifice alone. If you are not prepared for the sacrifice how can you expect freedom, for which other nations sacrificed their all? To attain liberty for 32 crores of people at the cost of a few lives was a cheap bargain and they must not grudge any sacrifice.'[210] He concluded his speech with stirring emotion, 'A country, which is ready to die cannot be kept in bondage by any country and shall surely win the fight.'[211] After his speech, Maulana Azad left for Calcutta the same day.

These speeches of Maulana Azad were certainly a source of discomfort and unease in government circles and they were looking for an opportunity to silence him, which they did on 21 August 1930, when he was arrested under Section 117 IPC, Section 4 of Ordinance 5 for delivering a speech at Meerut on 7 August 1930.[212] He was arrested in Calcutta and sent to Meerut by the Dehradun Express. He was made to disembark at Garh Mukteshwar and from there taken to Meerut in a lorry.[213] His arrest evoked severe criticism of the government and prompted many papers to come out with editorials. An important paper published from Allahabad, came out with a full-page editorial and questioned the wisdom in arresting him, 'was it indispensable for the purpose of good government that he should be arrested? The Government must naturally say yes. But as in respect of many other acts of authority we are unable to share their view of the demand for public safety.'[214]

During its course the movement touched a wider mass of the people where new sections of society were involved in national politics. However, there was also an opposite trend of declining participation of Muslims in the movement.[215] There were, however, several groups of Muslims, such as the Jamiatul-Ulema-i-Hind, Ahrar Party of the Punjab, the Khudai-Khidmatgars of NWFP and several nationalist Muslim groups who enthusiastically participated in the movement.[216] Maulana Azad too acknowledged the fact that so many Muslims had taken part in the movement, specially the members of the Jamiatul-Ulema-i-Hind, the Frontier and other Muslims.[217] He further pointed out that, 'it was an irony of fate that those Mussalmans who were from the fountain of modern learning had not joined the movement. But the members of the Jamiat, who were scholars of the Arabic on older lines had thrown themselves whole-heartedly into the fray.'[218] The level of participation of Muslims in the Civil Disobedience movement was a subject of curiosity even among journalists. In reply to a letter from the Secretary, Indian Journalist Association, Calcutta, Pandit Jawaharlal Nehru said, 'I am afraid I can't give any accurate figures for the numbers of Muslims who suffered imprisonment. The figure 12,000, which has often been mentioned is a rough estimate made by my colleague Syed Mahmood. We are now trying to get as accurate figure as possible and they will be incorporated in our annual report.'[219] Pandit Nehru was also conscious in pointing out that collating figures such as this would be rather difficult, 'But in no event we are likely to get accurate figures for different communities as our records are not made in this way.'[220] Despite such an assertion of Jawaharlal Nehru, the Congress consciously took note of Muslim participation in the movement and wished to thank them as such. In its meeting held on 6-7 June 1930, the CWC under the chairmanship of Motilal Nehru as acting president did take special note of Muslim participation in the movement. A resolution was adopted in this regard expressing satisfaction. It also said, 'In particular, the Committee puts on record its keen appreciation of the brave stand made by the Mussalmans of the NWFP, the Punjab and Bombay for the present Satyagrah campaign carried on by the Congress.'[221] The Bombay Provincial Congress Committee reported in response to a Congress circular to know from the provincial Congress committees as to the number of casualties in the wake of the police repression of those who took part in the movement. Its report contained several names such as Abdul Kadar Dawood, a member of the Azad Muslim Volunteer, who died in the Bhendi Bazar firing. In the same firing, a Khoja woman, called Fatmabai, too was killed. Then there was Dawood Munshi of Sankli state, not a Congress volunteer but all the same participating in the movement, who was badly assaulted and succumbed to his injuries in the Congress hospital on 17 July 1930. Mohammed Husain, who was jailed and after his release expired a broken man. One Jamiatul Ulema activist, Nizamud-din died due to injuries suffered at the hands of the police on 18 December 1930.[222]

With such involvement of various sections of the society, the Civil Disobedience movement was certainly a new political experience. But a mass movement of this magnitude was bound to taper off, as it had generated plenty of anxiety among sections of the business class as well as government circles too. In order to bring about rapprochement between the Congress and the government, Tej Bahadur Sapru and M.R. Jayakar were active for some time, which finally bore fruit on 26 January 1931, when Gandhiji and members of the Working Committee were released.[223]

Intense negotiations followed and finally the Gandhi–Irwin Pact was signed on 5 March 1931 under which the Congress agreed to suspend the Civil Disobedience movement while the British government agreed to release the prisoners and withdraw ordinances and notifications declaring organizations unlawful under the Criminal Law Amendment Act, restore forfeited property provided this had not been sold to third parties. It was agreed by the Congress not to press ahead for the boycott of British goods but peaceful picketing was to continue.[224] This enabled Gandhi to attend the Second Round Table Conference where he vehemently argued for a responsible government at the centre as well as in the provinces with immediate effect. However, he had to return to India empty handed towards the end of 1931. The political climate was ripe with possibilities of launching another phase of the Civil Disobedience movement, which actually started on 4 January 1932. This time around the policy of the government was to suppress the movement with a heavy hand by promulgating repressive ordinances and making mass arrests including that of the Congress president. It had already been resolved that the Congress president would nominate an acting president in succession of every arrest. Maulana Azad too had an opportunity to function as acting president and was prepared to face consequences. He was arrested on 12 March 1932 under the Emergency Power Ordinance. That day a protest was already organized against the arrest of Maulvi Kifayatullah, the leader of the Jamiatul-Ulema-i-Hind. When news broke about Maulana Azad's arrest, a few shops that were open too were closed in protest.[225] Azad was imprisoned in the district jail. Sarojini Naidu succeeded him as the sixth Congress president. After having served a term for about two months he was released on 11 May 1932 from the district jail of Delhi and immediately after that served a restraint notice.[226]

While the Round Table negotiations were on, the British Prime Minister McDonald announced the Communal Award on 16 August 1932, which conceded most of the Muslim demands. Apart from separate electorates for the depressed and backward classes, it allowed reservation of 89 seats for Muslims in the Punjab, which was a majority of two. In Bengal Muslims were allotted 119 seats, which constituted a majority of Indian seats. It also ensured a large weightage for Europeans so that they could maintain a balance between the two communities.[227] The Hindus with a sense of unease received the announcement of the Communal Award. It was felt that they were denied the minority rights where it was due to them.[228]

Azad personally did not approve of the Communal Award, and the failure of the efforts that he had made to reach some settlement on the communal demands made him quite unhappy.[229] All the same he was concerned that the minority problem be resolved in consultation with others. Azad was a part of endeavours made by men such as Madan Mohan Malaviya, Syed Mahmud and Shaukat Ali and for this purpose an All-Parties Muslim Conference was convened on 16 October 1932 at Lucknow in order to thrash out issues concerning constitutional arrangements, which would ensure that each community got what was its due. The discussion in the Conference centred around Jinnah's 14 points, introduction of provincial responsibilities on a priority basis, weightage on the model of the Premier's Award (McDonald Award). It was on the suggestion of Madan Mohan Malaviya that it was resolved to constitute a committee to negotiate with Hindus and others.[230] In view of this suggestion a committee consisting of men such as Maulana Shaukat Ali, Maulana Abul Kalam Azad, Nawab Mohammad Ismail, Zafar Ali Khan, Choudhary Khaliquzzaman and many others was constituted. A Unity Conference was organized at Allahabad on 3 November 1932 on the initiative of M.M. Malaviya,[231] and deliberations went on till 17 November 1932. The Committee did not oppose concessions to the Muslims in the Communal Award, but accepted the separation of Sind only on certain conditions, such as safeguards for minorities similar to those agreed to in the case of other provinces.[232] However, there was criticism of this Unity Conference.[233] Subsequent to the efforts made at the Unity Conference, an All-Parties Muslim Conference was held in Allahabad during 10-12 December 1932 to consider the proposal hammered out at the Unity Conference. Sir Zulfiqar Ali Khan, who presided over this Conference, hoped that the Unity Conference would eventually consider all the 14 points of M.A. Jinnah.[234]

In the background of these developments, the Unity Conference met for its second session at Allahabad on 16 December 1932, followed by yet another session on 23-4 December. And after intense confabulations an agreement was hammered out on several questions of constitutional importance. It said,

> The Conference therefore demands that control over the Government of India not excluding defence, foreign relations and finances should be transferred to the Indian people with only such safeguards, for a short period fixed by the statute, as may be shown to be demonstrably necessary in the interest of India. The Government in the provinces shall be autonomous and fully responsible to the legislature.[235]

The agreement also included points such as equality of all citizens before the law, protection of life and liberty, freedom of conscience, minorities rights to establish their, social, cultural, religious and education institutions. As regards the language/s it said, 'Hindustani shall be the language of the Central Government with the right to use either Hindi or Urdu character as the ordinary scripts, the use of English being permitted. In the provinces, the provincial language shall be the official language with liberty to use Hindustani or English.'[236] The agreement was presented by Maulana Azad, who delivered a long speech to highlight its importance in the present circumstances of political developments and had hoped, 'that the agreement that had been reached would be accepted by all the Organizations as every effort had been made to accept the demands of all the communities'.[237] For the efforts made at the Unity Conference, Maharaja of Alwar, Syed Mahmud and others profusely thanked Pandit Madan Mohan Malaviya and Maulana Azad.

These efforts to hammer out a solution to the controversy that had arisen due to the Communal Award did not bear fruit. The rival camps remained adamant in their respective approaches as regards the Award. This was particularly evident in Bengal where a series of meetings were organized to make claims and counter-claims. In a meeting organized by Muslims in Calcutta on 3 September 1933 an argument was made against any attempt to re-open the Award, as it would be considered ill advised and fraught with danger to the Muslim community and the country at large.[238] In the same meeting a resolution was adopted which warned, 'that any further attempt to change the Award would give rise to very intense feeling of discontent and disaffection among the Moslems of Bengal'.[239] In another meeting of some Muslims held at Howrah Town Hall in Calcutta on 2 October 1933 a resolution was adopted, which stated, 'the Award had already relegated Muslim majority in Bengal to Statutory minority and further that the participation of Muslims representatives in the Constitutional discussion had been on the clear assurance that the Communal Award was final'.[240] These assertions of the Muslims of Bengal did not go unchallenged. In a huge gathering of Hindus at the Albert Hall of Calcutta on 25 October 1933 the Communal Award was roundly condemned. The Poona Pact arrived at between Mahatma Gandhi and B.R. Ambedkar too was condemned. Bhai Parmanand, president of the Hindu Mahasabha was highly critical of the said Award, which he thought compromised Hindu interests.[241]

The bickering on the Communal Award was continuing on while the Civil Disobedience movement had already become considerably weak on account of the severely repressive policies of the British. As a consequence, Mahatma Gandhi decided to suspend the movement and he issued a statement to this effect on 7 April 1934.[242] Even after suspending the movement, the issue of the Communal Award lingered on. The Congress was unable to formulate an opinion, which would be acceptable to all. Finally in a meeting of the Working Committee of which Maulana Azad was a member, held on 17-18 June 1934, the Congress declared, 'The Congress claims to represent equally all the communities composing the Indian nation and therefore, in view of the division of opinion, can neither accept nor reject the Communal Award as long as the division of opinion lasts.'[243] Such a stand by the CWC came under intense attack not just by the adversaries of the Congress but many Congressmen themselves. In a sarcastic manner a letter was addressed to Nehru 'It is tantamount to passive acceptance rather than active rejection.'[244] It was emphasized, 'If the Congress declares itself against the Communal Award, it will lose nothing, but on the contrary it will regain much of its lost grounds, for by purifying itself of all the debilitating elements, it will become strong & not depend on the false allegiance of those who are at least themselves false to the principle of a united Indian nationality.'[245] This can be taken as an individual opinion of a member of the Congress. However, there was a far more organized response to the issue from other quarters. Organizations were formed with elected office-bearers expressly for the purpose of opposing the Communal Award. There was one based in Bombay, known as the All India Anti-Communal Award Conference, with Ramanand Chatterjee, editor *Modern Review* as its chairman, and persons like N.C. Kelkar as vice-chairman, which passed a resolution against the decision of the CWC.[246] It is interesting to note that opposition to the decision of the CWC was more vociferous in Bengal.[247]

The hands of the Congress were full with issues with considerable bearing on inter-community relations. A major challenge before it was how to move ahead in launching programmes and initiating policies, which would take everyone on board. In the immediate aftermath of the suspension of the Civil Disobedience movement, the ban on the Congress was lifted, still there was little scope for launching any political campaign, so the CWC decided to concentrate on the constructive activities in areas such as production of khadi, removal of untouchability, promotion of inter-community unity and many similar issues.[248]

Meanwhile, the report submitted by the Simon Commission along with other viewpoints gathered in the course of the three round table conferences provided substantial material to the Joint Select Committee of the British Parliament to work out constitutional arrangements for India. The outcome was the Government of India Act of 1935, which visualized a federal state with an effective responsible government in the provinces. Communal representation and safeguards for minority interests were ensured. Even though the Congress and League both criticized the Act, they eventually agreed to work it out. This was a momentous decision, a major move forward in constitutional development, which was to produce long-term consequences in terms of inter-community relations and national advancement.

NOTES

1. Asghar Ali Engineer (*Indian Muslims: A Study of the Minority Problems in India*, Ajanta Publications, Delhi, 1985) has argued that the Muslims of India during the latter half of the nineteenth and the first half of the twentieth centuries did not constitute a monolithic community. They were (as they are even today) divided horizontally as well as vertically into numerous regional and cultural groups on the one hand and into caste and class on the other (p. 1). In an almost similar vein Peter B. Mayor in 'Tomb and Dark Houses: Ideology, Intellectuals and Proletarians in the Study of Cotemporary Islam', in Imtiaz Ahmad, ed., *Modernisation and Social Change Among Muslims in India* (Delhi, 1983), has argued that any attempt to reify Islam would result in postulations of a Quranic political culture, which would be based on the formal theology of religion, instead of other considerations such as political ideas a particular group of Muslims would hold, and the relations between these groups and their social conditions (p. 5). The use of categories such as Hindus and Muslims should be seen in the light of the above statements.
2. Gail Minault, *The Khilafat Movement: Religious Symbolism and Political Mobilisation in India*, Oxford University Press, Delhi, 1982, p. 147.
3 K.N. Pannikar, *Against Lord and State: Religion and Peasant Uprisings in Malabar 1836-1921*, Oxford University Press, Delhi, 1989, p. 135.
4. Minault, op. cit., p. 149.
5. Abul Kalam Azad, *Khutba-i-Sadarat, Jamaitul-Ulama-i-Hind,* in Malik Ram, ed. *Khutbat-i-Azad*, Sahitya Akademi, Delhi, 1990, pp. 145-6.
6. Ibid., p. 147.
7. Ibid., p. 146.
8. Ibid., p. 152.

9. Ibid.
10. Minault, op. cit., p. 149. Also see Sumit Sarkar, *Modern India*, Macmillan, Delhi, 1983, p. 217.
11. Ibid., p. 149.
12. Mohammad Ali's speech at Erode near Madras on 2 April 1921 in *Mohammad Ali in Indian Politics: Select Writings 1920-23*, ed. Mushirul Hasan, Manohar, Delhi 1986, p. xxv.
13. Minault, op. cit., p. 141.
14. Ibid.
15. Ibid.
16. Ibid., p. 171.
17. Ibid., p. 178.
18. Mushirul Hasan, *Nationalism and Communal Politics in India, 1885-1930*, Manohar, Delhi, 1991. Hasan argued that the protagonists of Shuddhi and Sangathan conducted a more effective and ideologically cohesive campaign. Shuddhi Sabhas had started functioning since 1907 in order to re-convert the Malkan Rajputs back to Hinduism. The activities of the Shuddhi campaign were reinforced in 1923 when the All-India Hindu Mahasabha made it a part of its programme (p. 237).
19. Ibid. It has been argued that the organizers of Tabligh and Tanzeem groups defined their identity in explicitly religious terms. . . . They heightened the sense of community solidarity and religiosity by exhorting their followers to imbibe the Quran in letter and spirit. p. 232.
20. A.R. Malihabadi, *Zikr-i-Azad*, *Maulana Azad ki Refaqat mein Anrtees Saal*, Ujala Press, Calcutta, 1960, pp. 200-2.
21. Ibid., p. 273.
22. Ibid., p. 274.
23. Ibid. Also see, Ghulam Rasool Meher, ed., *Taburrakat-i-Azad*, Adabi Duniya, Delhi, 1963, for a similar opinion of Azad, while addressing the Special Session of the Indian National Congress, 1923.
24. V.N. Datta, *Maulana Azad*, Manohar, Delhi, 1990, p. 129.
25. Azad, Presidential address, 'Ajlas-i-Khusosi, Indian National Congress', 15 September 1923, in Malik Ram, ed., op. cit., p. 5.
26. Ibid., p. 196.
27. Ibid., p. 197.
28. Ibid., p. 198.
29. Ibid., p. 201.
30. Ibid., p. 202.
31. Ibid., p. 201.

32. Ibid., p. 206.
33. Ibid.
34. Ibid., p. 207.
35. *Al-Hilal*, vol. 1, no. 9, 8 September 1912.
36. Azad, Presidential address at the special session of the Congress in 1923, in Malik Ram, ed., op. cit., p. 205.
37. Ibid.
38. Ibid., p. 208.
39. Ibid., p. 203.
40. Ibid., p. 200.
41. Ibid., p. 209.
42. Azad, *Fitna-i-Irtidad aur Musalman*, in Ghulam Rasool Meher, ed., op. cit., p. 168.
43. Ibid., p. 169.
44. Ibid., p. 171.
45. Ibid., p. 169.
46. Ibid.
47. Ibid., p. 173.
48. Gail Minault, op. cit., p. 201.
49. Ibid.
50. Ibid., p. 203.
51. Ibid., p. 204.
52. Azad, *Masala-i-Khilafat*, in Ghulam Rasool Meher, ed., op. cit., pp. 178-9.
53. Ibid., p. 179.
54. Ibid., p. 184.
55. Ibid.
56. Datta, op. cit., p. 131.
57. As quoted in ibid.
58. AICC (Suppl.) File no. 50/1921-25, NMML, New Delhi.
59. Letter addressed to Mahatma Gandhi by B.S. Moonje dated 11 October 1924 in ibid. A copy of this letter was forwarded to Motilal Nehru too.
60. Ibid.
61. Ibid.
62. Joint statement of Pandit Motilal Nehru and Maulana Abul Kalam Azad on the Hindu–Muslim dispute at Nagpur, issued on 13 January 1925, AICC (Suppl.) File no. 50/1921-5.
63. Azad, speech at All India Khilafat Conference, Kanpur, 29 December 1925 in Malik Ram, ed., op. cit., p. 212.
64. Ibid., p. 213.
65. Ibid., p. 214.

66. Ibid.
67. Ibid., p. 218.
68. Ibid., p. 228.
69. Ibid., pp. 227-8.
70. Ibid., p. 230.
71. Telegram sent by Azad to Gandhiji, 8 May 1926, Gandhi Papers, File no. 11062, National Archives of India (NAI), New Delhi.
72 N.N. Mitra, ed., *The Indian Annual Register : An Annual Digest of Public Affairs of India* (hereafter *IAR*), serial no. 1, vol. II, July-December 1926, p. 26.
73. Ibid., serial no. 2, p. 90.
74. Ibid.
75. Ibid.
76. Ibid.
77. N.N. Mitra, ed., *The Indian Annual Register*, 1926, vol. II, New Series, Gyan Publishing House, New Delhi, 2000, p. 94.
78. Ibid., p. 95.
79. Ibid., p. 94.
80. G.R. Thursby, *Hindu-Muslim Relations in British India: A Study of Controversy, Conflict and Communal Movements in Northern India*, E.J. Brill, Leiden, 1975, p. 40.
81. Ibid., p. 41.
82. Ibid., p. 46.
83. Ibid., p. 47.
84. As quoted in ibid., p. 41.
85. Ibid., p. 42.
86. Refer to the footnote of G.R. Meher, *Taburrakat-i-Azad*, op. cit., p. 44.
87. Azad to Qasuri, 29 July 1927, in ibid., p. 44.
88. Ibid., p. 45.
89. Ibid., p. 46.
90. Ibid., p. 47.
91. N.N. Mitra, ed., *IAR*, 1927, vol. II (New Series), pp. 38-41.
92. Ibid., p. 55.
93. In a letter the Hindu Mahasabha protested by saying that the Congress being a political body should not have entertained questions relating to religion and religious practices. Regarding cow slaughter it said that, 'not likely to lead to unity and peace but on the contrary is calculated to lead to greater discord and strife'. AICC Papers, File no. G-64-66/ 1926, NMML.
94. 'Hindu feeling wounded by Calcutta Congress Committee passing resolution touching Korbani. . . . And promote disunion and

alienate large sections of people from Congress. In national interest earnestly request you to exert yourself and see that it is either not taken up by Congress or rescinded.' These organizations included, Sanatan Dharm Mandal, All India Cow Conference, Cow Protection Society, Marwari Association and Cow Preservation League, there were telegrams of protest from places such as Aurangabad in Maharashtra, Monghyr in Bihar, etc. AICC Papers, File no. G-64-66/ 1926 NMML.

95. Uma Kaura, *Muslims and Indian Nationalism: The Emergence of the Demand for India's Partition 1928-1940*, Manohar, Delhi, 1977, p. 29.
96. N.N. Mitra, ed., *IAR*, 1927, vol. I (New Series), p. 33.
97. Ibid.
98. Ibid.
99. Kaura, op. cit., p. 31.
100. N.N. Mitra, ed., *IAR*, vol. II, no. 5, July–December 1927, p. 402.
101. Kaura, op. cit., p. 31.
102. Dr. M.A. Speech at the Madras session of the Congress, *IAR*, 1927, vol. II (New Series), p. 372.
103. Ibid., p. 39.
104. Sind Hindu Association sent a telegram 21 December 1927 to Dr. Ansari, saying that it 'strongly opposes separation of Sind from Bombay on political and economic grounds . . . politically inexpedient in view of present tension between Mahomadans and Hindus.' AICC Papers, File no. G-64-66, 1926, NMML.
105. Ibid.
106. Ibid. The same telegram was also sent to Maulana Azad. In another telegram from Hyderabad, Sind, sent to Dr. Ansari on behalf of the Sind Panchayats. It said, 'All Panchayats of Sind strongly against separation of Sind from Bombay presidency . . . request Congress not to take any decision in the teeth of unanimous opposition of Sind Panchayats'. Similarly on 25 December 1927, 'Sind Sadhu Mandal unanimously resolved the separation of Sind question be dropped. Hindus are quite against it.' In yet another telegram sent to Dr. Ansari on behalf of Hindu Sabha on 27 December 1927, it was said, 'Sind separation ruinous to Hindus . . . and not risk alienation of Sind Hindus from Congress.
107. Telegram sent by the Sind Mohemadan Association, dated 23 December 1927, AICC Papers, File no. G-64-66, 1926. In

yet another telegram from Sheikh Tyab Ali Alvi to Rangaswamy Iyengar, secretary, Congress it was strongly pleaded that not only Sind be separated from Bombay, there should be reforms in the North-West and Baluchistan with provincial autonomy. It was further suggested that a national commission be constituted for framing of the national constitution on an universal basis.

108. *Bombay Chronicle*, 18 August 1928.
109. *Hindustan Times*, 16 August 1928.
110. Ibid.
111. Ibid.
112. Datta, op. cit., p. 135.
113. Ibid.
114. Hasan, op. cit., p. 256.
115. Ibid.
116. Kaura, op. cit., p. 39.
117. Ibid.
118. Ibid., p. 40.
119. The All India Muslim League Council, which included prominent names such as T.A.K. Sherwani, Dr. Ansari, Maulana Azad and many others did not entirely agree with the Report. *Bombay Chronicle*, 30 August 1928.
120. Ibid.
121. Ibid. In a significant manner they said, 'We the signatories are conscious of the fact that the All India Muslim League passed a resolution at Calcutta in 1927, which differs in material respects from the recommendations embodied in the report. We, however, in our individual capacity give our support to the Report and also give assurance that at the next session of the League we shall do our best to prevail upon the members of the League to ratify the same'.
122. 'The Muslim Case, Nehru Committee Report Analysed', article by Shaukat Ali, in *Bombay Chronicle*, 21 August 1928.
123. *Hindustan Times*, 15 September 1928. Important signatories included Firoz Khan Noon, Sir Mohammad Iqbal, Anwarul Aziz, MLA, Bengal and Sir Abdul Qadir.
124. Kaura, op. cit., pp. 40-1.
125. It seems this meeting had taken place a few days earlier, which was reported by the *Tribune*, later reproduced by the *Bombay Chronicle*, 21 September 1928.
126. Ibid.
127. Malihabadi, *Zikr-i-Azad*, op. cit., p. 354.

128. Ibid.
129. Ibid.
130. Ibid., p. 355.
131. Letter from Maulana Azad to Motilal Nehru, 4 September 1928, AICC (Suppl.) File no. 106, NMML.
132. Ibid.
133. Ibid.
134. A telegram sent by Motilal Nehru to Maulana Azad, dated 11 September 1928, AICC (suppl.) file no. 106, NMML.
135. A letter addressed by Maulana Azad to Motilal Nehru, dated 12 September 1928 in ibid.
136. Ibid.
137. Ibid.
138. Ibid.
139. *Bombay Chronicle*, 27 August 1928.
140. A letter from Maulana Azad to Motilal Nehru dated 1 October 1928, AICC (Suppl.) File no. 106, NMML.
141. Ibid. Azad was repeatedly hinting at spending money. At one point in the same letter he said, 'whatever he deemed fit he simply spent it'. It seems he did not mind using money power to buy consensus.
142. Azad to Motilal Nehru, 3 October 1928 in AICC (Suppl.) File no. 106.
143. Ibid. In another letter dated 5 October 1928, Azad again reminded Motilal about sending him funds to carry out the propaganda work.
144. *Hindustan Times*, 14 November 1928.
145. Ibid.
146. *Bombay Chronicle*, 22 December 1928.
147. Ibid., 26 December 1928. Headline of a report said, 'Nehru Report responsible for disunity in country, Maulana Mohammad Ali's fulmination at Khilafat Conference'.
148. *Bombay Chronicle*, 26 December 1928.
149. *Hindustan Times*, 10 October 1928.
150. Ibid.
151. *Hindustan Times* 10 November 1928.
152. *Hindustan Times*, 28 October 1928. This interview was given to the press soon after he returned from Europe. He also admitted that he had still not had enough time to 'digest' the Report but he had good idea about it and also expressed some reservations about it.
153. Ibid.

154. Ibid.
155. Ibid.
156. Malihabadi, *Zikr-i-Azad*, op. cit., p. 356.
157. N.N. Mitra, ed., *IAR*, vol. 1, January–June 1928, p. 97.
158. Hasan, op. cit., p. 277.
159. Ibid., p. 278.
160. Datta, op. cit., p. 136.
161. Ibid. p. 278.
162. Hasan, op. cit., p. 273.
163. *Bombay Chronicle*, 29 December 1928.
164. Ibid.
165. Kaura, op. cit., p. 49 Some of these fourteen points consisted of a federal constitution, residuary powers to be vested with provinces, effective representation of minorities in every province without reducing the majority in provinces where Muslims were in majority, one-third reservation for Muslims in the centre, etc.
166. Abdur Rahim, 'Nehru Report *vs* 14 Points Pettifogging and Communalism', in *Hindustan Times*, 6 July 1929.
167. Ibid.
168. *Bombay Chronicle*, 1 April 1929. In the Subjects Committee Raja Ghazanfar Ali moved a proposal on the same line as that of the Calcutta proposal of December 1928, and wished that the Subjects Committee should accept it. However it was not acceptable to people like Maulana Azad, T.A.K. Sherwani and others.
169. *Bombay Chronicle*, 4 April 1929.
170. *Bombay Chronicle*, 28 August 1929, N.C. Kelkar, while addressing a session of the Hindu Mahasabha, held at Dhaka, on 27 August 1929 argued that Hindus of India had to secure everything here only as they have no claim to support from any other quarter. He accused the Congress for allowing the Khilafat Committee to dominate it. After analysing the Nehru Report and issues concerning Hindu–Muslim relation, he obliquely hinted that in the event of no solution forthcoming, he might accept the solution given by the government of the day. He said this in view of the fact that intervention by Mrs. Naidu would not be acceptable since she was seen as too much pro-Muslim and Mahatma Gandhi, too generous. He added, 'For in his plenitude of generosity, he has more than asked Hindus to concede everything that the Muslims demand, in the interest, of course, of peace and harmony. We have therefore reached a position of stalemate.'
171. *Bombay Chronicle*, 16 July 1929.

172. Ibid.
173. Ibid., 19 July 1929.
174. N.N. Mitra, ed., *IAR*, vol. II, July–December 1929, p. 350, *Bombay Chronicle,* 29 July 1929. It was resolved to have its headquarters at Delhi.
175. Mitra, ed., ibid. *Bombay Chronicle*, ibid.
176. Mitra, ed., *IAR*, vol. II, July–December 1929, p. 350.
177. *Bombay Chronicle*, 29 July 1929.
178. Ibid.
179. The representation came from places such as Bengal, Bihar, U.P., Delhi, Punjab, NWFP, Bombay and Sind and Gujarat. AICC Papers, File no. 40, 1929, NMML.
180. Datta, op. cit., p. 137.
181. Kaura, op. cit., p. 52.
182. *Bombay Chronicle*, 20 July 1929.
183. Congress Muslim Party, 'A sign of Times', in *Pioneer*, n.d., reproduced by *Bombay Chronicle*, 15 July 1929.
184. 'I am glad you are having a Congress Muslim Party. If it is well supported and if it does not go to sleep, it must prove a tower of strength to the Congress and the institution will be of real service to India in general and the Muslim community in particular.' *Bombay Chronicle*, 29 July 1929.
185. *Bombay Chronicle*, 28 September 1929.
186. Ibid.
187. Ibid.
188. Ibid., 23 September 1929.
189. Datta, op. cit., p. 138.
190. Kaura, op. cit., p. 52.
191. Ibid., p. 53.
192. Ibid.
193. Ibid.
194. Ibid., p. 55.
195. Ibid.
196. Ibid., p. 58.
197. Gandhiji's draft note, AICC Papers, File no. 26, 1930.
198. Ibid.
199. Ibid.
200. These 11 points consisted of (1) Total prohibition, (2) Reduction of exchange ratio to 1s.4d, (3) Reduction of land revenue by 50 per cent, (4) Abolition of Salt tax, (5) Reduction of military expenditure by 50 per cent to begin with, (6) Reduction of salaries

of the highest-grade services by half, (7) Protective tariff on foreign clothes, (8) Passage of the Coastal Traffic Reservation Bill, (9) Discharge of all political prisoners except those condemned for murder, (10) Abolition of CID, (11) Issue of licences to use of fire arms for self-defence.

201. Mitra, ed., *IAR*, vol. 1, January–June 1930, p. 333.
202. Ibid., p. 437.
203. Ibid., p. 451.
204. Telegram from Jawaharlal Nehru to Maulana Azad, 27 March 1930.
205. Maulana Azad was the third acting president of the Congress after Pandit Motilal Nehru and Sardar Patel were arrested. Such nomination of the next president in the event of the arrest of the incumbent was part of the decision of the Congress. The party had resolved, 'In view of possible vacancies in the Congress Working Committee, arising out of Govt. action and in the event of normal procedure being rendered difficult, resolved that the following procedure be adopted—(1)The President may nominate his successor and the President for the time being shall have powers to fill up all vacancies in the Working Committee by his own nominations, (2) The working treasurer shall have power to nominate his own successor in case of similar emergency.'
206. *The Leader*, 8 August 1930. It was pointed out by Maulana Azad that the Nehru Report, which had created dissatisfaction in certain quarters was no longer, relevant. He appealed to all to sink their differences and join the country's struggle.
207. *The Leader*, 6 August 1930.
208. *Hindustan Times*, 8 August 1930.
209. Ibid.
210. Ibid.
211. Ibid.
212. *Hindustan Times*, 25 August 1930. It is important to point out that Maulana Azad's speech at Meerut was not as scathing an attack on the government as it was in Delhi.
213. Ibid. The reporter of the paper protested that the government was not showing enough respect to a leader of Maulana Azad's stature by taking him in a lorry instead of a car.
214. *The Leader*, 24 August 1930. The editorial comments also highlighted many qualities of Azad. It said, '—the Moulana commands an enviable position by virtue of his qualities of sincerity, uprightness, freedom from narrow communalism,

genuine nationalism, independence and patriotism. A reputed Arabic and Persian scholar, Moulana Abul Kalam Azad is one of the most graceful yet powerful orators in Urdu and holds audiences spell bound by the charm of his speaking.'

215. Sarkar, op. cit., p. 290.
216. Datta, op. cit., p. 138.
217. Maulana Azad had presided over a session of the Jamiatul-Ulema-i-Hind, held at Karachi on 1 April 1931. 'The Maulana spoke appreciatively of the part, which the Muslims generally and the Jamiat-ul-Ulema in particular played in last year's struggle. He also referred to the Frontier Muslims part.' Mitra, ed., *IAR*, vol. I, January–June 1931, p. 292.
218. Ibid.
219. Jawaharlal Nehru's reply to Secretary, Indian Journalist Association, Calcutta, 14 July 1931, AICC Papers, File no. G-1, 1931, NMML.
220. Ibid.
221. Mitra, ed., *IAR*, vol. I, January–June 1930, p. 441.
222. These names were out of a list of twenty-three deaths during the movement. AICC Papers, File no. G-1 (i) 1931, NMML.
223. Judith M. Brown, *Gandhi and Civil Disobedience: The Mahatma in Indian Politics, 1928-1934*, Cambridge University Press, Cambridge, 1977, p. 174.
224. Ibid., p. 186.
225. *Hindustan Times*, 14 March 1932.
226. Ibid., 12 May 1932.
227. Kaura, op. cit., p. 86.
228. Ibid.
229. Zia-ul Hasan Faruqi, *Maulana Abul Kalam Azad, Towards Freedom*, B.R. Publishing Corp., Delhi, 1997, p. 148.
230. Mitra, *IAR*, vol. II, July–December 1932, p. 288.
231. The Unity Conference too appointed a Committee consisting of Maharaja of Darbhanga, J.N. Basu, Ramanand Chatterji, Abul Kalam Azad, Shaukat Ali, Zafar Ali, Raja of Salempur, Sardar Sundar Singh, Sardar Ujjal Singh, Pandit Madan Mohan Malaviya, Dr. D'Souza and C. Raghavchariar and others to deals with issues, which demanded attention. Ibid., p. 295.
232. Text of agreement arrived at by the Committee of the Unity Conference, 18 November 1932, M.S. Aney Papers, as discussed and elaborated upon in Uma Kaura, op. cit., p. 90.
233. *The Leader* of Allahabad carried a story, which was not flattering

to the Conference. Some complained, 'chief goal before the Hindu leaders, who participated in the negotiations, was joint electorate but the price paid in the shape of the Hindus agreeing, among other matters, to statutory majority of Muslims in the Punjab and Bengal, conceding 32 per cent, representation to them in the central legislature and accepting the principle of separation of Sind was too exorbitant for the kind of joint electorate secured.' There was another observation about the role of many Congress leaders who took part in the Unity Conference. It was said, 'Such pro-Muslim attitude of the Congress Hindus was obviously the result of their fervent desire to achieve unity at any cost and they, therefore, had also to make repeated appeals to Hindus to make "supreme sacrifices" whenever any problem presented dead-lock.' Mitra, *IAR*, vol. II, July–December 1932, pp. 295-6.

234. Mitra, *IAR*, vol. II, July–December 1932, p. 302.
235. Ibid. p. 310.
236. Ibid.
237. Ibid., p. 314.
238. Ibid., 1933, p. 9.
239. Ibid.
240. Ibid., p. 11.
241. Ibid., p. 16.
242. Ibid., vol. 1, January–June 1934, p. 263.
243. Ibid., p. 300.
244. Dr. Shadi Ram Sharma's letter (a member of the Hoshiarpur City Congress Working Committee) to Pandit Nehru, n.d., AICC Papers, File no. G-24/1934, NMML.
245. Ibid.
246. Resolution of the All-India Anti-Communal Award Conference, Bombay, 27 October 1934, AICC Papers, File no. G-24/ 1934. It said, 'This Conference deplores the attitude of the Working Committee of the Congress which may be regarded as virtual acquiescence in that decision and is regrettable departure from the principle of nationalism which hitherto has been the proudest claim of the Congress to the support of the nation. . . .' The Conference also decided to form an All-India Anti-Communal Decision League to carry out continuous campaign against it (Communal Award).
247. The Congress Nationalist Party, Bengal, in its letter dated 6 August 1934 enumerated the Congress members opposition to the

decision by CWC at places such as Jessore, Calcutta, Pabna, Birbhum, Burdwan and the hill district of Bogra. The general tone of resolutions adopted in all these places was that CWC decision was a 'virtual surrender to communalism and goes against the best interest of the nation.' The Poona Sarvajanik Sabha too adopted a resolution, which considered the Award as 'anti-national'. 1934, AICC Papers, File no. G-24/1934, NMML.

248. Mitra, ed., *IAR*, vol. II, July–December 1934, p. 298.

CHAPTER FOUR

The Vision of Power-sharing and Cultural Identity, 1935-1940

The mid-1930s was a period of a real test of Azad's leadership. In the late 1920s and early 1930s he had already engaged himself in the struggle against growing communalism, which was undermining secular Indian nationalism. The impact of the introduction of communal representation under the Communal Award of 1932 was yet to be assessed. No one was sure if there would be collaboration between the Congress and political formations of the Muslims including the Muslim League. One thing was certain that serious efforts would have to be made to overcome the alienation of the Muslims at large from the Congress. How and what measures the Congress would initiate to re-establish its claim that it represented all Indians, remained a question mark.

I

Azad, like several other leaders of the Congress, reflected upon these issues. After the death of M.A. Ansari in 1936 his stature in the Congress attained greater heights. He was consulted on all issues of importance particularly those concerning Muslims. The Maulana was aware of his new role in the party but the job at hand was one of great challenge. Vast sections of the Muslims had become alienated from the Congress. He had therefore to work hard to bring them back to the party fold. He had to go beyond the realm of ideology; of composite Indian nationalism regarding which much had already been done in earlier years. His major concern at this time was to ensure that Muslims were reassured that the Congress was willing to share power with them in whatever manner was possible. At the same time he wished the

Congress would be more sensitive to issues of culture, the Urdu language and larger identity-concerns of the Muslims. In the present chapter an attempt is made to examine his standing in the Congress, his concerns about ensuring that Muslims stayed in the course of the nationalist movement, particularly under the aegis of the Congress, while taking care that they were accommodated in the power structure.

In his attempts in these directions, Azad received cooperation from some colleagues in the party, but there were others who did not share his thoughts. In the process several of his efforts stopped mid-way without healing the communally vitiated political climate. By the mid-1930s the social base of the Congress had considerably increased. The Congress was no longer merely an urban party since it was able to make deep inroads into rural areas, which produced a strange, politically radical but socially backward-looking mindset[1] with only limited sensitiveness about the cultural concerns of other religious communities and their identity perceptions.

The dust raised by the Communal Award of 1932 had hardly settled that the House of Commons passed the India Bill in June 1935, which received royal assent by August 1935. Thus the Government of India Act 1935 came into being. It was certainly an advance over all previous constitutional arrangements. It provided for two distinct units: one British India, the other an All-India Federation of British Indian Provinces and the Indian States.[2]

The Act of 1935 was condemned by almost all shades of political opinion. The Congress denounced the 'safeguards', rendering responsible government nugatory.[3] They demanded that Indians should frame the constitution through a constituent assembly, elected on the basis of universal adult franchise.[4] The All-India Muslim League too criticized the Act since it perceived the federal part of the Act as most reactionary.[5] It was feared that the structure of a federation was too unitary and hence subject to the dangers of Hindu-majority domination.[6] In spite of the fact that the Congress and the Muslim League, the two major players, had denounced the Act, they eventually agreed to contest provincial elections, which would help them to spread their political messages to the electorate.[7] Despite the decision by both the parties to contest elections, they did not enjoy parity in terms of the respective strength of their social base. While the Congress had emerged as a formidable force to reckon with at an all-India level, the claims of the Muslim League were yet to be tested in the light of the fact that it had not launched any movement worth the name which would necessitate mass mobilization. Not only this, there were some formidable Muslim leaders in the Muslim-majority provinces as well as certain Muslim-minority provinces who enjoyed greater social support than the Muslim League. Sikandar Hayat Khan and Khizr Hayat Khan in the Punjab, Fazlul Haq of Krishak Proja Party in Bengal, Khan Abdul Ghaffar Khan in NWFP and Allah Bux in Sind enjoyed great popular support. Similarly, the Muslim Independent Party in Bihar led by Maulvi Sajjad enjoyed broad-based social support. Therefore, much more than for the Congress it was likely to be a real test of the Muslim League's credibility and strength since it had to prove that it alone represented all Muslim political aspirations.

Preparation for the forthcoming elections may be said to have begun when Jinnah delivered a speech in Bombay in July 1936 in which he emphasized that the Muslim League must attain a status 'so as to speak with unchallenged authority for the eighty million Muslims in India'.[8] The Congress made an even more sweeping claim to speak for the whole nation,[9] despite the fact the party's base among Muslims had always been weak.[10] There were many Congress leaders who refused to acknowledge that there were very few Muslims in the party who would stand for elections on the Congress ticket. It was not for nothing that Syed Mahmud wanted the Congress to help out the Muslim Independent Party (MIP) in Bihar in the elections. Syed Mahmud's stance was based on an understanding that the MIP was a party of nationalist Muslims and shared similar ideological proclivities as the Congress and enjoyed considerable support among the Muslims there.[11] However, suggestions such as this by Syed Mahmud did not find favour with the leaders of the Congress.[12]

The Congress' predicament was that on the one hand it made legitimate claims to represent all sections of Indian society, but on the other the ground realities were changing. For instance, in the United Provinces, the dithering and delay in the selection of candidates led to several Muslims drifting to the Muslim League,[13] since there was lack of pressure on them. Nehru was to view it differently. 'Partly this is due to our own timidity as we ran few Muslim candidates. The burden of running over a thousand candidates (in the general constituencies) was great and we did not wish to add to it.'[14]

The results of the elections showed that the Congress was the dominant party. Of the 1,585 seats in provincial legislatures the Congress won 716. The victory was more impressive in the light of the fact that of the 1,585 seats only 657 seats were general. The party secured a clear majority in six out of eleven British Indian provinces, while it was the single largest party in three others.[15] The Muslim League won only 109 Muslim seats out of a total of 482. It performed poorly even in Muslim-majority provinces. It could not obtain a single seat in the NWFP and Sind. In the Punjab it got only one out of 86 Muslim seats and in Bengal only 37 out of 119 Muslim seats. It did better in the Muslim minority provinces. For instance in Bombay it won 20 out of 39 Muslim seats, in the United Provinces 27 out of 64 Muslim seats, in Madras 11 out of the 28 Muslim seats and in Assam 9 out of 34 Muslim seats. The Muslim League did not win a single Muslim seat in Bihar, Orissa and the Central Provinces.

The election results destroyed the very foundations upon which Jinnah had built his strategy ever since his return to India in 1934.[16] It was clear that the Muslim League was certainly not the party of choice for all Muslims at an all-India scale. But Jinnah was not someone who would easily accept defeat. He had sensed that the Congress would make a bid for power at the centre. In the event of such a development the Muslim-majority provinces would be forced to recognize their need to have a spokesman at the centre.[17] It was this perception, which made Jinnah believe that he as well as his party were relevant in Indian politics. He was also hopeful that something would happen in the present too to ensure some share in power for Muslim League legislators. This was the beginning of discussions about forming coalitions.

Maulana Azad's role was crucial since he was charged with responsibilities of government formations in several provinces.

He had the additional responsibility of making choices of Muslim ministers in other provinces as well.[18] Keeping in view Azad's position concerning Muslim affairs it was expected that he would be involved in negotiations as regards the possibility of a coalition ministry in the United Provinces. With regard to a possible coalition in another province, Bombay, there had been fear in Congress circles that with the entry of the Muslim League, the Cabinet would be pulled in different directions.[19] In the case of UP, it was clear to the Muslim League that the Congress was likely to form the government; Khaliquzzaman and Ismail Khan approached G.B. Pant in order to explore the possibility of some League members joining the ministry in the United Provinces. In the course of several meetings Khaliquzzaman told Azad that he would give a blank cheque to him (Azad), provided he and Ismail were taken in the ministry.[20] The CWC members were hardly able to appreciate the bargaining for the seats and Azad himself looked at all this with some suspicion.[21]

The Congress had put forward stringent conditions before Khaliquzzaman and Ismail were taken into the ministry. These conditions were,

> The Muslim League group in the UP legislature shall cease to function as a separate group. The existing members of the Muslim League party in the UP Assembly shall become part of the Congress party and will fully share with other members of the party their privileges and obligations as members of the Congress party. . . . The Muslim League Parliamentary Board in UP will be dissolved and no candidates hereafter be set up by the said Board in any by-election.[22]

After going through these conditions Khaliquzzaman told Maulana Azad that signing on these condition amounted to, 'signing the death warrant of the Muslim League Parliamentary Board as well as the Muslim League organisation, which I am representing there'.[23]

The conditions put forward by the Congress were certainly difficult to be accepted by the Muslim League. It is important to recall that, during elections, despite differences in ideological make-up and programmes *vis-à-vis* the Congress, there had been some common ground where the two could meet. Nehru remarked, 'During the general elections in the UP there was not much conflict between the Congress and the Muslim League. It was the desire of both parties to avoid a conflict as much as possible and to accommodate each other.'[24] Nehru went on to say, 'As we looked upon the election campaign it was a tussle with the Agriculturist Party, which was wholly a government party of big zamindars. The League was also opposing them and so inevitably our opposition to the League weakened. We did not want to split the forces opposed to pure reaction.'[25] But he spoke in a different voice later. Nehru did not like talks about a possible coalition ministry, 'I was feeling very uncomfortable and was instinctively repelled by all this talk on an opportunistic basis. I felt trouble would follow and the settlement would be temporary only.'[26] Others shared this view in the Muslim League too. Khaliquzzaman had said, ' . . . every effort had been made to make the Muslim Parliamentary Board manifesto as near to the Congress economic policy as possible.'[27]

In this letter, nowhere did Nehru refer to any clear-cut position taken by Maulana Azad as regards the formation of a coalition ministry. All that Nehru said was that, '*Maulana was also distracted*'[28] (Emphasis added). The use of an expression such as 'distracted' does not throw light on Azad's position on the subject. Azad did not share Nehru's perception in this matter. He reflected upon these developments twenty years later in *India Wins Freedom*. As he put it,

> After discussion with me, a note was prepared to the effect that the Muslim League party would work in cooperation with Congress and accept the Congress programme. Both Nawab Ismail Khan and Choudhary Khaliquzzaman signed this document and I left Lucknow for Patna as my presence was necessary for forming the ministry in Bihar.[29]

Azad was disconcerted when, a few days after this agreement, Nehru informed Khaliquzzaman and Ismail Khan that only *one* of them could be taken into the Ministry.[30] This was unacceptable to the duo since neither was in a position to come in alone. It was reported that

> the result of the negotiation with the Muslim League for a coalition in order to take *one or two* Muslim Leaguers as ministers is not yet known here. *It is believed in some Congress circles that the Muslim Leaguers might*

be available to join the Congress party by signing the Congress pledge but the Congress President seems to have also laid down some other conditions and that might be causing a hitch for (of) the Muslim League members to accept the offer of ministry.[31] (Emphasis added)

The report further stated that some people expected that the total strength of the Ministry could be either six or nine. However, in order to accommodate 30 per cent Muslims, 'it may be considered advisable to have ministry of nine with three Muslims and six non-Muslims'.[32] Such anticipation seemed fitting in the circumstances, since the only Muslim member of the Cabinet was Rafi Ahmad Kidwai.

Azad viewed this as the 'most unfortunate development',[33] because it was something which gave the Muslim League a new lease of life in UP.[34] He identified the person responsible for Jawaharlal's changed position,

> I found that Purshottamdas Tandon had taken a leading part in the whole affair. I did not have much respect for his views but I tried to persuade Jawaharlal to modify his stand. . . . Jawaharlal did not agree with me and held that his judgement was right. He argued that with strength of only 26 members, the Muslim Leaguers could not claim more than one seat in the Cabinet. When I found that Jawaharlal was adamant, I went to Wardha and sought Gandhiji's advice. When I explained the whole situation to him, he agreed with me and said he would advise Jawaharlal to modify his stand.[35]

Azad continued, 'I have to place on record that when Jawaharlal put the matter in a different light Gandhiji submitted to Jawaharlal and did not press that matter as he should have done. The result was that there was no settlement in UP.' [36]

Historians have viewed these observations of Azad with scepticism to the extent that in a recent work Azad's statements have been described as relying on 'hindsight and fading memory'[37] rather than on any serious reflection on historical developments. However, a scrutiny of sources establishes that Azad's observations are historically valid and not merely based on his 'hindsight' and 'fading memory'. Azad was keen to invoke Gandhiji's authority in the matter, and Gandhiji seemed to concur with Azad's position on coalition Ministry formation. This is borne out by a letter that Gandhiji wrote to Nehru on 22 July 1937,

Maulana Saheb stopped for a day in Wardha and we had a long chat. He showed me the draft agreement between the Muslim League members of the Assembly and the Congress members. I thought that it was a good document. But he told me that whilst you liked it Tandonji did not. I have written to the latter about it as the Maulana suggested I should. *What is the objection*?[38]

While Azad had clearly implied that it was Nehru who prevaricated, it is possible to argue that such a major decision may not have been any one person's work. Despite all these statements made by Azad as regards the coalition talks with the Muslim League in UP, what clearly emerges is that conditions put forth by the Congress essentially sought the merger of the Muslim League legislature party into the Congress rather than seeking formation of a coalition government. Another interesting aspect of the entire negotiations that Maulana Azad did not mention in *India Wins Freedom* is that when the final draft of conditions were presented to Khaliquzzaman again, on 26 July 1937, he in turn consulted Nawab Ismail and both met Maulana Azad on 28 July 1937 and expressed their feeling that the conditions were unfair. They also put forth some conditions before entering into the coalition. Those conditions were: 'inclusion of a clause in the agreement that communal matters such as the question relating to communal Award, language, culture, religious observances, etc., will be outside the scope of the agreement'.[39] It must have come as a surprise to Maulana Azad as he expressed his 'inability' in the matter but told Khaliquzzaman as reported by him, 'the Congress in its own interest would desist from raking up any communal controversies'.[40] In view of these facts it is difficult to fathom why did Azad say that talks failed due to Nehru's insistence alone on taking only one Muslim League member in the Cabinet, and not mention the conditions placed before the Congress by the UP Muslim League as one of the causes for the breakdown of the negotiations. It is another matter that earlier when the negotiations had just started even Azad held rather strong views as regards the coalition. As he put it, 'If any party wanted to join the Congress it must give up its separate identity and identify itself with the Congress.'[41]

An equally important point that needs attention is that

Maulana Azad was involved in mobilizing the Ulema to leave the Muslim League and join the Congress with considerable success.[42] In due course of time this success was further consolidated when four members of the Muslim League party joined the Congress by signing its pledge, which raised the strength of the members of Congress in the legislature to 139.[43]

In view of the above-stated facts, many historians would like to look at the whole process of coalition negotiations afresh. However, there are historians who have argued that Nehru was not directly involved in the negotiations and for that matter he may not even have been fully informed of developments.[44] Nehru himself implied that he alone was not responsible for the final decision. G.B. Pant, Rafi Ahmad Kidwai and Azad himself were instrumental in arriving at a decision not to form a coalition with the League.[45] 'It is true that the Congress did not need to form a coalition since it had a clear majority in UP.'[46] It is equally true that there was no prior agreement between the two parties (contrary to the impression that is given by some scholars).[47] However, it is a fact that 'there was no written pact between the Muslim League and the Congress for a coalition between the parties in the legislature, yet the amicable manner in which elections had been fought both by the Congress and League presaged a future settlement'.[48]

Though there was no need for a coalition, yet the texture of United Provinces' politics called for a new perspective.[49] The failure of negotiations because of the Congress' refusal to form a coalition was a serious error of judgement. This shattered the faith of the Muslims in the sincerity of the Congress.[50] The Congress seemed to be so self-centred. If even in the limited sphere of provincial autonomy it was not willing to share power with them then the community had reason to be concerned were the Congress to gain power at the centre.[51] Azad too had viewed this development rather despondently. His response could be described as *post-facto* reflections, nonetheless it deserves attention. He argued that 'Jawaharlal's action gave the Muslim League in UP a new lease of life. Mr. Jinnah took full advantage of the situation and started an offensive which ultimately led to Pakistan.'[52] These were strong conclusions, as he (Azad) did not refer to a highly assertive intervention by Jinnah, which did not let Khaliquzzaman enter into any bargain with the Congress.[53] Historians have continued debating over the impact of the failure to form a coalition ministry in UP. Not many have been sympathetic to the views of Azad. Some have argued that the absence of any agreement between the Congress and the Muslim League did not produce any 'weighty consequence'[54] whereas others believe that it was detrimental to the long-term political interests of India.[55] It is further argued that by not agreeing to form a coalition government the Congress did not merely act against one person or two but a whole section of the aristocracy which had rallied to organize itself in order to find space in the power structure.[56] The Congress' refusal has also been viewed as a case of poor statesmanship and indicating a lack of sensitivity to Muslims.[57] It would not have shattered Nehru's prestige if because of him the Muslims had got one ministerial post more than they were entitled to. If Khaliquzzaman had been made a minister, the Muslim League in Uttar Pradesh would most probably have dissolved itself.[58]

II

Azad was concerned that Muslims should view the Congress as a party willing to share power with them. This concern emanated from his perception that Muslims at large had become alienated from the Congress. Other Congress leaders did not share his concern, as they were simply guided by the numerical strength of the Muslims in the Congress rather than the policy of accommodation. In the context of provincial autonomy and ministry formations in various provinces, the desire to gain access to levers of power was bound to emerge. A mere mouthing of platitudes as regards Indian nationalism was not enough, as communities and groups yearned for political power as well. The only way to ensure that Muslims did not feel alienated and marginalized was to accommodate them in the power structure. It was with this conviction that Azad relentlessly pursued many Congress leaders.

One telling instance was an episode in Madras, under the premiership of Rajagopalachari. Soon after the formation of the Congress ministries there was an expansion of the Madras Cabinet.

Azad was keen that more than one Muslim member should be taken in the cabinet, as well as a Muslim among the parliamentary secretaries. Such a step, according to Azad, 'would surely have produced a very agreeable communal atmosphere'.[59] He was hopeful that this would create a good impression, which was essential for the smooth working of the government. In reply to his letter Rajaji said that the total strength of Muslims in the Congress did not justify more than one minister and one parliamentary secretary among the ministers and parliamentary secretaries. Rajaji further said, '*You can realise the trouble arising out of this proportion as you have had experience of it in U.P., Bihar and Bombay. That we have two members out of twenty among ministers and parliamentary secretaries is not bad*'[60] (Emphasis added). He added that, 'if we only had a large number of capable Musalmans in our party I would have doubled and tripled their number'. As an afterthought Rajaji also wished to remind Azad that there was no Christian among the ministers and only one Christian parliamentary secretary.[61] The contrast in approach to the problem of power-sharing among various religious communities is quite clear. Azad's concern was purely political—to win the confidence of the Muslims at large while Rajaji laid emphasis on technicalities and numerical strength in assigning positions of power to social groups.

Apart from Madras Province, there was a similar case in Orissa. In Orissa there was not a single Muslim member in the Cabinet, which Azad thought must be corrected by inducting one. He wrote to Rajendra Prasad, 'From several aspects it is vitally important that we induct one Muslim in the Orissa Cabinet. It would not make a difference except that we would give him a portfolio, but such a step would generate tremendous political impact, which would be invaluable for the Congress.'[62] The Maulana wished to assure Rajendra Prasad, 'Even our worst critic would be silenced that even when there was no compulsion, the Congress was generous enough to take a step such as this. This would please the Muslims there as well as making Muslims outside the state quite happy.'[63] Azad was not making these points out of context since similar voices were emerging from the ground. In a meeting of the Muslims at Cuttack a resolution was adopted to the effect that a deputation of representatives would meet Rajendra Prasad and Biswanath Das, leader of the Congress party in Orissa to pay attention 'towards the Mahomedan claim in respect of the Cabinet'.[64] In the same meeting another resolution was adopted to make an appeal to the Governor 'to exercise his special powers for selecting a Mahomedan in the Cabinet in case the Congress party refused to include one'.[65] Subsequently several communications were sent to the Governor to exercise his special power to secure one Muslim member of the Orissa Cabinet. However, the Governor in response to all these communications issued a communiqué saying, 'that it is not practicable in all circumstances to include a member of that community, nor has he grounds to suppose that the legitimate interest of the Muslim minority in Orissa will suffer as a consequence'.[66] It is interesting in this context to argue that Maulana Azad was neither making a technical point nor indulging in pious hopes whether the interests of the Muslims in Orissa would suffer or not. He was simply wanting to ensure that the Congress be seen as sharing power with Muslims so that the party's adversaries did not take advantage by charging that it was ignoring Muslims' claim to power. He also reminded Rajendra Prasad that during his last visit to Cuttack, when a delegation of Muslims had met him (Rajendra Prasad), he had responded positively, which made Muslims of Orissa quite hopeful of the inclusion of a Muslim in the Cabinet.[67] It was obvious that in the last two years no step was taken in this direction, 'frequent enquiries are made as why no step is initiated in this regard'. He also advised Rajendra Prasad that the Congress should ignore the fact that Maulvi Latifur Rahman was a member of the interim ministry in Orissa, as he was willing to sign the Congress pledge in order to join the ministry and work for the Congress. In yet another letter to Rajendra Prasad he raised the question of Orissa again. He argued that prior to the formation of the ministry there was no presence of the Muslim League in Orissa at all. However, now it seemed to have emerged there. In these circumstances if we take one Muslim in the Cabinet it would make quite an impact, not only on Muslims in Orissa but elsewhere too. Such a step would remove apprehension in the minds of Muslims.[68] Azad's pleading with other Congress leaders did not bear fruits.

Azad was struggling hard within his own party to convince the leadership to realize that it was not only necessary but also vital that the Congress bridge the gap between the party and Muslims at large in order to contain the communal propaganda of the League. One way of doing this was to secure Muslims in the power structure as much as it was possible under the circumstances. Another such occasion arose at the time of the formation of the ministry in Bombay.[69] Subsequently, when the ministry formation was announced it was decided to take Yasin Nurie as the Minister of Public Works.[70] On that occasion Maulana Azad availed the opportunity of making a statement that, 'as the result of his discussion with Sardar Vallabhbhai Patel, Mr. Kher and others it has been decided that Bombay should have two Muslim ministers, one of whom would be Mr. Nurie, who has already assumed office and the other name would be announced later'.[71] This statement of Maulana Azad was followed by another that he issued, reiterating his stand that the Bombay Cabinet should have two Muslims as ministers. He said that, 'in view of the prevailing circumstances it is better to have two instead of one Muslim in the Cabinet, the strength of which should accordingly be increased'. He continued on, ' . . . we have taken account of several important considerations and we had to face many difficulties, the Congress always considers such questions from the higher standpoint of the country's welfare and prepared despite these difficulties to arrive at a decision in spirit of generous mindedness.'[72] He also said that, 'for the other name I cannot come to an immediate decision. . . . I have no doubt that very soon we shall be able to fill up with an able and suitable Muslim the second seat in the Cabinet.'[73] It is significant to note that the Muslim League had become hostile to Yasin Nurie signing the Congress pledge before he joined the Bombay Cabinet. A meeting of the Bombay Presidency Muslim League Parliamentary Board held on 15 August 1937 under the chairmanship of M.A. Jinnah adopted a resolution condemning his action. The meeting also resolved to walk out when the Governor addressed the House and also not attend the Government House functions.[74]

The changed political realities put the Muslim League on a confrontationist course. They harped on the theme that 'Congress

Raj' was synonymous with 'Hindu Raj', where 'Islam was in danger'. The beginning of a bellicose politics by the Muslim League was made with the Bundelkhand by-election, held in July 1937. This was considered a trial of strength between the two. The Muslim League candidate Rafiuddin Ahmad defeated the Congress candidate N.A. Sherwani. In Nehru's analysis the Congress lost because of two reasons: First, 'the cry of Islam in danger, second, bribery on an extensive scale'. He went on, 'there was a third reason also—the strength of caste feeling. Quite 25% of voters were Malkan Rajputs and the Muslim League candidate belonged to the same brotherhood.'[75] Gandhi's reaction to the result was different. He said,

> I do not regard the Jhansi election as a rout. It was an honourable defeat, giving rise to the hope that if we plod away we can effectively take the Congress message to Musalmans. But I still abide by my opinion that the mere taking of the message unaccompanied by substantial work in villages, will not answer our purpose in the end. But it all depends upon the way in which we want to generate power.[76]

Unfortunately, the Congress relied more on uttering generalities about Indian nationalism than on doing work among Muslims. One such instance was the Muslim Mass Contact Programme launched by the Congress. Jawaharlal Nehru conceived of this in the light of the experience during the general elections in 1937 that the Congress had a weak base among the Muslims. To overcome this he thought the Congress should reach out to the Muslims directly. A cell in the AICC was created under the overall responsibility of K.M. Ashraf, who was personally not convinced that Muslims should be approached separately. Ultimately, in the absence of adequate funds and of support from several Provincial Congress Committees, the programme fizzled out.[77]

The failure of the mass contact programme affected the Congress adversely in several ways: it exposed differences of opinion within the Congress; everybody in the party was not as serious as Nehru about enlisting Muslims as Congress workers. The Muslim League saw it as a direct challenge to the rationale for its existence. From this time onwards, the Muslim League became increasingly

Plate 1: Congress Presidential Procession in Ramgarh, 1940.

Plate 2: A group of Congress and Muslim leaders at the Simla Conference, June 1945. (*Standing L to R:* G.B. Pant, M.A. Jinnah, C. Rajagopalachari and Maulana Azad.)

Plate 3: Congress President Azad arrives at the Viceregal Lodge, New Delhi to participate in the Cabinet Mission conference. Azad is seen in conversation with Stafford Cripps, A.V. Alexander and Pethic-Lawrence, 1946.

Plate 4: Maulana Azad along with others being administered Oath of Office, 15 August 1947.

Plate 5: Jawaharlal Nehru with Maulana Azad and others, n.d.

Plate 6: Maulana Azad with Jawaharlal Nehru, C. Rajagopalachari and Sardar Patel, n.d.

Plate 7: Prime Minister Nehru with Education Minister Azad at the Session of the Constitutent Assembly of India held at New Delhi on 16 May 1949.

Plate 8: Prime Minister Nehru with His Excellency C. Rajagopalachari and Maulana Azad at the Prime Minister's residence, 15 November 1949.

Plate 9: A group photo of Cabinet Ministers with H.E. C. Rajagopalachari, the retiring Governor-General, taken at his farewell party on 22 January 1950. *Seated (L to R):* Rafi A. Kidwai, Sardar Baldev Singh, Maulana Azad, Jawaharlal Nehru, H.E. C. Rajagopalachari, Sardar Patel, Rajkumari Amrit Kaur, John Mathai and Jagjivan Ram. *Standing (L to R):* N.V. Gadgil, K.C. Neogy, B.R. Ambedkar, Syama Prasad Mookerjee, Gopalaswami Ayyangar and Jairam Das Daulatram.

Plate 10: Pandit Nehru with Maulana Azad, 1951.

Plate 11: Inauguration of IIT Kharagpur by Maulana Azad, 18 August 1951.

Plate 12: Pandit Nehru looks on as Maulana Azad cuts the ribbon at the Opening Ceremony of the new CSIR building on 10 January 1953.

Plate 13: Prime Minister Nehru being greeted by President Rajendra Prasad and Maulana Azad at Palam Airport after his China trip, November 1954. Indira Gandhi can be seen standing behind Azad.

Plate 14: Jawaharlal Nehru in the background while Maulana Azad bids farewell to G.B. Pant prior to his departure from Palam Airport for Europe, 23 May 1955.

Plate 15: Jawaharlal Nehru with Maulana Azad, n.d.

Plate 16: Maulana Azad passes away. Nehru is standing next to the body.

belligerent towards the Congress. 'With the assumption of ministerships this Hindu Congress is now eliminating Muslim culture and Muslim religion with the help of administrative machinery. The only course for the Muslims is to organise in defence and to prepare for a fight with Hindus. All Muslim Congressmen are consciously or unconsciously traitors from the Muslim camp.'[78] In the same year, the Annual Session of the Muslim League was held in Lucknow, where the Congress was roundly criticized. In his presidential address M.A. Jinnah, accused the Congress of 'pursuing the policy, which is exclusively Hindu and . . . that the Musalmans cannot expect justice or fair play at their hands.'[79] He further argued that the 'Congress attempt under the guise of establishing the mass contact with the Musalmans is calculated to defeat and weaken and break the Musalmans and is an effort to detach them from their accredited leaders.'[80] On other occasions too Jinnah never missed an opportunity to castigate the Congress party and the Congress ministries. In his presidential address at Calcutta, he described the Congress as a 'Hindi body, which cannot be trusted by the Musalmans'.[81] The Congress Muslim leaders were described as Mir Jaffars. People like Maulana Azad and organizations such as Khudai Khidmatgars too were subjected to severe criticism, 'with Congress money, Congress propagandists and with the help of such persons such as Maulana Abul Kalam Azad, the Muslims of the Frontier were being de-Muslimised . . . the Khudai Khidmatgars were an all-India danger.'[82]

From this time onwards the Muslim League adopted a rather belligerent approach to all those whom they thought could pose an ideological and political challenge. Jinnah reiterated, time and again, the validity of his Fourteen Points. He put across other demands as well: (1) the share of Muslims in the state services should be fixed by the statutory enactment; (2) Muslim representation on local bodies should be governed by the principles of the Communal Award, separate electorates, and population strength; (3) coalition ministries should be formed and the Muslim League recognized as the sole representative organization of the Muslims; (4) Muslim-majority provinces should not be affected by any territorial adjustment; (5) Muslim personal laws and culture should be guaranteed by statute; (6) Muslims should have religious and cultural freedom; (7) Urdu should be the national language of India; (8) *Vande Mataram* should not be sung in public.[83]

These demands were a clear portent that in the coming days the communal situation was going to worsen. The Congress as a whole and Nehru in particular did not appear unduly perturbed. Nehru refused to consider Jinnah's demands. He told him that before taking demands into consideration, the political and economic background of the free India, they were all working for, had to be kept in mind.[84]

On another occasion, Nehru argued that there was no 'communal problem' that needed to be tackled; if there was any problem it was to fight the British.[85] Nehru's as well as Congress' consistent refusal to see the menace of growing communalism was to bear heavily upon politics and the freedom struggle.

III

These developments were taking place against the background of changing social realities. There was growing apprehension among Muslims about the political clout that Hindu political workers had started wielding. The growing base of the Congress had brought several sections of society under its influence, while the franchise base too was expanded.[86] The formation of Congress ministries in the Hindu-majority provinces provided a political incentive to the growth of this group of workers, who was politically radical but in social terms, backward looking.[87]

The language controversy was one such instance, which had emerged during the mid-1930s and can be seen in the context of this changing social base of the Congress. After all, it had been an avowed policy of the Congress, under Gandhi's influence to treat Hindustani in Nagari and Persian scripts as the national language since 1925.[88] Now the Hindi 'enthusiasts' had begun deleting many Persian and Urdu words from Hindi.[89]

Apart from the language question, other acts of commission and omission of the Congress ministries gave enough grist to the propaganda mill of the Muslim League, and aggravated the discontentment among Muslims, who saw deliberate provocation in the policies of the Congress ministries. Their discontent focused on issues such as Muslim school-children being forced to sing *Vande Mataram*, the Hindi–Urdu controversy, Muslim representatives being prevented from being elected to the local bodies, etc.[90] Other than the Pirpur Report, which looked into the grievances of the Muslims in the Congress-led provincial governments, another report prepared by the Muslim League exclusively looked into the grievances of Muslims in Bihar and described their pitiable conditions as they lived in fear of attack upon their lives and property.[91]

Maulana Azad dismissed the allegation of the Muslim League that the Congress governments deliberately adopt policies that were against the religious and cultural rights of the Muslims.[92] The main points in the Muslim League's propaganda against the Congress were that it was national only in name, and that the Congress ministries were perpetrating atrocities against the minorities.[93] Azad vehemently denied these charges. 'I can speak from personal knowledge that these allegations were absolutely unfounded.'[94] Azad was able to project his conviction that the Congress remained a body sensitive to the aspirations of all Indians including Muslims. He candidly expressed his disagreement with the Muslim League on many issues and rarely was there an occasion when he saw eye to eye with Jinnah. He did not hesitate in asking that the Congress declare not only the Hindu Mahasabha but also the Muslim League as communal bodies,[95] both of which falsely claimed to represent the interests of their respective communities. But the problem with the Congress was that it did not have any well laid out policy or the list of communal formations, in order to prevent members of the Congress from joining. An enquiry was made at the headquarters of the Congress, 'whether a Congress member can become a member of the Hindu Mahasabha? Is there any decision regarding this matter?'[96] A reply to this letter was quite interesting, and worth quoting in full. It cited Clause C of Article V which read,

No person who is member of any elected Congress Committee shall be member of any similar committee of communal organisation the object and programme of which involved political activities which are, in the opinion of the Working committee, anti-national and in conflict with those of the Congress.[97]

A more interesting part of the reply, which also betrayed total lack of clarity on the part of the Congress as to which organization or party could be declared as communal, was, 'No specific organisations are mentioned as communal. *If you think that the Hindu Mahasabha is such an organisation public opinion must assert itself and prevent the election of a member of Hindu Sabha to Congress Committee*'[98] (Emphasis mine). The important question is why should the Congress have left such a crucial decision to an individual or for that matter be waiting for 'public opinion' to assert itself. Maulana Azad did not agree with this approach of the Congress. He emphatically asserted that no person of the Congress executive could become a member of any communal body. If the Congress had not prepared a list of such formations in view of the fact that one required to be absolutely sure that any formation was communal, still then there was absolutely no doubt that the Muslim League and Hindu Sabha were certainly communal.[99] He further pointed out, 'our lax attitude in this regard has upset many people. Congress Muslims are seriously complaining'. The Congress Muslims felt that despite all kinds of opposition they did not join the League, and they expect that the Hindu members should reciprocate by not joining the Hindu Mahasabha.[100]

While denying the Muslim League any claim of legitimacy Azad was conscious that Muslims must maintain their distinct identity in the face of any difficulty. 'In India we have to simultaneously maintain a relationship between Islam and our Indianness. We, unlike the Europeans can not allow Islam which links us with millions of Muslims elsewhere to be completely merged in Indian nationality alone.'[101] It is important for us to remember that Azad had expressed this conviction steadfastly since the beginning of his political life. What prompted Azad to reiterate the same point all over again in the 1930s was that some measures were being initiated by Congress ministries in the realm of culture, which did not receive universal appreciation even within the party. Azad staunchly defended the Congress and the Congress-ministries but this did not make him abstain from internal criticism of the party. In the United Provinces Sampurnanand had declared that in the field of education, there should be no distinction between Hindus and Muslims. Azad did not agree with such an agenda and held a different view altogether.

> If Sampurnanandji has stated in the UP assembly that in matters of education as well as culture he does not wish to see any distinction between the Hindus and Muslims, then certainly he is talking about a thing which in no way can be acceptable to the Muslims. Neither such a policy has ever been a part of the Congress, nor would Muslims ever agree that in matters such as their education, culture, civilisation and other mark of identity formation should never be compromised and merged with the Indian national identity alone like the Germans and British.[102]

Azad asserted that the avowed policy of the Congress was to safeguard the culture, language and script of the minorities. 'The basic essence of the Karachi Resolution has been that Muslims would get to enjoy their distinct cultural identity rather than this being lost in Indian nationhood. Even the Congress does not visualise such a possibility.'[103]

Apart from this specific issue, Azad was particularly sensitive and assertive about the Urdu language and script. 'Whenever and wherever in any province Hindi script be adopted as the official script, in that case Urdu script shall be considered having come into force (as official script) automatically.'[104] But not everybody agreed with Maulana Azad. Sampurnanand as a minister in the UP Cabinet was held in high esteem. He generated another controversy by raising the question of national language and script in a speech at Banaras. He had said that irrespective of the presence of words of foreign origin, 'the name of our language should have been Hindi, whatever the number of Persian or Arabic words that may form part of it. Muslim poets in olden days have also called it Hindi Zuban.' However, it is difficult to miss his emphasis on Sanskrit in the whole project of the Hindustani.[105] Gandhiji in his reply to Sampurnanand said, 'I agree with what you have written. The Congress has named the language. It has not imposed any other limitations.' He continued on, 'those who are true will not boycott any word on Hindu–Muslim grounds. What can we say about others. Today it has become a fashion to oppose whatever the Congress or Congressmen say.'[106]

All those who were sensitive to the language question were not necessarily adversaries of the Congress. On the contrary, there were many Congressmen who thought that the party (Congress) and its leaders were not paying adequate attention to Muslim susceptibility as regards Urdu. It was felt that Hindi was favoured and promoted at the cost of Urdu. The portents of the issue were not in the best interests of national politics. Other than Congressmen there were fellow travellers who too thought that the Congress was ignoring the cause of Urdu.

The language controversy had begun picking up momentum even before the Congress had formed ministries. The protagonists of Hindi and Urdu had set up their respective camps. Even though it was considered as resolved that Hindustani in both scripts would be the national link language, a controversy flared up at the Nagpur session of the Bharatiya Sahitya Parishad on 24 April 1936. The general mood appeared to favour Hindustani, but of the kind, which Gandhiji described as 'Hindi yani Hindustani'.[107] Such a policy was bound to raise hackles, not only outside but also within the party. Syed Mahmud, a close associate of Jawaharlal felt disillusioned with such a stance of the Congress in general and Gandhi in particular. He wrote a long letter to Rajendra Prasad, charged with emotion.

> After having read your Nagpur address I could not help being emotional about it. It has been feeling rather heavy on my mind thus compelling me to have a dialogue with you, Pandit Nehru and Mahatmaji in order to know whether you people are serious at all about a united nationhood or not. If so then the language question can't be ignored. You may not be aware that after the Nagpur session the Muslims have been quite disturbed about it.[108]
>
> My objection is not like any other political issue. After Gandhiji's address people are talking that concept of the united nationhood seems to have been given up.[109] He reiterated that he would continue to draw inspiration from him (Rajendra Prasad), Gandhi and Nehru.[110] However, the Muslims think that the Urdu–Hindi question has vitiated the atmosphere. After all, it is not that big an issue, which the Hindus cannot concede.[111]

Perhaps a similar letter was addressed to Nehru too. While replying he took recourse to theoretical considerations. In the contemporary world there was a tussle between 'progress' and 'reaction' and in India particularly the vital factor was the problem of poverty and unemployment. All else was subsidiary to it and could only be considered in relation to it.[112] It was implied that the language question did not bother Nehru as much as it bothered Syed Mahmud. However, he stated emphatically, 'In our constitution, it is clearly stated that the language of the country and of the Congress is Hindustani. It is further stated that both the scripts, Nagari and Urdu, are to be officially recognised.'[113] He went on to reassure Syed Mahmud, 'In the Fundamental Rights Resolution of the Karachi Congress it is stated that "the culture, language and scripts of the minorities and the different linguistic areas shall be protected". Now this is as clear as could be.'[114]

Despite these protestations it is doubtful if all Congress members shared his views. The All-India Hindi Prachar Samiti based at Wardha released a pamphlet (in 1936) under the signature of Rajendra Prasad declaring its aims and objectives.[115] The objective of the Samiti was not to replace any provincial language; but to 'provide a language for all inter provincial business, in order to strengthen and cement bonds of nationalism'.[116] What came as a surprise was its declaration that to fulfil the aspiration of the nation, 'we should have a language that will do so not for any province or community but for the country as a whole. *Hindi has been accepted as the most suitable language for this purpose*'.[117] (Emphasis added)

It also said, in what appears as an afterthought. 'When we use the word Hindi, it is not used in a narrow sense, nor do we distinguish it from Hindustani,' since 'Hindi-Hindustani is the only language that can become the national language of India.'[118] Using 'Hindi' and 'Hindustani' as substitutable expressions produced a strange situation where it was not clear as to what the national language of India was? This ambiguity seemed to have been settled in favour of Hindi. In a letter to Nehru, Gandhiji expressed his views candidly, 'You should not hesitate to express the hope that as Hindus and Muslims are one day bound to be one at heart, they will also speak Hindustani, adopt one script, i.e. Devanagari, because of its being more scientific and being akin to the great provincial scripts of the languages descended from Sanskrit.'[119] It is disconcerting that while Nehru was making assertions about both the scripts being used for Hindustani, Gandhi moved away from his earlier position on the question of language and script. One would wonder about the relevance of the Hindustani Committee involving scholars such as Dr. Tarachand, Abdul Haq and Kaka Kalelkar, charged with the responsibility of preparing a Hindustani dictionary and textbooks. The growing differences on the language and script issue led many people to believe that, 'It will serve to indicate the strong public feeling against Hindustani which is calculated to do immense harm to Hindu culture and civilisation if not checked in time.'[120] Rajendra Prasad entertained similar misgivings about Hindustani.[121]

The controversy was to snowball into a major issue affecting the political atmosphere as well as inter-community relations. Muslim fears were not unfounded, particularly as regards the Hindi-Hindustani controversy.[122] The rise of Hindi extremism under the Congress seriously endangered the prospects of India's unity.[123]

Azad was understandably sensitive about the language and script question. His response to the issue was not guided by any grandiose theoretical or linguistic considerations. It was, rather, based on pragmatic considerations. He had reacted strongly when he learnt that in the NWFP, Dr. Abdul Qayum Khan had issued a circular declaring that Urdu alone would be the medium of instruction in the province. The justification given was that the state exchequer would be able to save about Rs. 40,000 annually.[124] This stance of the NWFP government apparently seemed to have been endorsed by the Urdu press. Azad reacted indignantly.

> It is a matter of regret that such a step is being considered a service to Urdu, which actually is fraught with danger. By stopping aid to girls schools run by the Sikhs the government won't save much. But imagine if similar steps were initiated in provinces such as UP, Bihar, Madras, Assam where Hindi was declared the only language and Urdu was deprived of funds! Then none of us would be able to speak up against it.[125]

Azad felt convinced that this step was a setback to any possible realization of minority rights. He raised many pertinent questions. How would the Urdu and Hindi-speaking section of society in Bengal react if Bengali was the only official language of the Presidency?[126] He was also fearful about the prospect of Bihar taking the cue from NWFP and adopting Hindi in Nagari script as the only language in the province for which efforts had been going on for quite some time.[127] Such a step would affect the Gurmukhi-based schools for Sikh girls, and a mirror-policy on the same logic would affect the Urdu-based schools in Bengal, Bihar, UP, Bombay, Central Provinces, Assam and Cuttack.[128]

For a while Azad's concern on the language question was in tune with Nehru's thinking. The latter, in his letter to Syed Mahmud, reflected on the question. 'It astonishes and grieves me to find that in the North West Frontier Province the Hindi script should be discouraged by the state. In your province of Bihar I understand that some people object to facilities being given to the Urdu script by the state. *That seems to me an utterly wrong-attitude*'[129] (Emphasis added). While referring to the language-script controversy, Nehru argued against linking a language with any specific religious community. He said, 'This talk of Muslim culture and Hindu culture in this connection astonishes me.'[130]

In other words, Nehru was opposed to linking any particular language with a religious community. Nehru's approach to the language question was not without its contradictions. The election results of 1937 had established that the Congress did not enjoy the confidence of the Muslim masses, and this led the AICC to launch a Muslim Mass Contact Programme. It was said that special efforts should be made to enrol the Muslim masses 'so that the struggle for freedom may become even more broad based than what it is'.[131] The circular issued by Nehru under his own signature said, 'Complaints reach our office sometimes that notices of meetings, etc., are not always issued in Urdu and so many people remain ignorant of our activities.'[132] Nehru also issued directives in this context to print notices in Urdu in all areas where there was an Urdu-reading population. This will apply more especially to the Punjab, Delhi and UP and to larger towns elsewhere.[133] Quite clearly, though unconsciously, Nehru conceded that Urdu was linked to Muslims. For this reason alone, perhaps, he stressed that to make the Congress more popular among the Muslims, Urdu should be used.

Nehru's concern on the language-script question was not a commonly shared experience within the Congress. On the contrary, the apprehension that there may be some opposition to Urdu was palpable. The interim government in Bihar had issued a circular known as the *Urdu Circular*, which made Urdu compulsory in academic curricula, though it was also interpreted to mean Urdu being made optional all over Bihar except the Santhal division[134] Azad's opinion was that such a major policy decision should have been taken only after consultation with all parties concerned.[135]

He was apprehensive that the Congress would oppose such a move by the interim government of Bihar. Therefore, he sounded a note of caution. 'Taking a pragmatic view of the developments it would be prudent that there should be no opposition from the Congress. And if at all there was any opposition it should be based on legal considerations that no community should ever pressurise others for a decision because this would lead to perpetual tension'.[136]

Azad added, 'The step taken in this regard does not confer on Urdu any primacy, instead at best it had been brought at par with Hindi. Had it been otherwise then the opposition to it would simply have been justified.'[137]

The fear, as regards the Congress' attitude to the language-script question, which was palpable in June 1937, gradually but steadily became more real. The Muslim League and the Urdu press charged that Urdu was being discriminated against. But they were not the only ones to do so. Even sympathizers of the Congress made similar charges against it. For instance, one Ahmad Makhdumi, who complained that literature concerning the Mass Contact programme, which was urgently needed had not reached him for quite some time. He bitterly attacked the Congress leadership for allowing the Haripura session of the Congress to take on Hindu colours (*Haripura mein All India Congress ka jo salana jalsa hua, usko bilkul hi Hinduana rang mein pesh kiya gaya*).[138] He said that apart from papers sympathetic to the Muslim League, a paper such as Medina from Bijnor too was highly critical of such biases.[139] He wanted to know from Muslim leaders of the Congress if they protested against such an attitude? He bemoaned that because of such attitudes Muslims were running away from the Congress. He asserted that, Muslims would not be lagging behind others in making sacrifices for the country's freedom if they (Congress leaders) showed sensitivities to Muslim concern for cultural and linguistic issues.[140] The Medina was known for taking a pro-Congress stand on several issues. It was also scathingly critical of the Congress. Referring to the Faizpur Congress and the neglect of Urdu, the paper said, 'the second biggest mistake of those responsible for running the affairs of the Congress is that the guide prepared for Faizpur Congress, is only in Hindi, Marathi and English language and script. By doing this they have given proof of their anti-Urdu stance'.[141] In its editorial comments it referred to the annual session of the Congress at Lucknow and said that similar complaints were raised then also. It commented further, 'we know that programmes, instructions and announcements of the district and subordinate Congress committees are issued in Hindi only'. It also objected to gates and arches being named after historical figures such as Shivaji while ignoring other such figures as Tipu Sultan.[142] The paper appealed to the Congress to keep itself free from the virus of communalism.

In view of these protests, the AICC issued a letter advising that in the coming session of the Congress in Mahakaushal, care must be taken that a number of gates and arches should be erected in commemoration of old Congress Muslim leaders; extensive use should be made of Urdu script side by side with Hindi; no propaganda in any form be carried on for cow protection and other similar movements; the presidential address as well as other proceedings . . . be translated and published in good and intelligible Urdu; no attempt should be made to prohibit the sale of meat in hotels and shops.[143] The letter sounded a little apologetic, 'I hope dear friend you will not misunderstand my sentiments on the point. I am in intimate touch with the Muslim press and I consider it my duty to inform you in good time.'[144] The ground for sounding so was presented in a manner as if these were not important issues before the Congress as they were meant to cater to Muslims sentiment, 'I know for a fact that apart from their exaggeration these are after all trifles and as a rule one ought to ignore them.'[145] This attitude of the Congress leadership to consider sensitive issues such as language, identity and culture as 'trifles' was not helping the party at all. It was frequently pointed out not just by foes but even friends of the Congress that it needed to sensitise itself on these questions. After all the Congress was not living in a political vacuum not to have realized that non-resolution of these issues was making it difficult to bridge the gap between the communities. There were occasions when the Congress wished to prod its members to take a sensitive view of issues under discussions. One such instance was the UP Provincial Congress Committee's communication which said, that all Congress Committees must be instructed that they should keep all important documents in Hindi and Urdu both. Even in speeches, simple words of Urdu and Hindi should be used. The Congress literature should not have any sign, which might give the impression of favouring any particular community.[146] This communication was prepared in the light of suggestions made by the Muslim members of the UP PCC in the context of the Muslim Mass Contact programme.[147] One might have hoped that letters and other communications specially the one addressed to the Secretary, Reception Committee of the Mahakaushal, would make a difference. But it did not appear to be the case. While the preparations to hold the annual session of the Congress at Tripuri were underway, a Congress worker from Jubbulpur who seemed to be involved in this complained,

> literature hitherto published and handbills printed in connection with the Congress are in language which is 90 per cent Hindwi Sanscrit. Then to begin the work "Shri Ganesha" is said and for all other purposes all gods are recalled such as Sarswati-Lakshmi. *Not one Urdu notice has been published and your Hindustani is buried deep in the river Narbada.*[148]

He brought a serious charge against the Congress that all those involved with the Tripuri Congress including the staff, paid and semi-paid were from the Hindu community. Shops are exclusively allotted to Hindus and every effort was made 'to make it look like a session completely Hindu'.[149] The list of charges appeared to be long. The letter said, 'Local Hindu Mahasabha leaders have been permitted to join the Reception Committee and they have been given high offices under it. This must react on Muslims.'[150] The concluding part of the letter was a significant pointer that due to developments such as these, 'it is certain that Mussalmans will desert it leaving us two or three old Congress Muslims to face the Music'.[151]

Apprehension was writ large in many such communications that insensitivity of the Congress in these matters might result in Muslims abandoning the party. This is true that the susceptibilities of Muslims as regards the Urdu question were quite high. Many Congress Muslim workers were showing similar concerns. It was pointed out by many that, 'there are two issues of special concern; one is that of Urdu and another of Congress and Muslims. They both are interlinked. The first issue is so important that Mr. Jinnah is repeatedly raising it. If the first one is not resolved, finding a solution to the second one can well nigh be difficult.'[152] Similarly, the Jamiatul Ulema-i-Hind was a fellow traveller of the Indian National Congress, ever since its formation towards the end of 1919. It always supported the cause of India's freedom. However, it remained sensitive to questions of identity, culture and religion of Muslims. It reacted rather sharply when the government of Orissa resolved that Oriya alone would be the medium of instruction.[153] It said that taking a decision such as this meant that not only Urdu would be wiped out but religion too.[154] In a similar fashion charges were brought against the Congress government in the Central Provinces that it was pursuing policies, which were against Urdu. Maulana Abdul Haq, famous scholar of Urdu, had alleged that in Betul and other places serious efforts were made to eliminate Urdu language from the curriculum of the school.[155] The significance of such an allegation was underlined, 'I feel that serious statements like this with the authority of Maulvi Abdul Haq behind them must be dealt with at the earliest opportunity. In any case the statements call for a clear declaration of Government policy on the subject of Urdu language and Muslim education in your provinces.'[156] The Government of Central Provinces and Berar issued a press communiqué, which tried to address some of the issues raised in regard to Urdu and education for Muslims.[157] Such a policy statement issued by the Government of the Central Provinces and Berar notwithstanding, the general impression persisted that the Congress was ignoring Urdu.

These observations were reflective of a deeper anxiety as to what would happen to Urdu and therefore Muslim culture. In this regard except Aftab Ahmad, no body seemed to have directly communicated with Maulana Azad. There does not seem to be a record of a reply from Maulana Azad to Aftab Ahmad, but it appears that Azad took serious note of it, which was amply manifested in his communications with other Congress leaders. He was quite disturbed by the attitude of his party, and felt that it was wilfully sidelining Urdu, contrary projections notwithstanding. He wrote to Rajendra Prasad rather curtly,

> Irrespective of the province the session of the Congress takes place its language policy must remain the same and be followed likewise However, this is not so because of the negligence of the reception committee. All signboards are put up only in Nagari. Tickets, receipts and other propaganda materials are published only in Nagari. *Nowhere is Urdu to be seen*. (Emphasis added)[158]

He added,

> If only such issues had not acquired a communal colour, then one could still ignore all this. But under the circumstances it is strongly feared that such things are noticed strongly and the message is widespread that the Congress is deliberately ignoring Urdu. [159]

For a person who was given to restraint in expression, it appears that a sense of frustration, led him to write, '*For several years this issue is being raised and by now not only our adversary but several Congress Muslims too are complaining of a similar attitude*'.[160] (Emphasis added)

After the Haripura Congress, the issue was discussed by the Congress Working Committee and it was resolved that such a lapse would not be allowed to take place in the future.[161] When the time for the Tripuri Congress approached, Azad was assured by Acharya Kripalani that Urdu would be used in the nameplates, banners, etc. In order to ascertain that adequate measures had been taken Azad went around the Congress Nagar only to discover to his dismay that Urdu was nowhere in evidence. 'After the session began I went around the Congress Nagar in order to ascertain the claim of Urdu having been used, it was nowhere to be seen.'[162]

He could not hide his anguish. 'Perhaps in order to please me, nameplates of the Working Committee members in Urdu were put up on their huts, except that Urdu was nowhere used.'[163]

Azad was worried as to what would happen since very shortly the Ramgarh session of the Congress was going to take place, which he was to address as President. He did not say much but at the same time he did not entertain much hope from the Congress, 'In this regard I look up to you only', he wrote to Rajendra Prasad.[164] Giving expression to his anger, he wrote,

> Please pay attention to such matters. Apparently a small thing such as this may cause big harm and instead of finding solutions to problems they are getting complicated. The moot question is whether the Congress has taken a decision about the national language in both scripts or not? If yes then shouldn't signboards in the annual session of the Congress be put up in Urdu as well? If this position is not disputed then we are duty bound to implement it.[165]

Azad let his mind be known on the eve of the Ramgarh session of the Congress, 'Whatever propaganda material the reception committee brings out in Hindi, they ought to be in Urdu as well.'[166]

Azad also asked for an Urdu typewriter to be available at the venue of the Ramgarh session. Towards the end of this rather long letter Azad sounded somewhat pessimistic as if he had no hope of a helpful response from the Congress. He said, 'Please inform me if arrangements would be made in this regard or not. If people don't agree with all this, I must know about it in advance.'[167] It seems that as regards its attitude towards Urdu the Congress was unable to inspire confidence even in a person like Maulana Azad, what to speak of ordinary Muslims who still wanted to remain on board. However, Urdu was not the only issue which caught the attention of Muslims, as there were many knotty issues, which too needed urgent attention by all, the Congress in particular.

IV

The language controversy was bad enough with the Congress not abiding by its own stand on Hindustani written in Persian and Nagari scripts. It was becoming clear that it favoured Nagari as a matter of deliberate policy. In this atmosphere of growing mutual distrust between the communities, an even more disturbing trend was seen—the blatant participation of several Congress members in communal riots. This serious charge was levelled not by the Muslim League, which could be considered motivated, but by Congress workers themselves. Jameel Ahmad Khan, a Municipal Commissioner and a member of the Congress, wrote that many Congress workers in Bhagalpur district had openly joined hands with the Hindu Mahasabha and delivered inflammatory speeches against Muslims. He said, 'Our leaders have remained completely communal before, during and after the riots.'[168] Several Congressmen also gave false statements about the Muslims there to the press.

Jameel Khan added, 'If such is the mentality of the Congress people, I do not know how far it can succeed in enlisting support and co-operation of any other minorities, who cannot think for a moment that their interests are safe in the hands of the Congress.'[169] For Azad, the disquieting aspect of the Bhagalpur riots was not merely that of Congressmen's involvement but the question of dual membership, where Congressmen could also become members of the Hindu Mahasabha.[170] He was apprehensive that if the situation was not checked the Congress would let all its gains go waste.[171] He demanded that the Congress should stop any member of its executive at any level from becoming a member of any communal organization.[172] He conceded that the Congress had not prepared any checklist of communal bodies as a guideline, but it was clear that at least the Muslim League and the Hindu Mahasabha were indisputably communal.[173] He cautioned, 'Not paying attention to these problems is lamentable, particularly to the Congress Muslims who argue that despite everything they do not enter the League. The Hindu Congress members should follow this policy.'[174] (Implying that they should not join the Hindu Mahasabha.)

Azad also pointed out that similar complaints had been received from the Central Provinces and advised that all such Congressmen be warned to keep away from the Mahasabha. At the same time he feared that the Congress might not pay heed to such warnings.

I have been having this constant feeling that these are issues to which we hardly pay any attention. However, if ever we were to take care of these issues they would go a long a way in winning over the Muslims who do not disagree with our objectives. But the problem is that we hardly bother about them.[175]

Azad was aware that resentment among the Muslim members of the Congress was growing. Increasingly instances were cited to prove a point that the party did not show adequate concern with regard to Muslim grievances. The Congress Muslims held a public meeting on 28 September 1938 in order to protest against the Congress high command and adopted resolutions. The first one read,

This meeting of all the Congress Muslims of Ranchi, appeal to the Provincial Congress Committee and All India Congress Committee that the party is ignoring them and the treatment that is meted out is deplorable. Therefore we appeal to the High Command to mend its way so that the party did not go further into abyss and it should work hard to make it popular.[176]

In the same meeting another resolution was adopted which sounded like a warning note to the high command of the Congress. It was concerning the ill treatment that was meted out to Shah Mohammad Zubair, vice-chairman, Gaya municipality, by the chairman of the same municipality on communal considerations. The resolution said, 'It condemns the silence of the high command and appeals to the provincial government and the Congress committee to conduct an enquiry and punish the chairman. Or else it would generate strong disliking and hatred against the high command.'[177] Azad's concern to assuage the hurt feelings of the Muslims in general and Congress Muslims in particular in places such as Bhagalpur, Ranchi, Gaya, etc., was strong. He wanted quick intervention in order to stem the slide. He sent a telegram to Rajendra Prasad seeking his personal involvement in the matter.[178]

It was not the first time Azad was raising all these issues. He had done so earlier too. In a letter he talked about issues which were raised by the Urdu press and argued that if immediate measures were not initiated, it would gravely hurt the long-term interests of the Congress.[179] He was very keen that the Congress be seen sharing power with Muslims, in order to allay their fears that their interests might be ignored in Congress-ruled provinces. He was equally anxious that the Congress be seen to be giving adequate representation to Muslims at various levels. As already stated, there were instances when the entry of Muslims into the elected bodies of the Congress was blocked.[180] The AICC office frequently received similar complaints from the Muslim Congress workers. In some cases remedies were sought, while other went unattended. A Muslim Congress worker from Orissa sent a complaint to the AICC office that discrimination was practised in electing delegates to the Provincial Congress Committee, on grounds of religious affiliations.[181] It was also stated that, 'this neglect on the part of the local Congressmen is extremely deplorable'.[182] This was not an isolated event as there were similar complaints pouring in from other parts of India too. Idris Khan Lodhi of Badaun had written to the AICC office that in spite of his twenty years of membership of the Congress and service to the cause of Indian nationalism he was not allowed to stand for the PCC. He was subjected to a highly objectionable propaganda campaign.[183] As a mark of protest he resigned, which was followed by 75 other Muslim members of the Congress on the same ground.[184] The Congress was receiving such complaints too frequently. The office-bearers at the AICC were responding to these issues from time to time more in a way of seeking the goodwill of the local Congress leaders. There were instances, where they sounded apologetic, a point, which has already been discussed earlier. Similar such complaint was received from Central Provinces. The Secretary, Hingan Ghat Muslim Mass Contact Committee, wrote that due to communal propaganda carried out by the Congress workers among the primary members, 'Muslim Congressmen generally fail to attract the primary members-electorate and are generally defeated in elections to the various Congress committees.'[185] It was further suggested by him that there should be reservation of seats for Muslims, at taluqa and town level committees. Similar reservation was suggested at the level of Provincial Congress Committees as well as AICC. It was argued that arrangements such as these alone would ensure Muslims' representation.[186] This was suggested in the hope that

Muslims would join the Congress in big numbers, which would be quite a rebuff to the Muslim League, which had said that the Congress was a Hindu party. But the AICC found the suggestion of reservation of seats for Muslims inconsistent with the party's constitution and ideals of nationalism. It was not explained if keeping Muslims outside the power structure within the party was the result of communalization of society and politics, but admitted that, '. . . in the last delegates elections, Congress Muslims found considerable amount of difficulty in getting themselves elected.'[187] In the light of these experiences it was suggested to form such constituencies as might consist of majority of members of the Congress. It was vainly hoped that such a step might be able to attract more Muslim to the Congress.[188]

Complains such as these persisted. It was almost a frequent experience of Muslim Congress members that despite their best efforts it was difficult if not impossible for them to get elected to various positions within the party. Maulana Azad, too was receiving letters, which bemoaned the attitude of the Hindu Congress members at the provincial and district level. Azad had been hinting at these developments for some time. Then came a time, when he found himself at the end of his tether,

> There is another important matter of membership of the Muslims in the Congress committees. I am thoroughly exasperated with the present developments. As a last resort I had proposed that the Constitution Sub-Committee of the Congress should bring about certain amendments, which would ensure certain seats being reserved for the Muslims in Congress bodies. We must do something about it.[189]

It is remarkable that Azad had to ask for reservation of seats for Muslims within the organizational structure of his party. This should not be confused with the Congress opposing reservation of seats for Muslims in the central legislature and in certain provinces (as demanded by the Muslim League and other Muslim leaders in 1928). After Azad's repeated reminders, one would have expected that the Congress would pay attention to these matters. But the complaint that entry of Muslims in the Congress was being blocked, continued unabated. Abdul Aleem Aabee wrote to Gandhi complaining that the Muslims' claim to various posts in the local board as well as the district board was deliberately ignored even though many able and nationalist Muslims had been enthusiastic about these elections, defying the call for boycott by the Muslim League.[190] The letter ended with an earnest appeal to the Mahatma to bring intractable problems such as these to an end.[191]

The complaints made against and objection taken to Congress policies on the issues, discussed so far, did not come from the Muslim League. There were Congressmen, who did not wish to compromise on their loyalty to the party, yet found its policies disturbing. There were individuals and groups outside the Congress too who raised similar objections to Congress policy as regards minorities. Sir Sultan Ahmad, a prominent barrister at Patna, wrote to Rajendra Prasad, 'When the Congress decided to accept office last year, no-one outside the Congress circle was more pleased than myself.' He continued,

> For a long time and even now I feel that those who are opposed to the Congress indulge in exaggeration and tall talk and for a long time I attached no importance to the catalogue of grievances placed before me, but within the last few months I was compelled to study the attitude of the Congress Ministry towards the Muslim community and other minorities. I have been led to most depressing conclusions.[192]

In response, Rajendra Prasad was not prepared to concede on the points raised by Sir Sultan. Instead he put the blame on others.

> I am aware that there is much propaganda against the Congress Ministry, particularly of Bihar, by League circles, by Bengalis and by Kisan Sabhaites. . . . So far as I am aware the Congress ministry has done nothing to the prejudice of Musalmans and if my impression is incorrect I should be obliged to be corrected so that any injustice which may have been done can be rectified.[193]

The overall response of the leaders of the Congress was to ignore complaints about the party and the government's style of functioning. Any complaint was automatically seen as the handiwork of adversaries.

The attack of the Muslim League on the Congress was yet to come, which it did at the special session held at Calcutta in 1938, where Fazlul Haq said that in the light of past experience, it was useless to expect from the Congress any fair play and equitable treatment.[194] In the same meeting, Jinnah thundered, 'But we cannot surrender, submerge or submit to the dictates . . . of the Congress high command which is developing into a totalitarian and authoritarian caucus.'[195] Such bellicosity was not without a basis, because the Congress particularly at provincial and local levels had acted very much contrary to the avowed policy of the party as regards inter-community relations. This behaviour was reflected in the report of the Sub-committee appointed by the Congress Working Committee to look into the matter. It said, 'It is evidently true that all over, Congressite Hindu friends have become openly communal.'[196] Despite this condemnation, there were leaders who still refused to admit the basis of these complaints not just from the Muslim League but from Muslim members of the Congress. C. Rajagopalacari was one—he advised Rajendra Prasad to ignore all this,

> I am afraid that we are going the wrong way to deal with these communal attacks. The Musalmans who refuse, without sufficient thought, to join the Congress, now see that there is no way to political influence and power. *They are desperate.* If we only allow them to work off their anger, I believe that large bodies of them will join the Congress at the next election.[197] (Emphasis added)

Such an outburst by a senior Congress leader was a sign that the Congress was not willing to look within with regard to infirmities of the party's policies.

The Muslim League itself took strong exception to certain other moves of the Congress, which, though meant to be people-oriented, did not go down well even with some sections of Muslims. These were the 'Wardha scheme of education', the singing of '*Vande Mataram*', the language-script question, and the Vidyamandir scheme of education.[198]

The League took full advantage of Muslim sense of unease and fanned the flames of discontent among the Muslim masses.[199] The League appointed a committee to look into Muslim grievances in Congress-ruled provinces, and later published its findings, popularly known as the Pirpur Report.[200] It was said in the Report rather bitterly:

The Indian National Congress' conception of nationalism is based on the establishment of a national state of the majority community in which other nationalities and communities have only secondary rights. The Muslims think that no tyranny can be (as) great as tyranny of the majority and they believe that only that state can be stable which gives equal rights and equal opportunities to all communities no matter how small. They attach great importance to this principle, which alone can safeguard the rights of the Muslims and other minorities. The Muslims have made it clear more than once that besides the question of religion, culture, language and personal laws; there is another question equally important for their future. They must secure definitely their rights and their due share in the national life, government and administration of the country.[201]

The common complaint of Muslims in the Congress-ruled provinces was that they were now much worse off than under the previous government.[202]

The irony of the political climate was such that not only were Muslims complaining against the Congress ministries, the Hindus and Sikhs too were complaining of discriminations in the Congress-ruled NWFP. In a printed memorandum addressed to Subhas Chandra Bose, they raised five issues: (1) Minorities were insecure in the Congress ministry; (2) Provincial Congress committee was under the influence of Red Shirts, and their sole aim was to destroy the Hindus. Conspiracies were organized in order to take away business and jobs from Hindus and Sikhs; (3) Sympathies were expressed with those who kidnap Hindu women. In Bannu and Dera Ismail Khan, no arrangements are made for the security of life and property of Hindus; (4) The '*Vande Mataram*' song was hardly sung as all the meetings of the Congress were started with recitation of the Quran and slogan of 'Nara-i-Takbir' rent the air; (5) The Agricultural Debtors' Relief Act, etc., were meant to drive the Hindus away so that a 'pure Muslim Raj' could be established.[203] It demanded creation of a permanent sub-committee in order to supervise the works of the Frontier Ministry as it also asked for an enquiry against Qazi Ataullaha Khan Sahib, the minister of education by judges from outside the province.[204] The basic problem around this time was that those who were at the helm of power, seemed to invoke majoritarian principles which was at variance with the perceptions of the minority.

The question that arises is whether the charges levelled against the Congress governments were true. It has been argued, 'It is worth the effort so as to place the Congress-baiting in perspective, and uncover the motives behind such a well-orchestrated campaign.'[205] What should be recognized is that the Congress ministries rushed towards legislative measures as regards certain issues particularly the ones that ameliorated the conditions of the cultivating class. In the NWFP, Naubat Chowkidari was done away with.[206] The Agricultural Debtors Relief Act, limited the rate of interest realized by moneylenders, and cancelled interest owed to creditors on 1 October 1937.[207] In UP, the Tenancy Bill was an important step to improve the lot of the tenant and was a precursor to the abolition of Zamindari in 1952.[208] Significant pieces of legislation were rushed through in the Central Provinces and Berar such as the Relief of Indebtedness Act, the CP revision of Land Revenue of Estates Act, the CP Tenancy Amendment Act, etc.[209] In Orissa as well as Bombay serious efforts were made through legislation to help tenants and save farmers from the clutches of the moneylenders.[210] These were steps initiated by the Congress ministries, which were in the larger interest of the masses. There were also instances where steps initiated by the provincial governments helped the Muslims at large. The Rural Development Scheme in UP benefited the Muslims, as they also fared well in public services. The Governors of CP, Bihar, and Bombay reported that in their respective provinces the Muslims did not suffer any serious injustice at the hands of the Congress ministries. These Governors also noted that the ministers were usually anxious to err on the side of generosity wherever Muslim interests were affected.[211]

Such instances notwithstanding, what mattered were measures adopted by the Congress as part of larger policies, which did not bring much cheer to Muslims. The Muslims felt considerably alienated. Around this time the Muslim League began claiming to be the sole spokesman for the entire Muslim community, while on the other the Congress claimed spokesmanship for the whole country.[212] The League began growing in status and strength since there was no other body with the credentials to articulate the 'Muslim' viewpoint. The League began making demands such as that any future constitutional arrangement should have the communities' consent as its basis.[213] Thus, under the leadership of Jinnah, the Muslim League began taking confident steps to make good its claims to represent all Muslims.

A year had passed since Azad in his letter to Rajendra Prasad had urged that the Hindu Mahasabha and the Muslim League be declared communal bodies.[214] The communal situation had not become any better. It was becoming more complex and ominous. Azad despite perceiving the Muslim League as a communal body expressed his desire that the Congress negotiate with it to arrive at a solution to the communal problem. Against the background of an appeal for communal harmony by Sikandar Hyat Khan, Azad said, 'After your discussion with Mahatmaji there should be no reason why the Congress and the Muslim League should not move closer to each other. Muslim League should appoint a few representatives.'[215]

Azad was eager that the Congress should respond immediately to overtures from the League. 'I have come to know from Choudhary Khaliquzzaman that the Muslim League Working Committee is meeting in Delhi. If you immediately send a letter to Sikandar Hayat Khan then it would have a positive effect on the League.'[216]

Why was Azad, who consistently since the days of *Al-Hilal* spoke against the Muslim League, starting to advocate negotiations with the League? One plausible answer could be that Azad was taking a pragmatic approach to a solution of a worsening communal problem. According to him, the communal impasse was the result of many factors, including the lethargic approach of the Congress. He did not mince words when he argued, 'The experiences of the last eighteen years are indications enough that the more we delayed efforts to find a solution to the communal problem, the more it became complicated and in the same proportion the demands of communal Muslims grew.'[217]

Wiser by hindsight, he wondered whether an opportunity had been lost when joint electorates, the cherished ideal of the Congress, could have been achieved by conceding certain demands raised by the League.

In 1926 the Muslim League had accepted joint electorates along with the separation of Sindh, reform in the Frontier and the notion of the majority in Bengal and the Punjab. Only if we had clinched the issue then the conflict would have been over forever. And above all the poison of separate electorates could have been wiped out.[218]

Almost a decade after the Nehru Committee Report to which Azad had extended all support, and had wanted other Muslims to support, he lamented that if the Congress had only agreed with Jinnah for reservation of seats in Bengal and Punjab in the absence of adult franchise, 'then by this time the situation would have improved'.[219]

Azad was convinced that the failure to concede the demands of the League had resulted in the imposition of the Communal Award because of which political unity and communal harmony had been jeopardized.[220] That was not all. Even the prospect of achieving joint electorates became bleak,[221] and the Congress was not able to reach definite agreements with others on communal issues.[222] Azad quite consciously was avoiding blaming the Congress squarely for having failed on the front of resolving communal tangles.

In the late 1930s Azad had three primary concerns. One was to bring about improvement in inter-community relations. In order to work towards it he did not miss any opportunity to remind the Congress that the issue required sensitive handling. This could be either by accommodating Muslims in the power structure or by making efforts towards communal reconciliation. In Bihar as elsewhere, the communal situation was worsening around this time. Azad was distressed about this. 'I strongly desire that all political questions must be kept aside for the time being and work towards improving relations between Hindus and Muslims, which have deteriorated in the last two years.'[223] This would go a long a way in keeping Muslims away from the League.[224]

Azad's second preoccupation was to dispel the impression that the Congress was unsympathetic towards Muslims. He defended Congress-led ministries against all criticism. His third concern during the late 1930s was to maintain discipline within the party. He was ideologically closer to those who were sceptical of the Congress Socialist Party and who did not sympathize with any radical programme.

Azad's stature in the Congress was moving upward during the late 1930s. On 16 April 1936 under Jawaharlal Nehru's presidentship of the Congress, Azad was elected a CWC member. He became a member of the Parliamentary Sub-committee along with Vallabhbhai Patel and Rajendra Prasad. This came to be known as the 'High Command' of the Congress. He tried his best to steer the Congress through a maze of complex political issues. He did not receive support from all the Congress leaders. Vallabhbhai Patel thought that the Maulana did not do enough to secure a better power position for the Hindu minority in Muslim-majority provinces. Patel wrote bitterly to Rajendra Prasad,

> It is not true that we have no policy in the minority provinces. The fact is that on the communal question our decisions in all matters rest with Maulana Saheb and these provinces are also under his charge. In Punjab we have done nothing to guide or advise in any matter and we have left the decisions in the province entirely to Maulana Saheb. He has even directed the Congress party to vote with the Government on (any) obnoxious measure. In Bengal, Mr. Huq meets him almost (every) other day and he himself being on the spot naturally is in sole charge.[225]

There was another occasion for Sardar Patel to take a jibe at the Maulana. Within the Congress circles it was quite clear that Subhas Bose might contest for the Congress presidentship again in 1939. There was some pressure on Azad to contest for the post, which he did not wish to.[226] Patel thought that Azad was himself angling for the post. He (Sardar Patel) wrote to Rajendra Prasad, 'I never dreamt that he (Maulana Azad) will stoop to such dirty and mean tactics for re-election to an office which is sacred and is held in highest esteem by all people of the land.'[227] These were strong words indeed, by one important leader about another respected figure in the Congress, devoted to the cause of freedom and harmonious inter-community relations. Azad was elected president of the Congress in 1940, but the question hangs, was he a unanimous choice or a compromise?

NOTES

1. B.B. Mishra, *The Unification and Division of India*, Oxford University Press, Delhi, 1990, p. 319.
2. Ibid., p. 325. For more details as regards provisions of this Act and their critique refer to Sumit Sarkar, *Modern India 1885-1947*, Macmillan, Delhi, 1983, pp. 336-7.
3. S.R Mehrotra, 'The Congress and Partition of India', in C.H. Philips and M.D. Wainwright, eds., *The Partition of India:, Policies and Perspective 1935-1947*, George Allen and Unwin, London, 1970, p. 189.
4. Ibid.
5. Anita Inder Singh, *The Origins of the Partition of India, 1936-1947*, Oxford University Press, Delhi, 1987, p. 2.
6. Sarkar, op. cit., p. 338.
7. Singh, op. cit., p. 2.
8. As cited in Salil Misra, *A Narrative of Communal Politics: Uttar Pradesh 1937-39*, Sage Publications, Delhi, 2001, p. 50.
9. Mishra, op. cit., p. 316.
10. Misra, op. cit., p. 72.
11. Mohammad Sajjad, review article of Salil Misra's *A Narrative of Communal Politics*, op. cit., in *Khuda Bakhsh Library Journal*, Patna, 2002, p. 18
12. Rajendra Prasad to Syed Mahmud, 5 October 1936, RP Papers, File no. 1/36 Collection II, National Archives of India (hereafter NAI). In this letter Rajendra Prasad replied, 'It seems to be unanimous opinion of us all that we must set up as many Muslim candidate as we can on behalf of the Congress directly. . . .'
13. Nehru to Rajendra Prasad, 21 July 1937, RP Papers, File no. 1/37(1-RP(PSF-1), 1937, vol. 1, NAI.
14. Nehru, as cited in B.R. Nanda, 'Nehru, the Indian National Congress and the Partition of India, 1935-47', in Philips and Wainwright, op. cit., p. 153.
15. Mehrotra, in ibid., p. 189.
16. Ayesha Jalal, *The Sole Spokesman: Jinnah the Muslim League and the Demand for Pakistan*, Cambridge University Press, Cambridge, 1985, p. 33.
17. Ibid.
18. Vallabhbhai wrote to Dr. Khare, on 11 July 1937, 'Secure Maulana Azad's sanction regarding Muslim members' choice', in P.N. Chopra, ed., *Collected Works of Sardar Patel*, vol. VII, p. 6 (hereafter

CWSP). Subsequently on 15 July 1937 Dr. Khare informed the Sardar that Usuf Sharif was taken in the Ministry at Nagpur.

19. Uma Kaura, *Muslims and Indian Nationalism: The Emergence of the Demand for India's Partition, 1928-1940*, Manohar, Delhi, 1977, p. 116.
20. Singh, op. cit., p. 21. However, Khaliquzzaman held a different opinion, 'Rafi Qidwai brought me a message from Pandit Pant that on his way to Wardha he would stay in Lucknow to meet me for a talk. . . . Pandit Pant, asked me how many seats in the Cabinet I would demand in case of a coalition between the Congress and the League, I replied: Three in nine and two in six, i.e. one-third of the total strength of the Cabinet whatever it may be.' Choudhary Khaliquzzaman, *Pathway to Pakistan*, Longmans, Pakistan Branch, 1961.
21. Ibid. Contrary to the suggestions made by Anita Inder Singh it appears that Azad instead of looking suspicious was taking quite an active part in the negotiations right through and regretted its breakdown, 'We regret that we did not fully succeed in our attempt in spite of the best endeavours on both sides.' *The Leader*, 4 August 1937.
22. *The Leader*, 4 August 1937. These conditions set before the Muslim League in UP were not known till such time as the negotiations broke down. Khaliquzzaman said that Maulana Azad presented these conditions to him in the presence of G.B. Pant on 15 July 1937 in Khaliquzzaman, op. cit., p. 160.
23. Khaliquzzaman, ibid., p. 161.
24. Nehru to Rajendra Prasad, File no. 1/37, 1-RP, PSF(1) 1937, RP Papers, NAI.
25. Ibid.
26. Ibid.
27. Khaliquzzaman, op. cit., pp. 156-7.
28. Ibid.
29. Azad, *India Wins Freedom: The Complete Version*, Orient Longman, Madras, 1988, p. 171.
30. Ibid.
31. *The Leader*, 20 July 1937.
32. Ibid.
33. Azad, *India Wins Freedom*, p. 171.
34. Ibid.
35. Ibid., p. 172.
36. Ibid.
37. Salil Misra, op. cit., p. 110.

38. Gandhiji to Jawaharlal Nehru, 22 July 1937, *CWMG*, vol. 72, 1937-8, p. 56.
39. Press statements of Khaliquzzaman, *The Leader*, 4 August 1937. Earlier, there was some speculation that the Muslim League too had put some conditions before the Congress. 'It is believed Maulana Azad has gone to Bombay for securing the approval of the Congress Parliamentary Sub-committee to the scheme evolved here by the League and Congress leaders for coalition by the League and Congress party in the UP, legislature.' *The Leader*, 20 July 1937. However, the next day it was reported in newpapers that Maulana Azad did meet Sardar Patel, regarding the Muslim member of the Bombay Cabinet. It did not mention any talk on coalition negotiations in UP. *The Leader*, 21 July 1937.
40. Ibid. Khaliquzzaman also stated that the 'talks started 3 months before thus failed on the 28'.
41. *The Leader*, 15 July 1937.
42. Khaliquzzaman, op. cit., p. 157.
43. *The Leader*, 25 July 1937.
44. Anita Inder singh, op. cit., p. 22.
45. Ibid., pp. 22-3. It has already been pointed out that Azad was the one who insisted that there must be a coalition government in the United Provinces.
46. Ibid., p. 23.
47. Bimal Prasad, 'Congress Versus the Muslim League 1935-37', in Richard Sisson and Stanley Wolpert, eds., *Congress and Indian Nationalism: The Pre-independence Phase*, Oxford University Press, Delhi, 1988, pp. 316-18.
48. Khaliquzzaman, op. cit., p. 153.
49. Mishra, op. cit., p. 318.
50. Ibid.
51. Ibid.
52. Azad, *India Wins Freedom,* p. 171. It is possible to argue that putting the blame at the door of Pandit Nehru was not a case of objective judgement. However, it remains a fact that after the failure of the negotiations Muslim League leaders thought in terms of downright opposition to the Congress rule. By doing this, 'we might be able to put life not only into the Muslim League organisation but also into the masses who had already become restive, and that with our opposition to the Congress policies the mass mind would begin to rally around the Muslim League'. Khaliquzzaman, op. cit., p. 164.
53. Kaura, op. cit., p. 116.

54. S. Gopal, *Jawaharlal Nehru: A Biography*, vol. 1, 1889-1947, Oxford University Press, Delhi, 1976, p. 229.
55. Kaura, op. cit., p. 135. She has argued that the failure of settlement between the Congress and League in the new context of provincial autonomy and federation had led the latter to search for an alternative scheme under which Muslims might be able to shape their destiny without any fear of interference from Hindu majority. This was to result very soon in the emergence of the demand for India's Partition.
56. M. Mujeeb, 'The Partition of India in Retrospect', in Mushirul Hasan, ed., *India's Partition: Process, Strategy and Mobilisation*, Oxford University Press, Delhi, 1993, p. 403.
57. Ibid., pp. 403-4.
58. Ibid., p. 404.
59. Maulana Azad to Rajaji, 29 August 1937, Rajaji Papers, File no. 5 Microfilm, reel no. 3 Nehru Memorial Museum & Library (hereafter NMML), Delhi.
60. Rajaji to Maulana Azad, 2 September 1937, Rajaji Papers, File no. 5, Microfilm, reel no. 3, NMML.
61. Ibid.
62. Maulana Azad to Rajendra Prasad, 13 July 1939, RP Papers, File no. xiv/40, Microfilm, reel no. 19, NMML.
63. Ibid.
64. *The Leader*, 19 July 1937.
65. Ibid.
66. Ibid., 23 July 1937.
67. Maulana Azad to Rajendra Prasad, 13 July 1939, RP Papers, File no. xiv/40, Microfilm, reel no. 19, NMML
68. Azad to Rajendra Prasad, 18 July 1939, RP Papers, File no. 53, letter no. nil, NMML.
69. *The Leader*, 21 July 1937. It reported that on 18 July 1937 Maulana Azad had come to Bombay and held prolonged consultations with Sardar Patel, 'regarding the Muslim member of the Bombay Cabinet'.
70. *The Leader*, 23 July 1937.
71. Ibid.
72. Ibid., 24 July 1937.
73. Ibid.
74. Ibid., 17 August 1937.
75. Nehru to Rajendra Prasad, 21 July 1937, File no. 1/37, RP Papers, NAI.
76. Gandhi to Nehru, 30 July 1937, *CWMG*, no. 35, p. 74.

77. For a detailed study of the Muslim Mass Contact Programme refer to Mushirul Hasan, 'The Muslim Mass Contact Campaign: Analysis of a Strategy of Political Mobilisation' in Mushirul Hasan, ed., *India's Partition*, pp. 133-59.
78. 'Some notes on the general approach and propaganda methods of AIML with special reference to inter-communal relations'. AICC papers, File no. G-32F 1938, NMML.
79. Ibid.
80. Ibid.
81. Ibid.
82. Ibid.
83. Kaura, op. cit., p. 119.
84. Ibid., p. 120.
85. Gopal, op. cit., p. 224.
86. Mishra, op. cit., p. 319.
87. Ibid.
88. Jyotindra Das Gupta, *Language Conflict and National Development: Group Politics and Language Policy in India*, Oxford University Press, Delhi, 1970, p. 111.
89. Mishra, op. cit., p. 320.
90. Kaura, op. cit., p. 124.
91. Sharif Report, as discussed in ibid.
92. Azad, *India Wins Freedom*, op. cit., p. 16.
93. Ibid.
94. Ibid.
95. Azad to Rajendra Prasad, 11 November 1938, File no. 4-A38, col. 6, Reel no. 12, RP Papers, NMML.
96. A letter from Secretary, Habibganj Sub-divisional Congress Committee, 18 November 1938, AICC Papers, File no. G-32/1938.
97. Ibid.
98. Ibid. Sadiq Ali, AICC Secretary's reply to the query.
99. Azad to Rajendra Prasad, 11 November 1938, File no. 4-A38, col. 6, Reel no. 12, RP Papers, NMML.
100. Ibid. Azad also referred to the same issue in the context of Bihar. He expressed the desire that the Bihar Provincial Congress Committee should issue a circular that no member of the Congress could remain a member of Hindu Mahasabha, which would positively influence Muslims. However, he was not particularly hopeful and said, 'but Congress Muslims think that we won't do this. I do not see any difficulty'.
101. Azad, 'National Tahreek: Wazarat Qabool Karne ke Baad League

wa Congress, Zuban-Wazarat', unpublished essay, ICCR, Delhi, p. 3.
102. Ibid.
103. Ibid., pp. 3-4.
104. Ibid., p. 4.
105. Sampurnanand addressed a letter to Mahadev Desai meant for Mahatma Gandhi, 5 September 1938, AICC Papers, File no. 30/1937. In this letter he made a point that in view of divergence between Hindi and Urdu, Hindustani was being popularized. But he also complained that, 'the difficulty today is that some people wish to propagate Urdu, under the name of Hindustani'. As a contrast he argued that a national language required to keep in touch with the people of Maharashtra, Gujarat, Bengal and Madras and, 'for their sake, we have to keep sufficiency of words of Sanskrit origin. Both the characters, Urdu and Nagari will of course remain for the present. . . . Sanskrit has such an intimate connection with the life of a large section of the population of this country that any language created by boycotting it would be artificial.'
106. Gandhiji to Sampurnanad, 8 September 1938, AICC Papers, File no. 30/1937.
107. Kaura, op. cit., p. 122.
108. Syed Mahmud to Rajendra Prasad, 3 August 1936, File no. xii, Reel no. 4, RP Papers, NMML.
109. Ibid.
110. Ibid.
111. Ibid.
112. Nehru to Syed Mahmud, 24 September 1936, File no. xi/36, Reel no. 4, RP Papers, NMML.
113. Ibid.
114. Ibid.
115. A pamphlet issued on behalf of the All India Hindi Prachar Samiti, Wardha. Reel no. 4, RP Papers, n.d. NMML. The pamphlet mentioned the names of office bearers and members as follows: Rajendra Prasad as the President, Seth Jamnalal Bajaj as Vice-President and Treasurer; M. Satyanarayan as Jt. Secretary. Among the members were the names of Mahatma Gandhi, Jawaharlal Nehru and P.D. Tondon.
116. Ibid., p. 5.
117. Ibid.
118. Ibid., pp. 6-7.

119. Gandhi to Nehru, 3 August 1937, *CWMG*, vol. 72, p. 91.
120. Parasnath Sinha, Secretary, Bihar Prantiya Hindi Pracharini Sabha, Patna, to Gandhi, 14 June 1941, File no. 3-c/41, RP Papers, NAI.
121. Rajendra Prasad to Kaka Kalelkar, 16 February 1942, File no. 1-H/42, RP Papers, NAI. In this letter he argued that it would be too much for any person to learn both scripts. He also stated that Hindiwalas might learn Urdu, which won't be reciprocated by Urduwalas.
122. Mishra, op. cit., p. 321.
123. Ibid.
124. Azad to Ghulam Rasool Mehar, 6 February 1937, in Malik Ram, ed., *Khutoot-i-Abul Kalam Azad*, Sahitya Akademi, Delhi, 1991, p. 252.
125. Azad to Ghulam Rasool Meher, 25 January 1937, in ibid., p. 246.
126. Ibid.
127. Ibid., p. 249.
128. Azad to Ghulam Rasool Meher, 6 February 1937, Malik Ram, ed., op. cit., p. 252.
129. Nehru to Syed Mahmud, 24 September 1936, File no. xi/36, Reel no. 4, RP Papers, NMML.
130. Ibid.
131. AICC circular no. 22, 31 March 1937, NMML.
132. Ibid.
133. Ibid.
134. Azad to Rajendra Prasad, 10 June 1937, File no. 11/37, Reel no. 5, RP Papers, NMML.
135. Ibid.
136. Ibid.
137. Ibid.
138. Ahmad Makhdumi, Secretary, Darul Islam, Paithana, Patna, wrote a letter to either Manzar Rizvi or K.M. Ashraf, which is not clear, asking for propaganda material, giving the impression that he was a sympathizer of the Congress. AICC Papers, File no. 30/1937.
139. Ibid.
140. Ibid.
141. *The Medina* published from Bijnor, 25 December 1936. The paper also said that the Congress had not adopted any resolution against Urdu, because they knew that it was the only language,

which was common to all. It did not behove an organization such as Congress to have invited Urdu-speaking people without the advantage of Urdu guide.

142. Ibid.
143. AICC letter, perhaps written by K.M. Asharaf to the Secretary, Reception Committee, Mahakaushal session, Jubbulpur, 25 July 1938. AICC Papers, File no. 30/1937.
144. Ibid.
145. Ibid.
146. Letter from Sandelvi, Publicity Dept. of UPCC to K.M. Asharaf, 19 August 1938, AICC Papers, File no. 30/1937.
147. Ibid.
148. Letter from Aftab Ahmad (Congress worker from Jubbulpur) to Maulana Azad, n.d. AICC Papers, File no. 30/1937. Copies of this letter were forwarded to Pandit Nehru, K.M. Ashraf, Mahatma Gandhi and Subhas Chandra Bose as well.
149. Ibid.
150. Ibid. This charge seems to be interesting in view of the fact that the Congress Working Committee had already resolved in the last week of December 1938 that the Muslim League and Hindu Mahasabha were communal organizations and no member belonging to their committees could ever become the member of the Congress committees. N.N. Mitra, ed., *IAR*, 1938, vol. II, p. 300.
151. Ibid. (Letter from Aftab Ahmad).
152. Chaudhary Liaqat Husain to K.M. Ashraf, 9 March 1938, AICC Papers, File no. 30/1937. In this letter he talked about a plan of the Congress to open a circulating library at Siana, Bulandshahr, which was to keep only Hindi books. He complained that such a decision would deprive Muslims and Urdu knowing Hindus. He also pointed out that despite his participation in Congress movements, there were occasions when he regretted it.
153. A letter from Abdur Rashid, Nazim, Jamiatul Ulema, Orissa to K.M. Ashraf, 10 June 1938, AICC Papers, File no. 30/1937.
154. Ibid. It attached resolution adopted by Muslims of Cuttack, which said that such a decision was against the spirit of the Karachi resolution, sub-clause III adopted by the Congress, which promised to protect the language, script and culture of the minorities.
155. A letter from K.M. Asharaf to Director Publicity, Central Provinces Government, Nagpur, 29 July 1938. AICC Papers, File no. 30/1937.

156. Ibid.
157. The communiqué stated that a training school for teachers had been opened at Wardha . . . a Mahomedan teacher had been appointed to teach Urdu. It further said that Urdu script was taught to all the pupil teachers so that they might be able to teach the same to Muslim boys admitted in Vidya Mandirs, if they so desired. 'It is be noted that this feature has been introduced to remove a Muslim grievance—that there is no provision in the primary schools at present to teach Urdu.'
158. Azad to Rajendra Prasad, 7 February 1940, File no. 14, RP Papers, NMML.
159. Ibid.
160. Ibid.
161. Ibid.
162. Ibid.
163. Ibid.
164. Ibid.
165. Ibid.
166. Ibid.
167. Ibid.
168. Jameel Ahmad Khan, 15 August 1938, File no. 3-B/38, RP Papers, NMML. The letter did not seem to have been addressed to any person but the High Command of the Congress.
169. Ibid.
170. Azad to Rajendra Prasad, 11 November 1938, File no. 4-A/38, RP Papers, NMML. This concern of Azad has already been discussed with reference fn. 96.
171. Ibid.
172. Ibid.
173. Ibid.
174. Ibid.
175. Ibid.
176. Abdul Majid, Asstt. Secretary, Muslim Mass Contact Committee, Ranchi sent this communication to AICC, 11 October 1938, AICC Papers, File no. 30/1937.
177. Ibid.
178. Telegram from Azad to Rajendra Prasad, 2 November 1938, File. no. 4-A/38, RP Papers, NMML. The content of this telegram reflected this concern, '. . . *Please decide Bhagalpore Gaya affairs. Removing Muslim complaints, which have perturbed Muslim nationalists. Immediate remedy necessary* . . .'. (Emphasis added)

179. Azad to Rajendra Prasad, 25 October 1938, File. no. 4-A/38, RP Papers, NMML.
180. A text giving details of such developments, particularly in the district of Bhagalpur was attached to a letter from Azad to Rajendra Prasad, 11 November 1938, File no. 4-A/38, RP Papers, NMML.
181. A letter from AICC to the General Secretary, Utkal PCC, 12 January 1939, File no. 30/1937.
182. Ibid.
183. A letter from AICC office to K.D. Malaviya, organizing secretary, UP PCC, 12 January 1939, File no. 30/1937.
184. Ibid.
185. A letter addressed to K.M. Ashraf, by the Secretary, Muslim Congress Party, 11 May 1938, AICC Papers, File no. 30/1937.
186. Ibid.
187. A letter from Political & Economic Information Dept. to the Secretary, Nagpur PCC, 26 June 1938, AICC Papers, File no. 30/1937.
188. Ibid.
189. Azad to Rajendra Prasad, 16 June 1939, File no. 24/40, RP Papers, NMML.
190. Abdul Aaleem (from Darbhanga, Bihar) to Mahatma Gandhi, 5 February 1941, File no. 1-A/41, RP Papers, NMML.
191. Ibid.
192. Sir Sultan to Rajendra Prasad, 16 November 1938, File no. 1-B/39, RP Papers, NAI.
193. Rajendra Prasad to Sir Sultan, 21 November 1938, File 1-B/39, RP Papers, NAI.
194. Deepak Pandey, 'Congress–Muslim League Relations 1937-39: The Parting of Ways', in *Modern Asian Studies*, Cambridge, no. 12, 1978, p. 635.
195. As quoted in ibid.
196. Ibid., p. 637.
197. C. Rajagopalachari to Rajendra Prasad, 21 November 1938, File no. 3-C/38, RP Papers, NAI.
198. Pandey, op. cit., p. 638.
199. Kaura, op. cit., p. 124.
200. K.K. Aziz, ed., *Muslims Under Congress Rule 1937-1939: A Documentary Record*, vol. I, Renaissance Publishing House, Delhi 1986. In this volume the Pirpur Report is incorporated in full, pp. 307-86.

201. Ibid., pp. 311-12.
202. Kaura, op. cit., p. 125.
203. Printed Memorandum to Subhas Chandra Bose by the Committee for Protection of Revenue Payers, distt. Peshawar, AICC Papers, File no. 30/1937.
204. Ibid.
205. Hasan, ed., *India's Partition*, p. 22.
206. Ibid.
207. Ibid.
208. Ibid., p. 23.
209. Ibid.
210. Ibid.
211. Ibid., p. 24.
212. Mishra, op. cit., p. 316.
213. Hasan, in M. Hasan, ed., op. cit., p. 26.
214. Azad to Rajendra Prasad, 11 November 1938, as already cited.
215. Ibid., 18 October 1939, File no. 15/40, RP Papers, NMML.
216. Ibid.
217. Azad to Rajendra Prasad, 21 April 1938, File no. 3-B/38, RP Papers, NMML.
218. Ibid.
219. Ibid.
220. Ibid.
221. Ibid.
222. Ibid.
223. Azad to Rajendra Prasad, 4 January 1940, File no. 14/40, RP Papers, NMML.
224. Ibid.
225. Sardar Patel to Rajendra Prasad, 15 October 1938, *Collected Works of Sardar Vallabhbhai Patel* (CWSVP), P.N. Chopra, ed., vol. VII, p. 179.
226. Pattabhi Sitaramayya, *History of the Indian National Congress*, vol. II, *1935-1947*, Padma Publication, Bombay, 1947, p. 102. Pattabhi argued in this context, 'Why did the Maulana withdraw? The Maulana alone knows and Gandhi might know.'
227. Sardar Patel to Rajendra Prasad, 2 November 1938, CWSVP, ibid., p. 201.

CHAPTER FIVE

Towards a United and Federated India, 1940-1947

In 1940 Maulana Azad was called upon to occupy the 'sacred office' of the president of the Indian National Congress and to preside over the Annual Session at Ramgarh in Bihar (now in Jharkhand). Ramgarh was not far from Moorabadi, where he had spent an internment from 1916-19. Azad had already presided over the Special Session of the Congress once in 1923, when he had skilfully averted a division in the Congress between the pro-changers and no-changers. However, presiding over the Annual Session was a more significant recognition of Azad's services in national politics and the freedom movement. Even before the date for filing nomination was finalized there was speculation that Maulana Azad might be 'requested to stand for election this year and his candidature will receive the official Congress support'.[1] Gandhiji too had endorsed his candidature.[2] Maulana Azad has acknowledged that when Gandhiji asked him 'to become the Congress President, I readily agreed'.[3] Once Gandhiji had thrown his weight behind Azad, the contest for the post was not likely to be serious. Azad himself was satisfied, 'There was no real contest for the presidential election, and the candidate who stood against me was defeated by an overwhelming majority.'[4] In *India Wins Freedom* he does not mention the name of his rival. It was M.N. Roy, who polled only 181 votes as compared to Azad's 1,841 votes, thus maintaining a lead of 1,660 votes.[5] 'While the Socialists everywhere voted for Maulana Azad, Communists remained neutral. There was no voting in Bengal and Delhi.'[6] Azad's victory in the election for Congress president was widely welcomed.[7]

This was the second time Azad became the Congress president. Earlier he had presided over the special session of the Congress in

1923. Between 1923 and 1940 much water had flowed under the bridge. The nationalist movement had gained much ground with a vastly-expanded social base for the Congress. This had earned the party the distinction of being the major representative voice of Indians. However, during the same period a disturbing trend had gained considerable momentum—this was the slow but steady alienation of Muslims from the Congress. In a certain sense the beginning had been made in the early 1920s, soon after the withdrawal of the Non-Cooperation–Khilafat movement. In the initial stage, Azad had sensed that this trend, if it persisted, might prove detrimental to nationalism and the interests of the Congress. He had tried to build bridges between communities, since the days of *Al-Hilal*. In his presidential address in 1923, he had highlighted the importance of Hindu–Muslim unity to the extent of being prepared for a delay in independence. He had declared, 'If an angel was to descend from the sky (High Heavens) and from the heights of the Qutb Minar ask us to abandon Hindu–Muslim unity and promise Swaraj within twenty-four hours I will refuse Swaraj but not the unity. Any delay in Swaraj would affect India but the end of our unity will be the loss of entire mankind.'[8] In the same speech Azad had stated, that he was convinced, 'Today in India we neither need a Hindu *sangathan* nor a Muslim *sangathan*. We are in need of only one *sangathan* and that is the Indian National Congress.'[9]

Azad had expected that this formulation would hold water and grow stronger with the passage of time. But it did not. Hindu–Muslim unity was strained in the 1920s and by the mid-1930s Muslims were considerably alienated from the Congress. By the end of the 1930s political bickering and struggle to occupy higher seats of power were in evidence. The Muslim League, which had earlier operated on the margins of political processes, metamorphosed into a party claiming to be the sole representative of the Muslims while denouncing the Congress as representative of only the caste-Hindus. Many individuals, groups and political formations among the Muslims challenged this claim of the League. In these circumstances Azad's challenges were many; his biggest challenge was to take the struggle for freedom forward; the second important challenge was to combat the Muslim League for its virulent communal and anti-Congress campaign. In a press interview Azad had said that, 'each day brings us nearer the coming struggle. All our attention should be centered round this very thing.'[10] In Lahore Maulana Azad addressed a public meeting[11] in which he advised his nine crore 'Muslim brethren that they should not look upon their countrymen with suspicion. Their rights were not at all in danger in the hands of the Congress. There was no other alternative for the Muslims than to join in the struggle for freedom of the country. . . . The doors of the Congress were open to all.'[12] These assertions of Azad were indicating towards the shape of things in the days to come. As regards Muslim concerns about their future Azad spoke in much the same language as he had done during the *Al-Hilal* days, when he exhorted Muslims to trust the Hindus, while struggling against the British. His assertion about the impending struggle was endorsed by the Congress Working Committee in its meeting held at Patna. A resolution was adopted, which clearly stated, 'the Congress withdrew the ministries from the provinces where Congress had majority in order to dissuade India from the war and to enforce the Congress determination to free India from foreign domination. This preliminary step must naturally be followed by civil disobedience in which the Congress will unhesitatingly resort. . . .'[13] The CWC also tried to assure the minorities that their rights would be protected. It appeared that Azad's leadership would sail smoothly.

Huge arrangements were made for the annual session of the Congress, in which Rajendra Prasad took personal interest since he was Chairman of the Reception Committee. The venue of this session was named after Mazharul Haq, a freedom fighter from Bihar and thus called Mazharpuri. On arrival at Ramgarh, Maulana Azad was given a warm reception by Congress workers and tribals of the area. Soon after reaching the venue he went to the cottage of Mahatma Gandhi to pay his respects.[14] On the day of the open session a torrential downpour inundated the Congress Nagar and yet the delegates stood in knee deep water with their umbrellas open to listen to Maulana Azad. Gandhiji in his characteristic style described this experience as, 'A Foretaste of the Suffering'.[15]

Azad, presiding over the Congress session on 19 March 1940 at Ramgarh delivered a long speech in chaste Urdu in which he addressed several issues of vital importance. He was conscious of the timing of his election as the president. As he put it 'By electing me the President you have reposed tremendous confidence in me at a critical moment. While it is a matter of honour, I look upon it as a major responsibility as well.'[16]

In his speech he surveyed the political scenario in the context of the Second World War, and tried to locate India's position in it, with a sense of grief that she was still not free to make choices. The Indians, he said, looked upon fascism and Nazism with a sense of revulsion, but they were as much disgusted with British imperialism and therefore not prepared to extend a hand of friendship to Britain.[17] He accused the British government of making attempts to generate all kinds of division. According to Azad, an alien government could survive only if a divide-and rule policy was successful. Azad admitted that he did not mean to argue that there were no internal problems; there were many, the problem of communalism being one.[18]

At this point Azad seemed to be making statements, which were at variance with Nehru's views on questions of communalism.[19] Azad admitted that the problem of communalism continued to exist, and it was one's duty that before any step forward as regards political development, one should look for means to resolve it. However, this problem should not detain us in the march forward.[20] He was anxious to reassure the Muslim and other minorities that:

- as and when a constitution was framed for India, it should have strong provisions for protecting minority rights.
- the protection required by minorities was a question that must be settled by the minorities themselves rather than by majority votes.[21]
- in the event of any situation where concerned groups could not reach an agreement, provisions could be made for arbitration,[22] and the Congress was committed to it.

Till this point Azad formulated points of assurance to the minorities in general and the Muslims in particular. The next part of his speech, discussed the apprehensions harboured by leaders of all hues of the Muslim-majority provinces—that the centre, which in any circumstances would remain Hindu-dominated, and therefore undermine the powers and privileges of the provinces. Such apprehensions had been publicly debated even during the preparation of the Nehru Committee Report. Azad was fully alive to these apprehensions. He thought they could be allayed by assurances that the future constitution of India would be federal rather than unitary. 'The future constitution of India irrespective of details of provisions shall be a constitution of All India Federations in which all units would enjoy autonomy of their subjects and functions, except in matter such as defense, foreign affairs and customs etc.'[23]

The best part of the speech was yet to come. In the concluding section he dilated upon the question of the heritage of Islam and of composite Indian nationhood. Azad said, 'I am a Muslim and proud of inheriting the glorious legacy of Islam.' He continued, 'I take pride in being an Indian and an essential part of indivisible Indian nationhood, without which its grandeur would never be accomplished. I shall never give up my claim to be an inalienable part of it.'[24] He emphasized that in eleven centuries of co-existence the mutual give-and-take have been such that they affected all aspects of life—language, literature, culture, taste and customs. Even in day-to-day life there is hardly any area which is untouched and unaffected by the achievements of our mutual interaction over the centuries. It is this heritage of composite culture, which is a treasure-trove of our united nationhood. We have to admit that by now we all are an indivisible nation. No vision of separation from each other can ever fructify. 'We all must accept with pride the common destiny shaped by history for us.'[25] He concluded the speech by paying tribute to Mahatma Gandhi for his leadership.

During the entire speech Azad's focus was on political developments now alight with the possibility of India moving closer to independence. Another concern was to allay apprehensions in Muslim minds and assure them that they too had a stake in the country's future. In Azad's scheme of things, such an assurance was vitally important in view of the campaign unleashed by the Muslim League, which was moving dangerously close to pronouncing the Muslims a distinct nation, which it did a week later on 23 March 1940 at Lahore.[26] M.A. Jinnah had already given a foretaste of things to come in an article titled as 'Two Nations in India' which was published in *Times and Tide*, and later reproduced by the *Hindustan Times*,[27] in which he had clearly argued that 'there are two different nations' in India. The pronouncements by the two Muslim leaders, Azad and Jinnah made a study in contrasts. One represented the Congress, committed to the cause of India's liberation while retaining its composite cultural ethos. The other represented the Muslim League whose only concern was to seek power for itself at the cost of negating a thousand years of history of co-existence between Hindus and Muslims.

Azad's pronouncements acquired importance in view of the fact that on the one hand Nehru was denying the existence of communalism and on the other hand Gandhiji was expressing helplessness to fight it out, 'I wish I could do something, but I am utterly helpless. My faith in unity is as bright as ever; only I see no daylight out of the impenetrable darkness and in such distress, I cry out to God for light.'[28] They both were concerned about the adverse effect communalism had generated in national politics. In marked contrast Azad's attempt was to hold out some hope to devise a strategy, which would counter the League's campaign and arrest the process of Muslims drifting away from the Congress.

Azad was taking upon himself and the Congress a gigantic task of resolving the intractable problems of communalism—when his own Presidentship stood on shaky ground. Aspersions were cast soon after his election as the president that the Congress had elected him to show that the party was truly national in character, representing the aspirations of all sections of Indian society. The *Manchester Guardian* remarked that Azad's election was prearranged. In view of the communal situation, it would be to the advantage of the Congress to demonstrate that it stood for the Muslims and the Muslims stood by the Congress.[29] Nehru defended the Maulana's election vehemently. 'We welcome therefore the elections of a Muslim. But it is wrong to think that Congress presidents are elected for communal reasons. Certainly not Maulana Abul Kalam Azad', Nehru went on, 'We welcome the Maulana's election because he represents in an eminent measure the Congress tradition and Congress viewpoint.'[30] Pandit Nehru continued,

> I do not speak of his great ability and learning, which he carries so lightly or his long and proud record of service in the cause of Indian nationalism and freedom, for every child knows about them. Of course, Maulana Azad is eminently qualified to tackle the communal problem and the Congress and the country should take full advantage of his services in this as other matters.[31]

Other than the questions about the timing of election as president of the Congress, Azad was getting into differences with Gandhiji. A few days before the annual session, the Congress Working Committee meeting was held on 15 March 1940. Gandhiji had come with a draft resolution prepared by Jayaprakash Narayan and wanted it to be adopted by the Congress. Azad, Nehru and Patel opposed this proposal. Seeing such opposition the proposal was dropped.[32] Gandhiji was not prepared to launch any civil disobedience since a resolution in this regard was already approved at AICC at Patna on 1 March 1940. Secondly, he (Gandhiji) was determined to ensure that the Congress did not initiate any programme, which might violate his creed of non-violence. Sensing the mood of several Congress leaders on the eve of the Ramgarh session, Gandhiji adopted a stern tone and said, 'An alternative occurs to me. I should be freed from the burden of my connection with you. And you go ahead. I keep myself in reserve.' 'However much you may agree with me, your *ahimsa* does not go as far as mine. And if after twenty years of practice of it I have not been able to win the affection and trust of Musalmans, my *ahimsa* must be of a very poor quality indeed.' Then he turned to the Maulana and said, 'There is no question of my distrusting you or other members of the Working Committee or the nation. It is a question of distrust in myself.'[33] Such a strong expression of Gandhiji shook Azad, since he was not able to reconcile himself to all that was said. He responded, 'You must not forget that it was at your command that I accepted to serve this year and you cannot now forsake me. One cannot think of civil disobedience without you.'[34] Azad further protested, 'You are always telling the people that they are not ready for a fight, this demoralizes them.'[35] Gandhi reacted to these statements of Azad rather curtly, 'If it does I cannot help it.' Differences between Gandhiji and Azad set the tone for future relations between the two. There were several occasions when Gandhi's assertions were not in tune with Azad with regards to several political developments.

II

The Maulana had to face several difficult questions. One of them was as to what would be the Congress' attitude towards the war in case the British were to concede India's demand for independence. The issue was debated at the CWC meeting in Delhi on 3-7 July 1940. The Committee resolved to organize effective defence of the country on condition that a declaration was made on her independence. The Congress demanded the setting up of a Provisional National Government, which 'commands the confidence of all elected elements in the Central Legislature and secures the closest cooperation of responsible governments in the provinces'.[36]

The passing of the resolution at Delhi had upset the equilibrium within the Working Committee as some members, particularly Abdul Ghaffar Khan, resigned from the Working Committee.[37] The differences came to a head at the AICC meeting held at Poona on 27-8 July 1940 where two resolutions were adopted. The first reiterated the conviction of the Congress in non-violence and the second declared that India's rightful place was in the democratic camp provided the country became free.[38] The Maulana's understanding was that faith in non-violence was fine, but there was room for disagreement with Gandhiji who thought the Congress should declare that free India would eschew violence and have no army for defence against aggression. This meant that the country would depend entirely on non-violence for dealing with internal disorders and external aggression.[39] Azad did not share this view, seeing the Congress only as a political body committed to the cause of independence. He declared,

> We had no courage to declare that we shall organize a state in this country without an armed force. If we did it would be wrong on our part. The Indian National Congress is a political organization pledged to win the political independence of the country. It is not an institution for organizing World peace.[40]

As a consequence of these developments, there were many Congress Working Committee members who felt uncomfortable about Gandhi's unwavering stand with regard to non-violence, and therefore to any participation in the war.[41] Then came a bombshell—a most unexpected letter signed by all the Working Committee members (with the exception of Jawaharlal Nehru, Rajagopalachari, Syed Mahmud and Asaf Ali) stating that they did not share Azad's view on India's participation in the war, and would resign.[42] Eventually all the signatories continued as members of the Working Committee. All the same, Azad, 'was deeply hurt to receive this letter'.[43]

Azad's predicament after becoming the Congress president was manifold. On the one hand he had difficulty in gaining the confidence of his colleagues in the Working Committee and of Gandhi. On the other hand, he had to shoulder the responsibility of countering the ideological campaign of the Muslim League based on the 'two-nation theory'. Jinnah perhaps realized that a campaign against the Muslim League and its demand for partition launched under a Hindu Congress leader would not carry as much conviction with the Muslims as one led by a Muslim leader such as Azad. Jinnah also knew that of all the Muslim Congress leaders Azad was the most learned and articulate and he could easily challenge the Muslim League in ideological and political realms.

Jinnah's attitude towards Azad was one of deep hostility. How else one can explain the tone of a letter that he addressed to Azad in response to a query by him (Azad) as to whether the Muslim League was interested in joining a Provisional National Government. Jinnah told Azad,

> I refuse to discuss with you by correspondence or otherwise as you have completely forfeited the confidence of Muslim India. Cannot you realize that you are made a Muslim Show Boy Congress President? You represent neither Muslims nor Hindus. The Congress is a Hindu body. If you have self respect resign at once. You have done your worst

against the League so far. I know you have hopelessly failed. Give it up.[44]

At this time Jinnah's arrogance and rudeness to Azad were misplaced, for several reasons: first, by merely adopting the 'two-nation theory' he did not get any authority to speak on behalf of all Muslims; second, even though the Muslims were alienated from the Congress, there were several political formations of the Muslims which were committed to the cause of Indian nationalism and willing to collaborate with the Congress; third, after the 1937 elections, no election had taken place which would have given the Muslim League an opportunity to test its popularity among the Muslim electorates. These were important considerations on which alone the League could have established the claim of being the 'Sole spokesman' of the community. In 1940, the available political factors were contrary to Jinnah's and the Muslim League's grandiose presumptions.

It is important to underline that Azad did not open this communication in his personal capacity as he was doing so on behalf of the Congress, which had envisaged a possibility of forming a Provisional National Government in the centre. He was explaining this position in order to take the general public in confidence. However, he was also expressing his regret that not many were coming forward to accept the Congress' offer.[45] Jinnah instead of accepting the offer chose to condemn and criticize it. He indignantly said that, 'so called National Government indicated in the resolution means a Congress Raj. The word nation has been flagrantly abused. The nation does not exist in India any more than in Europe or America.'[46] The bitter part of his statement was to follow. As he put it, '*If their demand is met, it will mean a Hindu majority government—a permanent Hindu majority government—a position which will never be accepted by Muslims. The Muslim League now firmly stands convinced that the only solution is a division of India as laid down by the Muslim League at Lahore.*'[47] (Emphasis added) Jinnah's outburst against the Congress seemed a sign of fear that he was not willing to concede.

However, Jinnah's charge against Maulana Azad that he represented 'neither Hindus nor Muslims' was not correct as Azad was held in reverence by a cross-sections of people. Two instances in this regard are interesting: first, the Ayyappankave Young Boys Association, based at Palaghat wrote a letter to Azad seeking his autograph to be put in a library;[48] second, the president, Sholapur City Congress Committee wrote to Azad, requesting him to visit Sholapur because many people, particularly Muslims wanted to have his *darshan* for a long time.[49] Instances such as these are reflective of the fact Azad was seen as a revered figure whose association in one form or the other was sought by diverse social groups cutting across boundaries. It seems that Jinnah lived in a make-believe world, when he ridiculed Azad. For this act of political and cultural indecency against him, Jinnah was roundly criticized. Asaf Ali took a jibe, 'Mr. Jinnah's reply to Maulana Azad who is universally respected by Indian Mussalmans makes a tragic and wanton lapse of decency.'[50] Another leader of standing, Yusuf Meherally, General Secretary of the Congress Socialist Party, too criticized Jinnah in quite strong words.[51] Not content with this he castigated Jinnah, 'to speak in the language he has chosen to do, shows that now he is at the end of his political resources and is resorting to abuse to bolster up a weak case'.[52] Apart from individual responses, there were organizations, which too condemned Jinnah for his rude reply to Maulana Azad. The Jamiatul-Ulema-i-Hind in its resolution took the view that, 'Maulana Abul Kalam Azad's telegram to Mr. Jinnah, expressing preparedness on behalf of the Congress to form the composite government commanding the confidence of all the parties including the Muslim League, in the Central Assembly provided a workable solution to the present difficulty.'[53] After assessing the conditions in which Azad had tried to open negotiations with Jinnah, the resolution went on to condemn him for the tenor of his reply.[54] Another organization, All India Majlis-e-Ahrar, too condemned Jinnah for his impolite and rude behaviour.[55] Such articulation of anger and condemnation by individuals and organizations through resolutions and statements was given concrete manifestation by organizing public meetings in open spaces. A public meeting organized in Urdu Park by the Jamiat-ul-Ulema-i-Hind was attended by more than 20,000 Muslims, who not only condemned Jinnah but also reposed confidence in the leadership of Maulana Azad. The meeting was addressed by the top echelons of the Jamiat.[56] These outbursts of indignation against Jinnah made it abundantly clear that Maulana Azad enjoyed the confidence not only of the Congress but Muslims too. Therefore, Jinnah was not only rude but highly presumptuous when he said that Azad had, 'forfeited the confidence of Muslim India'. At this stage of political developments if anybody suffered from a crisis of confidence, it was Jinnah in person and the Muslim League as a party, because there was hardly any electoral opportunity to test their popularity. And yet some feeble justification was marshalled to support Jinnah's stand. In response to the outpouring against Jinnah, Liaqat Ali Khan, General Secretary of the All India Muslim League, in his press statement said that, 'the language of a telegram is always necessarily condensed and therefore sounds more abrupt than that of a letter'.[57] He also said that Maulana Azad deserved such a treatment because of his support to the Congress ministries while a 'steamroller of oppression was moving fast in the Congress governed provinces and even the elementary rights of Musalmans were ruthlessly trampled upon. . . .'[58] Liaqat Ali Khan perhaps did not know that there was hardly any opportunity which Maulana Azad had missed in raising issues concerning Muslims, however, he did so within the Congress and its leaders instead of going public, a point which has already been discussed in detail in the earlier chapter.

The Muslim League's 'two-nation theory' or the Lahore resolution came under attack from diverse quarters. S. Srinivas Iyengar, former president of the Congress described this resolution as preposterous. He said, 'I can only hope they are not seriously meant. Neither the interest of India in general nor the interest of Muslims in particular from whatever point of view looked at can justify this preposterous demand.'[59] This understanding of Iyengar was shared by many Muslim organizations too. The Muslim Naujavan Party, based in Gujarat, passed a resolution opposing the Muslim League's scheme for the Partition of India.[60] In Amritsar, the Muslims had gathered at Khair Din's mosque for Juma prayer, where the tricolour flag was unfurled and speeches were made against the Muslim League. Ghazi Rahman Khan of Quetta in his speech argued that the Muslim League had squandered hard earned money in erecting pandals and other such things at Lahore, while the Muslim masses were suffering.[61] Another speaker Hamid Ali argued that the League was unnecessarily raising the bogey of Hindu domination. He said that Muslims had nothing to fear from Hindus. Muslims were exhorted to come under the Congress.[62] The most significant part of the whole exercise was that this meeting was not organized by any Congressite Muslim.

Asaf Ali described the stance of the Muslim League as nothing but cheap tactic.[63] Even a journal such as, the *Manchester Guardian*, which was not so friendly with the Congress, criticized the League's resolution, which struck at the heart of Indian unity. It went on to directly target Jinnah for re-establishing the reign of chaos in Indian politics and said that it is to be expected that, 'Lord Zetland will not be slow, when parliament meets to express disapproval with which the government must view this blow to Indian unity'.[64]

However, more organized opposition to the Muslim League's demand for Partition of India came from the All-India Azad Muslim Conference, a coalition umbrella of seven political formations of Muslims, representing diverse regions, classes, groups and interests with their commitment to Indian nationalism. In organizing this Conference, Maulana Azad acted as a source of inspiration, which further explains the reason for Jinnah's outburst against him (Maulana Azad). Within weeks of the passing of the 'two-nation theory' resolution of the League, preparations were underway to challenge it with the help of many nationalist political formations of Muslims as plans were also made to organize a major conference of such formations and the ordinary mass of Muslims. One secretary was also nominated for the purpose, who issued statements to the press from time to time. A press statement was issued on 3 April 1940, which clearly said that Muslims need to take cognizance of 'the disruptive and unconstructive' forces (implying the Muslim League and its resolution), which were bent upon undermining the interests of the country as well as the community.[65] This statement also said that the above-stated conference would take place on 27 to 29 April 1940 and invited Muslims to join the proposed conference in order to deliberate over issues with seriousness.[66] Support started pouring in from various quarters. Maulana Habibur Rahman of Majlis-i-Ahrar, while addressing a meeting in Delhi exhorted Muslims to join the conference. However, the most interesting part of his speech was the condemnation of the reactionary leadership of the Muslim League and its policy of communal settlement.[67]

As time moved on, the confidence of the organizers of the conference was bolstered as they claimed that, 'the conference will be more representative of the Muslim opinion in the country than the Muslim League session at Lahore'.[68] K.B. Jan Mohammad, MLC (Bengal) was nominated as the chairman of the reception committee. It seemed resolved that the proposed conference would have no official connection with the Congress. Maulana Azad was invited to address the conference, however, it seemed that he would not participate in the Subjects Committee proceedings.[69] A decision such as this was more to convey the impression that it was essentially an attempt on the part of Muslim political formations, independent of the Congress, which Maulana Azad represented.

Subsequently a joint statement was issued on behalf of the six constituents of the proposed conference, such as Jamiatul Ulema-i-Hind, Bihar Muslim Independent Party, Krishak Proja Party, All-India Momin Conference, Ahrars and Anjuman-i-Watan, explaining the reasons for convening a conference such as this.[70] After having stated the purpose of convening the conference it went on to castigate the Muslim League saying that it was the only organized platform of the Muslims, which regrettably depended more on the foreign government than the strength of the Muslims. And its present policy has, 'jeopardized the political future of the whole Muslim community and has made it possible for the enemies of India's freedom to make it appear that the Indian Muslims are not only opposed to freedom for their country but are frightened of the majority community'.[71] The signatories also appealed to Muslims to make this conference a huge success. While emphasizing the nationalist character of the constituents of this proposed conference, it was repeatedly pointed out that this had no connection with the Congress. It was also said that some of the delegates did not wholly approve of the Congress policies. It was further reiterated that the Muslim League leadership was reactionary and anti-national, which had caused a drift in Muslim politics.[72]

The press statements and mobilization for the proposed conference had a salutary effect on Muslims, particularly in Delhi. It was clear that the constituents of the All-India Azad Muslim Conference were against the Muslim League, its leadership and the demand for the Partition of the country. It was perceived to be not just anti-national but anti-Muslim too. The impact of this mobilization was considerably manifest when an 'Anti-Partition Day' was organized in Delhi, which was attended by more than 10,000 Muslims.[73] The most interesting aspect of the developments was that another meeting was convened on the same day by the Muslim League to mobilize support for its Partition scheme, in a park in the vicinity of Juma Masjid. But this meeting did not attract the audience.[74] This was a message to the Muslim League that its Partition scheme was out of sync with the popular mood of the Muslims at this point of time. Meanwhile preparations for the Azad Muslim Conference were going on feverishly. Important decisions were made and press statements kept the public informed about the proposed conference. The Reception Committee of the conference elected Khan Bahadur Allah Bux, ex-premier of Sind, to preside over the proposed conference, with full support of all the constituents of this conference. Allah Bux accepted his election to preside over the conference.[75]

The mass support for the groups, which constituted the Azad Muslim Conference, was a challenge to the League's claim to speak on behalf of the Muslims. The spatial distribution of these bodies was such that they represented Muslim-majority as well as minority provinces. This show of strength among the non-Congress nationalist Muslims was potent enough to have knocked the bottom out of the Muslim League's claim. Its socio-political strength was by any reckoning much larger than that of the League at this point of time.[76] The local Muslims too showed great enthusiasm for the conference. A number of crowded meeting were held at Ajmere Gate, Tiraha Bairam Khan and Jama Masjid in order to enlist support for the conference.[77] There were many provincial Congress leaders who mobilized support for the conference. For instance Mian Iftekharuddin, President Punjab Provincial Congress Committee, had issued circulars to friends and sympathizers to join the conference. Similarly, another well-known Congress leader, Mir Hilali was active in the NWFP in order to enlist the support of the Pathans.[78] It is significant to note the interest of the Congress leaders in the success of the conference, despite the fact it was repeatedly emphasized that the Azad Muslim Conference would have no official connection with the Congress. An equally significant aspect of the mobilization was the interest and support extended by the plebian classes. This was the greatest challenge to Jinnah's claim to be the 'sole spokesman' of Indian Muslims. Jinnah's hostility towards Azad in the context of these developments was understandable.

With the arrival of K.B. Allah Bux and other leaders and delegates, a huge procession was taken out through the streets of Delhi, in which about 50,000 Muslims participated. Streets were decorated and the scene was a reminder of the Khilafat days mobilization.[79] The procession terminated at Juma Masjid, in front of which a public meeting was held. Allah Bux addressed the meeting and said that the conference would give the right lead to the Muslims of India. He expressed happiness that the Muslims were behind none in their support to achieve freedom for India.[80] When the conference opened on 27 April 1940, the attendance was, 'not less than 75,000. The crowd inside and outside the pandal was in the neighborhood of one lakh people.'[81] This was considered one of the biggest possible meetings organized in Delhi by the contemporary observers. Its representative character was manifest through the delegates' participation from diverse regions of the country.[82] The larger message that emerged out of this conference was, 'We are Indians and India is our home', which was a fitting reply to the Pakistan cry of the Muslim League.[83] In his address Allah Bux, president of the conference, challenged the representative character of the Muslim League. He charged the Muslim League that it did not have the same electoral strength as compared to the Congress. He also argued that no Muslim with the slightest sense of self-respect would tolerate that he was made a scapegoat. He said that Indian Muslims were proud to be Indian nationals and equally proud that their spiritual level and creedal realm was Islam.[84]

The main resolution was moved by Mufti Kifayatullah and seconded by Yasin Nurie, former minister of Bombay. It said, 'India will have geographical and political boundaries of an indivisible whole and as such is the common homeland of all the citizens irrespective of race or religion, who are joint owners of its resources'.[85] He emphatically repudiated the charge that Indian Muslims were opposed to Britain granting freedom to this country. While addressing the conference, Maulana Habibur Rahman declared, 'that no sane Muslim could accept the Pakistan scheme, which was positively dangerous to their interests'.[86] He then went on to ask the audience to signify their disapproval of the Muslim League by raising their hands. '*The entire audience without a single exception raised their hands and shouted slogans of Pakistan Murdabad*'[87] (Emphasis added). Given the length of the proceedings and popularity of the conference, it was extended by another day till 30 April 1940. The Subjects Committee also went into intense deliberations about securing the future of Muslims by asking for a Constituent Assembly elected on the basis of adult franchise, which would frame a constitution for India. It was further resolved that, 'the safeguards for the protection of the rights and interests of Muslims shall be determined solely by the Muslim members of the Assembly. The representatives of other communities or any foreign power shall not have any right to interfere in their decision.'[88] In order to determine parameters for safeguarding minority rights, it was decided to constitute a Board of 27 members to be nominated by the president, Allah Bux.

This conference was the biggest possible challenge to the Muslim League, which felt uncomfortable about its huge success. It went into an attacking mode without any loss of time. Choudhary Khaliquzzaman, while addressing a conference of the Muslim League at Lucknow, criticized the constituents and the participants of the conference as 'half-hearted pseudo-nationalists' who would never be able to deliver any solution to the communal problem. Referring to the demands made by the conference about safeguards, Khaliquzzaman said this position was 'coincident with League demands and one may ask why don't they come to the League platform'.[89] Khaliquzzaman was off the mark when he took a jibe at the Azad Muslim Conference. Talking about the safeguards was important in the larger context of the political developments that were taking place since 1928, when the Nehru Report was formalized, without any success of generating consensus. The Muslim opinion was divided, as a sizeable group was willing to go with the recommendation of the Report, however, there were others who raised concerns about the constitutional guarantee for the future of Muslims. Even in the context of the Azad Muslim Conference, there was nothing new when it raised the issue of 'safeguards'. Another significant aspect of the issue was that unlike the Muslim League the conference did not raise the bogey of Hindu domination and therefore seeking the support to the British government. The conference was seeking a solution of the communal problem within the framework of India's unity with a sovereign constitution.

Hafiz Mohammad Ibrahim issued a rebuttal to the charges of Khaliquzzaman. He said that the question of safeguards was never a pre-condition for Muslims fighting for the freedom of the country. It was meant only to prepare the grounds for the well-being of Muslims as and when the Constitution was framed in order to ensure inter-communal harmony.[90] After having clarified the issue of safeguards, he went on to make a distinction between the stand taken by the Muslim League and the Conference. He argued that the Muslim League advocated a complete separation, forbidding Muslims from joining the Congress and relied on the support of the British government. Whereas the Conference believed in the oneness of India, it did not ban entry of Muslims into the Congress and advised them not to depend on foreign power.[91] However, despite these rebuttals the Azad Muslim Conference was repeatedly and bitterly attacked by the Muslim League press, 'the supporters and the workers of this organization are being as ruthlessly denounced as the Congress leadership. The most common note is that the Azad Conference is a clever ruse of the Congress to wean away the Muslims from the League and to bring them under the Congress domination.'[92] The fear as expressed in the *Khilafat* of Bombay was the real cause of worry for the Muslim League that its claim to speak on behalf of Muslims was challenged by the Conference. Therefore it is not surprising at all that the Muslim League press repeatedly attacked the Conference and Maulana Azad, about whom *Al-Aman* of Delhi, a pro-League paper said bitterly, 'Is it not a fact that Maulana Abul Kalam Azad who once enjoyed great popularity among the Muslims is now looked upon as a discarded and condemned leader. . . .'[93] Part of the explanation for such virulent attacks on Azad was also because he had clearly identified himself with the larger objective of the Azad Muslim Conference.[94]

The Azad Muslim Conference seemed to have clearly mounted the ideological attack on the Muslim League in its move to polarize Indian society in the name of religion and communalism, while expressing concerns for safeguarding the interest of Muslims. Around this time Maulana Azad's major concern was to question the machination of the British government, which was eager to extend support to the Muslim League. He had already hinted at this in his presidential speech—that an alien government would never wish internal solidarity and unity among the masses.[95] The 'August Offer' of 1940 was a case in point.

In this 'Offer' the government wished to take in some Indians into the Viceroy's Executive Council and to establish a War Advisory Council. However, in this 'Offer' there was no reference to India's Independence, but the Muslim League was encouraged to think that no constitutional changes would be introduced if the minority opinion disagreed. Even though a formal declaration in this regard was made only on 8 August 1940, the Viceroy had started corresponding with political leaders earlier. In one such letter to Azad, the Viceroy Linlithgow, wanted him to study the 'Offer' and reply by 21 August 1940.[96] The broad contour of the 'Offer' had already been enunciated without any serious negotiations among the concerned parties. Azad politely turned it down, 'When His Majesty's Government have already thought fit to announce a definite action, may I ask how far there still remains a chance of usefulness of further discussion.'[97] Upon receiving a fresh communication in this regard, he reiterated the point, adding, 'Apart from other fundamental questions there is not even a suggestion for a national Government.'[98] Meanwhile, he convened a meeting of the Congress Working Committee on 18 August 1940 at Wardha where the matter was considered in full and the Committee came to the conclusion that British authority had been continually operating so as to create, maintain and aggravate differences in India's national life. It also added that the Congress demand for a Constituent Assembly was never meant to coerce any minority and the government was using this issue to create barriers to India's progress.[99] Consequently, Azad informed the Viceroy that, 'the Working Committee are of the opinion that they cannot associate themselves in any way with these proposals'.[100]

After the outbreak of the Second World War, the unilateral declaration of India's participation in the war, and the resignation of the Congress ministries, this was the first time the government had thought of opening the doors of negotiations with parties including the Congress. And even this attempt was seen as half-hearted and insincere. The Congress Working Committee in its response to this 'Offer' was able to reflect the mood in the party closely.[101] The 'August Offer' remained a non-starter in view of the fact that the Muslim League was obliquely given a handle to act as a road block to any constitutional progress in the name of minority question. The British government pretended to ignore the fact that the League was not the only voice as there were many Muslim voices which were in consonance with Indian nationalism. One such voice was that of the UP Provincial Jamiat-ul-Ansar, which had raised a volunteers corps known as the Momin Ansar Scouts and Volunteers, and was willing to collaborate with any such voluntary bodies who were committed to the cause of India's freedom and communal harmony. This organization had resolved to work on 'the principles of non-violence and non-communalism'.[102] Similarly, the Azad Muslim Conference after having organized a hugely successful conference in Delhi towards the end of April 1940, had become active in various provinces. It was particularly active in the United Provinces as many of its provincial leaders were keen to spread the message of the Conference in the whole province.[103] As a result of these endeavours, many district level units of the Azad Muslim Conference were established in places such as Etawah, Lucknow and other places and their office bearers too were either elected or nominated. In several cases they compensated the resource crunch with enthusiasm for the success of their activities.[104]

They were also willing to collaborate with the Provincial Congress Committee, particularly with the Minorities Department, in order to propagate the good work done by the Congress during the period the party was in government, particularly in the United Provinces.[105] Z.A. Ahmad was quick to recognize the importance of the Azad Muslim Conference and felt the need of extending all possible support to it.[106] Confident of its ideological and political mooring the UP chapter of the Azad Muslim Conference was ever willing to take on the Muslim League. In his press statement Mohammad Faruqi frontally attacked the League. He referred to the success of the Conference in Delhi and support which was forthcoming from all quarters to the proposed conference at Lucknow to be held on 21-2 July 1940 and said, 'betray the trend of the time'.[107] He emphatically asserted that the Conference was 'representative of every school of progressive thought' which lent it a unique position in the country. 'In view of all these support to the Azad Conference can any one say that the Musalmans are with the reactionaries. No wonder the leaders of the reactionary school are fast losing ground.'[108] He also ridiculed Jinnah as 'the so-called Qaed-i-Azam of Musalmans', while referring to his dishonorable reply to Maulana Azad and concluded the statement with an appeal, 'to all freedom loving Musalmans to unite and work to further the objects of Azad Muslim Conference. . . .'[109]

With very little or no scope of any constitutional development, the Congress started contemplating political activities which had not been undertaken so far because Gandhi had insisted that if the British conceded India's Independence, the Congress might join the government in its war efforts. Therefore the options before the Congress were limited. In the Working Committee meeting held at Bombay on 13-17 September 1940, on Gandhi's insistence, a resolution on individual Satyagraha was passed (to be ratified by the AICC), instructing all Congress Committees and members to extend him (Gandhiji) the fullest cooperation.[110]

Subsequently Gandhi launched a limited Satyagraha movement on 18 September 1940. The issue was to protect civil liberty, the right of freedom of speech to propagate that India did not believe in the war and would dissuade people from assisting the war efforts of the government.[111] Azad did not fully share Gandhiji's approach in this matter and yet he went along with him 'Soon there was a nationwide movement of individual *Satyagraha*.'[112] Even to this limited Satyagraha, the government reacted sharply and arrested a large number of *Satyagrahis* across India. Azad was arrested on 31 December 1940 and sentenced to imprisonment for two years. He was detained in Naini Jail. Even while in jail he was in touch with the Congress leaders through his secretary, Ajmal Khan. Sadiq Ali, secretary of AICC wanted to know from him if Amtus Salam, a close associate of Gandhiji could interview him in jail.[113] Similarly, Azad was conveying his political opinion through his secretary. These correspondences are indicative of the fact that even in jail Azad was aware of and kept in touch with developments taking place. He was arrested for two years however, 'in December 1941, the Viceroy decided that Jawaharlal and I should be released. The decision was intended to test the Congress' reaction to the changed War situation.'[114] Azad did not seem to have been happy at his release. Moreover he 'felt that even though the war had been going on for over two years, we had not been able to take any effective steps for achieving Indian freedom. We seemed to be the victim of circumstances and not the master of our destiny.'[115]

After his release from jail, Azad realized that the debate on non-violence/violence continued. Differences between him and Gandhiji on this issue had persisted. 'I went to Gandhiji and immediately felt that we had moved further apart,'[116] on the question of non-violence. In order to thrash out the issue once again, a Congress Working Committee meeting was convened at Bardoli on 23-30 December 1941. The resolution as regards India's position on war as adopted at Bardoli, somehow endorsed Azad's reading of the prevailing situation in the country. While explaining the rationale for adopting a resolution to this effect he said, 'We had not moved an inch forward. It was not that we did not want to move. We wanted control of the government of our country; we wanted freedom and independence whether in times of peace or war.'[117] Gandhiji did not like the present stance of Azad and the CWC and subsequently asked Azad to relieve him of 'the responsibility laid upon me by the Bombay resolution, because he thought that only non-violence can save India and the World from self-extinction. Such being the case, I must continue with my mission whether I am alone or assisted by an organization or individuals.'[118] Gandhiji's request was conceded by the CWC held at Bardoli but Azad further qualified this that it was not correct to say that he (Gandhiji) was relieved so that the Congress could repeat its conditional offer of participation in the war. He went on, 'The bonds between the Congress and Gandhiji were indissoluble, and death alone could snap them.'[119]

It is quite clear that despite differences, Azad could not bring himself to sever links with Gandhi. Moreover, Azad had already undergone the bitter experience of resignation threats by several Working Committee members in 1940 soon after becoming Congress president. The issue at stake was not that of personal difference between the two leaders, but of devising strategies to attain freedom. Azad wanted to move fast but he was not free from constraints. Gandhiji was not moved by Azad's speech praising him at the AICC meeting. Gandhiji delivered a speech in which be clearly disagreed with Azad, 'I suggest to you that it is a grave mistake to contemplate its (non-violence) abandonment. It is hardly fair to describe my method as religious because it is new.' After having exhorted the AICC members Gandhiji went a step forward in expressing his anger, 'It (independence) cannot be obtained by joining the war. For the Congress to join any war before the attainment of complete independence is to undo the work of the past twenty years.'[120] He proceeded to declare, 'The article (non-violence) in my possession is an invaluable pearl. It has to be weighed in the proper scales, and those who can pay the price can have it. It cannot be bartered away even for independence.'[121] The differences over this resolution were apparent. While Nehru went along with it, Patel and Rajendra Prasad had reservations. Gandhiji went on to say, 'Colleagues like the Sardar and Rajender Babu are not happy over the resolution, but I am asking them not to leave the Working Committee.'[122]

Statements such as these were not calculated to build confidence in the Maulana as president. Ever since he had assumed the responsibilities of the president he had to contend with divergent trends within the party. Instead of being able to provide leadership, he was being pulled in different directions. It is no surprise that once he even thought of resigning.[123] Internal differences in the Congress leadership over certain principles and strategies were sapping the energy of the party and undermining the political initiative of Azad as president. The sword of Damocles of resignation by his Working Committee colleagues hung over his head. There were occasions when within Congress circles there were talks about suspending the Working Committee and electing Rajendra Prasad as Congress president.[124] However, ignoring internal bickering, he constantly endeavoured to extend political support to groups such as Azad Muslim Conference which were seriously challenging the ideological and political campaign of the Muslim League.[125]

The representatives of the government took a different view of these developments. Linlithgow in his communication with Amery described the All-India Azad Muslim Conference as 'so-called', and described a meeting in early March 1942 as 'stage-managed'. In the same communication, he talked about the All-India Momin Conference, a constituent of the Azad Muslim Conference, as an 'un-influential' body and said that many Momins were members of the League.[126] By any reckoning the All-India Momin Conference was a mass-based organization of Muslim weavers, numerous in UP, Bihar, Maharashtra and Bengal. Attempts to undermine the political importance of bodies such as these, committed to the cause of Indian nationalism, must have been motivated. Propping up the separatist claims of the Muslim League was more favourable an idea than to encourage nationalist Muslims' formations.

The tendency of the British to deprecate nationalist Muslims and encourage the Muslim League was amply manifested in the correspondence of those responsible for governing India. In view of the declining fortunes of the Allied Powers on the war-front, and of growing American pressure, the government thought of opening a dialogue with the Indian leaders. Even before Cripps came to India in March 1942 with a Draft Proposal for a future constitutional arrangement in India, some preparations were under way. Amery, the Secretary of State, wrote to Churchill that any declaration on Indian policy must reiterate the principles of 'the August Offer'. 'Our insistence on agreement has been widely taken' as a power of veto on all constitutional progress in India handed to Jinnah. Secondly, there should be a declaration that if the majority of provinces and princes agreed upon a constitution it would be accepted so far as they were concerned, leaving dissident states to stay out for the time being or even altogether.[127]

Cunningham, Governor of NWFP, wrote to Linlithgow in the context of the Cripp's Proposal that there were three ways of safeguarding Muslim interests. First, equality or something near equality of representation at the Centre; second, something on the lines of Pakistan; and third, transfer of some powers to provinces so that domination from the Centre would not greatly matter.[128] Cunningham conceded that he did not think that the average educated Muslims (implying NWFP) looked on the Pakistan idea as a practical solution.[129] It was against a background of such arguments that Stafford Cripps arrived in India with His Majesty's Government's Draft Declaration,[130] which became the basis for negotiations among Indian parties. There was a meeting between Azad and Cripps on 25 April 1942. Asaf Ali assisted Azad as interpreter. The Maulana assured Cripps that he would return to him after having discussed the Draft Declarations with his colleagues in the CWC.[131] In his meeting with Jinnah on the same issue, his sole concern was to know 'whether they (Muslim-majority provinces) would have the effective right to opt out of the Constitution in the event of their so desiring'.[132] While Jinnah was making these inquiries on 25 March 1942, he perhaps did not know that even if the Draft Declaration did not explicitly state what Jinnah had in mind as regards Pakistan, Amery had already conceded the same.[133] The Secretary of State was conceding a point against which a large number of Muslim political formations had arrayed themselves, and contrary to the stand of the Muslim League. The All-India Azad Muslim Conference held a meeting on 28 February and 18 March 1942, presided over by Allah Bux from Sind. It was demanded that the country must cease to be a dependency, and the speakers exhorted their countrymen to agitate to establish freedom. It also argued that it was a piece of special pleading by the Secretary of State that the League was projected as the authoritative spokesman of the Muslims.[134]

Ignoring the claims of other Muslim political formations and only focusing on the League was a case of deliberate mischief by the government in the context of the Cripps Proposals. On 28 March 1942 Cripps tried to reason with Azad about his proposals. He (Cripps) said, 'I do not think he was convinced.'[135] The following day Azad and Nehru met Cripps and suggested a scheme with regard to the Provincial option in which Muslim provinces could secede after five or ten years after the Union came into being. Cripps did not concede this. He concluded at the end of the meeting that the Congress appeared determined 'not to accept it and that it was not worth arguing or pressing'.[136] They (Azad and Nehru) met Cripps on 2 April 1942 again and gave him a final reply—that the Proposal was not acceptable to them on the grounds that it did not clearly refer to independence. The Draft Document had 'prejudiced any more favorable solution to the problem and they feared the partition of India and definitely thought that this encouraged it and that the principle of a united India was one for which they were prepared to go to almost any length'.[137] Subsequently Azad, in his communication with Cripps, unambiguously stated that his proposals were not acceptable to the Congress.[138] Cripps replied, 'I was extremely sorry to receive from you your letter of April 10, expressing the rejection by the Congress Working Committee of His Majesty's Government's Draft Declaration.'[139]

For a while after the failure of the negotiations with the Cripps Mission, the blame-game was carried out. Azad was to comment much later that Cripps tried to shift the blame on the Congress. He stated that 'if at all the British were sincere they should have sent through Cripps a declaration that Britain was ready to part with power. The offer of Cripps gave us nothing. If we had accepted his "Offer" we might have regretted it in the future.'[140] Cripps too in his press conference held on 11 April 1942 had remarked that the Working Committee was not prepared to accept the scheme or to enter a national government. 'The draft is therefore withdrawn and we revert to the position as it was before I came here.'[141]

The entire process of negotiation with Cripps Mission was rather tortuous. After it came to an end all the leaders returned to their respective places. So did Azad. However, the failure had generated terrible anxiety in the minds of people in view of the advancing Japanese army, which had already captured Burma. The Maulana thought that convening a meeting of the AICC would be advisable in order to explain the latest developments and remove confusion among Congressmen. Accordingly an AICC meeting was called from 29 April to 2 May 1942 at Allahabad.[142] At this meeting Azad delivered a speech referring to the negotiations with the Cripps Mission. He stated, 'The stand taken by the Working Committee with regard to the Cripps Proposals would have involved them in active participation in the War.' He continued, 'But he was happy to say that throughout the two weeks of negotiations these members viewed every proposal from the point of view of those colleagues who believed in the defense of their country by other than non-violent means. Whatever decisions they made were unanimous.'[143]

Patel seems to have anticipated the line of thinking of Azad. He issued a statement to this effect and held out threats of resignation from the Working Committee.[144] After the proceedings of the AICC had ended, the Sardar along with Rajendra Babu returned to Sevagram where Shankar Deo and Prafulla Ghosh had already arrived. Patel and Prasad addressed a letter to Azad saying they had apprised Gandhiji about developments at the Allahabad AICC meeting. It was pointed out that 'The views expressed by us in Allahabad have not been changed and we feel that the differences were fundamental and now those have effects in the work also, so it would be better that we go out of the Working Committee.'[145] They advised the Maulana, 'It is better that you have a discussion with Gandhiji. When we will not be there, if you think proper, you may call new members of the Working Committee. We have made known to you what we thought proper.'[146] The decision by Patel and Prasad to quit the Working Committee was endorsed by Gandhiji. In a letter to the

Maulana, Gandhiji said that, 'You ask Sardar and five or six other members to resign and constitute a new Committee. Now it is clear that when there are two opinions in the Committee, why should we pretend that we all are of the same view?'[147] Gandhiji's outburst against Azad was on the resolution that was adopted at Allahabad AICC, which he thought did not incorporate his views.[148]

In the light of such an attitude by the Working Committee members and Gandhiji—who threatened resignation—it is worth pondering what message they wanted to convey to Azad. Was it meant to convey that his presidentship depended on their support? Why did Gandhiji, considering his stature in the party and the country, have to resort to resignation threats? What was Azad's reaction to these developments? No definitive answer can be given in the absence of any hard evidence, but it can be surmised that Azad had little option except to act pragmatically. Despite being frequently threatened by resignations, he succeeded in carrying the AICC along his own line of thinking on a large number of issues. He openly admitted his differences with Gandhiji on the question of non-violence, but Azad always wondered why the Mahatma should make an issue of it. In his struggle within the party he received support from Nehru.[149] Apropos of Sardar Patel, Rajendra Parasad and Kripalani, Azad thought that they rarely tried to judge things on their own and they were accustomed to deferring to Gandhiji.[150] Whether this was true or not, it is clear that right from the time Azad became the Congress president, he had a difficult relationship with the stalwarts of Congress including Gandhiji, particularly on the question of non-violence.

A fresh round of demands for resignation was to follow. The Working Committee had gathered at Wardha to discuss the possibility of launching a mass movement under Gandhiji's leadership. The issue of non-violence once again came up, much to the chagrin of Gandhiji. He demanded that Azad resign from the Presidentship if the Congress wanted him (Gandhiji) to lead the movement. Gandhiji wanted Azad and Nehru to leave even the CWC. The Maulana was taken aback and only after Sardar Patel's intervention did Gandhiji agree to mollify the Maulana and withdraw the letter he wrote to him on 7 July 1942. The

Maulana yielded to his persuasion.[151] The meeting at Wardha was convened to discuss the proposed movement. Gandhiji was in an unusually militant mood.[152] For him the overwhelming consideration was to keep India away from the ravages of the war. The fear of the advancing Japanese army was palpable. The only way India could be saved was to launch a nationwide non-violent movement. In the course of discussion, Jawaharlal Nehru described the contemplated movement as non-violent open rebellion. Gandhiji seemed to like the expression and subsequently the Working Committee passed the 'Quit India Resolution' on 14 July 1942.[153]

Azad had some doubts about the timing and method of the proposed movement but he went along with the rest of the CWC. He forcefully defended the Wardha Resolution at the AICC meeting in Bombay on 7-9 August 1942. He declared, 'The slogan "Quit India" means nothing more and nothing less than the complete transfer of power to India's hands.'[154] He further elaborated upon the resolution that the 'Quit India' demand did not mean the physical removal of all British people from India. It only meant the transfer of political power to Indian hands. After the demand had been made by Gandhiji, Pandit Nehru and he went to Wardha to discuss the matter with Gandhiji, who made it clear to them that it only meant the transfer of power.'[155] Gandhiji while delivering a speech referred to the British evacuating from Burma, Malaya and other places in the hope of these places being recaptured,

> That may be their military strategy, but supposing they leave us, what happens to us. In that case Japan will come here. The coming of Japan will mean the end of China and perhaps of Russia too. In these matters Pandit Nehru is my Guru. I don't want to be the instrument of Russia's defeat nor of China's. If that happens, I would hate myself.[156]

Having elaborated upon the rationale behind launching the movement Gandhiji highlighted that non-violence alone, would be the guiding principle. 'But I must tell you that there is no change in me. I stick to the principle of non-violence as I did before. If you are tired of it then you need not come with me.[157]

It is difficult to say whether Gandhiji was simply reiterating his principle of non-violence or sounding a note of caution to

Azad and many like him who did not accept non-violence as a creed. Azad was already sceptical about a non-violent movement taking shape under existing circumstances. He thought, 'I could not for a moment see how the non-violent movement of Gandhiji's conception could be launched and maintained in war conditions'.[158] Clearly he apprehended that violence was likely to break out in the course of the movement. It is not surprising, therefore, that he said in a press interview on 17 July 1942, 'Gandhiji has been made to promise that the new movement will not be stopped merely for the reason that violence might be displayed. However, the Congressmen should never resort to or encourage violence.'[159]

It is difficult to establish whether Gandhiji really agreed to a condition such as this. In any case, the day after the passing of the 'Quit India' resolution almost all the leaders of the Congress including Maulana Azad were arrested. The 'Quit India' movement did emerge but outside the Gandhian framework in contrast to the two earlier mass movements. In the course of the 'Quit India' movement large-scale violence occurred. Consequently the British brutally suppressed the movement.[160] After his arrest Azad was taken to Ahmadnagar Fort, where he was jailed till April 1945. Thereafter he was removed to Bankura in Bengal and released on 15 June 1945. While in Ahmadnagar Fort Jail, he heard the news of his wife's illness. The Government of India was prepared to release him but he declined the offer. Some time later he received the sad news of his wife's passing away.[161]

While the leaders of the Congress were incarcerated in various jails, the Muslim League had an open field to expand its influence and broaden its social base among the Muslims. By 1945 the League enjoyed the status of the party controlling governments in Sind, NWFP, and Bengal and even in the Hindu-majority province of Assam.[162] The strength of the League had suddenly become formidable.

Gandhiji, was released in 1944, almost a year earlier than many of his colleagues. He opened a dialogue with Jinnah. Rajagopalachari had come up with a formula on the basis of which Gandhiji negotiated with Jinnah. The basic objective was to let Jinnah talk about the contentious issue, but he made it out that the Congress was endorsing his Pakistan scheme. In this context it is important to highlight the efforts made by the Azad Muslim Conference, a conglomerate of several Muslim political formations. Here was a Muslim coalition which had been consistently challenging the Muslim League, right since the time it had formulated the 'two-nation theory'. The Conference organized a session on 6-8 May 1944 at Delhi. Here it adopted two serious resolutions. The first emphasized that no satisfactory solution (of the communal problem) was possible till such time as a 'Real national government exercising full authority was formed at the centre'.[163] The second was far more interesting and with serious implications. For the sake of clarity it is useful to quote it in full, 'This meeting of the nationalist Muslims considers, in the best interests of the country that a Hindu–Muslim settlement is brought about without any delay.' It continued,

> In the opinion of this meeting a solution of the communal problem satisfactory to all parties concerned can be secured on the following fundamental considerations and such a solution will satisfy the needs and aspirations of Indian Muslims: (1) India should continue to remain a united country. (2) Her own people should frame the Constitution of India. (3) There should be an All-India Federation. (4) The units of Federation should be completely autonomous and all residuary power should be vested in them. (5) Every unit of the Federation should be free to secede from it as a result of plebiscite of all its adult inhabitants. (6) The religious, economic and cultural rights of minorities should be fully and effectively safeguarded by reciprocal agreement.[164]

After passing the resolution, three Conference leaders—S.A. Barelvi, Hafiz Mohammad Ibrahim and Dr. Shaukatullah Ansari met the press, further explaining the rationale for adopting the second resolution, which allowed secession as a choice for the provinces. They argued that it was done only to remove the apprehension in the minds of Muslims that there would be compulsion in forming the Federation. In order to remove such fears the 'Nationalist Muslims conceded the right of secession but advised the units not to exercise that right.'[165] The leaders further argued that what was proposed was not Pakistan but a plan that should let India remain united for all time to come. That was the fundamental difference between them and the League. 'They wanted to launch a campaign on the basis of this resolution in order to discredit the Muslim League and replace it as the "spokesman" of community.'[166]

Any alternative plan to the Muslim League's claim of Pakistan was bound to take into consideration the fear among many Muslims, particularly in Muslim-majority provinces. But the Congress did not view alternative plans thrown up by nationalist Muslims favourably. The government in any case had always displayed a propensity to ignore the claims of nationalist Muslims.

III

The government's stand on Indian participation in governance was indicated during the Simla Conference in June–July 1945. On 14 June 1945 Lord Wavell had in a radio broadcast announced that the government wished to engage Indian leaders in negotiations, with a view to forming a new Executive Council, which would be more representative of organized political opinion. The proposed Council would represent the main communities and include an equal proportion of caste Hindus and Muslims. It would work if formed under the existing constitution. It would be an entirely Indian Council except for the Viceroy and Commander-in-Chief, who would retain his position as War Member. It was also proposed that the portfolio of external affairs, hitherto held by the Viceroy, be placed in charge of an Indian member of Council, 'as far as the interests of British India are concerned'.[167] He added, the Viceroy would continue to exercise his constitutional power of control but would not exercise it unreasonably. This interim government would in no way prejudice the final constitutional settlement.[168] He fixed the date for consultations among the parties as 24 June 1945 at Simla.

On the day of the announcement itself the government ordered the release of the Congress Working Committee members. Most of them were released on 15 June 1945. It was indeed quite difficult for the Congress to arrive at a decision considering that many leaders had been in jail for about three years. Many of them were affected by personal losses and bad health. Yet this was one occasion, which held out hope of some settlement prior to India becoming independent. A Congress Working Committee meeting was convened on 21 June 1945 in Bombay to consider Wavell's initiative. It was agreed that Azad as the Congress president would represent the Congress as the chief negotiator.[169] Accordingly Azad sent a telegram to Wavell that he was authorized by the Congress Working Committee to accept his invitation to join the conference on 25 June 1945.[170]

Azad met Wavell on 25 June 1945 at Simla just before the conference. He was accompanied by G.B. Pant. He raised several issues with Wavell. One was the issue of parity between caste Hindus and Muslims. Azad said that the Congress would accept equality of caste Hindus and Muslims but would not compromise on the method of selection. Congress must have a voice in the selection of non-Hindus, and the Muslims in particular must not be selected by an exclusively communal body. This was vital to the Congress.[171] 'On the same day Jinnah had met Wavell and claimed that the Muslim League had the right to nominate all the Muslim members to the council.'[172] Wavell said he could not accept that. When Wavell mentioned that he intended to nominate a Muslim from among the Unionists, Jinnah retorted that the Unionist party members were traitors to Muslim interests and that the Punjab coalition ministry existed only by his tacit consent.[173] Wavell refused to give a pledge that the League should nominate all Muslims.[174]

With these clearly defined positions of the Viceroy, Congress and the League, the Conference began on 25 June 1945. The claims to represent an all-India interest by the Congress and the League's claims to represent the Muslims dominated the Conference. After a four-day gap the Conference convened on 29 June 1945. It was adjourned to meet again on 14 July 1945 in order to allow the parties to hold consultations among themselves.

Meanwhile on 7 July 1945, Azad submitted to Wavell a list of 15 members for the proposed Executive Council which, surprisingly, included the names of three Muslim League members and one Hindu Mahasabha member. The list makes an interesting reading. It was as follows: (1) M.A.K. Azad, (2) Jawaharlal Nehru, (3) Sardar Patel, (4) Rajendra Prasad, (5) M.A. Jinnah, (6) Nawab Liaqat Ali Khan, (7) Nawab Mohd. Ismail Khan, (8) Asaf Ali, (9) Syama Prasad Mookerjee, (10) Raj Kumari Amrit Kaur,

(11) Muniswami Pillay, (12) Radhanath Das, (13) Gagan Behari, (14) Ardeshir Dalal, and (15) Master Tara Singh.[175]

It is surprising that Azad should have chosen to include the names of Muslim League members in his list. The list presented to Wavell and his statements in *India Wins Freedom* are contrary to each other. In *India Wins Freedom* Azad wrote,

> Difference about the composition of the Council came into the open, after agreement had been reached on the political issue. When this general pattern had been accepted, the time came for the parties to suggest the names of their representatives. Naturally the first name in the Congress list was that of the Congress president. We included also the names of Jawaharlal and Sardar Patel. Regarding the other two names there was a good deal of discussion among us before we could come to an agreement. I was in favour of including one Parsee and one Indian Christian.[176]

It is true the list sent to Wavell included names of Raj Kumari Amrit Kaur, a Christian, and Ardeshir Dalal, a Parsee. Azad ignored the claims of Khizr Hyat Khan a Unionist. Instead Syama Prasad Mookerji's name was in the list—it is not clear as to what prompted Azad to include his name.

At another point he argued that Wavell wished to include the name of Khizr Hyat, which would have meant seven Muslims out of fourteen, half the total strength in the Executive Council. Azad stated that this was evidence of the generosity of the Congress and that it showed the stupidity of the Muslim League.[177] 'The League was supposed to be the guardian of Muslim interests and yet it was because of its opposition that the Muslims of India were denied a substantial share in the Government of undivided India.'[178] In any case Jinnah had already informed Wavell that, 'The Working Committee is emphatically of the opinion that the Muslim members in the proposed Executive Council should be chosen from the Muslim League, subject to a confidential discussion between Your Excellency and the President of the Muslim League, before they are finally recommended by you to the Crown for appointment.'[179] 'The Working Committee feels very strongly on this point and regards it as one of the fundamental principles.'[180] In view of Jinnah's correspondence with Wavell, the outcome was clear much before the Conference reconvened on 14 July 1945. All that was required was to make a formal statement about the Conference being brought to a close, which Wavell actually did.[181]

Before we proceed further, it is pertinent to consider a few important points touching the Wavell Plan with reference to Azad's assertions. First, in the entire *India Wins Freedom*, the details and description of the Wavell Plan do not match with other relevant evidence, whereas accounts about other developments do match the evidence. Why Azad did this remains inexplicable. Second, when Wavell already knew that Jinnah was likely to veto his plan what preemptive steps did he take? Could he have pressurized Jinnah to fall in line or would he have had to accept being kept out of the Executive Council in view of the fact that there were several able nationalist Muslims to fill positions. Third, can we discern some plan to let Indian groups fight among themselves, which would absolve the government and the Viceroy from any responsibility?

Apart from the discrepancy in Azad's account in *India Wins Freedom*, he squarely blamed the League and the Viceroy for the failure of the Conference. In his press conference soon after the Conference came to an end he said, 'The attitude of the Muslim League is responsible for the failure of the Conference.' He expressed his anger, 'For the communal situation in India as it is today, the British government cannot shirk responsibility. So long as the third party exists in India the same position will continue.'[182] Azad was furious about the role of the government in the whole affair. 'With a faltering step and wavering mind, we cannot reach our destination. It is good to think twice before taking a step forward, but when a step has already been taken hesitation is not a virtue but weakness. If the British government wishes to give shape to things they should have realized the communal situation. They should have been prepared not to surrender the right to veto to any group and thus block the path of progress.'[183] He also questioned the claim of the League to be the sole representative of the Muslims of India. 'There was a large bloc of Muslims who had nothing to do with the League.'[184]

Azad's assertion in the press conference was quite close to the mark as regards the Muslim League's strength among the Muslim masses. Many British officials had admitted only about a year earlier that while the League appeared to be growing in popularity in urban areas, 'it has still not made much headway outside towns. The Unionists scored a minor success the other day when their candidate for the senior vice-chairmanship of the Sialkot District Board defeated the League nominee by 31 vote to 10; the individual chosen was by no means a strong candidate so far as personal merits were concerned.'[185] It has been established that till around this time the Muslim League was struggling hard to find a viable foothold in Muslim-majority provinces. The British officials themselves admitted that the League was an urban phenomenon.

The capitulation of the British at the Simla Conference altered the scenario of the social support of the League. At least in the case of Punjab, Jinnah's share in the political market skyrocketed and several Unionist leaders switched sides to join the League.[186] The British were guilty of betraying the Unionists by allowing Jinnah to veto the inclusion of Khizr Hyat Khan in the Executive Council. The Unionists had been one group which had continuously cooperated with the government during the entire course of the war, in terms of the mobilization both of men and materials.[187] Azad had been much taken in by Wavell, 'I was impressed by the frankness and sincerity of the Viceroy as he described the proposal to me. I saw that his attitude was not that of a politician but of a soldier.'[188] However, the outcome of the Simla Conference could only lead one to conclude that he was very much a man representing imperial interests in India.

Azad had one more year as President of the Congress. The failure of the Simla Conference cast a shadow on the national political scene and Azad found he was left with little room for manoeuvring. However, this disappointment did not last long. In England, in the elections of July 1945 the Labour Party was swept to power. Labour's coming to power was viewed with optimism in Congress circles, Azad being no exception. Around this time his sole concern was to create a political climate where it was possible to accommodate Muslim aspirations despite the fear of a Hindu-dominated centre, and to outmanoeuvre the League in its pursuit of separatist politics. Given the pragmatic approach of Azad, he could not view the problem of communalism in the way Nehru did: 'Fundamentally, this communal problem as well as many other problems, if you analyse them, become a kind of conflict between medievalism and modernism, between the medieval outlook and modern outlook. Obviously it is not a question of a seat or job here and there.'[189] Azad thought differently. His understanding was that Muslims wanted a share in power, and the assurance that the power and authority in Muslim-majority provinces would not be tampered with.

Anticipating that the Labour government was shortly going to make an offer in connection with India's political future akin to the Cripps Offer, giving Muslim-majority provinces the right to secede, Azad thought of a strategy—if the Congress could make a similar offer on its own initiative it would have a positive effect on the Muslims. He said, 'they would have to admit that it was in the interests of Musalmans themselves to remain united with the rest of India rather than be separated from it'.[190] He also expressed optimism that 'if the Congress took a clear position on issues like this, it would help nationalist Muslims reorganize themselves better to convince the Muslims at large'.[191] Azad wanted to issue a press statement in this regard in the hope of a positive outcome. But Sardar Patel advised him not to do so since the matter was too important for individuals to express their opinions.[192] Before Azad wrote to the Sardar, he had already written a similar letter to Gandhiji, which was intercepted by the government agencies. A memorandum accompanied this letter. Azad had argued that the time had come to recognize that the communal problem did exist in the country and, that it demanded a solution based on a new approach to remove the Muslims' apprehension. Help from Muslims outside the League was necessary.[193] In the memorandum, which it would appear Azad himself had drafted, he said that any attempt to form a unitary government would fail. Partition would also fail, and was against the interests of the Muslims themselves. Azad regarded partition as a defeatist policy and could not accept it.[194] In this memorandum he suggested that it would be appropriate 'to leave entirely to Muslims the question of their status in the future constitution of India'. At the same time he feared that 'Unless Hindu Congress leaders take a new line, nationalist Muslims will desert them.'[195]

In this letter Azad seems to have taken a position as regards the solution of the communal problem, which was somewhat strong, and at variance with the dominant thinking in the Congress. In his scheme of things, holding out the hope of autonomy and freedom of choice was one possible way out of the stalemate. Gandhiji was not prepared to accept Azad's suggestion that there should be a convention by which the head of the Indian Federation in the initial period should be a Hindu and a Muslim by turn.[196] Gandhiji not only did not agree but he was angry too. He admonished Azad sharply. 'I do not infer from your letter that you are talking about "my Hindus". Whatever you have in your heart has not appeared in your writing.'[197] He did not stop here. 'Whatever you want to say about the communal problem should not be said without consulting the Working Committee. I am also of the opinion that it would be better to keep quiet. The Party can give its opinion after consulting with you. They have the right to do so. Besides, it is their duty.'[198] He concluded by saying, 'I do not feel the urge to do anything hastily.'[199]

In Gandhiji's perception even before Azad relinquished his presidentship, he was reduced to a position where he did not enjoy the authority of an elected president of the Congress. When he said that, 'The Party can give its opinion after consulting with you' did Gandhiji mean that Azad who was Congress President, had no authority to give statements or take positions while taking the party in confidence? This must have demoralized Azad.

That his plan of solving the communal problem was not viewed with favour in Congress circles was nothing new. As early as March 1942 Gopichand Bhargava, a prominent Congress leader from Punjab, complained to Rajendra Prasad that Azad seemed to have agreed with Sikandar Hyat Khan on certain conditions such as (1) complete provincial autonomy, (2) the centre to be given such power as are agreed to by the provinces, (3) residuary power to be with the provinces, and (4) the right of secession with the provinces.[200] Bhargava complained, 'There was a conference of Muslim Ulema. They adopted a similar resolution. It was alleged that Maulana Azad agreed with this resolution.[201] He concluded by saying that the 'Congress would suffer if this Pakistan or Zonal or similar scheme were agreed to without consultation.' ('People will have to be satisfied before the settlement becomes a fact'.[202])

Gandhiji's anger and Gopichand Bhargava's insinuation both seem to suggest that Azad had concurred with the Muslim League's view as regards provincial autonomy and the right to secession for the provinces. There were not many in the Congress willing to recognize that Azad was developing a parallel strategy to satisfy Muslims in Muslim-majority provinces in order to take the wind out of the sails of the League.

It is important to recall that in 1944 when all the Congress leaders were in jail and no political activity was possible, the Muslim League had ample room to manoeuvre and manipulate political developments to its advantage. The Azad Muslim Conference in its session at Delhi had raised similar demands as the Maulana did with Sardar Patel and Gandhiji. The constituents of the Conference were not conspiring but were openly challenging the League ideologically and politically. This Conference had enjoyed Azad's patronage right since the beginning in April 1940. After all, the nationalist Muslims needed some agenda and strategy to go to the masses in the face of the Muslim League's virulent campaign.

Azad had developed this scheme in view of the fact that the Congress was not able to reach out to the Muslim masses or offer assurances and commitments to instill confidence in them. Nehru was candid enough to admit as late as November 1945 in the context of UP that, 'It is pretty clear that we have long neglected the Muslim masses. The fault lies with us, not with them.'[203] Nehru was not alone in confessing Congress' weakness as regards Muslim support to the party. Sardar Patel too admitted in almost a similar tone, referring to Congress work among the Muslims of Bengal and Punjab, that, 'The Congress organization in both these provinces have been very weak. Congressmen have not worked in rural areas, and in the cities, they work only amongst non-Muslims.'[204]

Despite the frank admission that the Congress had very little presence among Muslims, the Congress as a body did not endorse the Maulana's formulation. The Congress Working Committee met on 12-18 September 1945 and again on 21-4 September 1945 and resolved, 'The Congress cannot agree to any proposal to disintegrate India by giving liberty to any component state or territorial unit to secede from the Indian union or federation. The Congress has been wedded to India's freedom and unity.'[205] Having declared the policy decision the CWC resolution admitted, 'Nevertheless, the Committee also declared, it cannot think in terms of compelling the people in any territorial unit to remain in an Indian Union against their established will.'[206]

While the Congress formulated its larger policy approach for maintaining the unity of India, the government announced on 21 August 1945 that general elections would be held in the following winter. This set the election preparations rolling, and the interested parties started preparing their election manifestos. Certain nationalist Muslim formations declared their strategy of boycotting the Muslim League in the elections and working towards national independence. In this they were guided by different considerations. The Shia Council strongly feared that if Pakistan came into being, the Hanafi School of Law would be established, something entirely unacceptable to them. Therefore the Council decided to work with those organizations that stood for the independence of India.[207] Similarly, the All-India Ahrar Conference in its meeting on 20-1 October 1945 condemned the Muslim League for crying hoarse about 'Islam in Danger'. Ahrar volunteers were exhorted to prevent the Muslim masses being misled by Jinnah and the League.[208] With identical ideological proclivities the Nationalist Muslims' Conference set-up a Nationalist Muslims' Parliamentary Board which decided to prepare its manifesto under the guidance of Maulana Azad. It condemned the Muslim League as a capitalist organization in league with the imperialist government to exploit Muslims.[209]

The battle for Muslim votes had reference to a small part of India's population. In British India the average percentage of enfranchised Muslims did not exceed 15 per cent in the Muslim-majority provinces.[210] In the course of its election campaign the League resorted to not only fair but also dubious means as well.

In several cases the tactics of the League was to disrupt the meetings of rivals and indulge in large-scale intimidation and blackmail.[211] Despite all these efforts the League's claim to represent all Muslims did not go unchallenged. The All-India Momin Conference put up stiff resistance to the League in the Bihar assembly general elections. Its main plank was that the League was a party of big landlords and reactionary elements and never represented the interests of working-class Muslims. The Momin Conference successfully defeated six League candidates.[212] No mean achievement. Many nationalist Muslim leaders were conscious that the limited franchise base was an advantage to the League, whereas universal adult franchise would have surely gone against it. The Nationalist Muslims' Conference in its meeting on 18 September 1945 had clearly stated that,

> This convention of various Muslim organizations feels that under the present circumstances only the votes of the wealthy and zamindar classes can be registered and there is no possibility of the Muslim masses recording their votes. It is therefore apparent that there is a clear danger of more reactionaries being returned.[213]

The declarations and protestations by so many Nationalist Muslim formations notwithstanding, the election results of 1945-6 gave the Muslim League the kind of electoral strength that it had been hoping for so that the party could be accepted as the only party of the Muslims. The League secured all the 30 seats reserved for Muslims at the centre, and 442 out of the 509 Muslim seats with 86.6 per cent votes.[214] This did not mean that the League's victory was a complete one.

In Bengal and Sind it had to depend on official and European support. In Punjab the Unionists were able to form a government with the help of the Congress and the Akalis. In NWFP and Assam, a province, which the League wanted to include in Pakistan, the Congress had comfortable majorities.[215]

The League, however, felt it had made good its claim to represent 'Muslim India'. It was convinced that in any future constitutional arrangement the League would negotiate from a position of strength, which it did during the Cabinet Mission negotiations.

The British government decided to send a Cabinet Mission to India. Prime Minister Attlee announced it on 15 March 1946. The Mission arrived in India on 23 March 1946, a three-man team, the Secretary of State for India, Lord Pethick-Lawrence, the president of Board of Trade, Sir Stafford Cripps and the First Lord of Admiralty, A.V. Alexander.[216] The mission had two clearly demarcated issues to negotiate with Indian political parties, particularly the Congress and Muslim League. The issues were—to form an interim government, and the principles and procedures for framing a new constitution for free India.[217]

In the tortuous negotiations among the parties, particularly with regard to independence and partition, one can discern a strange irony. There were two Muslim leaders, Maulana Azad representing the Congress, and Mohammad Ali Jinnah representing the Muslim League. The contrast between the two could not be greater. The one was a man imbued with religiosity but firm in his nationalist conviction that religions could not ever become the basis of nationality. The other was born and bred in the modern, liberal atmosphere of Karachi, Bombay and England, who, with the passage of time transformed himself to take political positions more suited to fanatics and bigots. One stood for Indian unity and the other would accept nothing short of India's division in order to make Pakistan.

Azad strove to meet the challenges of negotiation with a view to avert the Partition of India. In the course of negotiations with the Mission he sometimes walked the extra mile to accommodate the rival political opinion. There were occasions when he carried on negotiations with the Mission without a clear mandate from his party, because he was convinced of the power of his persuasive skills. There were occasions when he came up with ingenious ideas, which could have helped avert partition. At the same time, Azad's concern was that while protecting India's long-term interest, the interests of the Muslims too should be protected.

In his first meeting with the Mission he emphasized that it was the well-considered view of the Congress that any negotiation had to move on the solid basis of India's independence. He then moved on to argue that the Congress visualized a federal government with autonomous provinces, with residuary powers vested in the units themselves. However, this task had to be left with the constitution-making body. If afterwards some particular areas, which must be well-defined, should wish to opt out of the constitution so framed, they would not be compelled to come in.[218] He criticized the League's insistence on two sovereign states. This would mean that if Pakistan came into being the Muslims in the rest of India would be pushed into an alien status.[219] In this long interaction with the Mission, the Maulana was queried on several issues of vital importance. One poser put to Azad was whether he would contemplate a separate optional list for the Muslim-majority provinces. Azad strongly disagreed, arguing that this would be inconsistent with a single federal structure.[220] He underlined the fact that the Congress could never agree to the Partition of India and insisted that there should be no difficulty in forming an interim government.

These arguments convinced the members of the Mission. It noted, 'Only with great difficulty and after particular efforts by Azad himself has Congress come to this decision. If it had not been for his efforts the Congress would not have permitted any decision to be made.'[221]

By contrast, Jinnah in his meeting with the Mission said things diametrically opposed to what Azad had argued with them the previous day. There was no one India but many Indias held by the British as one.[222] 'The differences in India are far greater than between the European countries and compared to those, are of a vital and fundamental character. Even Ireland provides no parallels.'[223] In the course of his interaction he emphatically added, 'Fortunately in India the Muslims have their homeland and so let us divide India.'[224]

In his subsequent meeting with the Mission, Azad insisted that the constitution-making process be preceded by the formation of an interim government without any outside interference. Therefore the position of the Secretary of State would automatically become irrelevant. Once it was agreed that there would be a federal constitution no question would arise about India's bifurcation.[225] Azad also expressed his desire to bring the Congress and the League closer, about which the Mission expressed its inability at that moment.

Subsequently, with a view to requesting the Congress and League to nominate negotiators on behalf of their respective parties, the Secretary of State wrote to Azad that there could be a meeting ground between the Congress and League on the following consideration—that the future constitutional arrangements would be

> a union government with the following subjects; Foreign Affairs, Defense and Communications. There will be two groups of provinces, the one, predominantly Hindu provinces and the other predominantly Muslim provinces, dealing with all other subjects which the provinces in the respective groups desire to be dealt with in common. The provincial governments would deal with all other subjects and will have all the residuary sovereign rights.[226]

In his reply to Pethick-Lawrence, Azad disagreed on several points. The Congress would never accept the division of India into predominantly Hindu and predominantly Muslim provinces. He also objected to the use of expressions such as 'sovereign rights' of provinces and wanted this expression to be deleted in future.[227] He could not accept the proposal to create a sub-federation within the federal union. This would weaken the federal centre. 'We do not therefore favour any such development.'[228] Azad further elaborated upon the issue

> as you are aware, we have envisaged a federal union of autonomous units. Such a federal union must of necessity deal with certain essential subjects of which defence and its allied subjects are the most important. . . . Thus among the common subjects in addition to Foreign Affairs, Defence and Communications, there should be Currency, Customs, Tarrifs and other subjects as may be found on closer scrutiny to be intimately allied to them.[229]

On the question of sub-groupings of the federating units, Azad was more than emphatic. He said, 'We consider it wrong to form groups of provinces and the federal union and more so on religious or communal basis. It also appears that you leave no choice to a province in the matter of joining or not joining the group.'[230]

Maulana Azad also communicated to him that he was willing to join any negotiations along with three other colleagues, Jawaharlal Nehru, Vallabhbhai Patel and Khan Abdul Ghaffar Khan, that might take place. In reply Pethick-Lawrence said, 'We have taken note of the views you have expressed on behalf of the Working Committee of the Congress' and expressed satisfaction that the Congress agreed to enter the joint discussion with representatives of the Muslim League and members of the Cabinet Mission. Referring to the proposed terms of negotiations he said, 'these are our proposed basis for a settlement. . . .'[231] As the negotiations proceeded at Simla, Azad was not too satisfied with the proceedings. He said, 'I confess to feeling somewhat mystified and disturbed at the vagueness of our talks and some of the assumptions underlying them. . . . We must not deceive ourselves.'[232] He went on

> that the basic issue before us was that of independence and the consequent withdrawal of the British army from India, for there can be no independence so long there is a foreign army on Indian soil. We stand for the independence of the whole of India now and not in the distant or near future. Other matters are subsidiary to this and can be fully discussed and decided by the Constituent Assembly.[233]

The Cabinet Mission's suggestion of a sub-federation had exasperated him and his colleagues, as seen in the use of strong words, 'We are emphatically of the opinion that it is not open to the conference to entertain any suggestion for a division of India. If this is to come, it should come through the Constituent Assembly free from any influence of the present governing power.'[234]

In the positions taken by Azad one significant point is clear—that Azad was no longer in a position to pursue the line he had suggested to Patel and Gandhiji in August 1945. All that he was doing in the course of negotiations with the Cabinet Mission was to adhere to the Congress' well-considered position. In his communication to Pethick-Lawrence, he once again reiterated

> the necessity of having a strong and organic federal union. I have also stated that we do not approve of sub-federations or grouping of provinces in the manner suggested, and are wholly opposed to parity

in executives or legislatures as between wholly unequal groups. We do not wish to come in the way of provinces or other units cooperating together, if they so choose, but this must be entirely optional.[235]

Azad reasoned with Pethick-Lawrence that in view of the proposals sent by him, it appeared that 'two or three separate constitutions might emerge for the separate groups, joined together by flimsy common superstructure left to the mercy of the three disjointed groups',[236] because it was feared that such a proposed scheme would help the Muslim League more than anyone else.

It seemed clear that the League would never agree to one constitution-making body or the manner of forming the Constituent Assembly. Jinnah wanted not one Constituent Assembly but three, which would meet together only for the purpose of deciding the constitution of the union government.[237]

While negotiations about the technicalities of the future Constitution were carried out, the Cabinet Mission decided to make its own statement, which it did on 16 May 1946. It envisaged a federal union, controlling Defense, Foreign Affairs and Communications. The states were to be included in the federal union after negotiations. The powers of the federal union were reduced and the individual provinces had the liberty to form a subordinate union of their own. Each of these was to decide for itself the powers it would exercise outside the range of federal subjects. On the basis of the arrangement a Constituent Assembly would be convened to complete the constitution-making process.[238]

The Muslim League accepted the Cabinet Mission proposals in its meeting in Delhi on 5-6 June 1946. Its acceptance was because the party thought that in the proposed plan, 'The founding of Pakistan is inherent in the Mission's plan by virtue of the compulsory grouping of the six Muslim provinces in section B and C.'[239]

The Congress also accepted the Cabinet Plan—on completely different assumptions. Azad wrote to Wavell on 25 June 1946 saying, 'While the Committee has agreed to Congress' participation in the Constituent Assembly, it is in their opinion essential, that a representative and responsible provisional government be formed at the earliest.'[240] The letter also suggested that it had recommended the same for ratification at the AICC meeting to be held in Bombay on 6-7 July 1946.

The AICC met in Bombay on 6-7 July 1946. Two developments of importance took place: first, Jawaharlal Nehru replaced Azad as the Congress president, the other was a long debate on the Working Committee resolution of 26 June 1946 accepting the Cabinet Mission Proposal. Here, Azad made a strong plea with the AICC to ratify the decision of the CWC. He argued that, 'The Cabinet Mission Proposals also have once and for all time cleared all doubts about the questions of the division of India. These proposals have made it clear beyond a shadow of doubt that India shall remain an undivided single unit, with a strong Central Government composed of federating units.'[241] In the same breath he continued:

> For some time now, the Congress has been convinced that a completely unitary form of Central Government was unsuited for India as it is impracticable. The Congress also felt convinced that a division of India as demanded by the Muslim League would be disastrous for India. The Congress therefore decided for a middle course. That is the reason the Congress recommended a Federal format in the centre, with maximum autonomy to the federating units, including residuary powers. This helps to keep India undivided, at the same time ensuring utmost autonomy to the units to develop themselves individually and freely to the maximum extent.[242]

All members did not share Azad's perception with regard to the Congress' acceptance of the Cabinet Plan. Patel at the same meeting argued that 'The shape of the Central Government is a matter for the Constituent Assembly to decide,'[243] thus clearly and publicly repudiating Azad's enthusiasm about a 'Federal form at the centre'. Gandhiji in his speech argued for its acceptance but at the same time was able to see in this scheme nothing but 'darkness all around me'.[244] Nehru had the final word on all that was debated with regard to the provisions and conditions of the plan. In his speech he said, 'We are not bound by a single thing, except that we have decided for the moment to enter the Constituent Assembly.'[245] Nehru elaborated this in a press interview on 10 July 1946. 'The first thing is that we have agreed to the Constituent Assembly and we have agreed to nothing else.'[246] Nehru's statement was surprising in view of the fact that the AICC had already endorsed the resolution by a resounding majority of 204 in favour and 51 against it.

Nehru's approach surprised Azad. He thought it did damage the prospect of a united India. It is possible to argue that Azad might have hoped that once the League entered the Constituent Assembly on conditions agreed upon by both parties, it would be difficult for Jinnah to edge out, in view of the fact that any changes in the Constitution could take place only after ten years. By then the composition of the electorate would have undergone a major change in the sense of enlarging the franchise, therefore ensuring that elite-based Muslim League politics would lose its dominance.

Taking note of all this, the League changed its stand. It rejected the Cabinet Mission Plan on 27 July 1946. The Congress reiterated that it stood by the Cabinet Plan, which did not bring any change in the ground situation except that the Viceroy on 12 August 1946 called upon the concerned parties to constitute an interim government. The Muslim League refused to join since it was preparing for a 'Direct Action Day' on 16 August 1946, which it did by unleashing a torrent of violence in Calcutta in collusion with the League-led government of H.S. Suhrawardy.

It was under the shadow of riots and mayhem that the Congress decided to form the interim government at the centre under Nehru's leadership. In the course of the ministry-formation, the choice of someone under the Muslims quota was discussed. Many Congress leaders insisted that Azad must join to guide the ministry through difficult times. Azad initially was reluctant to join. However, under pressure, he agreed but insisted that he must enter the ministry under the *Congress* quota and not under the *Muslim* quota, or else he would serve the Congress as president again. Not many members agreed with him. Patel advised him against taking such a position. When Azad further insisted Sardar Patel told him, 'You are suffering from indifferent health',[247] as if Azad in poor health could serve as a minister under the *Muslim* quota but not as the President of the Congress. Azad's marginalization in the Congress was tragically evident. He did not have many friends in the party to listen to him. His suggestion to accommodate one more nationalist Muslim in the cabinet, over and above the quota of five was resisted.[248] Azad was a pragmatist to the core. He accepted things stoically. He entered the interim government with the education portfolio.

On 26 October 1946, Wavell succeeded in persuading the League to join the interim government, without the League accepting either the long-term or the short-term provisions of the Cabinet Plan. It is a matter of common knowledge that the League's joining the government did not help matters. On the contrary, it made smooth functioning of the government almost impossible. Out of exasperation nine members of the interim government wrote to the Viceroy demanding that the League members resign. The League made a counter-demand that the Constituent Assembly which had met for the first time on 9 December 1946, be dissolved.

While the bickering went on endlessly, on 20 February 1947 Attlee announced in Parliament that the British would withdraw from India by 30 June 1948. Simultaneously he also announced that a new Viceroy would replace Wavell. In the third week of March 1947 Mountbatten arrived in India, and immediately got into hectic consultations with a number of members of the Congress and the League as well as accredited leaders of these parties and others. Maulana Azad was one such leader with whom Mountbatten held some consultations.

The first opportunity was to discuss Gandhiji's suggestion to Mountbatten that Jinnah be invited to form a new government, which he could constitute entirely from League members or as a coalition.[249] Mountbatten asked Azad for his opinion. Azad said that Gandhiji had the capacity to persuade the Congress to accept his plan. However, if it were left to him (Azad), he would prefer the Cabinet Mission Plan, if accepted whole-heartedly by all parties.[250] The Maulana reiterated the same in another meeting with Mountbatten on 12 April 1947. Mountbatten reported,

> Maulana Azad volunteered to go to any length to support me in trying to get the Cabinet Mission Plan accepted by both Congress and the League. He told me that whatever any body else told me it was his conviction that if Mr. Jinnah really accepted the Cabinet Mission Plan,

at almost any stage within the next few months, the chances of Congress accepting it were really fair.[251]

Azad suggested to Mountbatten that if he could revive the Cabinet Mission Plan it would be a good idea.[252] And he would persuade the Congress to do the same.

Azad was in effect flogging a dead horse in the vain hope that the Cabinet Mission Plan would avert Partition. For the first time it seemed as if he was dreaming of an impossible situation. Within two days of the last letter from Azad to Mountbatten, V. P. Menon wrote to Mr Abell, 'even if Jinnah accepted this proposal (the Cabinet Mission Plan), which is a remote possibility, I have myself no doubt that Azad will find it difficult to get the Congress to accept it'.[253]

Azad was perhaps unaware that the leaders of the Congress had practically given up on the Cabinet Mission Plan. Secondly, no one any longer favoured the idea of a weak federal centre since they believed that only a strong unitary centre was the need of the hour.[254] Azad was careful enough not to raise this issue with other Congress leaders. In any case political developments were moving on the fast track. After having assessed the political situation in India, Mountbatten came up with his own proposals for the future of India on 3 June 1947, known as the Mountbatten Plan. This envisaged India's Partition in order to let Pakistan come into being but not with the whole of Punjab and Bengal as these provinces too were to be divided.

The Third June Plan needed to be endorsed by parties concerned. The Muslim League had difficulty in accepting a truncated Pakistan. The dilemma before the Congress was that acceptance of the Third June Plan was an ideological defeat in view of the fact that the Congress had steadfastly stood for a united India. But under the circumstances, it had no option but to give in. With this in mind an AICC session was convened on 14 June 1947 for the ratification of the CWC decision to accept the Third June Plan. A resolution to accept the Third June Plan was moved by Govind Ballabh Pant and seconded by none other than Azad. In this session Gandhiji pleaded that, 'We had come before the AICC to urge the acceptance of the resolution. Sometimes certain decisions, however, unpalatable they might be, had to be taken.'[255]

After Gandhiji's speech, J.B. Kripalani spoke. After that the mover of the resolution, G.B. Pant, while accepting the Third June Plan, spoke that 'this was the only way to achieve freedom and liberty for the country. It would assure an Indian union with a strong centre, which could ensure progress and help the country, take her rightful place in the world.'[256]

In the course of his speech Pant had also said that the Third June statement was better than the Cabinet Mission Plan. Azad strongly disagreed, and emphatically asserted that 'the Cabinet Mission Plan was the best solution of the problem'.[257] Azad did not think this was the best decision; the indecision and drift in the party had forced it to accept the Plan. He pointed out that even at this stage the Cabinet Plan had not been shelved. But the decision had to be taken by the people of the areas concerned.[258] Hoping against hope, Azad said wistfully, 'The decision is only of the map of the country and not in the hearts of the people, and I am sure it is going to be a short-lived partition.'[259] At the end of his speech, the Maulana became a little apprehensive that the Muslims at large may face difficulties on account of the impending Partition. He cautioned the party, 'Our attitude towards our countrymen should not undergo any change by reason of the fact that certain parts had elected to secede.'[260]

After having seconded the resolution Azad must have known that all that was left now was to wait for 15 August 1947 to see India formally declared independent. His hope that partition would be short-lived remained a dream never to come true. His faith in united India had remained unshaken. In *India Wins Freedom*, which he dictated till a few months before his death, he wanted to relive the days that he had spent negotiating with members of the Cabinet Mission, which could avert Partition even if that meant making more concessions to the Muslim-majority areas.

Azad was given to philosophical disposition. He had reflected upon this in *Ghubar-i-Khatir*, the epistles he composed in Ahmadnagar Fort Jail. He talked about the Epicureans and Stoics. Except for a brief period of epicurean life Azad was generally, given to stoicism. He accepted the Partition of India stoically. Yet it did not undermine the gravity of a political tragedy. He had grappled with several difficulties and suffered many tragedies. However, the greatest tragedy in his life was that at the dawn of independence, politically he did not have a following in his own community as well as among his countrymen.

NOTES

1. *Hindustan Times*, 20 January 1940.
2. Ibid. 4 February 1940. Gandhiji in an interview had said, 'Under the circumstances Maulana Abul Kalam Azad was the best choice' and he hoped that his election would be unanimous.
3. Abul Kalam Azad, *India Wins Freedom: The Complete Version*, Orient Longman, Madras, 1988, p. 29.
4. Ibid.
5. *Hindustan Times,* 16 February 1940.
6. Ibid.
7. One Raghubir Sahai from Badaun wrote a letter to the editor of the *Hindustan Times*, 21 February 1940: 'His election should be an eye opener to those opponents of the Congress both Indian and foreign who dub it purely as a Hindu body. . . . The election is a fitting reply to the taunt of Lord Zetland that the Congress is not taking up the minorities question in right earnest. . . . Maulana Abul Kalam Azad can be safely trusted to see that the Congress deals with the Muslim minority not justly but generously.'
8. Azad, Presidential address to Special Session of India National Congress, 1923, in *Khutbat-i-Azad*, ed. Malik Ram, Sahitya Akademi, Delhi, 1990, p. 205.
9. Ibid., p. 208.
10. *Hindustan Times*, 19 February 1940. While talking about the struggle Azad was visualizing the launching of 'civil disobedience'. He had also said that resolving the Hindu-Muslim problem would be part of his endeavour, however, he had no hesitation in saying, 'the struggle for the achievement for independence could not await the settlement of internal problems'.
11. Ibid. It was reported that, 'it was one of the biggest meetings held in Lahore in recent memory and included a very large number of Muslims'.
12. Ibid.
13. *Hindustan Times*, 2 March 1940.
14. Ibid., 16 March 1940.
15. Ibid., 20 March 1940.

16. Azad, Presidential Address to Indian National Congress in 1940 at Ramgarh, in *Khutbat-i-Azad*, ibid., p. 270.
17. Ibid., p. 272.
18. Ibid., p. 286.
19. Nehru had made his famous statement that anybody who talks about communalism must be talking about a problem in the air, in N.L. Gupta, ed., *Nehru on Commuanalism*, Sampradayikta Virodhi Committee, Delhi, 1965, p. 197.
20. Azad, Presidential Address to Indian National Congress, 1940, in Malik Ram, ed., op. cit., p. 287.
21. Ibid., p. 288.
22. Ibid., p. 289.
23. Ibid., p. 294.
24. Ibid., p. 298.
25. Ibid., pp. 299-300.
26. Latif Ahmad Sherwani, *The Pakistan Resolution,* Quaid-i-Azam Academy, Karachi, 1986, pp. 15-16.
27. M.A. Jinnah, 'Two Nations in India, Western Democracy Unsuitable: Mr. Jinnah Expounds Muslim League Case.' As reproduced in *Hindustan Times*, 14 February 1940.
28. Gandhiji to Jinnah, 22 March 1937 in *CWMG*, vol. LXV, Delhi, 1976, p. 231 as quoted in Bimal Prasad, 'Gandhi and India's Partition', in A.K. Gupta, ed., *Myth and Reality: The Struggle for Freedom in India 1945-47*, Manohar, Delhi, 1987, p. 114.
29. *Selected Works of Jawaharlal Nehru*, vol. 10, ed. S. Gopal, Orient Longman, Delhi, 1977, p. 495.
30. Ibid.
31. *Hindustan Times*, 28 February 1940.
32. *Rajendra Prasad, Correspondence and Select Documents*, ed. Valmiki Choudhary, vol. 5, Allied Publishers Ltd., Delhi, 1986, p. 246.
33. Ibid., p. 248.
34. Ibid.
35. Ibid.
36. R. Coupland, *The Constitutional Problem in India* as quoted in V.N. Datta, *Maulana Azad*, Manohar, Delhi, 1990, p. 162.
37. Datta, ibid., p. 162.
38. Azad, *India Wins Freedom*, pp. 32-3; Datta, ibid., p. 162.
39. N.N. Mitra, ed., *Indian Annual Register* (hereafter *IAR*), vol. II, 1940, p. 193.
40. *IAR*, vol. II, July–December, 1940 as quoted in Z.H. Faruqi, *Maulana Abul Kalam Azad: Towards Freedom*, B.R. Publishing Corporation, Delhi, 1997, p. 187.

41. Azad, *India Wins Freedom*, p. 33.
42. Datta, op. cit., p. 163.
43. Azad, *India Wins Freedom*, p. 34.
44. M.A. Jinnah's letter to Azad, as quoted in Pattabhi Sitaramayya, *History of the Indian National Congress*, vol. II, *1935-1947*, Padma Publication, Bombay, 1947, p. 202; and as cited by Datta, op. cit., p. 164. It is suggested that the said letter was perhaps written in the first week of July 1940.
45. Maulana Azad's speech as reported in the *Hindustan Times*, 9 July 1940.
46. *Hindustan Times*, 10 July 1940.
47. Ibid.
48. A letter from A.K. Swaminatha Iyer, secretary, Ayyapankave Young Boys Association, Palaghat, Kerala to Maulana Azad, 17 July 1940. The letter said that the organization wanted to put up his as well as Mahatma Gandhi's autographs in the library, which was run by the said organization. G-1, 1940, AICC Papers, NMML.
49. A letter from Keshavlal Veerchand Shah, president, Sholapur City Congress Committee to Maulana as Azad, 17 July 1940 in ibid. This request was made in the hope that as Azad was to visit Pune towards the end of July to attent a meeting of AICC, therefore it would not be difficult for him to visit Sholapur.
50. *Hindustan Times*, 14 July 1940. In his statement Asaf Ali also said by this act Jinnah had shut the door of any consultation and negotiation with him if not necessarily with the League. He accused Jinnah for dictatorial behaviour and warned the Muslim League that if it did not assert through its council at an early date, it would soon rule itself out of public life.
51. Yusuf Meherally had said, 'Mr. M.A. Jinnah himself had begun destroying the great Jinnah legend, firstly by Deliverance Day, then the Pakistan scheme and this uncommonly rude reply to the Congress President.' *Hindustan Times*, 18 July 1940.
52. Ibid.
53. The resolution of the Jamiatul-Ulema-i-Hind as reported in the *Hindustan Times*, 15 July 1940.
54. Ibid. The above-stated resolution said, 'the tone of Mr. Jinnah's reply to Maulana Abul Kalam Azad is against all standards of decency and public discussions of political questions. It further demonstrated Mr. Jinnah's indifference towards the present need of the hour and his desire to thwart the progress of the country.'
55. The Ahrars also analysed reasons for this behaviour of Jinnah. It said that Jinnah felt threatened because of negotiations, which

Sikandar Hyat Khan and Fazlul Haq had opened with Maulana Azad 'despite injunctions of Mr. Jinnah'. *Hindustan Times*, 15 July 1940.

56. *Hindustan Times*, 16 July 1940. This meeting was presided over by Maulana Husain Ahmad Madani and addressed by Maulana Hifzur Rahman and Habibur Rahman and others. It was said in the course of the meeting that the Muslim League had no representative character and therefore no authority to speak on behalf of the Muslims.
57. Liaqat Ali Khan's press statement, in *Hindustan Times*, 21 July 1940.
58. Ibid.
59. S. Srinivas Iyengar's interview, in *Hindustan Times*, 29 March 1940.
60. *Hindustan Times*, 30 March 1940. The said resolution also expressed confidence in the leadership of Maulana Azad and the Congress' demand for framing a constitution for India.
61. *Hindustan Times*, 2 April 1940.
62. Ibid.
63. Ibid. Asaf Ali had issued a press statement criticizing the League. He also said, 'As for the Muslim minorities in the rest of India, it is well known that he has clearly told them that they must struggle as best as they can themselves against the enemy the League is creating for them. Those who could realize this implication even before Mr. Jinnah's declaration have already begun to repudiate the League's lead.'
64. The London correspondent of the *Hindustan Times* reported publication of the said article, 3 April 1940.
65. Press statement of the secretary, Independent Parties Muslim Conference, *Hindustan Times*, 3 April 1940.
66. Ibid.
67. Maulana Habibur Rahman's speech, as reported in the *Hindustan Times*, 9 April 1940.
68. *Hindustan Times*, 14 April 1940.
69. Ibid.
70. *Hindustan Times*, 16 April 1940. The press statement said that 'the Indian National Congress, the only national organization in the country was facing the situation boldly. At such a critical period, the nine crores of Indian Musalmans also have to define their position and status in a free and self-governing India. The Muslims have to play their part in the struggle for freedom.'

71. Ibid.
72. *Hindustan Times*, 17 April 1940.
73. *Hindustan Times*, 20 April 1940. It is not clear in the report as to which organization and leaders were behind organizing this meeting. However, known anti-Muslim League leaders addressed the meeting. Maulana Hifzur Rahman, while addressing the meeting argued that the Muslims in general had already condemned the partition scheme. He also said that, 'the idea of partition was diametrically opposed to the basic idea of independence and therefore the two could not go together'.
74. Ibid. It was reported that till the scheduled time of the meeting there were barely 50 people. However, after a lot of effort around 500 people could be mobilized. Liaqat Ali Khan and others addressed the meeting and defended the Lahore resolution. Some speakers used abusive language against the Hindus and the Congress.
75. *Hindustan Times*, 22 April 1940.
76. W.C. Smith, *The Modern Islam in India: A Social Analysis*, Victor Gollancz Ltd., London, 1946, pp. 231-2.
77. *Hindustan Times*, 23 April 1940. In order to mobilize support several other meeting were lined up to be held in Paharganj, Bara Hindu Rao, Karol Bagh, Balli Maran and other Muslim localities. A large number of Muslim organizations including the local Jamiat-ul-Ulema-i-Hind, Majlis-i-Ahrars, Azad Muslim Party, Nationalist Muslim Youth League, Anjuman-i-Saiful Islam, Anjuman-i-Mujahidul Islam, Meo's Association, Karol Bagh Muslim Students' Association, Tibbia College extended their support for the Conference. The most interesting aspect of the support was that, 'Tonga, Thela and Water Carriers' Association have offered their cooperation.'
78. Ibid.
79. *Hindustan Times*, 27 April 1940.
80. Ibid. It was reported that 'important consultations went on throughout yesterday among the leaders. It appears the general aim of the Conference is a united India, a free India and agreed scheme of effective safeguards for the minorities and the speedy attainment of India's political goal.'
81. *Hindustan Times*, 29 April 1940.
82. The break up of delegates was as follows; United Provinces 357; Punjab 155; Bihar 75; Bengal 45; NWFP 35; Sind 42; Baluchistan 25; Bombay 40; CP 12; Madras 5; Orissa 5; Ajmer-Marwar 12;

Assam 5; Delhi 112; Indian states 12. According to a general rule laid down by the conveners, for every ten delegates a member could be sent to the Subjects Committee. Thus it consisted of 198 delegates. The small provinces were given special representation on the Subjects Committee. *Hindustan Times*, 28 April 1940.

83. *Hindustan Times*, 28 April 1940.
84. Ibid.
85. Ibid., 29 April 1940.
86. Ibid., 30 April 1940. Habibur Rahman also said that the sponsors of the Pakistan scheme were the same old allies of British imperialism.
87. Ibid.
88. Ibid.
89. Ibid., 6 May 1940.
90. Ibid., 25 May 1940.
91. Ibid.
92. *Urdu Press Review* (for the month of June 1940). It was a report prepared by Z.A. Ahmad, who looked after the Minorities Department of the UP Provincial Congress Committee, AICC Papers, File no. 7 of 1940. It was also reported that the *Khilafat* of Bombay, a pro-Muslim League paper, deplored the fact that the Muslim League did not capture the Azad Muslim Conference. It contended that if this organization is allowed to grow and to constitute its local branches, it would soon become a rival of the League. It also suggested that instead of breaking the Azad Muslim Conference meetings with brickbats and stones, Muslim League should now concentrate on winning over the rank and file of the Conference through arguments and reason.
93. *Urdu Press Review* (for the month of July 1940) in ibid.
94. *Hindustan Times*, 1 May 1940. Initially the expectations were that Maulana Azad would be able to address the Azad Muslim Conference session in Delhi. However, due to some reason he could not do so but sent a goodwill message, which said, 'Please convey best wishes to the Conference. May its deliberations be fruitful for the great cause of the country and the Muslims.'
95. Azad, Presidential speech in Malik Ram, ed., op. cit., p. 28.
96. Linlithgow to Azad, 4 August 1940, File no. G1, 1940, AICC Papers, NMML.
97. Azad to Linlithgow, Telegram, 8 August 1940, G1, 1940, AICC Papers, NMML.
98. Azad to Linlithgow, Telegram, 10 August 1940, in ibid.

99. CWC meeting at Wardha 18-22 August 1940, N.N. Mitra, ed., n. 28, 1940, vol. II, p. 197.
100. Azad to Linlithgow, 19 August 1940, File no. G1, 1940, AICC Papers, NMML.
101. R.H. Gadre, a member of the Maharashtra Provincial Congress Committee had addressed a letter to Maulana Azad on 12 August 1940 in which he had said, 'the goal of complete independence does not appear to be even within the distant vision of the Viceroy. Dominion Status—so much clamoured for and enamoured of by the Hindu Sabha, the Liberals and even the *Times of India*, does not find any place in the Viceroy's declaration. Even the most sober and elementary demand about the formation of a National Cabinet at the Centre has been trampled down, and instead we are asked to be content with the nomination of a few more Viceroy's puppets.' File no. G-1, 1940, AICC Papers, NMML.
102. A letter from Istafa Husain to the Secretary, Minorities Department, UP Provincial Congress Committee, 1 August 1940, File no. 8/1940, AICC Papers, NMML.
103. A letter from Mohammad Faruqi, Convener, UP Azad Muslim Conference, 15 July 1940. Name of the addressee is not clear in this letter. File no. 1 of 1940, AICC Papers, NMML. There was another letter issued on 22 June 1940 addressed to prominent Muslims of Gorakhpur, Bahraich and Muradabad, which exhorted them to establish an unbroken and stable chain of the work started by the Azad Muslim Conference in different parts of the country, which would establish Muslims' willingness to sacrifice for the country.
104. A letter from Abdul Aleem, UP Azad Muslim Conference, Lucknow unit, 10 July 1940, File no. 1 of 1940, AICC Papers, NMML. Even in this letter the name of the addressee is not clear.
105. Mohammad Faruqi addressed a letter on 15 July 1940 perhaps to Z.A. Ahmad, who looked after the Minorities Department of the UP Congress requesting him to send literature, highlighting the work done and concessions given to Muslims during the Congress' rule so that a pamphlet could be prepared to let Muslim know the reality. File no. 1 of 1940, AICC Papers, NMML.
106. Z.A. Ahmad had issued a circular suggesting that, 'the achievements of this Conference may, however, be lost if we do not take some practical steps to popularise its resolutions and decisions. Our province can give a lead in this matter to the rest of India

provided we meet from time to time in order to review the political situation and to chalk out our line of action.' File no. 1 of 1940, AICC Papers, NMML.

107. Press statement issued by Maulana Mohammad Faruqi, convener, Azad Muslim Conference, UP, File no. 2 of 1940, AICC Papers, NMML.
108. Ibid.
109. Ibid.
110. CWC Resolution at Bombay, 13-17 September 1940 in N.N. Mitra, ed., n. 28, 1940, vol. II, p. 222.
111. Datta, op. cit., p. 166.
112. Azad, *India Wins Freedom*, p. 36.
113. Letter from Sadiq Ali to Ajmal Khan, 21 June 1941. It is not clear from the letter the purpose of such a proposed interview. For a while there was some speculation that Maulana Azad might be transferred from Naini Jail to some cooler place.
114. Azad, *India Wins Freedom*, p. 37.
115. Ibid.
116. Ibid., p. 38.
117. Azad's speech at AICC meeting, 15-16 January 1942, in N.N. Mitra, ed., *IAR*, vol. I, p. 279.
118. Gandhi to Azad, 30 December 1940, RP Papers, File no. 2-A/41, AICC, NMML.
119. Azad's speech at AICC, 15-16 January 1942, in N.N. Mitra, ed., *IAR*, vol. I, p. 280.
120. Gandhi's speech, ibid., p. 281.
121. Ibid.
122. Ibid.
123. Nehru to Azad, 18 October 1940, *SWJN*, vol. II, p. 247. Nehru in this letter referred to *Hindustan Standard* from Wardha, which had carried an item stating that Azad had offered to resign.
124. Pattabhi Sitaramayya as cited in Datta, op. cit., p. 165.
125. Azad, while addressing the Lahore session of Jamiatul-Ulema-i-Hind on 22 March 1942 argued with Muslims that they must not stand in the way of freedom. He exhorted Muslims that unless they were free from British imperialism, no other question should be raised. Muslims should not ask for any safeguards but should try to attain the country's freedom first., in Mitra, ed., op. cit., 1942, vol. 1, p. 232.
126. Linlithgow to Amery, 7 March 1942, *TOP*, vol. 1, pp. 161-2.
127. Amery to Churchill, 25 February in ibid., p. 240.

128. Sir G. Cunningham to Linlithgow, 22 March 1942, ibid., p. 256.
129. Ibid.
130. For a brief account refer to *SWJN*, vol. 12, p. 183.
131. Notes by Sir Stafford Cripps, *TOP*, vol. 1, p. 479.
132. Ibid., p. 480.
133. Amery to Linlithgow, 24 March 1942, MSS. EUR. F. 125/11. In this letter Amery said, 'Jinnah, I should have thought, will be content to realize that he has now got Pakistan in essence, whether as something substantive or as bargaining point, though no doubt the purely provincial declaration will want a good deal of adjustment so as to secure what he calls, "Zones".'
134. Linlithgow to Amery, 2 March 1942, op. cit., p. 293.
135. Notes by Cripps, 28 March 1942 in ibid., p. 514.
136. Notes by Cripps in ibid., p. 530.
137. Notes by Cripps, 2 April 1942 in ibid., p. 609.
138. Maulana Azad to Cripps, 11 April 1942, G-1/1942, AICC Papers, NMML. In this letter Azad clearly exposed the insincerity of the British government in negotiations as regards the constitutional advancement of India. He clearly charged, 'We are convinced that if the British government did not pursue a policy of encouraging disruption, all of us, to whatever party or group we belonged, would be able to come together and find a common line of action. But, unhappily, even in this grave hour of peril, the British Government is unable to give up its wrecking policy. We are driven to the conclusion that it attaches more importance to holding on to its rule in India, as long as it can, and promoting discord and disruption here with that end in view, than to an effective defence of India against the aggression and invasion that overhang us.'
139. Cripps to Azad, 10 April 1942, *TOP*, vol. I, p. 732.
140. Azad, *India Wins Freedom*, p. 62.
141. Cripps' press conference on 11 April 1942, in Mitra, ed., op. cit., 1942, vol. 1, p. 247.
142. Azad, *India Wins Freedom*, p. 72.
143. Azad's, Speech at AICC, 29 April to 2 May 1942, in Mitra, op. cit., 1942, vol. I, p. 291.
144. Sardar Patel's statement, 25 April 1942, *CWSP*, vol. IX, p. 112.
145. Sardar Patel and Rajendra Prasad to Azad, 3 May 1942, *CWSVP*, vol. IX, p. 113.

146. Ibid.
147. Gandhi to Azad, 9 May 1942 in *CWSVP*, vol. IX, p. 114.
148. Ibid.
149. Azad, *India Wins Freedom*, p. 76.
150. Ibid.
151. Ibid., p. 77.
152. Sumit Sarkar, *Modern India*, Macmillan, Delhi, 1983, p. 388.
153. Azad, *India Wins Freedom*, p. 78.
154. Azad, Speech at AICC meeting, 7-9 August 1942, in Mitra, ed., op. cit., 1942, vol. II, p. 237.
155. Ibid.
156. Gandhiji's speech at AICC meeting, 7-9 August 1942, in ibid., p. 244.
157. Ibid., p. 242.
158. Azad, *India Wins Freedom*, n. 1, p. 77.
159. Justice Wickenden's Report, *Historic Judgement on Quit India*, P.N. Chopra, ed., p. 71 as cited in Datta, op. cit., p. 167.
160. For details about the movement and the British response refer to Gyanendra Pandey, ed., *Indian Nation in 1942,* K.P. Bagchi (Calcutta, 1988), Sumit Sarkar's *Modern India*, F.G. Hutchins' *Spontaneous Revolution: The Quit India Movement*, Manohar, Delhi, 1971.
161. Datta, op. cit., p. 170.
162. Ibid.
163. *Proceedings of Azad Muslim Conference*, 6-8 May 1944, in Mitra, ed., op. cit., 1944, vol. I, p. 243.
164. Ibid., p. 244.
165. Statements of S.A. Barelvi, Haji Mohd. Ibrahim and Dr. Shaukatullah Ansari on 8 May 1944 in ibid., vol. I, p. 244.
166. Ibid.
167. Wavell's radio broadcast on 14 June 1945 in ibid., 1945, vol. I, p. 247.
168. Ibid.
169. Azad, *India Wins Freedom*, p. 111.
170. Azad's telegram to Wavell, 21 June 1945. File no. G-26/1945, AICC Papers, NMML. In this telegram Azad had also requested Wavell to make it convenient to see him before the conference. Azad was accompanied by two secretaries to the conference.
171. Wavell to Amery, 25 June 1945, *TOP*, vol. V, p. 1152.
172. Ibid., p. 1153.
173. Ibid.

174. Ibid. It seems Wavell had assured Azad too that the government would not support the claims of the Muslim League, *India Wins Freedom*, p. 112.
175. Azad to Wavell, 7 July 1945, *TOP*, vol. V, pp. 1203-4.
176. Azad, *India Wins Freedom*, p. 119.
177. Ibid., p. 121.
178. Ibid.
179. Jinnah to Wavell, 7 July 1945, *TOP*, vol. V, p. 1205.
180. Ibid.
181. Mitra, ed., op. cit., 1945, vol. I, p. 240.
182. Azad's press conference, 14 July 1945, in ibid., 1945, vol. I, p. 241.
183. Ibid., p. 242.
184. Ibid., p. 243.
185. Sir B. Glancy to Wavell, 23 August 1944, *TOP*, vol. IV, p. 1224.
186. Ian Talbot, *Punjab and Raj, 1849-1947*, Manohar, Delhi, 1988, p. 199.
187. Ibid.
188. Azad, *India Wins Freedom*, p. 113.
189. Nehru's press statement after failure of the Simla Conference, in Mitra, ed., op. cit., 1945, vol. II, p. 133.
190. Azad to Sardar Patel, 13 August 1945, *CWSVP*, vol. 10, pp. 80-1.
191. Ibid., p. 81.
192. Sardar Patel to Azad, 29 August 1945, ibid., p. 82.
193. Intercepted letter of Azad to Gandhiji 2 August 1945 in Sir E. Jenkins to Mr Abell, in *TOP*, vol. VI, pp. 155-6.
194. Ibid., p. 156.
195. Ibid., pp. 156-7.
196. Ibid.
197. Intercepted letter from Gandhiji to Azad, 16 August 1945, in Sir E. Jenkins to Mr Abell, 28 August 1945, *TOP*, vol. VI, p. 172.
198. Ibid.
199. Ibid.
200. Gopichand Bhargav to Rajendra Prasad, 26 March 1942, RP Papers, File no. 2-C/42, NAI.
201. Ibid.
202. Ibid.
203. Nehru to Azad, 27 November 1945, *SWJN*, vol. 14, p. 124.
204. Sardar Patel to Shanti Prasad, 26 March 1946, *CWSVP*, vol. 10, p. 212.

205. CWC resolution of September 1945 in Correspondence and Select Documents of Rajendra Prasad, vol. 6, Appendix, p. 346.
206. Ibid.
207. Mitra, ed., op. cit., 1945, vol. II, p. 162.
208. Ibid., p. 163.
209. Ibid., p. 140.
210. Ian Talbot, *Provincial Politics and the Pakistan Movement*, Oxford University Press, Karachi, 1988, Talbot has roughly approximated this percentage particularly in the Muslim majority provinces. More exact figures as regards the enfranchised Muslims across the British Indian provinces are as yet to be explored.
211. Ibid. Talbot has explained various methods of the Muslim Leagues mobilization techniques and has reached this conclusion.
212. Hasan Nishat Ansari, *The Momin-Congress Relation: A Socio-Historical Analysis*, Patna, 1989, pp. 17-18.
213. The Nationalist Muslims Conference meeting on 18 September 1945 in Mitra, ed., op. cit., 1945, vol. II, p. 164.
214. Sumit Sarkar, *Modern India*, n. 82, p. 426. For a detailed break up of election results refer to Anita Inder Singh, *The Origins of the Partition of India*, Oxford University Press, Delhi, 1988, pp. 118-41.
215. Ibid. (Sarkar).
216. Datta, op. cit., p. 172.
217. Sarkar, op. cit., p. 428.
218. Records of the meeting between Cabinet Delegation, Wavell and Azad on 3rd April 1946, *TOP*, vol. VII, pp. 111-12.
219. Ibid.
220. Ibid., p. 114.
221. Ibid.
222. Records of the meeting between Cabinet Mission and Jinnah, *TOP*, vol. VII, p. 118.
223. Ibid., p. 119.
224. Ibid.
225. Records of the meeting of the Cabinet Delegation with Maulana Azad on 17 April 1946, *TOP*, vol. VII, p. 259.
226. Pethick-Lawrence to Azad, 27 April 1946, *TOP*, vol. VII, p. 352.
227. Azad to Pethick-Lawrence, 27 April 1946 in ibid., p. 353.
228. Ibid., 28 April 1946 in ibid., p. 357.
229. Ibid., 28 April 1946, File no. 40, 41/1946-47, AICC Papers, NMML.

230. Ibid.
231. Pethick-Lawrence to Azad, 29 April 1946, File no. 40, 41/1946-47, AICC Papers, NMML.
232. Azad to Pethick-Lawrence, 6 May 1946, File no. 40, 41/1946-47, AICC Papers, NMML.
233. Azad to Pethick-Lawrence, 6 May 1946, ibid., p. 433.
234. Ibid., p. 434.
235. Azad to Pethick-Lawrence, 9 May 1946, File no. 40, 41/1946-47, AICC Papers, NMML.
236. Ibid.
237. *TOP*, vol. II, pp. 475-6 as cited in Singh, op. cit., p. 163.
238. Datta, op. cit., p. 173.
239. Muslim League meeting held on 5-6 June 1946, in Mitra, ed., op. cit., 1946, vol. I, p. 183.
240. Azad to Wavell, 25 June 1946, in ibid., vol. I, p. 176.
241. Azad, Speech at AICC session, 6-7 July 1946, in ibid., 1946, vol. II, p. 133.
242. Ibid., p. 134.
243. Sardar Patel's speech, in ibid., p. 135.
244. Gandhiji's speech, in ibid., p. 137.
245. Nehru's speech, ibid., p. 143.
245. Nehru's press interview 10 July 1946, in ibid., p. 146.
246. Patel to Azad, 20 August 1946, *CWSVP*, vol. 10, p. 261.
247. Patel to Azad, 23 August 1946, p. 263 in ibid.
248. Meeting between Mountbatten and Gandhi, 2 April 1947, *TOP* vol. X, p. 83.
249. Meeting between Mountbatten and Azad, 2 April 1947, *TOP*, vol. X, p. 86.
250. Record of Mountbatten's interview with Azad, 12 April 1947, *TOP*, vol. X, p. 215.
251. Azad to Mountbatten, 14 April 1947, *TOP*, vol. X, p. 234.
252. V.P. Menon to Abell, 16 April 1947, *TOP*, vol. X, p. 265.
253. A.K. Natrajan wrote a letter to B.G. Kher on 21 July 1947, congratulating him on his radio speech emphasizing the need for India to have a strong central government. He said, 'As you know, nobody dared to say so, barely two months ago. The utmost that a man who counted in practical politics would go was a weak shadowy centre. I do not know how Maulana Abul Kalam Azad would take your categorical assertion.' B.G. Kher Papers, File no. 26, part I, NMML.

B.G. Kher replied on 24 July 1947, saying 'I am glad you liked what I said about the necessity of a strong centre', B.G. Kher Papers, File no. 26, part II, NMML

254. Gandhiji's speech at AICC session 14 June 1947, in Mitra, ed., op. cit., 1947, vol. I, p. 127.
255. G.B. Pant's speech at AICC, 14 June 1947, in ibid., p. 128.
256. Maulana Azad's speech at AICC, 14 June 1947, in ibid., p. 129.
257. Ibid., p. 130.
258. Ibid.
259. Ibid.
260. Ibid.

CHAPTER SIX

Building Academic, Scientific and Cultural Institutions for the Nation, 1947-1958

Maulana Azad had hinted that he was not willing to join the interim government, which was formed in September 1946, a point already discussed in the preceding chapter, albeit briefly. Azad's reason for not joining this government was borne out of considerations that he did not want to be appointed out of the Muslim quota as he expected that being a senior leader of the Congress, he at best could move into the government out of the Congress quota. It was perhaps for these considerations he kept himself out and suggested the name of Asaf Ali to be taken into the interim government.[1] However, after the Muslim League moved into the government, difficulties arose within the executive, as a result of quite frequent friction. 'Thus the question again arose about my participation in the government. Gandhiji pressed even more strongly than before that I should join.'[2] Azad suggested that even Pandit Jawaharlal Nehru too was keen on his joining the government, which he did on 15 January 1947 with the responsibility of looking after education. He took over education from Rajagopalachari. V.N. Datta, in his biography of Azad has argued that, 'it seems that Gandhiji was not in favour of his appointment as Education Minister'.[3] However, contrary to this perception Azad, rather emphatically asserted that, 'Gandhiji suggested that Education would be the most appropriate subject for me and also in the true national interest. He said that the pattern of future education was a basic question for free India.'[4] It was perhaps not Gandhiji but others who did not wish Azad to join the interim ministry.[5]

Contrary to these assertions by Azad, there are scholars who do not share his perceptions and think that Azad was not assigned the portfolio which was in keeping with his stature, 'and we empathize with his disappointment at being given the education portfolio in Nehru's cabinet, but we can hardly miss noticing the moral authority he wielded while he steered educational and cultural policies in the first highly sensitive decade of independence'.[6] Despite such perceptions of scholars, it is difficult to ascertain the occasion and the manner in which Azad might have given reflections of his 'disappointment'. Besides the considerations of historical circumstances in which he took up responsibilities of steering the Ministry of Education, it is important to underline the manner in which he strove hard to refashion the educational map of India.

He was no educationist by training. He had not seen the gate of a college or university as a student. His training was in religious studies, which his father Maulana Khairuddin had arranged for, at his residence in Calcutta. When he grew up, his voracious appetite for books resulted in Azad educating himself. In the course of time he earned a name for himself as a scholar of Islam. Before he took up the ministerial responsibilities, he had barely contributed to the field of education in any formal manner. And whatever little he did, had no relationship with the formal structure of education. For instance, during the days of internment in Ranchi (1916-19) he had started a Madrasa Islamia in 1917, with the intention of propagating and imparting Islamic knowledge to the local Muslims. Similarly in the wake of the Non-Cooperation–Khilafat movement in 1920 he started another madrasa in Calcutta with a view to express solidarity with Gandhiji, in boycotting the English system of education. Beyond these experimentations the Maulana had very little to do with formal education. He was barely involved in formulating any major policy in this regard. And yet in sovereign India his mandate was to cover the distance in an uncharted territory in view of his background and training. Two tentative suggestions can be made in this regard. First, despite no formal education, Maulana Azad's scholarship, intellectual prowess and vision about India's future were never in doubt. Second, in sovereign India the need of the hour was to work out a mechanism and build infrastructure, which would ensure that education, did not remain an elite affair as it moved closer to the larger mass of the people. Such a project in independent India required the stewardship of a person whose political understanding and vision was based on sound principles. In this context it is interesting to underline the distinction made by Susanne Hoeber Rudolph and Lloyd Rudolph, between the politics of education and politicization of education. According to them, the politics of education requires a certain kind of wisdom and vision to build institutions while the other is to make political capital out of them.[7] In the light of such theoretical formulations, Maulana Azad can easily be seen invoking the sound principles of the politics of education in order to usher sovereign India into a stage of development in the field of education, which would sustain its growth and development. After all, a democratic society required democratization of knowledge too, which, however, was possible only through the democratized institutional structures, accessible to a larger mass of the people hitherto outside the purview of formal education.

II

Maulana Azad's challenges were manifold. First, education was not in the list of central subjects as per the provisions of the Government of India Act 1935. It was clearly stated that this subject would be within the purview of the state subjects. In view of this the Ministry of Education under Maulana Azad had an important responsibility of initiating policies and taking decisions in order to promote education without undermining the authority of state governments and yet acceptable to them. Second, it was vitally important to understand the subject with utmost sensitivity, while laying down infrastructures and building institutions.

Conscious of his new responsibilities, he got down to dealing with the subject even before India became independent. Surveying the existing system of education, Maulana Azad argued that it was 'shaped by non-nationals in non-national interests'. He argued that despite this, it could perhaps not be denied that it opened a new world of science and modern technology[8] and yet, 'the greatest charge against the present system of education is that it has not led to the development of a national mind'.[9] Azad expressed his concern for initiating programmes for reconstruction of education, however with a clear focus on improving the status and conditions of teachers. He also hoped that the new National Government of India would recognize this as the foremost task. In order to underline the importance of education in the life of a free and sovereign nation, Azad argued, 'Education should have the highest priority in our national budget and should take place immediately after food and clothing. In fact, a proper system of education is necessary in order to tackle satisfactorily even these problems.'[10] He concluded his press conference with the hope that India would make a determined and concerted effort in order to take education on par with its status in other civilized countries of the world.

Azad was clearly marking priorities as regards the future steps in the field of education. He was aware of the limitations under which he had to discharge his responsibilities, particularly the financial one. Another difficulty was the question of initiating policies, which would revamp the entire education system, however, it was not possible till such time as India became sovereign. Equally daunting was the task of formulating policies and their implementation in politically tumultuous times, when Partition-related riots engaged the attention of the national leadership in controlling them as well as providing relief to the riot victims. Yet another limitations under which Azad had to labour was the constitutional constraints, for education was a subject in the state list at the time of independence and even after the sovereign Constitution of India came into effect. Azad was conscious of these daunting challenges. He acknowledged that there were many difficulties. He said, 'I know that on account of the happenings in the recent past, the attention of the Government and the people has often been diverted from the constructive work.'[11] After stating the difficulties, he highlighted the importance of education, '*After full considerations of all these factors, I would still assert that education cannot wait*.'[12] (Emphasis added)

Azad started identifying areas of education, which needed the immediate attention of the entire nation. For instance, he was simultaneously concerned about education for schoolgoing children as well as adults. He calculated that there would be roughly three crore children in the age group of 6-11 and even if three teachers were provided for 100 pupils, there would be need of about 9 lakh teachers, which he considered as an 'impossible task'.[13] In order to meet this challenge, he exhorted all educated men and women to come forward to share this burden of the government by volunteering to teach.[14] Azad's concern was so pronounced that he went to the extent of suggesting, 'We may also consider some kind of conscription for the purpose.'[15] It is another matter that Azad's suggestion for conscription was never put to practice, all the same he exhorted, 'if two lakhs of educated men and women come forward every year, we can in five years have the minimum number of teachers necessary for our plans'.

Adult education was another area of Azad's concern for expanding the education base particularly among those who were illiterate. He attached importance to this segment in view of the fact that with the coming of democracy, 'the problem of adult education has become even more important than it was in the past'. He highlighted the need of doing so on two counts: first, arrangements for making adults literate; second, the provision of measures to enlarge their minds and enable them to take intelligent interest in the affairs of the country. Aware of the resource constraints, he sought the help of government employees who could render great help in their spare time by working in night schools as well as Sunday schools, with a view to spread literacy among their subordinates.[16]

These were his early statements, as he needed more time to formulate long-term policies for the ministry under his charge. After all the basic and adult education alone were not the need of the nation as there were more pressing areas which too needed government attention in order to fix priorities, so that the limited resources were not frittered away 'in attempting too many things simultaneously'. These seemed the guiding principles for laying down priorities in the field of education so that the time lag and deficiency created by foreign rule could be wiped out.[17] The priorities that were identified by his ministry were as follows: (1) the provision of basic education on an universal, free and compulsory basis for all our school-going children; (2) the provision of adult education in order to wipe out the colossal illiteracy of our masses; (3) the improvement and expansion of technical education in order to solve the problem of manpower for industrial and technical development; (4) and finally the re-organization and improvement of university education from a national point of view.[18] After highlighting the priority areas for education, Azad reminded the members of the Central Advisory Board of Education (CABE) that despite these conceptions and planning a major constraint was mobilizing finance to meet the expenses on education. However, it was not easy as the main burden on finances was on account of the huge expenditure on the import of food, rehabilitation of refugees and defence. He said, 'It is obvious that welfare services cannot be expanded till these burdens are lightened.'[19]

Despite these limitations, the need of the hour was to make moves and take initiatives, which would refashion the educational map of India. Out of these four priority areas, the one to which more importance was attached to begin with, was higher education and for this purpose a University Education Commission was constituted in 1948 under the able leadership of an educationist and philosopher, S. Radhakrishnan. The Commission was also known as the Radhakrishnan Commission. The Commission worked with considerable seriousness and was able to submit its report to the Government of India almost within a year. The guiding philosophy of the Commission was to take into account past experiences, which included India's heritage in the field of education, art and culture, while blending them with future possibilities. The objective of the Commission set before itself was,

> If India is to face the confusion of our time, she must turn for guidance, not to those who are lost in the mere exigencies of the passing hour, but to her men of letters and men of science, to her poets and artists, to her discoverers and inventors. These intellectual pioneers of civilization are to be found and trained in the universities, which are the sanctuaries of the inner life of the nation.[20]

After having identified the high moral and philosophical objective, the Commission slowly moved closer to identifying the nuts and bolts of higher education in sovereign India. It identified, 'the three divisions (natural sciences, social sciences and humanities) to deal with facts, events and values. Their methods are different, though they are used in all studies in different degrees . . . whatever be our subjects of study, we must be able to observe carefully, think effectively and use our judgment properly.'[21] According to the Commission, in order to meet the challenges of widespread poverty and inequalities it was important that educational institutions were able to turn out scientists, technologists and administrators so that distributive justice was done to the millions of Indians. It considered the blending of professional ethics with social responsibilities. The Report said, 'while graduates in law, medicines and engineering acquire specialized information and technical skill, they should also be inspired by high social aims as no group can pursue private ends without regard to the social consequences of their activities . . . Individual freedom entails social responsibility.'[22]

After detailing the larger aims and objectives of higher education in sovereign India, the Commission made a set of broad recommendations in order to restructure this sector of education so that a high level of proficiency was maintained. These recommendations ranged from better salaries and service conditions for teachers to developing library and laboratory facilities. It suggested that admission to universities should be after 12 years of schooling, however, in order to reduce pressure on the universities, occupational institutions should be provided and students from the general stream diverted to education and training therein at the end of 10 and 12 years of schooling.[23] As regards postgraduate education and research in arts and science, the Commission underlined both the quantitative expansion and qualitative improvement through better provision of material assistance, increased research grants and scholarships. It recommended opening of new departments and strengthening the existing ones as well as appointing additional teachers through improvised selection process.[24] The ways and means of improving the teaching and learning process in the field of Agricultural Science, Commerce, Education, Law, Medicine and Engineering and Technology were suggested. However, the most significant part of the recommendations was the medium of instruction in colleges and universities. The realization among all the concerned and the Commission in particular was that the English language had acted as an impediment in the spread of education, specially, higher education. In a democracy, the democratization of knowledge too was vital, which however could be possible only with the introduction of a system accessible to a larger number of people. Keeping this in mind the Commission recommended, 'that for the medium of instruction for higher education, English be replaced as early as possible by an Indian language'. It further added that, 'higher education be imparted through the instrumentality of regional language with the option to use Federal language, as the medium of instruction either for some subjects or for all subjects. The Commission took cognizance of the importance of English language and therefore did not want to dispense with it altogether. It suggested, 'that English be studied in High Schools and in the Universities in order that we may keep in touch with living stream of ever-growing knowledge.'

The recommendation of the Commission on the question of medium of instruction that regional language/s should replace English in more ways than one was the meeting ground of Maulana Azad's thoughts on the matter. He had clearly defined the position as early as December 1947.[25] Elaborating upon the issue, he said that there were aspects of the language issue—one, concerned government offices and the other, education. He argued that,

> so far as education is concerned the following should be the programme: (1) We should decide that the medium of instruction throughout will be regional language; (2) So far as elementary and secondary education is concerned there is no obstacle in our way. But we have to make provision for higher education. We have to make a start straightaway. Here too we have to fix a time limit of five years.[26]

In spite of such a policy statement, Azad was conscious of the importance of English as an international language. He admitted, 'It is in our interest that we should make the best use of our knowledge of English and continue its study in our educational institutions.'[27]

Another area of convergence between the recommendations of the Commission and the ideas of Maulana Azad was imparting instruction in religion/s. He was keen that instruction in religion should take place under the supervision of the government. He believed that millions of Indians would not like their children to be brought up in an irreligious atmosphere. Referring to the recent communal upheavals in the wake of Partition, Azad said that, 'our present difficulties, unlike those in Europe, are not creations of materialistic zealots but of religious fanatics'.[28] Keeping this in view Azad sounded keen to find a solution to problems such as these at least at the elementary stage of education. However, the divergence between Azad's thoughts and the recommendation of the University Education Commission was that it wanted religious education even at the higher level of education. And yet keeping in mind the multiplicity of religions in the country, the Commission recommended that all educational institutions should start work with a few minutes of silent meditation. In the first year of the Degree course, lives of great religious leaders such as the Buddha, Confucius, Jesus, Prophet Muhammad, Zoroaster, Nanak, Mahatma Gandhi and others be taught. It also suggested that in the second year some selection of the universalist characters from the scriptures of the world be studied, followed by the philosophy of religion.[29]

Apart from many recommendations that were made by the Commission, the one for establishing a Central Grants Commission, which in due course of time came to be known as the University Grants Commission (UGC), turned out to be of considerable significance. The idea behind this was to allow the central government to keep a body under its control for the purposes of finance, coordination of facilities in special subjects, adoption of national policies, ensuring minimum standards of efficient administration and liaison between universities and national research laboratories and scientific surveys, etc. Democratization of the university structure too was a part of many recommendations in order to ensure that mechanism of checks and balances was in place.[30]

The University Education Report has been subjected to criticism, which any document of national importance should be. It is said that the Commission was prematurely appointed as a result of which, the rebuilding of an educational pyramid started from the wrong side because socio-economic and political realities had hardly crystallized for educational imperatives to be clearly known. For its limitations, it is not the Commission but the people who set it up who should be held responsible.[31]

This criticism was not subscribed by everybody, as there are scholars who have argued that efforts were made not only to strengthen higher education but basic and secondary education too. It is argued that when India became independent, the most spectacular change at the primary stage was the implementation of Basic Education, which was accepted as the national system of education. New schools were established and the existing schools were converted into Basic Schools.[32] And for this purpose many Basic Training Institutions were opened in various parts of the country in order to train teachers, who could be absorbed in this sector of education. The secondary stage of education was considered a problem area, which required serious attention. It was felt that the courses offered in schools were academic and unrelated to life. The system of instruction was such, which had limited appeal. For all these reasons it was considered necessary to revamp secondary education. As a result of this realization a Secondary Education Commission was constituted in 1952, which submitted its Report in 1953. This Commission was also known as Mudaliar Commission, after the name of its chairman, A.L. Mudaliar. The Commission felt that education, particularly the secondary stage, must make its contribution to the development of habits, attitudes and qualities of character, enabling its citizens to be worthy of a democratic society. Education must also help to improve productive efficiency, to increase the national wealth and thereby raise the standard of living of the people.[33] Keeping these aims and objectives in mind the Commission recommended reorganization of secondary education, which was divided into junior secondary, for a period of three years, and higher secondary, for four years. One year was added to the existing high schools to make a total of eleven years of schooling, after which a student could either find a job or enter a college.[34] It recommended that at the junior secondary level, the curriculum should include languages, social studies, general science, mathematics, art and craft, music and physical education. At the higher secondary stage the curriculum should have core subjects and optional subjects.[35]

The Government of India as well as most state governments accepted the recommendations of the Commission. With the implementation of these recommendations, there was considerable expansion of secondary education in the country.[36] In order to diversify secondary education and to prepare children for different walks of life, the Commission recommended the establishment of multipurpose schools. As a follow up during the First Five-Year Plan, 374 such schools were opened, as the number went up to 2,115 by the end of the Second Five-Year Plan.[37]

Many institutions were a reminder of past experience. For instance the CABE had already prepared a report on the Post-War Educational Development in India in 1944 but in sovereign India the role played by such an organization needed to be defined afresh, hence these commissions and their mandate. While addressing the fourteenth session of the CABE on 13 January 1948, Azad stated, 'I think we should call it the inaugural session of the Board since the first thirteen took place during British rule, which on 15 August 1947 came to an end and with it a long chapter of Indian history.'[38] He was candid in admitting, 'whatever depth of vision and sympathetic imagination the Board might have tackled the educational problems in the past, it could not escape the fact that there was no free National Government to support it'.[39] Under these political circumstances of independence and desire to deal with the subject of education seriously, the appointment of the two commissions, one for higher education and another for secondary education was indeed a step forward to work out a possible course of action to disentangle education from the influence of a colonial hangover.

In the light of the recommendations made by these commissions, particularly the University Education Commission, the Ministry of Education initiated steps to constitute the UGC. It is interesting to note that even prior to attempts to establish the UGC, some years ago a University Grants Committee had been established on 4 June 1945. Subsequently the constitution of the Committee was amended and its scope was enlarged on two occasions, one in July 1946 and another in December 1947. However, the Committee went into abeyance since 1950, pending considerations of the recommendations of the University

Education Commission by the Government of India.[40] It was further recommended that allocation of both recurring and capital grants to universities from the centre was fundamental to their proposals for improving and developing university education in India. The CABE and Inter-University Board endorsed these proposals with further suggestions that such a commission should function on the lines of a similar committee in the United Kingdom.[41] After careful thought to these considerations it was decided to establish immediately a UGC with the following functions: (1) To advise the government on the allocation of grants-in-aid from public funds to the central universities; (2) To advise the government on the allocation of grants-in-aid to other universities and institutions of higher learning, whose case for such grants might be referred to the Commission; (3) To advise universities and other institutions of higher learning in respect of any question referred by the government.[42]

After delineating the aims and objectives of this Commission the government discussed its structure and resolved that it would be headed by a chairman appointed by the Government of India, and work as a whole-time officer. There would be three non-official members appointed by the Government of India for a term of six years. There would also be two representatives of the Government of India, one from the Ministry of Education and the other from the Ministry of Finance. It was said these officers would be in office during the government's pleasure.[43]

Finally the Ministry of Education issued a press release announcing that, 'Government of India have accordingly nominated the following to constitute the Interim University Grants Commission; Dr. S.S. Bhatnagar, Chairman, Dr. A.L. Mudaliar, Acharya Narendra Dev and Mr. Wadia, who was the Vice-Chancellor of Bombay University as non-official members.' The government representatives were K.G. Saiyidain and K.R.K. Menon, who represented the Ministry of Education and the Ministry of Finance respectively.[44]

The making of the Commission had evoked considerable interest among the important and influential sections as many prominent persons expressed their desire to join it. In several cases recommendations too were sought to strengthen their candidature.

One such instance was the interest shown by Radha Kumud Mookerji to serve in some capacity in the UGC. He sought the intervention of Dr. Rajendra Prasad, the then President of India, who wrote to Maulana Azad for considering his name for the Commission.[45] Azad did not make any commitment.[46] This was one side of the picture; the other side of it was to seek opinions and suggestions from educationists. Maulana Azad had personally wished to know the names of persons who could be nominated to the UGC. In response to such an interest shown by Azad, A.L. Mudaliar responded by sending a list of six vice-chancellors, out of which any one could be nominated to the UGC.[47] Out of these six names when the final selection was made only Navroji J. Wadia was taken in the UGC. Voluntary interest shown to work for it was largely ignored.[48]

In 1953 the UGC was established only through a resolution of the central government and enjoyed only an interim status. However, after about three years of its functioning and evaluation the need to accord it statutory status was felt by the Ministry of Education and accordingly initiatives were taken to introduce a bill in Parliament and after due process it became an Act, thus it came to be known as the University Grants Commission Act 1956. With the coming of the Act the composition of the Commission was to be different from what it was in 1953. Provisions were made for a chairman, three vice-chancellors, three eminent educationists and two representatives of the ministries of Education and Finance. Maulana Azad took personal interest in its establishment. He was careful in making the selection of the people who would constitute this Commission. The notings in the Ministry of Education files makes it abundantly clear, 'The Minister has directed that University Grants Commission should be constituted as follows: Chairman, Dr. C.D. Deshmukh. Three vice-chancellors nominated by the Government: (1) Dr. John Mathai (2) Dr. A.L. Mudaliar (3) Prof. N.K. Sidhanta. Distinguished educationists: (1) Dr. Zakir Husain (2) Pt. H.N. Kunzru (3) Dr. M.S. Thacker. Two Representatives of the Ministry of Education and Finance.'[49] After all these decision-making processes the Ministry of Education issued a notification on 1 November 1956 to be published in the *Gazette of India*, confirming all the above names in their respective positions. However, it became clear through this notification that K.G. Saiyidain, Secretary, would represent the Ministry of Education and P.C. Bhattacharya, Secretary, Ministry of Finance.[50]

The establishment of the UGC, first through a resolution of the central government and subsequently through an Act of Parliament, was indeed a major step towards streamlining higher education in India. Its mandate was broad based since it was not confined to merely sanctioning grants to the central universities as it was also involved in supervising further expansion of university education in the country. The foundation of the Commission was laid on solid grounds that this institution is serving the nation well.

III

There were initiatives, which might not have had the same significance as the founding of the UGC, however, they were no less important. One such step was according the Visva-Bharati the status of a central university. It is interesting to note that the University Education Commission had recommended that, 'Visva-Bharati at Santiniketan and Jamia Millia at Jamia Nagar be given provisional charters as universities, and be given suitable capital and recurring grants.'[51] This recommendation posed serious legal difficulty before the Ministry of Education, as it was not sure if it could take recourse to granting the charter to these institutions to become universities. Taking advantage of the recommendations of the University Education Commission, the Visva-Bharati, moved a proposal for legislation for the establishment of the university at Santiniketan, however, not to be called a provincial university.[52] The ministry concurred with the proposal and thought this institution not only had a national but international character too, and in view of its importance it intended to give statutory recognition to the institution by the central government.[53] The authorities at the Visva-Bharati had intended to accept lower pay scale for its staff and yet the total financial implication involved was Rs. 3,62,000 (recurring), including the sum of Rs. 90,000 a year, which the central government had given as a grant to Visva-Bharati and Rs. 5 lakh (non-recurring). In view of all these developments, the Ministry of Education thought that, 'since there was no provision in the Constitution to give a Charter to any University, it is proposed to enact the Visva-Bharati Act'.[54]

Maulana Azad was quite keen about this proposal to elevate the Visva-Bharati to the level of a central university. In a note prepared by Humayun Kabir, the then Secretary, Ministry of Education, he clearly stated, 'As Finance Secretary is aware, both HPM (perhaps implying the Hon'ble Prime Minister) and HM Education have generally agreed to the proposal during the course of their discussion with deputation led by Mr. Rathindranath Tagore. HM Education is particularly anxious that the proposal may be approved in principle by the Cabinet before he goes abroad on July 19th 1950.'[55] Humayun Kabir, prepared a note stating, 'when Tagore was alive, the Visva-Bharati derived advantages both in prestige and financial assistance from the esteem in which he was held by the people in India and outside.'[56] Finally a five-page note was prepared for the Cabinet,[57] which was approved and Maulana Azad wanted the Ministry of Law to prepare the Bill so that it could be introduced in the ensuing session of the Parliament commencing from 5 February 1951, which it did rather in a fast mode. After the Bill was prepared, the next important stage was to seek presidential assent, a necessary step since it involved expenditure from the consolidated fund of India, so that it could be presented to the Parliament. Azad was to leave for Europe on 2 May 1951 and was keen to present the Bill before that date.[58] On the same note Dr. Rajendra Prasad put his signature with 'recommended' in his own writing. Thus an institution, Visva-Bharati founded by Rabindranath Tagore, in 1921 became a central university in 1951 and inaugurated on 22 September 1951 by Maulana Azad. In his inaugural speech he highlighted the sense of humanism of Rabindranath Tagore, which in essence was a result of the mingling of the Sufic poetry and philosophy of the Upanishads. He continued that, 'It was this consciousness of the fundamental spiritual unity of man that led Gurudev to found the Visva-Bharati, where the world could unite in common brotherhood and realize the ideals of peace, goodness and unity.'[59] While referring to the *Shantam*, *Shivam*, *Advaitam*, the driving philosophical objective at the time of the founding of the Visva-

Bharati, Azad said that it could not be included in the Act because there were objections about invoking the name of God in matters of legislation and yet its eternal values could never be denied. He argued, 'we have a conception of God which rises above all narrow limitations of race, religion or creed. I may also like to tell you that if the term Advaitam is translated into Arabic, it would read as Wahidahu La Shariq: the One who has no second, which is the highest affirmation of the monotheistic belief.'[60] Highlighting the uniqueness of this institution further, Maulana Azad reminded the Visva-Bharati fraternity that, 'with the passing of the Act a new order has started for you, but you must always remember that yours is a unique institution. You should therefore not merely try to imitate what other institutions do, but on the contrary try to set an example to them. You should derive your inspiration not from the practice or profession of other universities, but from the lofty ideals of Gurudev.'[61] Maulana Azad concluded his speech with a wish for the future of the Visva-Bharati in consonance with its past, 'I wish you godspeed in your new career as a Central University in the name of the One Supreme Being who is *Shantam*, *Shivam* and *Advaitam*.'[62]

The Jamia Millia Islamia was another institution, which had come into existence, in protest against the colonial system of education in October 1920 in the wake of the Non-Cooperation–Khilafat movement. A number of eminent Muslim leaders were involved with its foundation and later on made great efforts in sustaining it. The Gandhian philosophy of education, *Bunyadi Taaleem* (Basic Education), which evolved in consultation with Zakir Husain, was put in practice in the Jamia Millia Islamia. Many intellectuals of national and international repute were invited here to make presentations, so were eminent nationalist leaders, including Gandhiji, Pandit Jawaharlal Nehru and others. It was perhaps for these reasons the University Education Commission had recommended that the Visva-Bharati and Jamia Millia Islamia be elevated to the status of universities.

Despite similar trajectory they moved in different directions after Independence. The people responsible for managing the affairs of Visva-Bharati were quick to take the initiative for its recognition as a university and the Ministry of Education adequately responded to them. No such step seemed to have been initiated by Jamia Millia for its recognition as a university. On the contrary it was struggling hard for recognition of its degrees and diplomas by the Ministry of Education and other institutions. In this regard a representation was made to the Minister of Education requesting his help to advance the educational prospects of the Jamia Millia, 'something more than a symbol or an experiment'.[63] The letter highlighted the fact that as early as 1944, the then Government of India had appointed a committee to examine if it could recognize the examinations of the Jamia Millia as 'equivalent to the corresponding examinations of High School and Intermediate Boards of Indian Universities. The Committee in their Report, submitted in January 1945, recommended the recognition of all examinations and degrees of the Jamia Millia (Vide para. 72 of the Report) but the Government of India recognized only our matriculation and Diploma of Basic Training.'[64] The letter also stated that subsequently the matter was pursued further with Dr. Sargent and Dr. D.M. Sen and they advised that it was not worthwhile to pursue the matter just then. In view of these developments the letter said, 'I would request you to have the question of recognition taken up now, as the further development of our work now depends entirely upon the recognition given to it by the Government of India.'[65]

The Minister of Education noted in the file, 'There are two applications from Jamia Millia, Delhi. Secretary may please see and then discuss the matter with me.' And the two applications were: one for the recognition of Jamia's diplomas and degrees and the other was concerning the grants to Jamia Millia. In response to Azad's notings the process was initiated by asking Jamia Millia to furnish relevant papers showing the courses of study, syllabus and method of examinations, etc. Prof. Mujeeb, the then Vice-Chancellor, Jamia agreed to furnish them. The Ministry of Education prepared a note in this regard, which said that the matter was referred to the Inter-University Board, which in turn referred the same matter to its standing Committee.[66] The Standing Committee could not make up its mind as it wanted to wait for the opinion of the University Commission. In order to avoid the delay in taking a decision in the matter it was resolved,

'A Committee to consider the question whether Jamia degrees could be recognized for purposes of Government employment should be appointed at an early date.'[67] Finally a Committee consisting of the following was constituted: (1) Joint Educational Advisor to the Government of India; (2) Mr. G.C. Chatterji, Member, FPSC; (3) Principal Gurmukh Nihal Singh of Ramjas College, Delhi; (4) Representative of the Ministry of Home Affairs; and (5) Mr. H.S. Verma, Under Secretary, Ministry of Education, who was to act as the Secretary to this Committee. Later on Maulana Azad concurred with the opinion of Humayun Kabir to have one more member from the Inter-University Board.[68] The first meeting of this Committee was to take place on 17 October 1950. However, details of the proceedings of this Committee are not available in the files of the Ministry of Education. But the decision of the said Committee came to light when Aligarh Muslim University (AMU) expressed its desire to recognize the degrees of Jamia Millia in subjects such as History, Politics, Economics, Urdu, Education (Teaching) and Law, and sought the Ministry's approval. In response to such a request, it was observed, 'The request of the Aligarh Muslim University (AMU) is in accord with the recommendation of the Inspection Committee recently appointed by us and which recommended that the BA Degree of Jamia Millia Islamia should be considered as equivalent to the similar awards by other Universities. The Report of the Committee has been approved by us.'[69] Despite such a recommendation, the difficulty was with the Act of AMU, according to which, it could recognize a degree awarded by an institution established by law, which was was not applicable in the case of Jamia Millia. In view of this Zakir Husain, Vice-Chancellor, AMU made a plea with the ministry that as and when the Act would be revised, provision should be made to accommodate degrees awarded by institutions such as Jamia as well.[70]

Despite no such efforts on the part of Jamia Millia as well as the Ministry of Education, the good work done by Jamia was well recognized by the ministry. For instance Idara Talim-o-Taraqqi was engaged in the field of adult education for quite some time. It ran five adult education centres in Delhi. These centres conducted the following activities: (1) Literary classes in Urdu and

Hindi; (2) Study circles for social education; (3) Parents Association; (4) Children's Club; (5) Youth Clubs; (6) Libraries and reading rooms; and (7) Recreational activities like indoor games.[71] This Idara was also engaged in preparing literature series for the same purpose. Some officers of the ministry visited this Idara in order to assess the financial requirements, as was demanded and they found themselves quite impressed with their activities.[72] It was suggested that the government might think of, 'how help could be given to their organization for the preparation of literature'. The Idara was seen as an important link to the efforts of the ministry to spread the social education, where supply of literature at a nominal cost was an important factor. Humayun Kabir prepared a note suggesting that a 'people's encyclopedia' could be prepared in the most simple language and style, which could focus on History, Geography, Agriculture, Craft, Health and Education, etc. It could also contain elements on rights and duties as enshrined in India's Constitution. Fearing that a project such as this might take a long time, it was suggested,

> In the meantime, we may take advantage of the work done by Jamia Millia who have produced large number of such pamphlets. The Ministry proposes to publish out of them about 100 pamphlets in Hindi, in editions of 10,000 copies each. The Jamia have also posters, which are likely to be of great use in this connection. If HM approves, we may therefore, make a grant-in-aid of 2¼ lakh to Jamia Millia for purpose of production of these pamphlets.[73]

What emerges as an interesting point in the entire episode of the demand for recognition of the degrees awarded by Jamia Millia Islamia, a nationalist institution, which had a sense of dedication to the cause of education as well as the nation building processes is that it had to seek the recognition of its degrees instead of demanding to be elevated to the status of a university as the authorities at Visva-Bharati had done. While the ministry responded to its desire favourably, at no stage it suggested even vaguely that Jamia Millia too could be given the status of a university. It had to wait for another decade before it earned the distinction of a deemed university in 1963 and much later a central university in 1988. The questions that arise are: was it due to diffidence on the part of Jamia Millia to raise an issue such as the above? Or was it because the ministry was too preoccupied with other pressing demands than to elevate an institution to the level of university on its own initiative? Both the questions are in the nature of conjectures in the absence of any hard evidence.

In the field of higher education, there were unsuccessful attempts to start a central university for the Punjab, Patiala and East Punjab States Union (PEPSU) and Himachal Pradesh which was formed in July 1948. Gopichand Bhargava, Chief Minister of the Punjab, made this suggestion.[74] This suggestion was made in view of the fact that the Punjab University was located in Lahore, which after partition went to Pakistan, necessitating its relocation. In response to this proposal, Tara Chand said that he would discuss the matter with Maulana Saheb and assured Gopichand Bhargava, 'we will give our best consideration to your proposal', which the Ministry of Education did. Later a note was prepared, which said, 'As desired by the HM, a preliminary examination has been made of the possibility of converting the present Punjab University into a Central University to serve Punjab, PEPSU and adjoining areas.'[75] The urgency to start a central university was felt due to 'explosive language problem', and it was suggested, 'As a border state of India, it is particularly necessary to ensure that at any rate the younger generations are kept free of undesirable influences.'[76] The Ministry of Education approached the Ministry of States in this regard, which agreed with the proposal, but made suggestions to, 'secure the agreement of the participating units. In view of this suggestion a Conference of the representatives of three states was convened on 9 September 1952, which was chaired by Maulana Azad, who wanted the Conference to ponder over the desirability of having a central university instead of separate universities for these units. He stressed that the system of university education prevalent in India needed considerable reorganization to satisfy the real needs of the country. He also said, 'In view of this the proposed University if established should set a model for the rest of the country.'[77] In this Conference, the Chief Minister of PEPSU, theoretically did not disagree with the proposal to start a central university, catering to the needs of all these provinces, however, he stated that the public opinion in his state was to have a separate university for which a Bill was already prepared. Later on it came to be known that the PEPSU government was determined to have a university of its own instead of agreeing to the idea of a central university for three states. The matter was brought to the notice of Maulana Azad, who in his ministerial note said that in view of such an opposition from PEPSU and the decision of the Punjab government to have a university in the new capital, the matter should be treated as closed.[78] It brought the curtain down to a distinct possibility of a central university in the Punjab, PEPSU and Himachal Pradesh.

While the above-stated efforts made by the Ministry of Education came to nothing there were others who were seeking Azad's blessings to start a university in Calcutta. The Chief Minister of West Bengal, was keen to elevate the National Council of Education at Jadavpur to the status of a university, for which he assured all possible central help, however, he was told that the main burden would be on the provincial government. It was also planned to start a College of Engineering and Technology and the Polytechnic for diploma courses as well as a College of Arts and Science, catering to about 1,500-2,000 students.[79] For these efforts B.C. Roy, Chief Minister of Bengal was assured, 'Maulana Saheb is agreeable that in case you are able to find funds for the National University of Jadavpur, there is no objection to your doing so.'[80] He (B.C. Roy) also wanted to know from Azad, if it was a good idea to associate the name of Sri Aurobindo with this proposed university since he was the first principal of the National College. Maulana Azad said that the 'Mother' of Sri Aurobindo Ashram at Pondichery wished to start a university in his name, therefore he advised against associating the name of Sri Aurobindo with this new university.[81]

The concerns of the Ministry of Education while expanding higher education were to invite public initiatives in this field. Maulana Azad had discussed this problem with the Secretary and Deputy Secretary and it was felt that there was a growing tendency among the people to rely solely on the government. Whereas it was possible to create space for public initiatives, where the ministry could cooperate.[82] Another area of concern expressed by Azad was, 'the question of the great poverty of general knowledge displayed by most of the students in our colleges and universities and stressed the desirability of taking adequate steps to improve their general standards of cultural and intellectual interests as well as knowledge of their world and country.'[83] In this regard he advised that the ministry should approach the universities and other institutions of higher learning to institute 'general education' courses. He also suggested a broad outline of action to be initiated in this regard such as arranging trips, excursions and visits by select groups of students to places of historical interest. Trips to important scientific and technological projects, including the headquarters of the provincial and central governments were considered desirable. In order to strengthen this part of the curriculum in colleges and universities, Azad advised his ministry to address the vice-chancellors offering all possible help from the ministry.[84]

As a follow up, K.G. Saiyidain addressed a letter to vice-chancellors of all universities, underlining the need to introduce the component of 'General Education Course' in the universities. In the letter he highlighted the points raised by the minister. He further added, that the Public Services Commissions at the centre as well as states 'have drawn pointed attention to the fact that a large majority of our students, including many of those who have obtained high honours and first class marks, are woefully ignorant about the culture and social life in other parts of the country and the various activities going on in different states'.[85] This initiative of the ministry received considerable response from universities such as University of Delhi, Calcutta University, Aligarh Muslim University, Jammu and Kashmir University, Osmania University, Agra University and SNDT University. Most of them showed willingness to introduce this subject in their curriculum, while some others said, a similar subject had already been introduced.

The enthusiasm of the universities notwithstanding, a major concern was the financial difficulties faced by them, which was taken note of by the ministry.[86] Doubts expressed by the Ministry of Education were almost confirmed by the Ministry of Finance. In its note it appreciated the idea of organizing tours, excursion, etc., to places of historical, sociological and technological importance, but at the same time it was apprehensive. It said, 'Apart from the financial difficulties, which can easily be removed if the scheme is accepted under the "Five-Year Plan" it is prudent to proceed in this matter cautiously.'[87] Thus a scheme such as this, to build larger perspective among the students could not take off due to financial constraints. Innovative ideas and their implementation involved a cost to be borne by the concerned agencies, without which, they remained confined to the files of the Ministry of Education.

The records in the Ministry of Education do give the impression that there was an over-emphasis on higher education. It was perhaps for this reason some scholars have taken a critical view of such an approach of the ministry.[88] It is further argued that this approach could be justified only on superficial grounds, that India was in need of leaders at all levels, therefore priority attention was paid to the university education. However, the author has taken an extreme view of developments in the field of higher education, 'But unfortunately there are no short cuts to education. Probably the choice of the leaders was instinctive and the result of the tradition of building from the top downwards, which is hierarchical and feudal heritage of mankind.'[89] Contrary to such harsh criticism, the long-term projections of the Ministry of Education were in favour of universal elementary education as well and not just confined to higher education. This was adequately manifested in the 'Draft-outline for educational development in the Second Five-Year Plan.'

The draft seemed a careful document as regards building infrastructure for elementary education. It stated,

> In formulating a draft outline of the Second-Five Year Plan, so far as education is concerned, certain basic principles and considerations have been kept in view. *Of them the first and foremost is the necessity to provide a certain minimum standard of education for all citizens in order to ensure that the needs of a democratic republic are adequately met.*[90] (Emphasis added)

The ministry was conscious 'at present educational opportunities are by and large dependent on the economic status of the family. This results in large-scale national loss as many children or adolescents of brilliant promise have to give us (up) studies prematurely.'[91] It was pointed out that, at the beginning of the First Plan, the country was still suffering from the after-effects of war and partition. There was acute shortage of food and raw materials. It was thus understandable that greatest emphasis in the First Plan was placed on making good these deficiencies. With the success in these fields, the case for increasing the provision of social services has become much stronger. Among the social services, the greatest stress should perhaps be placed on education as the quality of our manpower will determine progress in all fields and the quality will depend on the effective system of national education.[92]

After having highlighted the broad policy contours of the ministry, the draft document went into examining the possibilities of expanding education, in a sector-wise manner. Its target for elementary education was projected to cover 75 per cent children in the age group of 6-11 and 30 per cent of children in the age group of 11-14. In order to meet this target it was considered important to hire good teachers with enhanced salary structures and opening of new schools.[93] As regards the adult education the draft proposal stated, 'There is no need to stress the importance of social education. Without the support of the adult—and in India about 90 per cent of the adults are illiterate—no programme of education and indeed any national development can be sustained.' In view of the existing conditions it was proposed that in the Second Five-Year Plan there should be establishment of a community centre in each Community Project Block, a literacy centre on a somewhat more modest scale in each National Extension Block and one Janata College in each division.[94] It also envisaged training of social education workers and considerable strengthening of the Social Education Organization in the district and state headquarters. As far as the secondary level education was concerned the draft said, that the ministry intended to implement the recommendations of the Secondary Education Board as revised by the Central Advisory Board of Education. This would require conversion of a large number of schools into multi-purpose schools. Attempts would be made to introduce diversified courses, as also the standards of the secondary education would be raised so that the intermediate examination would be eliminated. As per the plan proposal, 20 per cent children would be covered under this head.[95]

As regards the technical education, the draft proposal of the ministry clearly stated that in view of the expansion of industry, it was important to start technical training centres. And for this purpose, it was proposed to establish a number of junior technical schools in different parts of the country. It also suggested starting 'apprenticeship-training-cum-schools of Industry for high school leavers'. It was felt necessary to upgrade the quality of teachers in these technical institutions.[96] The ministry wanted to keep the momentum of the higher technical education. It said, 'provision has been made for continuing the development of the Kharagpur Institute and the establishment of the Western and the Southern Higher Institutes'. It was also suggested to increase the plan outlay from 25 crore to 80 crore.[97] Till this point it seems that the ministry was laying more emphasis on elementary, secondary and technical education. Under the head of higher education in colleges and universities, there was very little that was demanded by way of plan outlay. The ministry proposed that a universal three-year degree course would be introduced throughout India, starting from July 1956. This might require downgrading of some of the colleges as well as upgrading of still some other colleges, which, however, might require additional funding. In order to improve quality teaching, the ministry emphasized the need to employ first-rate teachers, by enhancing the scales of teachers in universities and colleges. It underlined the fact that, 'the amount involved for improving the scales of teachers in universities and colleges is fortunately small and manageable'.[98] The education for physically handicapped was another area that was identified by the ministry.

The most interesting aspect of the draft proposal was the ministry's desire to intervene in the social aspect of education. Its projection seemed inspired by the principles of social justice without much sloganeering. It is worth quoting the entire paragraph. It said,

> The democratization of education also requires that there must be general provision of scholarship and other assistance to deserving pupils at all levels from the primary to the university including Technical Education. The institution of scholarships to Scheduled Castes, Scheduled Tribes and Other Backward Classes has led to an enormous increase in the number of students from these groups. From outside

these communities also, there are many children who are meritorious but because of lack of resources are compelled to give up studies prematurely. In a rich country like the United Kingdom, as already pointed out, 70 per cent of all university students are in receipt of public support. In a university like Oxford about 85 per cent of the students are scholars or stipendiaries. In India, on the other hand, perhaps not more than 10 to 15 per cent of the students receive public assistance and in most cases this assistance is not adequate to meet their needs. For all these miscellaneous projects an ad hoc provision of Rs. 40 crore is proposed for the second plan period.[99]

By the time the Ministry of Education was preparing the draft proposal for the Second Five-Year Plan, it was fully conversant and confident of issues concerning the ministry and direction in which it wanted the entire education to move. However, it was conscious of the fact that education was not a subject in the central list of subjects, it was not even in the concurrent list, which could have given the ministry much greater freedom to initiate measures. However, under the existing provisions of the Constitution, involvement of the provincial governments was necessary, which indeed was a cumbersome process. Another desire on the part of the ministry was to take steps in order to standardize education across the country. The need to do so was felt as a result of the experience for some years that the pace and standard of education was not the same everywhere. Therefore the ministry made preparations for bringing about changes in the constitutional provisions so that it could exercise unfettered power and authority on the subject under its control. Keeping these considerations in view, the Ministry of Education made a suggestion that, 'University education should be transferred from the state list to the Concurrent List. If on further consideration it is felt that "co-ordination of facilities and maintenance of standards at all stages of education" should be made a Central responsibility by appropriate Amendments of the List of Entries.'[100] Since suggestions such as this, involved making changes in the Constitution, the Ministry of Law was consulted to give its opinion and it did not consider that such an amendment was in order in the larger context. It suggested that it was 'difficult to appreciate why any such co-ordination is necessary in regard to elementary and secondary education or how exactly it will be achieved by the Centre.' It was further opined by the Ministry of Law, 'would it not be better to limit it to higher including technical and scientific education and research'?[101] In addition to this suggestion, the Ministry of Home Affairs too suggested that 'as the proposal cannot be finalized without ratification by the state legislatures, consultation with the state governments is essential, if not now, at later stage'.[102] It was further pointed out that in the matter, the Ministry of Education should obtain the views of the state governments on the proposal in the first instance and place them before the special committee of the cabinet dealing with the constitutional amendments.[103] Contrary to these suggestions, Maulana Azad held a different view, as he wanted the proposal to go through the cabinet sub-committee first before consulting the state governments.[104] Keeping this desire of the Maulana in view the ministry prepared a four-page note for consideration of the cabinet sub-committee. The note in its preamble said

> The Constitution provides that education, including universities shall be a State subject, excepting for certain special items mentioned specially in the Union list. In the Union list, an exception is made in favour of certain institutions declared by law to be institutions of national importance and union agencies and institutions for certain special types of training and study. Vocational and technical training of labour has been placed on the Concurrent list. The coordination and determination of standards in institutions for higher education or research and in scientific technical institutions is however an exclusively Central responsibility.[105]

It was further noted that since university education and scientific education both involved heavy expenditure and utilization of funds, a mechanism of coordination was required in order to avoid duplication. The note highlighted the importance of elementary as well as secondary education too under the central responsibility with a view to maintain standards and coordinate facilities and they 'should be so designed as to turn out the kind of citizens that free India requires'.[106] Keeping all the above objectives in mind the note reiterated, 'The Ministry of Education are therefore of the view that determination of standards and inter-state coordination of facilities at all stages of education should be a central responsibility.'[107] After building its case for bringing education under the purview of the centre, the ministry made recommendations to amend the relevant sections of the Constitution: (1) For the entry 66 of List I, substitutes: '66. Determination of Standards, and inter-state coordination of facilities, at all stages of education.' (2) For entry 11 of List II, substitutes: '11. Education subject to the provisions of entries 63, 64, 65 and 66 of List I and entries 25 and 25A of List III.' (3) After entry 25 of List III insert: '25A. Universities and other institutions for higher education or research subject to the provisions of entries 63, 64, 65 and 66 of List I.'[108] The proposal to bring about amendments in the list of subjects was made in consultation with the Ministry of Law. After going through the required exercises the matter was placed before the cabinet sub-committee, whose meeting took place on 20 May 1955, which was chaired by Pandit Jawaharlal Nehru, the Prime Minister of India.[109] The cabinet sub-committee appreciated the need for ensuring proper standards for coordinating facilities at all stages of education, however, it felt that the proposed amendment might not be the most suitable means of achieving that object. 'The Prime Minister suggested, and the Committee agreed, that in these matters indirect control would be more acceptable and effective. The Committee was, therefore of the view that the Ministry of Education should impress upon the State Governments the gravity and urgency of the problem and seek their advice and assistance in achieving a satisfactory solution.'[110]

IV

The proposal for amending the List of subjects was not endorsed by the cabinet sub-committee and it must have disappointed Maulana Azad. He did not seem to give any such expression immediately. However, later on he did reflect on the issue and the impression that emerges is that he would have appreciated if others in the government too shared his views. While addressing the 25th meeting of the Central Advisory Board of Education, he was introspecting on the tasks fulfilled in the field of education during the years it was under his stewardship. In the course of his address he said, 'when I assumed charge of education in 1947, I immediately saw that there could be no solution of our educational problem without the fullest cooperation of the Centre and the provinces. Education no doubt was a provincial subject but it was my considered opinion that this distinction could be maintained only when our educational targets have been achieved'.[111] The difficulties that the Ministry of Education faced during the last ten years were many but one crucial aspect of the issue was that, 'some of my colleagues have regarded education to be purely provincial subject and did not therefore think it necessary that the Central Government should provide adequate funds for education'.[112] He also lamented the fact that education was not considered a subject, which could give a quick return as other subjects could. He protested, 'even when the Planning Commission was set up, the situation did not at first change. When the first draft of the First Plan was made, education was almost completely ignored.'[113] In the course of this evaluation Azad candidly admitted that from the point of view of desirability the results were not satisfactory. He added, 'If, however, we consider the situation in which India attained her freedom and the difficulties which we have had to face since then, I am glad to say that there is no need to be apologetic for what has been achieved during the last ten years.'[114]

The spread of technical education was one area, which gave Maulana Azad some sense of satisfaction. He argued,

> you will be glad to see that there has been a remarkable expansion both in quality and quantity of education in this field. In fact this is perhaps the area where the most remarkable progress has been achieved. . . . We can confidently say that if this rate of progress is maintained, India will soon be able to meet all her requirements for technical personnel and perhaps help some of our neighbouring countries.[115]

He drew particular satisfaction on account of the establishment of the Indian Institute of Technology at Kharagpur, West Bengal. He said,

> the Act incorporating the Indian Institute of Technology, Kharagpur has been brought into effect and the Institute is functioning as an autonomous organization. Its progress has been fully maintained and I

would like to compliment the Director and his colleagues for their meritorious work.[116]

Maulana Azad had reason to mention the name of Indian Institute of Technology (IIT), Kharagpur with a sense of fulfilment in the field of technical education. He knew the role he had played in its establishment in times when resources were scarce. It is not surprising that even today the IIT at Kharagpur recalls his services with a fine sense of gratitude, 'Maulana Azad was not only one of those who established this Institute he also retained to the last day of his life, kind and affectionate interest in its affairs.'[117] The IIT at Kharagpur in its previous incarnation was 'Eastern Higher Technical Institute' which was barely one-year old since it was founded in March 1950 in Hijili campus as a result of recommendations made by a Committee headed by Nalini Ranjan Sarkar in 1946. However, the political climate of the country was not conducive to give shape to these recommendations, as they had to wait for another four years. Dr. J.C. Ghosh was appointed its Founder Director. Within a very short period of time the Ministry of Education resolved to rename it as Indian Institute of Technology, Kharagpur.[118] This Institute was modelled on the Massachusetts Institute of Technology, USA. Dr. B.C. Roy, the Chief Minister of West Bengal assigned 1,200 acres of land to this institute. Maulana Azad formally inaugurated it on 18 August 1951. In his inaugural speech he said,

> It has been clear to me from the very beginning that this Institute must provide instructions of the highest standard, under the supervision of recognized authorities in their respective fields. We have intended that only men of highest quality should be in charge of different departments, and we have not hesitated even to go outside India to recruit professors wherever necessary.

While underlying the importance of the choice of right personnel and curriculum design, Maulana Azad emphasized that the ministry needed to satisfy itself that, '(a) properly qualified and experienced personnel has been secured to run the course, and (b) that the industrial and technical development of the country need the provision of such a course.'[119] In the establishment of this Institute, he pledged government support in every possible manner, however, at the same time he also solicited support from industry, 'I would like to make a special appeal to our industrial and business magnates to take an active interest in the development of this Institute. . . . Industry can assist financially by establishing chairs in subjects in which it is specially interested.'[120] He, in the concluding part of his speech thanked Ardeshir Dalal for mooting the idea and Nalini Ranjan Sarkar for drawing up the plan for the Institute.

In 1951 the undergraduate course leading to the Bachelor's degree was offered in Civil Engineering, Electrical Engineering and Mechanical Engineering.[121] In due course of time the number of courses offered by the Institute went up to 13 which were Mechanical Engineering and Production Technology, Heavy Electrical Engineering, Electrical Communication Engineering, Civil Engineering and Building Construction, Architecture and Town Planning, Naval Architecture, Geology and Geophysics, Chemical Engineering with special reference to Combustion Engineering and Fuel Economy, Agricultural Engineering, Mathematics, Physics, Applied Chemistry and Humanities.[122]

However, while the IIT was growing, a major concern remained about the status of its degrees since it did not enjoy any statutory position. The Founder Director, Dr. J.C. Ghosh as early as November 1952, raised the issue with S.S. Bhatnagar, Secretary, Ministry of Education, 'I consider that the time has now come when Government should make the Institute into an autonomous body like the Central Universities of Benaras, Aligarh and Delhi.'[123] However, the Ministry of Education at this stage was not prepared to concur with Dr. Ghosh's perspective in the matter. It was of the opinion, 'the proposal to convert the Institute into a Technological University was completely ruled out'. As regards it being set up as an autonomous institution, it was suggested that there was hardly any need to disturb the present set up.[124] Even Maulana Azad as Minister noted that, 'I do not consider it necessary that this question deserves consideration at the moment. It is a matter, which has many important considerations, and unless these have been considered fully, decision cannot be taken. We shall consider this in future at some appropriate stage.'[125] The apprehension in the Ministry of Education around this time was on account of the fact that if the Institute was elevated to the status of a university, it would come under the purview of the UGC and 'there was the danger that the University Grants Commission might not allocate as large amounts as were proposed to be spent on the Institute by the Government'.[126]

And yet the concern of the Institute persisted as regards its degrees and other matters in the absence of any statutory recognition of the Institute. The new Director of the Institute, Dr. S.R. Sengupta was equally keen for a statutory provision for the Institute. He pursued the matter with Humayun Kabir, suggesting that 'the Institute should be set up under a Statute, it need not be called a University'.[127] The anxiety was on account of the fact that it needed to award degrees such as B.Sc, B.Tech, M.Sc, M.Tech, D.Phil and Ph.D, etc. His arguments were based on sound logic and justifying why it was important to bring the Institute under statutory provisions on distinct grounds: (a) Recognition by various Public Service Commissions for employment would be easy; (b) Recognition by Indian universities for the purposes of employment as teachers and for admissions in postgraduation courses; (c) Recognition by foreign universities would become easier with statutory awards.[128]

In view of these arguments the ministry prepared a note reiterating the history and importance of the Indian Institute of Technology and suggested an enactment empowering the Institute with the authority to confer degrees and sought the approval of the Minister.[129] He concurred by putting a note in Urdu, '*han zaroori karwai karni chahiye. Cabinet ke liye ek note tayyar kiya jaye*' (Yes, the necessary steps should be taken. A note for the cabinet should be prepared). The ministry took the necessary step of preparing a note for the approval of the cabinet for introducing a Bill in this regard on the lines of, 'The Kharagpur Institute may be declared an Institution of national importance and incorporated by an Act'.[130] Finally the ministry moved the cabinet for introducing a Bill in Parliament to declare Indian Institute of Technology, Kharagpur as a statutory body. The Bill became an Act and came to be known as the Indian Institute of Technology (Kharagpur) Act 1956 and came into force on 1 April 1957, which declared the Indian Institute of Technology, Kharagpur an

Institution of National Importance with powers to grant Degrees, Diplomas and other academic distinctions.[131] Thus this Institute earned the distinction of being the first among the chain of Indian Institutes of Technology and in due course of time emerged as a kind of beacon light in the field of technological education. It is not surprising at all that Maulana Azad looked at the founding and evolution of this institution with a sense of pride and placed it among his achievements and an example for the nation to follow.

The case of IIT Kharagpur was an example of the initiative taken by the Ministry of Education in order to build institutions, which would meet the requirement of technological education indigenously and collaborate with industries. In this regard Maulana Azad had solicited support of the industrial houses in extending all possible facilities including financial support. However, the case of Indian Institute of Science was a case of converse experience, where private initiative of an industrial house was nationalized in the best interest of education in the field of science and technology.

The House of Tatas founded the Indian Institute of Science in the year 1909 with a view to step into the field of scientific education and over the years it was able to earn a distinction for itself. The best of scientific brains were associated with this Institute including the Nobel Laureate C.V. Raman. However, with the dawn of independence, the Ministry of Education, on the recommendation of the Nalini Ranjan Sarkar Committee geared itself to move into this sector of education in a big way. It was with this purpose in view the government appointed a Committee,

> to review the working of the Institute with special reference to the purpose for which it was founded and if any changes were considered desirable in the organization and activities of the Institute for the better achievement of those purposes, to make recommendation accordingly but with due regard to the Institute's actual or reasonably augmentable financial resources.[132]

The Committee consisted of Sir Alfred Egerton of Imperial College, London as the chairman and Sir Ben Lockspeiser and Dr. J.N. Mukerji as members. G.K. Chandiramani acted as its secretary.[133]

The committee assembled at Bangalore in August 1948, interacted with a large number of people associated with the institute in the present as well as the past through informal discussions, personal interviews and in some cases through correspondences. The committee also interacted with the senate and council of the institute and was able to submit its report, which was sent to the council of the institute as well as the Tata family for their comments. Only after having satisfactory perusal of the report and comments thereupon, the President of India accepted a revised scheme for the administration and management of the properties and funds of the institute.[134] Consequent upon the recommendation of the committee the institute was placed under the purview of the Ministry of Education through the President of India as its visitor. The new arrangement for the administration and management of the Indian Institute of Science came into force on 1 January 1951. It was clearly stated that the President of India would be ex-officio visitor of the institute. The visitor would have the authority to review the work and progress of the institute periodically, order enquiries into the affairs of the institute to pass orders on the recommendations of the reviewing and enquiry committees, which would be binding on the institute. The powers of the visitor also included approval of appointments as provided by regulations.[135] The power structure of the institute was considerably democratized, as it was not kept concentrated in a single authority or person and was divided among ten such agencies: (1) Visitor, (2) Court, (3) Council, (4) Finance Committee, (5) Senate, (6) Faculties, (7) Board of Management, (8) Board of Trustees, (9) Director, (10) and such other authorities as might be declared by the regulations to be the authorities of the institute.

As regards the objects of the institute, it was resolved that it would

> (i) provide for advanced instructions and conduct original investigation in all branches of knowledge as likely to promote the material and industrial welfare of India, (ii) establish and maintain Chairs and Lecturerships in Science, Arts and Technology, (iii) provide suitable libraries, laboratories and equipment, (iv) cooperate as far as possible with such recognized institutions as exist or are founded in future for

cognate objects in India, (v) do all such things as might be incidental, necessary or conducive to the attainment of all or any of the objects of the Institute.[136]

While setting out objects of the institute as stated above, a possibility for the future too was kept in mind in terms of collaboration with other institutes of similar character. It was done so, in the hope that as and when a Higher Technological Institute would be established for the Southern region, it could well be located in Banglore. In such an event the Indian Institute of Science should be able to collaborate with it, so as to 'provide the total facilities envisaged in the Sarkar Committee Report on "Higher Technological Education", the broad division of work being that the Indian Institute of Science would provide mainly for the post-graduate level of instruction and research and the contemplated institute would provide for the rest.'[137] However, such contemplation never materialized since such a Higher Technical Institute for the Southern region was proposed at Madras.[138]

The Council of Scientific and Industrial Research was another scientific organization, which was considered important in the reconstruction project in independent India. The then British colonial government founded this council in 1942 in order to meet the wartime requirements on the 'model' of the Department of Scientific and Industrial Research founded in Britain during the First World War.[139] The Council was founded as an autonomous body due to the efforts of eminent scientists such as Ramaswamy Mudaliar and S.S. Bhatnagar and was registered under the provisions of the Registration of Societies Act XXI of 1860.[140] Some of the functions of this Council were clearly enunciated in its constitution, which were as follows: (1) The promotion and coordination of scientific and industrial research in India including the institution and the financing of specific research; (2) the establishment or development and assistance to special institutions or departments of existing institutions for specific studies of problems affecting particular industries and trades; (3) the establishment, maintenance and management of laboratories, workshops institutes and organizations to further scientific and industrial research and to utilize and exploit any discovery or invention likely to be of use to Indian industries; apart from many other functions.[141] With these functions the Council was working for the above stated objectives. However, after Independence the Council was placed under the charge of the prime minister, who became the president of its governing body and the Minister of Education its vice-president.[142]

Maulana Azad referred to the Council with a sense of satisfaction that it was performing a bigger role in the national reconstruction. While inaugurating the Central Road Research Institute in New Delhi on 16 July 1952, which was under the purview of the CSIR, Maulana Azad said

> It is true that the Council of Industrial and Scientific Research was established in 1942 but its activities were concerned mainly with the increase of the country's war potential. It is after the formation of the National Government that its activities have been expanded to cover all aspects of national life and progress made at a pace that would reflect credit on any government. In the brief course of the last four years, not only have the activities of the Council expanded but a new department of Scientific Research has also been set up by the Government. This Department has now reached a stage where it has become a full-fledged Ministry.[143]

Pandit Nehru was gracing the occasion and Azad took that opportunity to acknowledge his leadership in these developments,

> I have no hesitation, Mr. Prime Minister, in saying that this remarkable progress is due entirely to your leadership and inspiration. In spite of all your pre-occupations as Prime Minister in a most difficult time, you undertook direct responsibility for the Department of Scientific Research and all its work was done under your personal guidance.[144]

The autonomy that the Council enjoyed was one of the factors for its rapid success. Azad clearly suggested this,

> and it appears to me that the one reason for its splendid success is that the Council is an autonomous body with its own budget and free from formalities and red-tape, which slow down the administrative machine of the Government. Even the minister-in-charge who supervises the activities of the Council does so not as a minister but as an office bearer of the Council . . . and to a large measure the success of the Council is due to this fact.[145]

V

The cultural reconstruction of the nation in post-independent India was an equally significant aspect of the engagements undertaken by the Ministry of Education under the charge of Maulana Azad. It was the considered view of Azad that during colonial rule, the cultural life of Indians was not given adequate representation. This imbalance was needed to be corrected in independent India in a variety of ways.

In this regard one of the early steps that was initiated by the ministry was to create an institutional mechanism to popularize the National Anthem. Azad prepared a two-page note in Urdu on its importance in the life of a nation. He began with the following statements, 'In almost all the countries of the world it is the practice that National Anthem of the country is learnt by all the children in the school and all of them sing it with great enthusiasm. There would be hardly any child in France who won't memorize La Marsellaise . . . and be able to sing it solo as well as in chorus.'[146] He commented on conditions during the British rule, when nothing was adopted as the National Anthem, except for the fact that in Congress sessions '*Vande Mataram*' was sung. He added, now that the Government of India has adopted Tagore's '*Jana Gana Mana*' as the National Anthem, 'there was hardly any reason, why our schools and colleges must remain deprived of its melodious and overwhelming tunes'.[147] He considered the matter too important from the national point of view to be left to the discretion of the state governments, therefore making a plea for a decision by the centre in order to ensure its applicability to all parts of the country.[148] He desired that through a resolution of the Government of India, it was possible to ensure that the National Anthem was taught in all schools and colleges on tunes, which are determined for this Anthem. He also advised that in schools, children could sing this Anthem in chorus instead of two-three children singing it and the rest could remain silent. Keeping all these in mind he advised, 'Secretary may please take necessary action in this regard'.[149]

In response to these considerations of Azad, the ministry took steps in order to popularize the singing of the National Anthem.

It issued a circular to the provincial governments. The circular stated, 'The Government of India, therefore, feel that *Jana Gana Mana* should be regularly taught to all the pupils in schools and colleges so that they are able to sing it in the tune officially adopted for it, not only individually but also in chorus'.[150] However the circular also clarified, 'Before the Government of India considers what steps should be taken they would like to know what actually is being done in this regard in the different states.' The ministry also wanted to know from the state governments as to what steps they might have already taken or propose to take.[151]

The replies that the Ministry of Education received from different provincial governments as well as some directorates of education were quite revealing and interesting. For instance, the Directorate of Education of the Delhi state in its reply admitted that, 'The position with regard to this is that so far no training is given in any systematic or uniform manner. Actually there is still confusion in many places about the position of the song "*Bande Matram*" and in schools the headmasters and headmistresses have been making use of one or the other according to their whim in the matter.'[152] The ministry was assured that steps in this regard would be initiated. However, a major difficulty that these institutions faced, that there was no authoritative version available in the gramophone records which had been prepared either by HMV or other gramophone companies. It was further suggested that there was a necessity of prescribing certain set rules for the National Anthem and also the manner, which would show total reverence to the Anthem.[153] In this regard an interesting suggestion was made that, 'as a practical step that the government should supply each school with a gramophone record of the National Anthem correctly recorded in the tune officially adopted.'[154] On the issue of the National Anthem, the Ministry of Home Affairs too was consulted, however, a major difficulty was that it had, 'only the military band version of "*Jana Gana Mana*" which had so far been played on official and ceremonial occasions in India.'[155] It tried to assure the Ministry of Education that the Ministry of Information and Broadcasting was taking steps to obtain copyrights of the orchestral and vocal version of the Anthem from the parties concerned namely Mr. Murrills and Rathindranath Tagore of the Visva-Bharati respectively.[156] The Ministry of Home Affairs further said, 'we are doing all that is possible to expedite this matter' and regretted that they were unable to supply to the Ministry of Education any 'authorized form of the vocal version of the *Jana Gana Mana*'.[157] A suggestion too was made that the prime minister's secretariat might be consulted in the matter.

About five years after the suggestion was made by Maulana Azad to popularize the National Anthem and an initiative taken by the Ministry of Education in this regard, an organization called the Bharat Sewak Samaj, Cultural Division drew a scheme to popularize the National Anthem and made a suggestion that

> with the help of the Education Ministry, a nation-wide directive should be sent that in all schools, colleges and other institutions work should commence either by the entire institution collecting to sing the National Anthem, if the members of the institution normally congregate for other purposes or that each class should commence work for the day with the chorus singing of the National Anthem.[158]

The Ministry of Education brought it to the notice of the prime minister's secretariat that it had already issued a circular to state governments for encouraging community singing of the National Anthem in all education institutions.[159] However, in pursuance of the wishes of the prime minister, the Ministry of Education issued another circular with additional emphasis, 'Since then the matter had been discussed further in the Government of India and the Prime Minister has himself been taking a keen interest in the whole question.'[160] The difference between the earlier initiative and the latest one was that then concerned agencies were not sure about the standardized 'vocal version' of the '*Jana Gana Mana*' about which there was some certainty and confidence so that the Ministry could say that the Ministry of Information and Broadcasting was arranging to bring out a record of the National Anthem, 'which will give the standardized vocal version as approved by the Prime Minister'.[161]

In the realm of re-building the cultural institutions Maulana Azad as Minister of Education, had smooth sailing. One of the institutions established under the auspices of the ministry was the Sahitya Akademi in 1952. In order to establish this organization, a Conference of Letters was convened on 15 March 1951, which was attended by representatives from 19 state governments as well as representatives of various Assamese, Bengali, Gujarati, Hindi, Kannada, Marathi, Malayalam, Oriya, Sanskrit, Tamil, Telugu and Urdu literary organizations.[162] Maulana Azad addressed this Conference and in his preliminary remarks said that in India there was a long tradition of state patronage of men of letters, which was absent during the colonial rule and the time had come to revive the old tradition. In order to create conditions in which 'our languages can develop their innate potentialities and contribute to the heritage of the world',[163] and in this regard, the first issue of consideration for this Conference is a proposal for the establishment of an Indian Academy of Letters, 'which will coordinate literary activities in all Indian languages'. He also assured that, 'the Government should certainly help both by material assistance and by creating an atmosphere congenial to cultural activities. . . . The scope of non-official activity in these fields is unlimited and can never be overemphasized.'[164] The Conference requested the minister to appoint a Committee to draft a constitution and lay down the functions of the National Academy of Letters. Subsequently the Committee was appointed,[165] which prepared the constitution of the proposed Academy and it suggested that, 'The name of the Indian National Academy of Letters shall be Bharat Bharati', and its headquarters 'shall be at New Delhi' which could be shifted to another place with the agreement of three-fourths of the members. It also said that the object of the Bharati would be to foster and develop Indian languages and literature, to promote the cultural unity of the country and to maintain high literary standards.[166]

The draft of the constitution was circulated among the representatives for comments and there were not many responses but the one from the Madras government clearly stated that it would prefer the Academy to be known as 'Indian National Academy of Letters' and desired that 'Bharat Bharati' might be omitted. In view of this objection the ministry officials made a suggestion that the Academy could perhaps be called 'Sahitya

Akadami'[167] Maulana Azad did not agree with this suggestion initially as he was of the opinion that for the present the issue of the Hindi technical terms had not been resolved, therefore it was not advisable to rush for Hindi names and as of now 'confine ourselves to English names. As soon as the problem of Hindi technical terms will be resolved, Hindi name shall be adopted'.[168] However, on the advice of Maulana Azad, the ministry officials consulted the Hindi section to find a suitable Hindi name for the Academy and two names were suggested; 'Sahitya Bharati' and 'Sahitya Niketan'. Despite these suggestion it was felt that 'Sahitya Akadami' would be proximate translation of the 'Academy of Letters'. Azad finally concurred, 'I agree that its Hindi name would be Sahitya Akadami'.[169]

After going through all this motion, the Ministry of Education issued a resolution to be published in the *Gazette of India* for general information. It stated,

> Whereas it is considered expedient to establish a national organization to work actively for the development of Indian letters and to set high literary standards, to foster and coordinate literary activities in all the Indian languages and to promote through them all the cultural unity of the country, it is hereby resolved as follows: A National Academy of Letters to be called 'Sahitya Akadami' shall be established.[170]

While defining its functions, the Resolution said, 'To promote cooperation between literary associations, universities and cultural organizations and to encourage the establishment and development of representative literary associations concerned with the development of language and literature.'[171]

In order to give greater respectability to the founding of the Sahitya Akadami, Maulana Azad proposed the name of Pandit Jawaharlal Nehru as its first president, (which meant as chairman) and said that he (Jawaharlal Nehru) had given his consent in this regard.[172] In view of the desire expressed by Maulana Azad to have Pandit Nehru as its founding chairman, the ministry prepared a note for the President of India, who alone had the power to appoint the Chairman, who would hold office for a term of five years. It was stated that, 'It was the intention of the framers of the constitution that the chairman should be a person of high national standing who also has intimate knowledge of letters and who will command general confidence and respect among writers. The Minister of Education suggests the appointment of Shri Jawaharlal Nehru as the first Chairman of the Academy for a period of five years.'[173] The note concluded, 'Approval of the President is solicited to the above proposal.' Before sending a note to the office of the president, for appointing Pandit Nehru as the first Chairman of the Academy, the Ministry of Education had made it clear to the prime minister's secretariat that his (Pandit Nehru's) nomination was not on account of his being the prime minister but in his personal capacity as 'a man of letters'.[174]

About the appointment of Pandit Nehru as the first Chairman, Maulana Azad acknowledged that,

> He has been appointed not because he is the Prime Minister but because he has carved out for himself a distinctive place as a writer and author. . . . The Ministry of Education offered the Chairmanship to him, as it was beyond dispute that from every point of view he is the best man we could have selected for the first Chairmanship of India's National Academy of Letters.[175]

With such credible names the Sahitya Akadami was formally inaugurated on 12 March 1954. While delivering his inaugural speech, Maulana Azad stated that there were some people who thought that the Akadami should not have been established in this manner and the prime minister too for a while seemed to share the same opinion as it was regarded as an imposition from above. They thought that the growth of academies should have been encouraged from below and allowed individuals and societies to establish such academies and then 'the Government's function should have been merely to recognize them'.[176] Azad candidly stated that he did not agree with this approach. In defense of his stand he cited the example of the European experience and said, 'Since the Renaissance, many academies have been established in Europe. Today there is hardly any country in the Western world, which does not have one or more national academies. All these academies were established by the Government under letters-patent of the Sovereigns or by legislation.'[177] He also emphasized the importance of maintaining the high standards of literary output in the country, failing which the purpose of establishing an Academy such as this would be lost.

After founding of the Sahitya Akadami, another cultural institution of national importance, the National Academy of Art, to be called Lalit Kala Akadami was established in 1953. In order to establish an institution such as this, a small committee of artists and art critics was set up in March 1953 to draw up a constitution for the Academy of Art. The Committee in its meeting held on 4 April 1953 drew up a constitution and the draft constitution was circulated among the state governments for their comments.[178] Subsequently the Ministry of Education, in view of the Committee's recommendation and the proposed constitution adopted a Resolution, which stated, 'Whereas it is considered expedient to establish a national organization to foster and coordinate activities in the sphere of visual and plastic art and to promote thereby the cultural unity of the country, it is hereby resolved as follows: A National Academy of Art, to be called Lalit Kala Akadami shall be established.'[179] It was decided that the headquarters of the Academy would be at New Delhi, which however could be shifted to another place with the consent of four-fifths of the members of the Academy. While outlining its functions the Resolution said that the Academy would encourage and promote study and research in the fields of paintings, sculptures and architecture and applied arts. Apart from various other functions it would also strive to foster national and international contacts through exhibitions, exchange of personnel and art objects, etc.[180] However, unlike the Sahitya Akadami, the chairman of the Lalit Kala Akadami was to enjoy a term only for three years. With these and other conditions it was ordered on 7 October 1953 that the said Resolution be published in the *Gazette of India*.[181]

The next in order in the line of establishing cultural institutions was the Sangeet Natak Akadami, which was founded on 31 May 1952 and inaugurated by Dr. Rajendra Prasad, the President of India on 28 January 1953. Maulana Azad, in the course of his welcome address at the inauguration of the Indian Academy of Dance Drama and Music, with its Hindi name, Sangeet Natak Akadami said that in August 1949 a Conference on Art was convened in Calcutta, which resolved that there should be committees to look into the possibilities of founding not only an academy of this kind but also academies such as Academy of Letters and Art.[182] The Central Advisory Board of Education accordingly approved these suggestions and a Committee was entrusted with responsibilities of drafting a constitution for it. The Committee, when drafting the constitution, named it as 'The Constitution of the Academy of Hindustani Music.'[183] While outlining the object of the proposed Academy, it said,

> The objects of the Academy will be to foster and develop Hindustani music (including dance) and in relation to it, to encourage the study of other schools of Indian Music. The Academy will accordingly make provision for instruction and research in theory and practice of Hindustani music and will also endeavour to bring about a closer understanding not only between Hindustani music on the one hand and other schools of Indian music on the other.[184]

The proposed Academy was to have its headquarters at Lucknow and therefore keeping that in mind it was said that the Education Minister of Uttar Pradesh would be the president for the first three years and thereafter, the president would be nominated by the Government of India.[185]

When this constitution was circulated among the member states for their comments and suggestions, the Education Minister of UP, Dr. Sampurnanand raised certain objections as regards the financial powers, 'The constitution says nothing about the manner in which the Academy will be financed.' He raised another objection, 'No power vests anywhere to compel any other state to give an appreciable money grant and yet the UP government gets a minority representation on the general council and most of the other members are also nominees of the Government of India.'[186] In this communication he almost declined the possibility of associating himself with the Academy on account of the fact that the term of the president was meant to be only for three years. He complained, 'After three years the Government of India will be free to nominate some person not belonging to UP to the key position of the President of the Academy. If this draft embodies the final opinion of the Government of India, I am sure you will realize my difficulty in associating myself with it.'[187] In reply to these objections raised by Sampurnanand, Dr. Tarachand did his best to reason with him that his apprehensions were not based on sound ground since the government grants to the Academy should be as secure as the grants to universities and other institutions.[188] As regards the position of the President of the Academy, he said, 'the President can obviously be nominated only by the government of India; otherwise, it would be difficult to satisfy the claims of the participating State Governments'.[189] In the letter Tarachand hoped that Sampurnanand would find these explanations satisfactory and proceed in the matter so that the Academy could be established by the end of the financial year.

It seems Dr. Sampurnanand was not convinced, and did not take an interest in the matter, resulting in inordinate delays in communication. In view of this delay in replies, the Ministry of Education at the centre suggested that the establishment of the Academy might be proceeded with without waiting for replies from the UP government any further. Maulana Azad concurred and wrote a curt note on the files, 'There has to be a limit in the matter. We have given the UP government enough time to take a decision. There is no point in waiting any further. Lets proceed in the matter.'[190] A suggestion came up that instead of Lucknow, the Academy could possibly have its headquarters in Bombay. However, even before a final decision was taken about the headquarters of the Academy, the Ministry of Education sent a communication to the Department of Education, Government of Uttar Pradesh saying that, 'the Government of India have most reluctantly decided to take further steps towards the establishment of the Academy on the assumption that the Government of Uttar Pradesh do not desire to have the headquarters of the Academy at Lucknow.'[191] The loss of Lucknow, resulted in the gain of Delhi to have the headquarters of the Academy and instead of Dr. Sampurnanand, Dr. P.V. Rajamannar became its founding chairman.

In his welcome address, Azad highlighted the achievements of India over the centuries in the field of music, dance and drama. He said, 'India can be proud of a long heritage and traditions in the field of dance, drama and music. In the field of fine arts, as in those of philosophy and science, India and Greece occupy an almost unique position in human history.'[192] He felt that breadth and depth of Indian music was perhaps unrivalled as it was integration of vocal and instrumental music. While commenting on the achievements in the field of drama, he paid a glowing tribute to Indian genius, 'Kalidasa may be compared with the greatest among the Greek dramatists. We have also the works of Bhasa, Bhavabhuti and Banbhatta who raised the Indian drama to a level which is not inferior to that attained by the Greeks.'[193] Similarly, he praised Indian achievements even in the fields of dance, whether classical forms as they developed in temples or the folk dances as they developed in different regions of the country.[194]

The above-discussed cultural institutions, while being founded, were visualized to bring diverse cultures within the country closer to one another in order to foster a sense of unity through the medium of culture. Maulana Azad visualized another cultural institution, which could bring India closer to a large number of countries through a programme of exchange of literature, culture and personnel associated with these fields. However, there was hardly an institution, which could cater to such requirements and hence the need to establish one was felt rather seriously. In order to explore such a possibility, a Conference for Cultural Co-operation between India and Asian Countries was convened at New Delhi, on 21 August 1949. While addressing this Conference, Azad, highlighted the importance of developing closer cultural ties among the countries of Asia and argued,

> We want to deepen our friendship and contact not only with Iran but also with Turkey and the countries of the Middle-East and China and our neighbours and in South-East Asia. Such cooperation is also necessary from an international point of view. If we can create large blocks of goodwill in different areas of the world, grounds for suspicion and hatred will be removed and we can contribute to increased international understanding and unity.[195]

In the course of the same speech, he underlined the importance of developing such contacts, 'Political alliances are based on a spirit of bargaining, while cultural contacts deepen mutual understanding. Such understanding is more important today in view of the new awakening, which is taking place throughout the Eastern world.'[196]

Azad, stressed that India in recent years was brought closer to countries of Europe and America and in the process neighbouring countries were kept out of this ambit. Now the time had come to get closer to neighbours and in this regard, 'we must on one hand, establish closer contacts with Turkey, Afghanistan and the Middle-East countries. On the other we should also develop closer relations with China, Japan and the countries of South-East Asia.'[197] For all this to be translated into realities, he proposed the creation of a body to be named as 'Indian Council of Cultural Cooperation'. He invited intellectuals and members of the intelligentsia to associate themselves with the proposed body and prepare a constitution for it, through a Provisional Committee and its sub-committee so that this Council could formally be launched by early November (perhaps the same year 1949).

It could not be possible to launch the proposed Council in November 1949, as it had to wait for some more months and it could be launched only on 9 April 1950. In his inaugural address Maulana Azad informed that the Provisional Committee met on 27 November 1949 and accepted the draft constitution of the Council, which was named as Indian Council for Cultural Relations.[198] He expressed satisfaction that the decision to establish a Council such as this was warmly welcomed by countries such as Egypt, Syria, Lebanon, Iraq, Iran and Afghanistan. Burma, Ceylon and the Republic of Indonesia too expressed strong support for the Council. The headquarters of the Council was established at Hyderabad House, New Delhi with a library and other facilities. He (Azad) donated his personal library to this Council. The Ajit Ghosh collection was bought for the same purpose. The Council proposed to publish two quarterlies; one in Arabic and another one in English. It was suggested that the Arabic journal would be a vehicle of cultural exchange between India and the Middle-East, whereas the English journal would perform the same role with the Eastern and South-Eastern countries. In this context Azad hoped, 'that the work of this Council will encourage the study of Sanskrit, Arabic, Persian, Chinese and other Oriental languages which have contributed to the development of human culture and civilization'.[199]

Even though the Council was started to build cultural relations with the countries as stated above, to begin with it had only one division to deal with the Middle-East, Turkey and Egypt. About eight years later, and one week before his death, Azad revealed the reasons to launch a division such as this in the Council, while delivering his presidential address at the General Assembly meeting of the Council. He said that soon after Independence and Partition, there was a climate of communalism and hatred due to Partition-related violence on both sides of the divide. However, regrettably Pakistan launched a propaganda campaign against India, which clouded the thinking of many Muslim countries and they thought that, 'India now meant solely a Hindu country. They came to believe that even if a few Muslims remained in India, they had no religious and civic freedom.'[200] He also cited the example of how the Indian Ambassador to Egypt, Syed Husain was perceived to be ambassador of Pakistan due to such misperceptions, which needed urgent correction. And with the founding of the Council and publication of an Arabic Quarterly, *Thaqafat-ul-Hind*, all these countries realized that, 'the Indian Government was not a government of Hindus alone but a truly national Government of all Indians'.[201] The Council started another quarterly in Persian, *Hind-wa-Iran*, which was published by the Indo–Iran Society of Calcutta for the Council. These efforts resulted in dispelling misconceptions and 'the same people who had formerly distrusted India now became India's warmest friends'.[202] After the successful functioning of this division in the Council, another division for South-East Asia was added in order to bring the people of this region closer to India since a vast majority of them in this region felt close affiliation with India on account of the fact that they were either Buddhists or Muslims. With this purpose in mind a journal, *Indo Asian Culture* was started, which became popular with students of Buddhist history, philosophy and culture.[203] In this speech Azad also visualized the possibilities of starting a division in the Council to deal with the Commonwealth countries.

Interestingly, a representative of Pakistan too was attending this Conference and Azad took a special notice of his presence and welcomed him in the hope this would mark a further strengthening of the ties between the two countries. Acutely aware of the autonomous realm of culture, Azad stated, 'We have been separated on political grounds, but we have been one people and cultural life is such that it cannot be divided without loss to both.' The concluding lines of Maulana Azad, were inspiring. He said, 'I hope our contacts with all these countries will continue to increase and the Council will play an increasing role in bringing our peoples closer to one another.'[204]

These were some of the educational, scientific, technological and cultural institutions that were founded under the aegis of Maulana Azad as the Minister of Education from 1947-58. The breadth of vision that went into the making of these institutions and the depth of foundations ensured that they would continue to serve the nation much after he was gone. A cursory glance at these would convince that they are still serving the nation well.

It is futile to think what would have happened to the country if these institutions had not been established. The fact is that they came into existence as a response to specific needs of the time. There were some, which were a product of imaginative anticipation, visualization and planning. In these enterprises of the Ministry, Azad was so very ably supported by men of standing such as S.S. Bhatnagar, Humayun Kabir, Dr. Tarachand and K.G. Saiyidain. There were still many others whose names did not appear in public but they played an important role in formulating policies in the ministry, such as Ashfaq Husain and G.K. Chandirmani and others. The ministry under Azad's stewardship had a fair share of critics but then in a democratic set up, who is spared of criticism. Azad took all this in his stride while he moved on to deepen the foundation of education and culture so that India could prosper not just educationally but culturally as well.

Azad barely lived about a week after delivering this address as he fell in his bathroom and broke his hip. He fell unconscious and never recovered.[205] Dr. B.C. Roy came down from Calcutta to examine him but it hardly made any change in his condition. Jawaharlal Nehru too paid a visit to him. 'While he was lying on his death-bed on 22 February 1958, he caught hold of Jawaharlal Nehru and his last words were "Jawahar, Khuda Hafiz".'[206] Thus an intellectual, nationalist and institution builder of modern India was laid to rest in the vicinity of Delhi's Juma Masjid.

NOTES

1. Maulana Abul Kalam Azad, *India Wins Freedom: The Complete Version*, Orient Longman, New Delhi. 1988, p. 188.
2. Ibid.
3. V.N. Datta, *Maulana Azad*, Manohar, New Delhi, 1990, p. 224.
4. Azad, *India Wins Freedom*, p. 188.
5. Khwaja Abdul Majeed wrote to Azad on 28 December 1946 pleading with him that he should not join the interim ministry for the reason that India was still not independent. However, in the event of his joining the ministry he would have to take the oath in the name of the British Crown, which he did not appreciate. It was for this reason he expressed his resentment against Pandit Nehru for taking an oath in the same manner. Despite this Khwaja said that Azad was hugely capable of handling any responsibility that was given to him.
6. Krishna Kumar, 'Education and Culture: India's Quest for Secular Policy', in Krishna Kumar and Joachim Oesterheld, eds., *Education and Social Change in South Asia*, Orient Longman, Delhi, 2007, pp. 210-11.
7. Susanne Hoeber Rudolph and Lloyd I. Rudolph, *Education and Politics in India: Studies in Organisation, Society and Policy*, Oxford University Press, Delhi, 1972, pp. 8-9.
8. Maulana Azad's press conference held on 18 February 1947 in *Speeches of Maulana Azad 1947-1958,* Publications Division, New Delhi, 1989, p. 1.
9. Ibid., p. 2.
10. Ibid., p. 9.
11. Maulana Azad's address to the All India Educational Conference, New Delhi, 16 January 1948 in ibid., p. 29.
12. Ibid. Azad asserted, 'that even if other nation building activities of the Government have to be slowed down or deferred on account of such difficulties, education at any rate must be pushed forward as rapidly as possible. We must not for a moment forget that it is the birthright of every individual to receive at least the basic education without which he cannot fully discharge duties as a citizen.'
13. Ibid.
14. Ibid. Azad made a passionate appeal, 'I would urge upon every educated man and woman to regard it a sacred national service to come forward and serve as a teacher for at least two years. They should regard it as a sacrifice to the national cause and accept for

their services whatever allowance the state may afford.'

15. Ibid., p. 30.
16. Ibid., pp. 32-3.
17. Maulana Azad's address to the Central Advisory Board of Education, Cuttack, 8 January 1950, in *Speeches of Maulana Azad 1947-1958,* Publications Division, New Delhi, 1989, p. 126.
18. Ibid., pp. 126-7.
19. Ibid., p. 130.
20. Report of the University Education Commission, Government of India, Ministry of Education (December 1948-August 1949), vol. I, New Delhi, 1949, p. 33 as cited in D.P. Nayar, *Towards a National System of Education*, Mittal Publication, New Delhi, 1989.
21. Ibid., p. 41.
22. Ibid., p. 47.
23. Nayar, *Towards a National System of Education*, p. 386.
24. Ibid., p. 387.
25. The Convocation speech at Patna University on 21 December 1947 in which he said, 'The position that English occupies today in our educational and official life cannot be sustained in future. It is but essential that Indian languages should find their legitimate position.' In *Speeches of Maulana Azad 1947-1958,* p. 16.
26. Ibid., p. 18.
27. Ibid.
28. Azad's presidential speech at the 14th session of the Central Advisory Board of Education, 13 January 1948, in *Speeches of Maulana Azad 1947-1958*, p. 25.
29. Nayar, *Towards a National System of Education*, p. 396.
30. Ibid., pp. 402-3.
31. Ibid., p. 370.
32. T.M. Thomas, *Indian Educational Reforms in Cultural Perspectives*, S. Chand and Company, New Delhi, 1970, p. 101.
33. Report of the Secondary Education Commission, New Delhi, Ministry of Education, Government of India, 1953, as cited in ibid., p. 103.
34. Thomas, op. cit.
35. Ibid.
36. Kartick C. Mukherjee, *Underdevelopment, Educational Policy and Planning*, Asia Publishing House, Calcutta, 1967, p. 72.
37. Ibid., p. 73.
38. Azad's presidential speech at the 14th session of the Central Advisory Board of Education, 13 January 1948, in *Speeches of Maulana Azad 1947-1958*, p. 23.

39. Ibid.
40. Ministry of Education, Government of India, File no. 30-4/52 G 3 U 2, National Archives of India, New Delhi.
41. Ibid.
42. Ibid.
43. Ibid.
44. Ministry of Education, Press Note issued on 10 November 1953, in ibid.
45. Rajendra Prasad, President's Camp (Jagdalpur), India, 23 March 1953 to Maulana Azad, Ministry of Education, Government of India, File no. 30-5/52 G 3 (U 2), National Archives of India, New Delhi.
46. Letter from Maulana Azad to Rajendra Prasad, 27 March 1953 in ibid. Azad only said, 'Thanks for your letter dated 23 March 1953, regarding Radha Kumud Mookerji. When the time comes, his name will be considered.' Ministry of Education, Government of India, File no. 30-5/52 G 3 (U 2), National Archives of India, New Delhi.
47. A.L. Mudaliar's confidential letter to Humayun Kabir, 5 September 1953. He suggested the names of six vice-chancellors, 1. V.S. Krishna, V.C., Andhra University, Waltair, 2. Hansa Mehta, V.C., University of Baroda, 3. Navroji J. Wadia, V.C.; University of Bombay, 4. Pandit K.L. Dubey, V.C., University of Nagpur, 5. G.S. Mahajani, V.C., University of Delhi, 6. R.P. Tripathi, V.C., University of Saugar. Mudaliar explained the reasons for recommending these names, 'The names I have suggested are of those who have, in recent years, taken keen interest in the Inter-University Board and have attended all the meetings of the Board. Four of them are actually members of the Standing Committee but that did not influence me in suggesting their names.' Ministry of Education, Government of India, File no. 30-5/52 G 3 (U 2), National Archives of India, New Delhi.
48. I.S. Avinashlingam from Coimbatore, in a letter dated 19 April 1953, offered his candidature for either chairmanship or membership of the Commission. Similarly Detaram Makhijani in his letter dated 19 November 1952 made a strong case for himself. The most interesting part of the letter was, 'I am strong in physique, young in spirit and I am confident that my work will be appreciated as a member of the Commission.' Ministry of Education, Government of India, File no. 30-5/52 G 3 (U 2), National Archives of India, New Delhi.

49. Ministry of Education, Government of India, File no. 24-18/56 A 1(U 2), National Archives of India, New Delhi.
50. Ibid.
51. Ministry of Education, Government of India, File no. 40-5/1950 D 3.
52. Ibid.
53. Ibid.
54. Ibid.
55. Ibid.
56. Humayun Kabir's note prepared on 25 July 1950 provided the rationale for making Visva-Bharati a central university. The note also said, '. . . it will also help the institution indirectly by giving a greater market value to its degrees and diplomas. During Tagore's days his personal prestige was so great that students were attracted from India and outside even though they knew that the degrees and diplomas of Visva-Bharati were not recognized for purposes of employment. Today such recognition is necessary if the institution is to continue to play a useful part in interpreting India to the world outside and developing several important aspects of Indian culture.
57. Ibid. The last paragraph of the note said, 'HM Education therefore requests that the approval of the Cabinet may be given to the proposal to introduce during the next session of the Parliament legislation for instituting Visva-Bharati into a Central University. Further steps will then be taken in consultation with the Ministry of Law.'
58. Ibid. Humayun Kabir prepared a note for the Presidential assent on 9 April 1951. It said that, 'As HM Education is very anxious that necessary legislation may be enacted before he leaves for Europe on 2 May, we will be grateful if the recommendation of the President be secured and conveyed to us as early as possible.'
59. Address at the formal inauguration of Visva-Bharati as a central university, Santiniketan, in *Speeches of Maulana Azad 1947-1958*, p. 164.
60. Ibid., p. 165.
61. Ibid.
62. Ibid., p. 166.
63. A letter from Jamia Millia Islamia, dated 27 April 1949. It is not clear from the file as to who signed this letter. Ministry of Education, Government of India, File no. 73-216/49 D III A1.
64. Ibid.

65. Ibid.
66. Ibid. The note said that, 'the Standing Committee is of the opinion that it is not desirable to recognize as universities, institutions which have not been given statutory recognition. It will be open to the Governments, Provincial and Central to recognize for the purposes of public appointments the qualifications of such institutions as are not statutorily established as universities.'
67. Ibid. Noting on files of the Ministry of Education.
68. Ibid.
69. Ministry of Education, Government of India, File no. 26-5/51 G III A 1.
70. Ibid.
71. Ministry of Education, Government of India, File no. 43-75/50 B 1.
72. Ibid. The officers prepared a report, which said, 'We saw some of these and we were impressed by the industry and pains taken by the organizers for preparing the series. Most of these have done in Urdu and some in Hindi. We understood that they also intend to prepare these publications in other languages if adequate help and necessary demand were there. It was understood that about twenty-five manuscripts in Hindi and as many in Urdu were ready for publication and for want of financial help they have not been able to move much in the matter.' It was admitted that their work was not only intrinsically but educationally sound and of competitive merit.
73. Ibid. Note prepared by Humayun Kabir on 9 March 1950. Maulana Azad concurred with this suggestion and wrote in Urdu, '*Han, Yeh Nihayat Zaroori Kaam Hai. Zaroor Anjam Diya Jaye.*'
74. Ministry of Education, Government of India, File no. 29-54/51 G 3 KW. Gopichand Bhargava addressed a letter to Dr. Tara Chand, the then Secretary of Education dated 28 April 1951. He said, 'Considered from all points of view, I believe the suggestion of having a University for this region under a Central Act, financed by the Government of India, the state of Punjab, Himachal Pradesh and PEPSU, if possible, is a sound one. It will materially raise the standards of higher education in this part of the Republic.'
75. Ibid. A note was prepared by Humayun Kabir on 5 February 1952.
76. Ibid. It was further suggested, 'HM is aware that we are proposing to approach the Cabinet to earmark the amount which will be available under the American Emergency Food Aid Act fund for

the rehabilitation of our Universities, viz., Punjab and Calcutta should be given special treatment. If the Cabinet accepts our proposal, the entire cost of Laboratory and equipment of the Punjab University which falls to the share of the Centre may be met out of that fund.'

77. Ibid. Proceedings of the Conference held on 9 September 1952.
78. Maulana Azad's note dated 11 January 1953 in ibid.
79. Ministry of Education, Government of India, File no. 23-27/55 A 1 (U 5). B.C. Roy, Chief Minister, West Bengal, wrote a letter to Maulana Azad, dated 20 August 1955, detailing the manner in which the proposed University would be shaped.
80. Ibid. B.C. Roy said, 'I am writing to you for your blessings and support for this small University. . . .'
81. Ibid.
82. Ministry of Education, Government of India, File no. 29-16/51 G III.
83. Ibid.
84. Ibid.
85. Ibid. K.G. Saiyidain's letter addressed to all vice-chancellors, dated 15 January 1951.
86. Ibid. A note prepared in the Ministry of Education on 19 September 1951, said, 'It would appear that the one snag is Finance. Because we have taken the initiative, our universities want us to find funds for implementing a scheme, which would cater to their wants. But in the present financial set-up we hardly could expect M/Finance to favour the idea.'
87. Ibid. A note prepared by the Ministry of Finance dated 7 January 1953
88. Nayar, *Towards a National System of Education*. The author has argued that such an approach was taken due to the University Education Commission, which was prematurely appointed, as a result there was rebuilding of the educational pyramid from the wrong end, p. 370.
89. Ibid., p. 371.
90. Ministry of Education, Government of India, File no. 10-2/55 A 1 (U 5), 'Draft-outline for educational development in the second five-year plan', which said, 'The Constitution has prescribed that every endeavour should be made to provide by 1960 universal compulsory, free elementary education to all children up to the age of 14.
91. Ibid.

92. Ibid. It was further stated that, 'it is sometimes overlooked that no permanent improvement of the economic condition of a country is possible without an improvement in the quality of manpower. The Ministry of Education pressed this point of view even at the time of the formulation of the first plan.'
93. Ibid.
94. Ibid.
95. Ibid.
96. Ibid.
97. Ibid.
98. Ibid.
99. Ibid.
100. Humayun Kabir's letter dated 23 November 1953 to the Ministry of Home Affairs initiated the discussion in the Government circles as to how to go about the proposal of the Ministry of Education. Ministry of Education, Government of India, File no. 33.36/55 A1.
101. Ibid. These comments were made by the Ministry of Law on 14 October 1954, almost about a year after the original proposal was made by the Ministry of Education.
102. Ibid.
103. Ibid.
104. Ibid. Humayun Kabir in his noting on the file recorded, 'I have discussed with the Minister. He is of the view that the proposal should first be considered by the Sub-Committee of the Cabinet. The State Governments should be consulted only after the Government of India have made up their mind in the matter.'
105. Ibid. The four-page note prepared by the Ministry of Education. It was pointed out that in the light of the experience of the working of the Constitution, it was felt that there was need to extend the scope of Central responsibility and provide for coordination of facilities and maintenance of standards also at the elementary and secondary levels. Standards could not be maintained in the universities, unless the students received adequate training in the lower stages. It also suggested that since only a small fraction of the population would receive higher education, it was imperative that elementary and secondary education should be so designed as to turn out the kind of citizen that free India requires.
106. Ibid.
107. Ibid.

108. Ibid.
109. Ibid. Apart from Jawaharlal Nehru, other members of this sub-committee were, Govind Ballabh Pant, Minister of Home Affairs, Jagjivan Ram, Minister of Communication, Dr. Kailashnath Katju, Minister of Defence, T.T. Krishnamachari, Minister of Commerce and Industry, C.C. Biswas, Minister of Law and Minority Affairs. Maulana Azad too attended this meeting.
110. Ibid.
111. Maulana Azad's presidential address to the 25th meeting of the Central Advisory Board of Education, New Delhi, 6 February 1958, p. 407. It is interesting to note that he delivered this speech just sixteen days before he passed away on 22 February 1958.
112. Ibid., p. 408.
113. Ibid. It is interesting to note that Azad was making these statements in the context of evaluation of the functioning of his Ministry for he had set out two criteria: 'The first is to look at what has been done from the point of view of what was desirable. The second is to do so from the point of view of what was possible in the circumstances.'
114. Ibid., p. 407.
115. Ibid., p. 412.
116. Ibid.
117. *A Walk Through History: 50 Years of IIT Kharagpur*, Indian Institute of Technology, Kharagpur, 2002, p. 31.
118. Ibid., p. 29. Also refer to a Notification of the Ministry of Education, which said, 'The following amendments have been made to Resolution no. F-10-2/49-T.2, dated 24 February 1950 'for the word "Eastern Higher Technical Institute, Hijli" wherever they occur, the words "Indian Institute of Technology, Kharagpur" shall be substituted.' Ministry of Education, Government of India, File no. 20-87/50 T6.
119. Opening address at the Indian Institute of Technology, Kharagpur, 18 August 1951 in *Speeches of Maulana Azad 1947-1958*, p. 160.
120. Ibid., p. 161.
121. *A Walk Through History: 50 Years of IIT Kharagpur*, p. 34.
122. Ministry of Education, Government of India, File no. 20-87/50 T6.
123. Ibid. Dr. J.C. Ghosh also suggested that in case there were difficulties in converting the Institute into a university, then it could be made an autonomous body under the management of a high-powered Board of Governors.

124. Ibid.
125. Maulana Azad's noting on the file dated 24 August 1953, Ministry of Education, Government of India, File no. 20-87/50 T6.
126. Ministry of Education, Government of India, File no. 20-87/50 T6.
127. A letter from S.R. Sengupta, Director, IIT Kharagpur to Humayun Kabir dated 22 April 1954, Ministry of Education, Government of India, File no. 20-87/50 T6.
128. Ministry of Education, Government of India, File no. 20-87/50 T6.
129. Ibid. In the same note it was suggested that the minister himself from the beginning had insisted that the Institute must be a research institution of a high order. Its products must, therefore be able to find place in universities in India and elsewhere as teachers and researchers, which however was not possible without a statutory authority for its degrees.
130. Ibid.
131. *A Walk Through History: 50 Years of IIT Kharagpur*, p. 41.
132. Ministry of Education, Government of India, File no. 8-17/1949 T.1.
133. Ibid.
134. Ibid.
135. Ibid.
136. Ibid.
137. Ibid.
138. Opening address at the Indian Institute of Technology, Kharagpur, 18 August 1951, in *Speeches of Maulana Azad, 1947-1958*, p. 412.
139. V.V. Krishna, 'Organisation of Industrial Research: The Early History of CSIR, 1934-47', in Roy, Macleod and Deepak Kumar, eds., *Technology and the Raj: Western Technology and Technical Transfers to India, 1700-1947*, Sage Publications, Delhi, 1995, p. 289.
140. Ibid.
141. Ibid., p. 299.
142. CSIR Handbook, CSIR, New Delhi, 1989, p. 1.
143. Inaugural address of Maulana Azad, in *Speeches of Maulana Azad 1947-1958*, p. 210.
144. Ibid.
145. Speech at the opening of the Central Building Research Institute at Roorkee, on 12 April 1953, in ibid., p. 241.

146. Maulana Azad's note in his handwriting on the issue of National Anthem, Ministry of Education, Government of India, File no. 49-111/50 D-3.
147. Ibid.
148. Ibid.
149. Ibid.
150. Circular issued by the Ministry of Education, Government of India, in ibid.
151. Ibid.
152. Letter from the Directorate of Education, Delhi State, 28 September 1950 in ibid.
153. Ibid.
154. Letter from the Directorate of Public Instructions, Madras, 3 October 1950, in ibid.
155. Notes of the Ministry of Home Affairs, 30 October 1950 in ibid.
156. Ibid. They also said that after securing the copyrights, they would be able to supply the standard form of the vocal version, which would be sung in schools and colleges.
157. Ibid
158. Letter from the Bharat Sewak Samaj, Cultural Division signed by one J.N. Sahni. This letter was addressed to the prime minister, who suggested the issue should be taken up with the Ministries of Education and Information and Broadcasting. Pandit Nehru, on 24 May 1955 noted, 'perhaps the Education Ministry might deal with the matter in cooperation with I&B Ministry of Education, Government of India, File no. 27-1/55 P E 4. This suggestion was the most ironical in the sense that matter was referred to the Ministry of Education, which had already initiated a step in this regard about five years ago in 1950.
159. Humayun Kabir's letter dated 5 April 1955 in ibid.
160. Circular issued by the Ministry of Education dated 31 May 1955 to the secretaries of Education Department of the state governments, in ibid.
161. Ibid.
162. Ministry of Education, Government of India, File no.10-7/52 G II 1A.
163. Ibid.
164. Ibid.
165. Ministry of Education, Government of India, File no. 6-4/51 H2 A. This Committee consisted of secretary, Ministry of Education,

Shankar Rao Deo, Nilmani Phookan, Mahamahopadhya Datto Vaman Potdar, Kaka Saheb Kalelkar, Pt. Amarnath Jha, Dr. Zakir Husain, Dr. Syama Prasad Mookerjee and Sardar Teja Singh.

166. Ministry of Education, Government of India, File no. 10-7/52 G II 1A.
167. Ministry of Education, Government of India, File no. 6-4/51 H2 A.
168. Ibid.
169. Ibid.
170. Ministry of Education, Government of India, File no.10-7/52 G II 1A.
171. Ibid.
172. Azad's noting in the file in Ministry of Education, Government of India, File no. 6-4/51 H2 A.
173. Ibid.
174. Ibid.
175. Maulana Azad's speech at the inaugural meeting of the Sahitya Akadami on 12 March 1954, in *Speeches of Maulana Azad, 1947-1958*, p. 296.
176. Ibid., p. 292.
177. Ibid.
178. Ministry of Education, Government of India, File no. 16-8/53 H 2.
179. Ibid.
180. Ibid.
181. Ibid.
182. Welcome address by Maulana Azad on 28 January 1953, in *Speeches of Maulana Azad, 1947-1958*, p. 226.
183. Ministry of Education, Government of India, File no. 4-5/49 G 2 AI. It is not clear from the records of the Ministry as to when it was decided to name this Academy as the Sangeet Natak Akadami.
184. Ibid.
185. Ibid.
186. Letter from Sampurnanand to Dr. Tarachand, dated 4 January 1951 in ibid.
187. Ibid.
188. Dr. Tarachand's reply to Sampurnanand, dated 31 January 1951.
189. Ibid.
190. Maulana Azad's notes in the file of the Ministry, ibid.

191. Communication from the Ministry of Education, Government of India, dated 15 November 1951 in ibid.
192. Welcome address by Maulana Azad on 28 January 1953 in *Speeches of Maulana Azad, 1947-1958*, p. 227.
193. Ibid., p. 229.
194. Ibid.
195. Maulana Azad's address at the India and Asian Countries was convened at New Delhi, on 21 August 1949 in *Speeches of Maulana Azad, 1947-1958*, p. 104.
196. Ibid., p. 105.
197. Ibid.
198. Maulana Azad's inaugural address at the Indian Council for Cultural Relations, on 9 April 1950 in ibid., p. 132.
199. Ibid., p. 134.
200. Maulana Azad's Presidential address to the General Assembly meeting of the Indian Council of Cultural Relations, 14 February 1958 in ibid., p. 416.
201. Ibid.
202. Ibid., p. 417.
203. Ibid., p. 418.
204. Ibid., p. 419.
205. V.N. Datta, *Maulana Azad*, Manohar, Delhi, 1990, p. 227.
206. Ansar Harvani, 'As I Knew Him', in Syeda Saiyidain Hamid, ed., *India's Maulana, Abul Kalam Azad, Centenary Volume I*, Vikas Publishing House, Delhi, 1990, p. 121.

Conclusion

As the study has shown, Maulana Abul Kalam Azad like so many other Indian leaders, was deeply involved in the political processes in order to reinforce Indian nationalism as an integral part of the anti-colonial struggle. However, what sets him apart from other leaders, particularly, the nationalist Muslim leaders, was that he showed an early concern with regard to constructing an ideological framework that would ensure Muslims' participation in the nationalist movement as a religious duty rather than merely indulging in political activism for its own sake. He thought that aloofness of Muslims from the ongoing freedom struggle in the early part of the twentieth century was an undesirable fact to be accepted. It was for this purpose, as other considerations such as changing the whole mindset of the Muslims of his generation, that he decided to launch a journal called *Al-Hilal* in July 1912. The clarion call of this journal was to oppose British rule in India in every possible way. He argued that such was the duty enjoined upon a Muslim by the Quran. With the launch of *Al-Hilal*, Azad had launched himself as well on the firmament of India's struggle for freedom. He was able to earn recognition for himself as a nationalist without having participated in any struggle, except for a brief stint with the extremist political formation called Yugantar, in the wake of the anti-Bengal partition agitation in 1906. Later his nationalist concerns drew quite heavily from pan-Islamism, which had emerged in the late nineteenth century but acquired serious form in the beginning decades of the twentieth century. However, there were many nationalist Muslim leaders who too started their political journey in the course of this pan-Islamic upsurge. For instance, the Ali Brothers, Mukhtar Ahmad Ansari and Hasan Mahmood, were part of the same phenomenon. This generated a possibility of Muslim leaders moving away from the shadow of a culture of mendicancy, as was the practice in Aligarh since the late nineteenth century due to the impact of Sir Syed Ahmad Khan, who had tried to seek reconciliation with the British and continued to plead the same till he was alive. He was of the opinion that seeking confrontation with the British was injurious to the interests of Muslims.

In the course of his nationalist articulation Azad was influenced by his vast knowledge not just about India but other countries as well—such as Egypt, Iraq and Turkey, where rumblings of nationalist upsurge had begun rather loud, which found adequate space in the pages of *Al-Hilal*. By starting a journal such as the one under discussion Azad was breaking no new ground since many nationalist leaders had already done so in the past. For instance, Lokmanya Tilak in the late nineteenth century, had launched *Kesari* and *Maharatta*, with the help of which he was able to spread the message of nationalism. It has to be recognized that a nationalist movement in a colonial society was bound to be a slow and evolutionary process more so in the specific context of India where the collective existence of the people was based on religion, caste and linguistic affiliations. The major task of the nationalist movement was that without undermining these affiliations, the communities needed to be welded into a single nationhood, which was possible only by involving them in the nationalist political processes. In the course of making this possibility as a distinct reality many nationalist leaders thought of religion as an entry point and made good use of it. The politics initiated by Tilak, Sri Aurobindo and Bipin Chandra Pal fit into this scheme. It is another matter that in due course of time the same phenomenon did not remain static as it gave way to coalescing the communities into a political society purely on political considerations, without which the nationalist movement would have remained considerably weak.

In *Al-Hilal*, Azad was following much the same line by invoking the authority of religion in order to galvanize Muslims for political action. However, Azad made a distinction for himself in the course of religion-based articulation by emphasizing the need for Hindu–Muslim unity right since the beginning. In his scheme of things this unity was the cornerstone of any political action. One can argue that ideological formulation for political action was certainly couched in exclusivist terms but the larger objective that Azad never lost sight of was to bring communities into the nationalist political activities. However, Azad's manner of expression while formulating ideas and making arguments in *Al-Hilal* gave the impression that he was speaking from a high pedestal, as a *pir* or an *imam* who only needed to be heard and paid obeisance to by the followers. This impression one is able to arrive at, despite several disclaimers by Azad that he did not like the culture of *piri-muridi* as was the tradition at his home till his father, Maulana Khairuddin, was alive. Despite conscious rejection of such a culture, Azad seemed to have come under its influence unconsciously. It seems that the die was cast rather early in his life and he found it difficult to overcome it in the days to come. There were reasons for such an approach. Azad was convinced that considering his family background, scholarship and sharp intellect he could only provide leadership to the people, particularly the Muslims, as partners in the freedom struggle. He was rarely swayed by populist considerations, as was the case with Jinnah, who was prone to be swayed by the popular mood.

In the course of an articulation such as the above there were occasions when Azad too seemed to have been swayed by the popular mood. There was an instance to this effect in the context of the First World War, in which Turkey had arrayed itself in the camp of Germany. The breaking out of this war had generated a lot of heat particularly among the Muslims of India, who were given to entertain the idea that the Sultan of Turkey was truly the khalifa of all Muslims the world over. Their concern was borne out of the consideration that the Sultan was also the custodian of the holy places of Islam. The upsurge in the popular mood was amply reflected in the Urdu press. Azad too as stated earlier came under its influence and went to the extent of describing the seat of the Sultan of Turkey as the seat of the khalifa, which might be looked upon as the political centre of Muslims across the globe. It is surprising that a conscious and politically aware person like Azad was talking in the language of a supra nationalist. Given his capacity to move his audience by his writings as well as oratory such a formulation could have produced an undesirable consequence for the future of India. Fortunately Azad had an opportunity to quickly revise his opinion in the context of the Non-Cooperation–Khilafat movement. As compared to other Khilafat leaders it was Azad who argued that the whole struggle in the context of the Khilafat agitation was only to free India from the British rule. He used religious idioms to construct a powerful anti-colonial ideology. It is another matter altogether that when he wished to refer to his political activities and ideological construction he always wanted to impress his audience that he consciously maintained a linear continuity from the days of *Al-Hilal*, which, however, was not the case. Not only this but on other occasions too he emphasized the same point that despite shifts and adjustments that he made in the course of the changing political circumstances, a linear continuity was maintained. Whereas the fact remains that his changing stances did not reflect continuity as claimed by Azad, in the changing context of political developments.

It is observed in the course of the present study that Azad mostly relied on his own formulations since he was self-assured about his intellect and articulation. The problem that one confronts in the context of Azad's changing stances are that once he became a public figure then any transformation of ideological as well as political stand required consultations with others in a broader sense, which Azad was not willing to do as he always looked upon himself as someone only to provide leadership in every respect. It is possible to argue that he was making shifts and changes in his stand because he was not a part of any political formation and was accountable to nobody except himself. Another aspect that requires to be underlined is that even though he was formally not a part of any organization, he was consciously projecting an image of a public figure, which in some measure had become the reality. Azad perhaps did not realize or ignored the facts that once he became a public figure his activities—intellectual or political—were under public scrutiny. Therefore any change of stance should have taken the public perception into account, which mostly did not happen.

While arguing that Azad had an independent mind and he never allowed the masses to influence him, it has to be admitted that precisely because of this reason there emerged a fault-line between him and Muslims at large. He desired to lead Muslims in the nationalist politics but in reality they started moving away from him. Part of the explanation for this could be that in the course of an evolutionary journey, Azad covered a wide spectrum of political positions starting from extremist politics to pan-Islamic ideological moorings to joining the Indian National Congress. In all circumstances he was mostly led by his conviction and analysis of the changing political circumstance, irrespective of the perception of the common Muslims.

In the course of the extremist politics Azad was not uncomfortable that only Hindu symbols such as Kali, Durga (Hindu goddesses), etc., were pressed into the cause of nationalist awakening. It was beyond the imagination of an average Muslim to have identified with these symbols. But this was also the time when the Maulana had not even thought of mobilizing Muslims for political action. The thought of involving Muslims in political action came to him later, in 1912, when he launched his papers *Al-Hilal* and later *Al-Balagh*. These papers were able to draw significant response from the Urdu-reading sections of Muslim society. The Maulana was able to convince his readers about the efficacy of pressing Islam in the service of the nation by arguing that Muslims must come forward to free India from British rule. In other words he was able to convince his readers that a fight against the British enjoyed the sanction of Islam.

In the process of building an ideological framework which was his own and not a borrowed one, he went to the extent of arguing that Muslims in India must be their own leaders and not follow others, since they were expected to provide leadership to the larger society. This argument along with a large number of developments associated with the First World War generated plenty of political upheaval among Muslims. In due course some Muslim formations too came up. The Central Khilafat Committee and Jamiatul-Ulema-i-Hind were two such formations, which channeled the political energies of Muslims into the nationalist movement in the name of the Khilafat issue. It was a defining moment as regards Muslims' participation in the freedom struggle on a mass scale. Azad was closely associated with these groups during the Khilafat movement and made use of their platforms to enunciate powerful anti-colonial arguments. The hallmark of the success of the movement was large-scale mobilization and participation by Muslims. Its linkages with the Non-Cooperation movement under Gandhiji's leadership made it a formidable force. The movement held hopes that in the days to come the unity between Hindus and Muslims would emerge as a formidable force to reckon with. However, the edifice of such a political unity crumbled in the wake of the withdrawal of the movement after the Chauri-Chaura incident on 5 February 1922. This was the beginning of the alienation of Muslims from the Gandhian framework of political agitation and personally from Gandhiji himself as well as the Congress.

While the long drawn-out alienation of Muslims from the Congress was beginning, Azad in a reverse manner started moving closer to the party. The fault-line between Azad and Muslims started appearing. While addressing the Special Session of the Congress at Delhi as its President in 1923 he argued with all, and Muslims in particular, that the country did not need any *sangathan*, either of Hindus or Muslims since the Congress was capable of representing everyone. Azad's assertion was not in conformity with his own political preaching in the preceding period when he had insisted on Muslim leadership for Muslims in a manner as if a religious community could also simultaneously act as a political entity. It is argued that such thoughts were formulated at a time when there was little participation of Muslims in the nationalist movement in an organized manner.

A person of sharp intellect such as Azad might have been able to evaluate the political situation and come to certain conclusions that under the changed circumstances a new political strategy was the need of the hour rather than sticking to earlier formulations. The Maulana was at liberty to choose a quick transformation of his convictions in terms of associating himself with the Indian National Congress, more so when he was offered an opportunity to become its President in the special session at Delhi in 1923. However, the real problem was that since the days of *Al-Hilal* Azad had started imagining himself as a national leader representing Muslims and when it came to making a quick transformation he seemed to have moved much ahead of his co-religionists, without having waited for consultations and their response. It must be admitted that in large measures the Maulana's writing and speeches over a decade starting from the *Al-Hilal* days till the Khilafat movement was set rolling, had produced substantial impact on average Muslims and prepared them for political action. But when Azad made a shift in favour of the Congress, this newfound position was seen as an abrupt act. Any serious study of leadership might recognize the fact that a leader's capacity to lead would be recognized by the followers only till such time as the gap between the two does not increase beyond certain acceptable limits. In this case, soon after Azad joined the Congress in 1923 the gap between the two became visible and in due course of time steadily increased. It is true that even after changing his stance his concerns for Muslims remained undiminished. As a result he and the Muslims started drifting apart from each other. It is difficult to fathom as to why he did so except that he might have thought that the only way to stem the tide of communalism would be to abandon pursuit of a distinct community-based political formations and formulations.

The drift continued even in the context of the Nehru Report, which did not adequately take care of the concerns of Muslims particularly in the Muslim-majority provinces. One can argue that Azad supported the Nehru Report, but had some reservations about it and hoped that at some point of time the Congress might like to review it. Many of Azad's associates whom he patronized and collaborated with, did not extend any support to the Nehru Report. The Jamiatul-Ulema-i-Hind was one such body, which did not approve of the Report. It emphasized that complete independence should have been the only option rather than the Dominion Status as it was enunciated in the said Report. It was also argued that the Report ignored the aspirations of Muslims in Muslim-majority provinces by advocating a unitary constitution. The All Parties Conference held at Calcutta in December 1928 clearly indicated that the Hindu Mahasabha had cast a shadow on the future of the Report. In the popular perception of Muslims the Congress did not appear sincere in making provisions which would take care of Muslim concerns for a share in power.

Azad's support for the Report did not go down well with the Muslims. The *Rangeela Rasool* controversy too had vitiated the political atmosphere in the country. Many Muslims were quite agitated about it but the Maulana tried to reason with them that an emotional outburst on an issue such as this was avoidable. Azad's attempt to pacify the Muslims took place despite his strong displeasure that some people should choose to express disregard to Prophet Muhammad. These developments produced unpleasant consequences.

Maulana Azad was conscious of the growing gap between Hindus and Muslims as regards joint political action. He strongly felt that such a gap if allowed to grow would harm the long-term interest of the country. This realization was not new but he became more concerned about improving the communal situation. In the mid-1930s, particularly with the entry of the lower middle classes into the Congress it increasingly acquired cultural colours associated with Hindus. Once again the issue of respecting the cultural identity of Muslims was seriously debated. Azad emphatically argued that it was beyond imagination that Muslims should submerge their cultural identity in the process of nation-building. Unlike the European experience of total subordination of cultural identity to the national identity, Indian Muslims would like to preserve their distinct identity. He was also keen that the Congress be seen as willing to share power with Muslims. Azad thought that this would help the party to convey an impression that it represented all, not only ideologically but in power-sharing arrangements too. All did not share Azad's concern. There were many Congress leaders who did not agree with Azad's views. This heightened Azad's predicament—on the one hand he was considerably alienated from the Muslims, while on the other his party colleagues did not support him.

Azad was apprehensive that the Muslims might be pushed closer to the Muslim League. His apprehension was borne out in the context of the 1937 elections when the Muslim League did not get sufficient electoral support from Muslims. But while the Muslims did not get closer to the League, they did not repose their confidence in the Congress either. The Congress made no special effort to overcome this except to conduct a half-hearted

Muslim Mass Contact Programme. Azad became critical of the Congress for its slack response to questions concerning Hindu–Muslim relations, till 1938. In this regard it was Azad who took the initiative to get the Hindu Mahasabha and the Muslim League declared communal bodies. He was critical of the party for having missed several opportunities to clinch the issue of joint electorates by making concessions to certain Muslim political groups particularly in the Muslim-majority provinces. He suggested that the Congress should try negotiating with the Muslim League to resolve the communal tangles. Azad was critical of the fact that not many Muslims were accommodated in the party structure. He demanded that if this was on account of lack of support for Muslim candidates for positions in the party, then there should be provision of reservation to ensure better representation for Muslims. Azad was trying to project an image of the Congress as representing all communities. However, he never allowed his differences with party colleagues to come to the surface. The Congress did not help Azad in his relationship with the Muslim masses. The alienation that had started in the 1920s continued except that in the 1930s Azad tried to retrieve lost ground—without much success. Despite the fact that all these years he was continuously making arguments to keep Muslims within the fold of the Congress, he was not able to do much for several reasons. One was that Azad was considerably circumscribed by the limitations of various programmes and policies of the Congress, which had no blue print in order to keep Muslims within its fold. There were general policies about the constructive work to be undertaken, preaching against intoxicants, removal of untouchability, etc., but no specific programme to target Muslims as an important social base of the party. The second was that there were several political formations, which were making claims to represent Muslims interests, for instance the Unionist Party in the Punjab. The third was that Azad at this point of time did not have a larger space for political initiatives, which attracted all, Muslims in particular. His collaboration with other nationalist Muslims formation was to materialize only in the 1940s. Therefore his attempts to retrieve lost ground were mostly taking place within the Congress where he was trying to convince top leaders of the party for greater sensitivity to issues concerning Muslims. However, these attempts did not have much visibility to let Muslims gain impression that Azad was concerned about them.

Azad's election as Congress president in March 1940 was a recognition of his services to the cause of India's freedom from British rule. However, his election coincided with the Muslim League's passing of the 'two-nation theory' resolution on 23 March 1940, which became the basis for the demand for partition of India. The Congress rejected this. But the biggest ideological challenge to the Muslim League came from the Azad Muslim Conference, a coalition of several nationalist Muslim formations to which Azad extended all support. While he was engaged in questioning the legitimacy of the Muslim League's claim to represent all the Muslims of India, his presidentship of the Congress itself was on shaky grounds. The frequent threats of resignation held out by his Working Committee colleagues must have weakened his authority as the president. He was left with very little room to take political initiative. Even when he tried doing so he was advised against it. There were occasions when doubts were cast over his integrity and political wisdom.

It was with considerably compromised authority that Azad negotiated with the Cripps Mission in 1942 and the Cabinet Mission in 1946. While negotiating with both the Missions his sole concern was to protect India's integrity as a united entity. However, during his negotiations with the Cripps Mission, short of accepting a province's right to secede he was in favour of a federal structure, which would remove the fear in the Muslim-majority provinces that a Hindu-dominated centre would override their interest. Not many in the Congress agreed with him, as most leaders wanted a unitary centre. This issue dominated the negotiations with the Cabinet Mission. Azad's contention was that if the Congress conceded the right to provinces to secede then that would help in taking the wind out of the Muslim League's sails. These political thoughts of Azad once again were not in tune with many Congress stalwarts. Due to his unflinching commitment to Indian nationalism he was struggling with various formulations and political action, which would prevent India from being partitioned.

However, not many scholars have viewed Azad's efforts to prevent the partition of the country with sympathy. One such scholar was Mushirul Haq, who in his book *Muslim Politics in Modern India, 1857-1947* quoted a long passage from *India Wins Freedom*,

> It is one of the greatest frauds on the people to suggest that religious affinity can unite areas which are geographically, linguistically and culturally different. It is true that Islam sought to establish a society, which transcends racial, linguistic, economic frontiers. History has however proved that after the first few decades, or at most after the first century, Islam was not able to unite all the Muslim countries into one state on the basis of Islam alone.

Haq argued that such an assertion by Azad, in the context of partition politics came rather too late. Haq observed, 'had Azad emphatically expressed this opinion when it was needed probably, one may say, the situation would have been different. But he did not dare say so at that time and his main opposition to the idea to Pakistan was similar to that of any other *alim*.' One can argue that Haq was quite off the mark in his assessment of Azad. It has been shown in the preceding chapter that all through he tried his best to fight back the separatist politics of the Muslim League, more so in 1940s not as an *alim*, religious scholar of Islam, but as some one who could easily claim that he was an integral part of the nationalist political process and as a leader tried his best to steer the nationalist movement in its most difficult times. While he was engaged in an exercise such as this there were the limitations of an individual, who could not have gone beyond a point in preventing partition. Moreover in a democratic political process he could only have gone with the majority opinion within the Congress rather than his own. One statement or two were not likely to stem the tide of the Pakistan movement.

Haq's observations about the role that Azad played in the context of the Pakistan movement were certainly harsh. But other scholars too have argued that Azad's leadership was a failure that he could not win the confidence of his co-religionists in order to keep them within the fold of the Congress. These observations have been made by V. N. Datta in *Maulana Azad*. However, Datta has analysed the personal failure of Azad in a much broader context and argued that in many ways the partition of India could be seen as a failure of the Congress led nationalist movement that it could not keep the Muslims within its rank. The editors, Gail Minault and Christian W. Troll annotated *Maulana Abul Kalam Azad: An Intellectual* and *Religious Biography* by Ian Henderson Douglas, too seem to suggest much the same argument. Then it becomes necessary to ask a question: was he truly a failure? In many ways one would agree with Datta and the editors of Douglas' volume on Azad that he failed in his endeavours. However, there is still some room for a new interpretation that despite many of his failures, the short as well as long-term efficacy of his ideological formulations remained valid. For instance, he never wavered in his conviction that religion could ever become the basis of formation of nationhood and therefore communities would have to be coalesced into a single nationhood. However, Azad was not merely being theoretical as he had practical suggestions to make in regard to accommodating all communities, Muslims in particular, in the power structure in order to develop their stake in the political process.

It was in the context of this understanding that he talked about the disregard shown by many top Congress leaders to the growing communal problem. Azad was aware that the communal problem was going to hinder the future march of the Indian nation. But unlike many other leaders it was Azad, who from time to time kept on coming up with various suggestions in order to stem the growing tide of communalism and save the nationalist movement from difficulties. His suggestions were practical and not theoretical. For instance in the exercise of government formation by the Indian National Congress after the 1937 elections, Azad showed his keenness that the policy to accommodate Muslims in the power-structure was a vitally important element. But this was largely ignored. Azad's understanding was that the growing alienation of Muslims from the Congress could be stemmed only by convincing them that it too was concerned about their share in power. There were issues of cultural identity of the Muslims as well particularly with regard to the language question as to whether Hindi or Hindustani would become the national language of India. Except lip service, many leaders had moved closer to accepting Hindi in Nagari script as the national language. These were issues which affected the inter-community relation as they affected the future prospects of the nationalist movement.

Azad was acutely conscious that by ignoring these issues nobody would be able to serve the cause of India's future. Thus his substantial political energy was consumed in making arguments for resolving these issues while the nationalist movement moved on in its march forward. Therefore it may appear that he was spending more energy on seeking a better inter-community relation than serving the cause of the freedom movement. The only plausible explanation that can be extended in this regard is that the evolutionary trajectory of Indian nationalism was such that inter-community relations in whatever form did affect it. Therefore in Azad's scheme of things it was important to retain those Muslims who were not under the influence of the Muslim League, within the fold of the nationalist movement. However, only ideological slogans would not attract them as concrete plans would. With the growing belligerence of the Muslim League in the late 1930s and 1940s the lines suggested by Azad were relevant but it required a different strategy, which could not be devised. Azad did not give up. He did not give vent to his differences within the Congress publicly since he thought that adversaries of the Congress would benefit. But at the same time he did not miss an opportunity to remind his fellow colleagues the necessity of initiating measures to retrieve lost ground. Even in the 1940s when the Muslim League, after adopting the 'two-nation theory' in March 1940, went to town declaring that the Muslims of India constituted a distinct nation, it was left to Azad to mobilize those Muslims and their political formations, who were still committed to the cause of the composite Indian nationalism. However, electoral success eluded them when it came to the crunch in the elections of 1945-6 as the Muslim League was able to carry the day.

The Partition of India on 14 August 1947 in order to make Pakistan as demanded by the Muslim League was a sad day in the annals of her long history. It saddened everybody, as Azad too was deeply sad that with the arrival of independence the unity of India was gone. He feared that such cataclysmic development would affect those Muslims who would not go to Pakistan and stay back might be considered alien in their own homeland. He also hoped that Pakistan would be a short-lived phenomenon. His fear did take shape in one form or the other but his hope remained a distant dream.

Historians have considered the Partition of India as a failure and defeat for Azad. However, it needs to be added that it was a political and electoral defeat. Ideologically Azad still held on to his ground that the notion of a religion-based nation was nothing short of 'fraud'. It is another matter that the die was already cast. Despite the best of energy, intellectual as well as political, there are times in the lives of men when unfolding historical circumstances overwhelm them.

The role that Azad played in the years preceding Partition was that of a one-man army against Muslim alienation from the Congress, and the Congress' indifference towards sensitive issues of identity, culture and desire for power-sharing. In his struggle Azad found himself mostly alone. Jawaharlal Nehru was the only colleague whom he looked to for support. He was sustained by his conviction in a united India. India's partition saddened him. But he knew that despite Partition his political philosophy was still relevant. When Muslims wanted to return to him after India's Partition, he did not say no to them. He admonished them but did not abandon them out of anger or frustration. He welcomed and exhorted them to come forward to reclaim their share in the national life. While addressing a gathering of Muslims from the Jama Masjid in Delhi in October 1947, Azad in order to instill a sense of confidence among them had suggested that some pages of history were still blank, which they could fill with their contributions. When Azad became independent India's first Minister of Education, and the manner in which he undertook the arduous task of reconstruction of the educational life of India, it seemed he was doing so on behalf of the entire nation, Muslims in particular and filling the 'blank pages of Indian history'. Whether before or after Partition, Azad's central concern was to work out an ideological framework and develop a political ethos, which would make it possible for communities to coalesce into a single nationhood.

Bibliography

PRIMARY SOURCES

Writings by Abul Kalam Azad

Afkar-i-Azad: Hazrat Maulana Abul Kalam Azad Saheb ke Achoote Khayalat ka Muraqqa, compiled by Mohammad Usman Farqalit, Maktaba-i-Azad, Lahore, 1945.

Aina Abul Kalam Azad, Ateeq Siddiqui, ed., Taraqqi-i-Urdu Hind, Delhi, 1976.

Al-Hilal volumes, 1912, 1913-14.

Al-Jihad fi Sabeelillah, Nizamia Khilafat Store, Muradabad, n.d.

Azad ki Taqreerain, ed. Anwar Arif, Adabi Duniya, Delhi, 1961.

Azeemat wa Dawat, Etaqad Publishing House, Delhi, n.d.

Dars-i-Wafa, New Taj Office, Delhi, n.d.

Dawat-e-Haq, Kitabistan, Delhi, n.d.

Diwan-i-Abul Kalam Azad, compiled by Abdul Ghaffar Shakil, Adara Tahqeeqat-i-Urdu, Patna, 1991.

Falsafa: Usool wa Mawadi ki Raushni Mein, New Taj Publishers, Delhi, n.d.

Ghubar-e Khatir, Sahitya Akademi, Delhi, 1983.

India Wins Freedom: The Complete Version, Orient Longman, Madras, 1988.

Intekhab-e-Al-Hilal, Adabistan, Lahore, 1960.

Islam aur Azadi, Imdad Sabri Publishers, Delhi, 1957.

Islam ka Nazaria-i-Jung, compiled by Ibn Raee, Bisat Adab, Lahore, 1965.

Khutba-i-Sadart Tahreeri, Jalsa-i-Jamiatul Ulema-i-Hind Lahore, Qaumi Darul Ashat, Meerut, 1921.

Khutbata-i-Azad, Urdu Kitab Ghar, Delhi, 1959.

Khutbat-e-Azad, ed. Malik Ram, Sahitya Akademi, Delhi, 1990.

Makateeb-e-Abul Kalam Azad, compiled by Abu Salman Shahjahanpuri, Sindh, Karachi, 1968.

Malfuzat-e-Azad, compiled by Ajmal Khan, Urdu Academy, Delhi, 1959.

Maqalat-e-Abul Kalam Azad, Chaman Book Depot, Delhi, n.d.

Masala-i-Khilafat wa Jazeeratul Arab, Al-Balagh Press, Calcutta, 1920.

Maulana Azad aur Madaris Islamia: Nadwatul Ulema ki Tareekh ka ek Baab, compiled by Qamar Aastan Khan, Khuda Bakhsh Khan Oriental Public Library, Patna, 1992.

Maulana Azad ne Burre Saghir Hind wa Pak ke bare Mein kya Kaha Tha, compiled by Ahmad Husain Kamal, al-Darul Aleema, Delhi, 1973.

Mazameen-e-Abul Kalam Azad, compiled by Syed Sifarish, Urdu Academy, Delhi, 1944.

Mazameen-e-Al-Balagh, ed. Mahmudul Hasan Siddiqui, Hindustani Publishing House, Delhi, n.d.

Mazameen-e-Al-Hilal, Adam Ishatul Quran, Delhi, n.d.

Mazamin Lisanul Sidq, compiled by Abdul Qavi Dasnavi, Nasim Book Depot, Lucknow, 1967.

Mera Aqeeda, Maktaba Jamia, Delhi, 1959.

Musalman aur Congress, Azad Book Depot, Lahore, n.d.

Naqsh-i-Azad, compiled by Ghulam Rasool Mehar, Kitab Manzil, Lahore, 1958.

'National Tehreek: Wazarat Qubool Karne ke Baad League wa Congress Zuban-Wazarat', unpublished essay, ICCR Library.

Nigarishat-i-Azad, Maktaba 'Mahol' Delhi, 1960.

Numud-i-Ghubar, compiled by Sharafat Husain Mirza, Apna Kitab Ghar, Bijnor, 1991.

Qaul-i-Faisal, Taj Publishers, Delhi, 1967.

Rasool-i-Rahmat, compiled by Ghulam Rasool Meher, Etaqad Publishing House, Delhi, 1982.

Sada-i-Haq, Maktaba Ashaat-ur-Quran, Delhi, n.d.

Shahadat-i-Husain, Etaqad Publishing House, Delhi, 1959.

Subah-i-Ummeed, compiled by Faiyyaz Ahmad, Sangam Kitab Ghar, Delhi, 1959.

Tabarrukata-e-Azad, Ghulam Rasool Meher, ed., Adabi Duniya, Delhi 1963.

Taleemi Turke Mawalat ka Maqsad, Om Press, Meerut, n.d.

Tarjumanul Quran (4 vols.), Sahitya Akademi, Delhi, 1964.

Tazkirah, Sahitya Akademi, Delhi, 1968.

Tehreek-e-azadi wa Yek Jahti, Shaheen Book Centre, Delhi, 1960.

PRIVATE PAPERS (INDIVIDUAL COLLECTIONS)

Abdul Majid Daryabadi Papers, Nehru Memorial Museum & Library (NMML), New Delhi
Ajmal Khan Papers, NMML
B.G. Kher Papers, NMML
Bhulabhai Desai Papers NMML
C. Rajagopalachari Papers (Microfilm), NMML
Gopichand Bhargava Papers, NMML
Habibur Rahman Ludhianvi Papers, NMML
Humayun Kabir Papers, NMML
Husain Zaheer Papers, NMML
Jayaprakash Narayan Papers, NMML
Mahatma Gandhi Papers, National Archives of India (NAI), New Delhi
Maulana Azad Papers, NMML
Mirza Ismail Papers, NMML
P.D. Tandon Papers, NMML
Rajendra Prasad Papers (Microfilm), NMML
Rajendra Prasad Papers NAI

ORGANIZATIONAL RECORDS

AICC Files, NMML
Files of the Ministry of Education

GOVERNMENT RECORDS

Home Political Files

PUBLISHED SOURCES

Collected Works of Mahatma Gandhi, vols. 1-75, Publications Division, Delhi.

Collected Works of Maulana Abul Kalam Azad, vols. 1-11, ed. Ravindra Kumar, Atlantic Publishers and Distributors, Delhi.

Patel: Collected Works, vols. 1-15, ed. P.N. Chopra, Konark Publishers, Delhi.

Rajendra Prasad: Correspondence and Select Documents, ed. Valmiki Choudhary, vols. 1-12, Allied Publishers, Delhi.

Selected Works of Jawaharlal Nehru, vols. 1-15, S. Gopal, Orient Longman, Delhi.

Speeches of Maulana Azad, 1947-1958, Publications Division, Delhi, Ministry of Information and Broadcasting, 1989.

The Indian Annual Register Volumes, 1926-1947, ed. N.N. Mitra. Calcutta.

The Transfer of Power 1942-47, vols. 1-12, Her Majesty's Stationery Office, London.

SECONDARY SOURCES

BOOKS

Abdul Mughani, *Maulana Abu Kalam Azad*, *Zehan wa Kirdar*, Anjuman Taraqqi Urdu, Delhi, 1989.

Ahmad, Aziz, *Islamic Modernism in India and Pakistan*, Oxford University Press, London, 1967.

Ahmad, Malikzada Manzoor, *Maulana Abul Kalam Azad*, *Fikro Fun*, Nasim Book Depot, Lucknow, 1978.

Ahmad, Qeyamuddin, *The Wahabi Movement in India*, Firma K.L Mukhopadhyaya, Calcutta, 1966.

Ahmad, Syed Nesar, *Origins of Muslim Consciousness in India: A World System Perspective*, Westport, Greenwood Press, 1991.

Akbaraabadi, Maulana Sayeed Ahmad, *Maulana Abul Kalam Azad Marhoom*, *Sirat-o-Shaksiyat aur Ilmi aur Amali Karname*, compiled by Abu Salman Shahjahanpuri, Maulana Sayid Ahmad Akademi: Karachi, 1986.

Al-Namar, Abdul Muna'm, *Maulana Abul Kalam Azad: Ek Mufakkir Ek Rahnuma*, vols. I & II, Urdu translation from Arabic, Maulana Azad Memorial Akademi, Lucknow, 1989.

Anjum, Khaliq, ed., *Maulana Abul Kalam Azad*, *Shaksiyat aur Karname*, Urdu Akademi, Delhi, 1986.

——*Hasrat Mohani*, Publication Division, Delhi, 1994.

Ansari, Asarbin Yahya, *Maulana Azad: Ek Siyasi Diary*, Aaliya Publications, Dhulia, 1982.

Ashraf, Ali, *Dawn of Hope*, *Sections From the Al-Hilal of Maulana Abul Kalam Azad* (translation), Indian Council of Historical Research, New Delhi, 2002.

Ashraf, K.M., *An Overview of Indian Muslim Politics*, *1920-1947*, Manak Publications, Delhi, 2001.

Azami, Abdul Latif, *Mu'tarizeen Abul Kalam Azad*, Ilmi Adara, Delhi, 1990.

Brass, Paul R., *Language*, *Religion and Politics in North India*, Cambridge University Press, Cambridge, 1974.

Brown, Judith M., *Gandhi and Civil Disobedience: The Mahatma in Indian Politics*, *1928-34*, Cambridge University Press, Cambridge, 1977.

Butt, Abdullah, *Abul Kalam Azad*, Qaumi Kutub Khana, Lahore, 1986.

Cabral, Amilcar, *Revolution in Guinea*, *Select Text*, Monthly Review Press, New York, 1969.

Chakrabarty, Bidyut, ed., *Communal Identity in India: Its Construction and Articulation in the Twentieth Century*, Oxford University Press, Delhi, 2003.

Chandra, Bipan, *Essays on Colonialism*, Orient Longman, Delhi, 1999.

Chopra, P.N., *Maulana Abul Kalam Azad*, *Unfulfilled Dreams*, Interprint, Delhi, 1990.

—— *Maulana Azad Select Speeches and Statements*, *1940-47*, Reliance Publishing House, Delhi, 1990.

Cohen, A.P., *The Symbolic Construction of Community*, Ellis Horwood Limited, Sussex, 1985.

Copland, Ian, *India 1885-1947: The Unmaking of an Empire*, Pearson Education Limited, London, 2001.

Daryabadi, Abdul Majid, *Urdu ka Adeeb-i-Azam*, *Maulana Abul Kalam Azad ke Husn Insha'a par ek Nazar*, Adara Tasnif wa Tahqueeq Pakistan, Karachi, 1986.

Dasgupta, Jyotindra, *Language Conflict and National Development: Group Politics and Language Policy in India*, Oxford University Press, Delhi, 1970.

Dasnavi, Abdulqavi, *Hayat-i-Abul Kalam Azad*, Modern Publishing House, Delhi, 1999.

—— *Ma'asirin wa Mutalluqat Maulana Azad*, Nai Awaz, New Delhi, 1996.

—— *Talsh-i-Azad*, *Hayat*, *Shaksiyat*, *Khidmat*, *Chand Jhalikyan*, Dashavi, Bhopal, 1990.

Datta, V.N., *Maulana Azad*, Manohar, Delhi, 1990.

Desai, Mahadev, *Maulana Abul Kalam Azad: A Biographical Memoir*, George Allen and Unwin, London, 1946.

Douglas, Ian Henderson, *Abul Kalam Azad: An Intellectual and Religious Biography*, Oxford University Press, Delhi, 1988.

Esposito, John L., *Islam the Straight Path*, Oxford University Press, New York, 1991.

Faruqi, Ziayul Hasan, *The Deoband School and the Demand for Pakistan*, Asia Publishing House, Bombay, 1963.

——*Maulana Abul Kalam Azad: Towards Freedom*, B.R. Publishing Corporation, Delhi, 1997.

Farooqui, Mohammad Abdur Razzaq, *Maulana Abul Kalam Azad ke Taleemi Tasawwurrat*, *Unke Mazhabi*, *Siyasi and Samaji Afkar ke Pase Manzar Mein*, Anjuman Hayat-i-Now, Gulbarga, 1985.

——*Abul Kalam Azad*, *Fikr-o-Nazar ki Chand Jehatein*, Maktaba Jamia: Delhi, 1994.

Gandhi, Rajmohan, *Eight Lives: A Study of Hindu-Muslim Encounter*, Roli Books, Delhi, 1985.

——*India Wins Errors: A Scrutiny of Maulana Azad's India Wins Freedom*, Radiant Publishers, Delhi, 1989.

Gilmartin, David, *Empire and Islam: Punjab and the Making of Pakistan*, Oxford University Press, Delhi, 1989.

Gopal, S., *Jawaharlal Nehru: A Biography*, Oxford University Press, London, 1975.

Hameed, Syeda Saiyedain, *Islamic Seal on India's Independence: Abul Kalam Azad*, *A Fresh Look*, Oxford University Press, Karachi, 1998.

Haq, Mohammad Alam Mukhtar, *Maulana Abul Kalam Azad: Ek Nadir Rozgar Shaksiyat*, Ghulam Rasool Meher, Lahore, 1994.

Haq, Mushirul, *Muslim Politics in Modern India*, *1857-1947*, Meenakshi Prakashan, Meerut, 1970.

Hardy, Peter, *Partners in Freedom and True Muslims*, Green Wood Press Publishers, London, 1985.

——*The Muslims of the British India*, Cambridge University Press, Cambridge, 1973.

Hasan, Mushirul, *A Nationalist Conscience: M.A. Ansari*, *the Congress and the Raj*, Manohar, Delhi, 1987.

——*Communal and Pan-Islamic Trends in Colonial India*, rvd. edn. Manohar, Delhi, 1985.

——ed., *India's Partition: Process*, *Strategy and Mobilisation*, Oxford University Press, Delhi, 1993.

——ed., *Islam and Indian Nationalism: Reflections on Abul Kalam Azad*, Manohar, Delhi, 1992.

—— *Mohammad Ali: Ideology and Politics*, Manohar, Delhi, 1991.

——*Nationalism and Communal Politics in India*, *1885-1930*, Manohar, Delhi, 1991.

——*Nationalism and Communal Politics in India*, *1916-28*, South Asia Books, Delhi, 1979.

Husain, Abid S., *Destiny of Indian Muslims*, Asia Publishing House, Bombay, 1965.

Hutchins, F.G., *Spontaneous Revolution: The Quit India Movement*, Manohar, Delhi, 1971.

Iyer, Subramonia R., *The Role of Maulana Abul Kalam in Indian Politics*, Abul Kalam Azad Oriental Research Institute, Hyderabad, 1968.

Jalal, Ayesha, *Self and Sovereignty Individual and Community in South Asia Islam Since 1850*, Routledge, London, 2000.

—— *The Sole Spokesman: Jinnah, the Muslim League and the Demand for Pakistan*, Cambridge University Press, Cambridge, 1985.

Jha, Padmasha, *Maulana Abul Kalam Azad and the Nation*, Rajesh Publications, Delhi, 1998.

Ghosh, Ratna and Mathew Zacharia, eds., *Education and the Process of Change*, Sage Publications, Delhi, 1987.

Karandikar, M.A., *Islam in India's Transition to Modernity*, Orient Longmans, Bombay, 1968.

Kaura, Uma, *Muslims and Indian Nationalism: The Emergence of the Demand for Partition of India*, Manohar, Delhi, 1977.

Khan, Mohammad Ajmal, *Maulana Abul Kalam Azad ke Adabi Khutoot wa Jawabat-i-Azad*, Sangam Kitab Ghar, Delhi, 1966.

Khan, Rashiduddin, ed., *Abul Kalam Azad Ek Hamagir Shaksiyat*, Taraqqi Urdu Bureau, Delhi, 1989.

Kumar, Krishna and Joachim Oesterheld, eds., *Education and Social Change in South Asia*, Orient Longman, Delhi, 2007.

Kumar, Ravinder, ed., *Essays on Gandhian Politics: The Rowlatt Satyagrah of 1919*, Clarendon Press, London, 1971.

Malihabadi, Abdur Razzaq, *Azad ki Kahani Khud Azad ki Zubani*, Maktaba Ishatul Quran, Delhi, 1965.

——*Zikre Azad, Maulana Azad ki Rafaqat mein Anrtees Saal*, Ujala Press, Calcutta, 1960.

Malik, Ram, *Kuch Abul Kalam Azad ke Bare Mein*, Maktaba Jamia, Delhi, 1989.

Malsiyani, Arsh, *Abul Kalam Azad*, Publications Division, Delhi, 1976.

Meher, Ghulam Rasool, *Maulana Abul Kalam Azad, Ek Nadir Rozgar Shaksiyat*, compiled by Mohammad Mukhtar Haq, Meher Sons, Lahore, 1994.

Metcalf, Barbara D., *Islamic Revival in British India: Deoband 1860-1900*, Princeton University Press, New Jersey, 1982.

Minault, Gail, *The Khilafat Movement, Religious Symbolism and Political Mobilisation in India*, Oxford University Press, Delhi, 1982.

Mishra, B.B., *The Unification and Division of India*, Oxford University Press, Delhi, 1990.

Misra, Salil, *A Narrative of Communal Politics: U.P. 1937-39*, Sage Publications, Delhi, 2001.

Mujeeb, M., *The Indian Muslims*, George Allen and Unwin, London, 1967.

Mukherjee, Kartick C., *Underdevelopment Educational Policy and Planning*, Asia Publishing House, Calcutta, 1967.

Nanda, B.R., *Gandhi, Pan-Islamism, Imperialism and Indian Nationalism*, Oxford University Press, Bombay, 1989.

Naqvi, Mushtaq, *Partition the Real Story*, Renaissance Publishing House, Delhi, 1995.

Nayar, D.P., *Towards a National System of Education*, Mittal Publication, Delhi, 1989.

Nizami, Khaliq Ahmad, *Maulana Azad: A Commemorative Volume*, Adar-i-Adabiyat-i-Delhi, Delhi, 1990.

Page, David, *The Prelude to Partition: The Indian Muslims and the Imperial System of Control, 1920-1932*, Oxford University Press, Delhi, 1982.

Pandey, Deepak, *The Role of the Muslim League in National Politics, 1935-47*, Tiwari Publications, Delhi, 1991.

Pandey, Gyanendra, *Indian Nation in 1942*, K.P. Bagchi, Calcutta, 1988.

——*Remembering Partition: Violence, Nationalism and History in India*, Cambridge University Press, Cambridge, 2001.

—— *The Ascendancy of the Congress in Uttar Pradesh, 1926-34: A Study in Imperfect Mobilisation*, Oxford University Press, Delhi, 1978.

Panikkar, K.N., *Communal Threat and Secular Challenge*, Earthworm Books, Madras, 1997.

—— *Against Lord and State: Religion and Peasant Uprising in Malabar 1836-1921*, Oxford University Press, Delhi, 1989.

Piscatori, James, *Islam in a World of Nation States*, Cambridge University Press, Cambridge, 1986.

Prasad, Beni, *The Hindu-Muslim Questions*, Kitabistan, Allahabad, 1941.

Prasad, Bimal, *Pathway to India's Partition*, vol. II: *A Nation Within a Nation 1877-1937*, Manohar, Delhi, 2000.

—— *Pathway to India's Partition*, vol. I: *The Foundation of Muslim Nationalism*, Manohar, Delhi, 1999.

Qadri, Khalid Hasan, *Hasrat Mohani*, Adara-i-Adabiyat-i-Delhi, Delhi, 1985.

Qamar, Jamshed, *Maulana Azad ka Qeyam-i-Ranchi*, *Ahwal wa Aasar*, Maulana Azad Study Circle Ranchi, Patna, 1994.

Qarshi, Afzal Haq, ed., *Abul Kalam Azad: Adabi wa Shaksi Mutala*, al-Faisal, Lahore, 1992.

Qureshi, I.H., *Ulema in Politics: A Study Relating to the Political Activities of the Ulema in South-Asian Subcontinent, 1556-1947*, Ma'aref Ltd., Karachi, 1972.

Qureshi, Mohammad Faruq, *Maulana Abul Kalam Azad aur Qaum Parast Muslamano ki Siyasat*, Takhliqat, Lahore, 1997.

Rajput, A.B., *Maulana Abul Kalam Azad*, Lion Press, Lahore, 1946.

Ramnathan, G., *Educational Planning and National Integration*, Asia Publishing House, Bombay, 1965.

Rasool, Abduhu, G., *The Educational Ideas of Maulana Abul Kalam Azad*, Sterling Publications, Delhi, 1973.

Rizvi, Syed Sifarish Husain, *Partition End Product of the Trend*, Khuda Baksh Oriental Public Library, Patna, 1998.

Robinson, Francis, *Islam and Muslim History in South Asia*, Oxford University Press, Delhi, 2000.

Sabri, Maulana Imdad, *Imamul Hind Maulana Azad*, *Maulana Abul Kalam Azad ke Sawanah Hayat*, *Shaksiyat wa Sirat aur Khidmat ka ek Dilawez Tazkira*, Maktaba Rashidiya, Karachi, 1986.

Saiyidain, K.G., *The Faith of an Educationist: A Plea for Human Values* Asia Publishing House, Bombay, 1965.

Sarkar Sumit, *Modern India*, Macmillan, Delhi, 1983.

Shadai, Shamshul Haq, *Maulana Abul Kalam Azad: Some Personal Glimpses*, Academic Publishers, Dhaka, 1991.

Shahjahanpuri, Abu Salman, *Maulana Azad ki Sahafat*, Adara Tasnif wa Tahqiq Pakistan, Karachi, 1989.

—— ed., *Maulana Abul Kalam Azad aur unke Ma'asirin*, Adara Tasnif wa Tahqiq Pakistan, Karachi, 1996.

Shaikh, Farzana, *Community and Consensus in Islam: Muslim Representation in Colonial India, 1860-1947*, Cambridge University Press, Cambridge, 1989.

Shakir, Moin, *Khilafat to Partition 1919-1947: A Survey of Major Political Trends Among Indian Muslims*, Kalamkar Prakashan, Delhi, 1970.

Shan Muhammad, *Sir Syed Ahmad Khan: A Political Biography*, Minakshi Prakashan, Meerut, 1969.

Sherwani, Riyazur Rahman Khan, *Mir-i-Karwan Abul Kalam Azad: Nisf Sadi ke Mutale aur Mushahide ki Dastan*, Adara Tahqeeqat afkar wa Tahreekat-i-Milli, Karachi, 1988.

Singh, Anita Inder, *The Origins of India's Partition 1936-1947*, Oxford University Press, Delhi, 1987.

Smith, W.C., *Modern Islam in India: A Social Analysis*, Victor Gollancz, London, 1946.

Syed, Masihul Hasan, *Havashi Abul Kalam Azad*, Urdu Akademi, Delhi, 1988.

Syed, Qasim, *Abul Kalam Azad ek Taqabli Mutala'a*, Aijaz Publication House, Delhi, 1992.

Talbot, Ian, *The Provincial Politics and the Pakistan Movement*, Oxford University Press, Karachi, 1988.

——*The Punjab and the Raj 1849-1947*, Manohar, Delhi, 1988.

Tara Chand, *History of the Freedom Movement in India*, vol. III, Publications Division, Delhi, 1971.

Thomas, T.M., *Indian Educational Reforms in Cultural Perspective*, S. Chand & Co., Delhi, 1970.

Thursby, G.R., *Hindu-Muslim Relations in British India: A Study of Controversy, Conflict and Communal Movements in Northern India, 1923-1928*, E.J. Brill, Leiden, 1975.

Tirmizi, S.A.I., *Maulana Azad: A Pragmatic Statesman, A Documentary Study 1923-42*, Commonwealth Publishers, Delhi, 1991.

Usmani, Masudul Hasan, *Abul Kalam Azad, Ahwal wa Aasar*, Maulana Azad Memorial Akademi, Lucknow, 1977.

Zaidi, Ali Jawwad, *Anwar-i-Abul Kalam Azad*, Saqafat Sub-committee, Jashne Bahar Kashmir, Srinagar, 1959.

Zakaria, Rafiq, *Rise of Muslims in Indian Politics, An Analysis of Developments From 1885 to 1906*, Somaiya Publications, Bombay, 1970

ARTICLES

Ahmad, Ejaz, 'Azad's Career: Roads Taken or not Taken', in Mushirul Hasan, ed., *Islam and Indian Nationalism: Reflections on Abul Kalam Azad*, Manohar, Delhi, 1992.

Azaimabadi, Suhel, 'Maulana Azad Ranchi Mein', *Payam-i-Watan*, Azad Number, Delhi, 1977.

Deutsch, K.L., 'Sri Aurobindo and the Search for Political and Spiritual Perfection in Political Thought in Modern India', in Thomas Pantham and K.L. Deutsch, eds., *Political Thought in Modern India*, Sage Publications, Delhi, 1988.

Dixit, Prabha, 'Political Objectives of the Khilafat Movement in India', in Mushirul Hasan, ed., *Communal and Pan-Islamic Trends in Colonial India*, Manohar, Delhi, 1985.

———, 'Ideology of Hindu Nationalism', in Thomas Pantham and K.L. Deutsch, eds., *Political Thought in Modern India*, Sage Publications, Delhi, 1988.

Engineer, Asghar Ali, 'Theological Creativity of Abul Kalam Azad', Delhi, unpublished paper, 1988.

Hasan, Mushirul, 'Religion and Politics in India: The Ulema and Khilafat Movement', in Mushirul Hasan, ed., *Communal and Pan-Islamic Trends in Colonial India*, rev. edn., Manohar, Delhi, 1985.

——'The Muslim Mass Contact Campaign: Analysis of a Strategy of Political Mobilisation', in Mushirul Hasan, ed., *India's Partition: Process, Strategy and Mobilisation*, Oxford University Press, Delhi, 1993.

Kripalani, J.B., 'The Voice of Reason', in Humayun Kabir, ed., *Maulana Abul Kalam Azad: A Memorial Volume*, Asia Publishing House, Bombay, 1959.

Mehrotra, S.R., 'The Congress and Partition of India', in C.H. Philips and M.D. Wainwright, eds., *The Partition of India: Policies and Perspectives 1935-1947*, George Allen and Unwin, London, 1970.

Minault, Gail, 'The Elusive Maulana: Reflections on Writing Azad's Biography', in Mushirul Hasan, ed., *Islam and Indian Nationalism: Reflections on Abul Kalam Azad*, Manohar, Delhi, 1992.

Mujeeb, M., 'The Partition of India in Retrospect', in Mushirul Hasan, ed., *India's Partition: Process, Strategy and Mobilisation*, Oxford University Press, Delhi, 1993.

Nizami, K.A., 'Abul Kalam Azad: An Assessment', Iran Society, Calcutta, 1988.

Pandey, Deepak, 'Congress-Muslim League Relations 1937-39: The Parting of Ways', *Modern Asian Studies*, no. 12, 1978.

Prasad, Bimal, 'Congress vs the Muslim League 1935-37', in Richard Sison, and Stanley Wolper, eds., *Congress and Indian Nationalism: The pre-Independence Phase*, Oxford University Press, Delhi, 1988.

——'Gandhi and India's Partition', in A.K. Gupta, ed., *Myth and Reality: The Struggle for Freedom in India 1945-47*, Delhi, Manohar, 1987.

Ray, Rajat K., 'Revolutionaries, Pan-Islamists and Bolsheviks: Abul Kalam Azad and the Political Underworld in Calcutta, 1905-1925', in Mushirul Hasan, ed., *Communal and Pan-Islamic Trends in Colonial India*, rev. edn., Manohar, Delhi, 1985.

Robinson, Francis, 'Islam and Muslim Separatism: A Historical Debate', in Mushirul Hasan, ed., *Communal and Pan-Islamic Trends in Colonial India*, rev. edn., Manohar, Delhi, 1985.

Syed Jamaluddin, 'The Brelvis and the Khilafat Movement', in Mushirul Hasan, ed., *Communal and Pan-Islamic Trends in Colonial India*, rev. edn., Manohar, Delhi, 1985.

UNPUBLISHED WORKS

Azad, 'National Tehreek: Wazarat Qubool Karne ke Baad League wa Congress Zuban-Wazarat', unpublished essay, ICCR.

Singh, Hulas, 'Cultural Consciousness in 19th Century Maharashtra', unpublished M.Phil dissertation, JNU, 1984.

Index